# MUD, MEN & MEMORIES

*Research for this book revealed the amazing existence of this old team photograph of an Oxford City Rugby Union team in 1886–7! Were these boys the forerunners of the Oxfordshire Nomads formed in 1909?*

*Back row, left to right:*
*W Pike, AR Fernsby, GW Cook, HFJ Hart (Capt), WJ Wake, JH Nancarron, HT Walker.*
*Middle row: W Butler, Rev M Kirkby, JRF Turner, GW Harris, W Clifton.*
*Front: H Smith, CH Head, B Ostler, ED Walden.*

# MUD, MEN & MEMORIES

The Continuing Story of
Oxford Rugby Football Club

The Middle Years
1960 to 1987

By
Richard Tyrrell

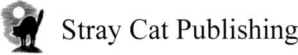
Stray Cat Publishing

MUD, MEN AND MEMORIES
The Continuing Story of Oxford Rugby Football Club
The Middle Years 1960–1987

First published in March 2017 by
Stray Cat Publishing
Telephone: 01865 377366

@Text and illustrations copyright Richard Tyrrell

All rights reserved.
Without limiting the rights under copyright reserved
above, no part of this book may be reprinted or reproduced or
utilised in any form or by any electronic, mechanical or other
means including photocopying and recording, or in any
information storage or retrieval system, without the permission
in writing from the Publishers.

Printed by Parchment of Oxford, Printworks, Crescent Road,
Cowley, Oxford OX4 2PB
Telephone 01865 747547

Distributed by Stray Cat Publishing
159, Banbury Road, Kidlington, Oxford, OX5 1AL, England

Set in Times New Roman

ISBN 978-0-9557188-1-6

Design by Wild Boar Design Limited,
21 Cumnor Road, Wootton, Boars Hill,
Oxford OX1 5JP
www.wildboardesign.co.uk

# Contents

| | Page |
|---|---|
| **Acknowledgements** | 6 |
| **Foreword** | 7 |
| **Introduction** | 8 |

**Chapter 1 – Looking back**   11
A brief resume of the first fifty years

**Chapter 2 – Swing Low**   19
1960–61, 1961–62, RFU Sevens restrictions, 1962–63

**Chapter 3 – Second Coming**   47
1963–64, 1964–65, 1965–66, Oxfordshire County Championship semi finalists

**Chapter 4 – Broken wings and treading water**   81
1966–67, 1967–68, 1968–69

**Chapter 5 – Home, sweet home**   113
1969–70, Oxford RFC buy own ground

**Chapter 6 – Up for the Cup!**   127
1970–71, Oxford's inaugural Oxfordshire Cup win, 1971–1972, 1972–73, 1973–74, 1974–75, 1975–76, 1976–77, 1977–78

**Chapter 7 – Let there be light**   197
1978–79, Oxford's new floodlights turned on, 1979–80, 1980–81

**Chapter 8 – The times they are a-changin'**   217
1981–82, 1982–83

**Chapter 9 – 75th Anniversary with Merit**   233
1983–84, Merit Table entry, 1984–85, Oxford's 75th Anniversary season, 1985–86, 1986–87, league placings announced

# Acknowledgements

Richard Tyrrell would like to thank all of the following for their special help in making this project a reality:
Chris Price, Thom Cooper, Mrs Wilhelmina Church, Ron Salter, Don Barrett, Peter West, Gordon Skates, Frank Webb, Ray Hance, Michael Rhymes, Ian Moffatt, Ray Tapper, Sarah Bagnall, Sally Mills, Gareth Lewis, Keith Jenkins, Eileen Mawle, Neville Worsfold, Clive Bevan, Graham Barrett, Steve Wheeler, Lynn Evans, Vic Gordge, others who have contributed in 'bar-room' conversations and anybody else whose contribution may have been inadvertently omitted.
Particular thanks to Bob Sankey for his contribution and also patience in reading and correcting the script.
And, of course, to the long suffering Sandra Tyrrell once again for her continued support, patience and fortitude!

**Photographic contributions from:**
*Oxford Mail and Times*
Oxfordshire History Centre
*Rugby Post*
**With reference to:**
Rugby World
Winning Rugby – Richard Sharp
Golden Jubilee 1932–1982 – Oxfordshire Rugby Football Union
*Green, White and Black*
Front and rear cover – Oxford v Gordon League, 26th February 1977

# Foreword

Can you recall how in some crime fiction novels or films the principal character is introduced as his mobile phone rings and the plot begins to unfold? Well ... my mobile phone rang. I was sitting next to Carlos Barbieri, the Presidente of the Confederacion Sudamericana de Rugby in the Estadio Charrua, Montevideo, Uruguay. England were about to play a warm up game against a CONSUR Team prior to playing two test matches in Argentina. "Hello Spud" (my nickname) the voice said. "Look across to the stand behind the goal." There I can see Tubby Tyrrell and Roy Holt waving to me. I am half way round the world and two friends from Oxfordshire following their passion for Rugby just give me a call to say hello. Like them I was also at the match to support the England Team but as President of the Rugby Football Union.

Anybody interested in sport and Rugby Union in particular will find this second book by Richard, his first was titled "Green, White and Black", an informative read about Oxford RFC. Richard has been a stalwart of Oxford RFC for 47 years and his historical knowledge and painstaking research is both skilful and boundless. He draws out the essence of club rugby supported by factual information.

This second book, Mud, Men & Memories, covers the next period of Oxford RFC history. The book maps the journey the Oxford Club has made through 27 rugby seasons from 1960 to 1987 in a period before the pressures of the current professional era and league rugby. It gives an historical account of the clubs success in the then new Oxfordshire RFU County Cup, the contribution to County Rugby and the club's rivalry with Henley RFC. It chronicles the various seasons with details of the teams, players and match results. The struggles at the club to obtain fixtures against 1st class opponents and an innovative club feeder system is explored. The purchase of the Southern by-Pass ground, merit tables and the impact of the first Oxfordshire club with a floodlit pitch are all examined. Players, Teams, Coaches and Administrators, both past and present are thoughtfully covered with many great rugby anecdotes. These stories are supported by illustrations, memorabilia and photographs which show the passage of time.

I have known Richard since my own playing days and our paths have crossed on and off the playing field as he has followed his passion for rugby. We have met in as far off places as Rome, Hong Kong, Buenos Aires and as previously mentioned Montevideo. Naturally there have been a few beers at the Southern Bypass Ground or at social gatherings of a rugby nature in the local Oxfordshire rugby scene.

As a past player of the Oxford Club, albeit briefly due to injury, I can personally relate to so much of the enjoyable content contained within the covers. I am sure you will enjoy Richard's skills as a wordsmith as his all-encompassing passion for the Oxford Rugby Club comes through in his writing of this book. An essential read for the rugby alikido, I can thoroughly recommend it.

**Paul Murphy BEM**
Past President Rugby Football Union (2012–2013)

# Introduction

Following the plaudits I received after the publication of what has and will become the first of the trilogy of the continuing story of the Oxford Rugby Football Club, "Green, White & Black", I must apologise to those of you who have been waiting patiently for this, the second book in the 'series'. I hope that when you glance through the pages you will appreciate the amount of time it has taken through continual research to produce it. Rest assured work has already started on the third and final edition which I hope will bring us up to date.

In the time since the last book was completed the Oxfordshire Record Office has moved lock, stock and barrel from its old location in the Westgate Centre to new premises at the former St Luke's Church in Temple Road, Cowley. This immediately changed my approach from hopping onto a city centre bound bus to an eighteen mile round trip in the car to enable me to scroll through miles of microfiche. It is no coincidence that the church bells rang out to provide a regular fifteen minute beat that echoed around Cowley thus bringing some order to the days of my youth and later working life.

It does sound as if this has been something of a chore and certainly when, after a good few hours of research, I time and again realised that there was still much to do. But far from it. The experience has again brought me much enjoyment as well as a sense of achievement and as the third edition starts to unfold I can now refer to my own archive saved and collected from the days when I produced the club match day programmes in the late 1980s and early 1990s.

The number of people who have passed through the club over the years since 1909 must number in thousands each with a story to tell and, by its very nature, a book of this nature can only scratch the surface of a rich and massive history. But I hope that if you are a player you can be entertained by, perhaps, dropping into the time zone when you gave sweat, blood and maybe some tears in the name of Oxford RFC to be reminded of your era and the events that took place in those times.

Ron Grimshaw, whose reports have been the mainstay in my research for this book, had been reporting on rugby at Oxford RFC since the late 1940s and soon became the *Oxford Mail*'s chief rugby correspondent. He was also a club member where he was able to pick up 'snippets' for his regular column. This could have caused the odd challenge of double jeopardy but Ron was nothing but fair in his match reports and wrote how he saw it much to the chagrin, on occasions, of some Oxford players. "You'll have to play better if you want me to write good things about you" he'd say. A fond recollection of mine was at the University's Iffley Road ground which happened to be on my beat as a Police Officer. The home Wednesday afternoon games attracted a crowd in those days and as the safety of gate money was a concern I was often posted to the ground for that reason. I would appear at the top of the Pavilion steps to see what was going on and Ron would say "Ah, good, Tubby's here. We can start now." At half time he would disappear to ring the first half report in for the late edition and always missed the start of the second half. "Have I missed anything?" he'd say. I often thought that I could have told him anything and he'd write it down but it was, of course, not worth it at the expense of a sporting friendship.

Becoming a Station Duty Officer at Cowley Police Station gave me ample opportunity in the small hours of the monthly cycle of night duty to produce a newsletter which I circulated to all members of the Force rugby team across the three counties that now make up Thames Valley Police. A4 'skins' attached to the oily drum of the old Gestetner duplicating machines will bring back memories for some and of black fingers for me! But it was well received

*Ron Grimshaw with Lynn Evans after the 1971 Oxfordshire Cup Final. Lynn holds on to the Cup!*

and I always sent a copy to Ron who was then able to give the team some much appreciated publicity in our fight for the cause.

Later I progressed to producing the Oxford RFC First XV match day programmes. Arranging the art work and advertisements, writing, typing, printing the editorial parts, assembling them and then selling them at the ground was often a race against time, especially as I was running the Vikings XV at the time with Graham Barrett. It was at this time that Ron said to me "You should write the club history." There was no way at that point but his remark sowed a seed and I am now well on the way along that road thanks to Ron's copious reports over the years stored in various archives.

When Ron died in 1987 a splendid trophy was commissioned to be presented annually in his memory to the 'Man of the Match' in the Oxfordshire Cup Final. It took the form of an oblong shield with a stand out bronze figure thereon and it became a feature of the occasion for many years. Sadly the trophy went missing and had to be replaced after the recipient in 2009 failed to ensure its safe return. Perhaps it's time now that the original was given back?

The name and history of the club is undoubtedly remembered world-wide. In 2011 I was privileged to spend some time in New Zealand during the Rugby World Cup and was invited to attend the South Canterbury v North Otago match at the Alpine Energy Stadium in Timaru. This was the very ground that became home to the South Canterbury Rugby Union founded by Alfred St George Hamersley quite a few years before he retired to England and Oxfordshire to co-found the fore runner of Oxford RFC, the Oxfordshire Nomads. I was collected by the South Canterbury Rugby Union historian, Jeremy Sutherland, who led me around on what he called the

*Jeremy Sutherland displays the splendid Hamersley Cup in 2010.*

'Hamersley Trail', ie the hotel and offices where discussions took place in 1879 regarding the formation of the South Canterbury Union, the church where he prayed and the grave of one of his sons at a cemetery in an area known as Watlington after the area in Oxfordshire where Alfred was born. Then it was on to the ground, a seat in the stand and, after an exciting match, the exchange of our club's shirts. I was shown the iconic 'Hamersley Cup', a beautiful 186cm tall silver trophy which cost $NZ7000, commissioned in 2010 in honour of the man who founded both the South Canterbury Rugby Football Club in 1875 and Oxfordshire Nomads in 1909. The winners of the Senior Championship clubs have their names engraved on the trophy from as far back as 1888 with room for many more in the future. A memorable occasion.

In 2013 Alfred St George Hamersley was inducted into the World Rugby Hall of Fame. His name lives on, as it should do.

As the years go by the members and players of Oxford Rugby Football Club write their own history. Let's hope that future club history is at least as rich as what we look back on today. I hope that you enjoy the book.

**Richard Tyrrell**
February 2017

*On one of my research visits to Chris Price, a former Oxford RFC player from the 1950s, I was handed this picture and asked if I recognised anybody. I didn't, but wait. Who is that person second from the right in the back row? Yes, it's Martin Johnson when he was playing in New Zealand. And the older gentleman standing on the left, second row up? Why, that's John 'Chippo' Wood, a prop forward at Oxford RFC in the early Fifties, coaching in New Zealand. Maybe we could claim some input into England's World Cup win in 2003?*

# Chapter 1 –
## Looking back.

Suddenly, Oxford Rugby Club was fifty years old! Members and guests who attended the Golden Jubilee Dinner at the Randolph Hotel in Beaumont Street, Oxford, on Thursday 8th October 1959 were in high spirits. So many people had passed through the club since its formation in June 1909 and, although there had been many peaks and troughs along the way, the future was bright and the members had much to look forward to. There would have been many reminiscences of the 'old days' that night, and many of those days over the fifty years would have seemed like yesterday. A lot of those who attended would have recalled

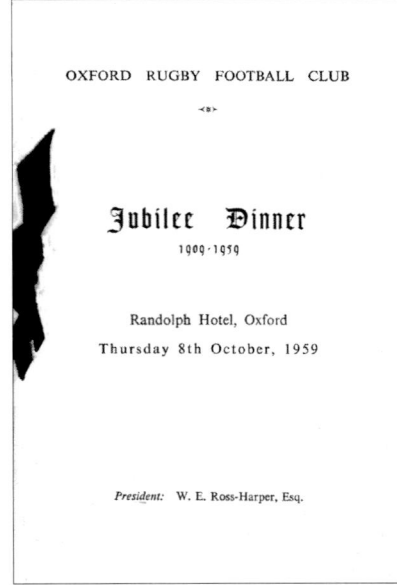

*This Menu survived the revelry of the celebration Dinner.*

*The Fixture Card also celebrated 50 years of Oxford rugby.*

the impromptu scrum down which followed in the hotel foyer between players and Vice Presidents when Frank Webb, a successful Captain in the mid 1950s, numbered amongst the casualties when his new DJ trousers were irreparably split! Those who had founded the Oxfordshire Nomads club in 1909, James Mathew Eldridge and Alfred St George Hamersley, could have hardly known what they had started and would have been justifiably proud!

It had not been an easy thing to do. Forming a rugby club in Oxford in those times was one thing but keeping it going forward in the shadow of University sport was another. Rugby Football had been played in the city in the 1870s and the 1880s but had foundered in the early 1890s due to the increasing popularity of Association Football when, due to the easier nature of the game, clubs and teams had sprung up around the city and Rugby outside the University gradually died out, leading to a barren number of years. The odd game was played occasionally however, arranged by people who had left Oxford colleges amongst others, but who were still keen to play.

One such person was the young solicitor, James Eldridge, a local lad born in the St Ebbes area of West Oxford in 1879. James came from a slightly privileged family that lived in a private house next to the Gas works where his father was an Engineer and Superintendent. He was educated at the Dragon School then Cheltenham College and, finally, gained an MA at Pembroke College, Oxford, leaving in 1905 to start practicing as a Solicitor in Oxford at Lloyds Bank Chambers, Carfax. James would have probably learnt to play Rugby at the Dragon School and might have continued when he was at College, but where would he and people like him play the game when they had left the University? What was needed in Oxford was a club for townsfolk and so a friendship, probably through the Law profession, with Alfred St George Hamersley led the way. It was to the Bank Chambers at Carfax that people were asked to send a postcard noting their interest in forming a rugby club in

*A public meeting was held in the Clarendon Hotel, Oxford, on Monday, 7th June 1909, when it was decided to form the Oxfordshire Nomads R.U.F.C. Mr. A. St. G. Hamersley was elected President, and Mr. J. M. Eldridge Hon. Secretary. Mr. Basil Blackwell was a member of the Committee.*

Oxford. The return must have been good because a notice appeared in the Oxford Times on 5th June 1909 to announce a Public Meeting on Monday 7th June in the Clarendon Hotel, Cornmarket Street, "to inaugurate the formation of a Rugby Football Club for Oxford and district", Alfred Hamersley was to Chair the meeting. Alfred was a much travelled and respected man, and would give much credibility to the venture. He was also a local man, well, almost. Born in 1848 he originated from the family home at Pyrton Manor, near Watlington, Oxfordshire, and would have learnt to play rugby when the game was very much in its infancy, at Marlborough School, Wiltshire. Following in his father's footsteps into a career in Law he qualified as a Solicitor and moved to further his career to London where he became a member of the Marlborough Nomads Rugby club based there, one of the leading clubs in England at the time. A meeting in January 1871 resulted in the formation of the Rugby Union, and a sub-committee was elected to choose a team to meet a challenge issued by the Scottish members of the Union. Alfred was chosen to represent England in the first ever Rugby International played in March 1871 in Edinburgh. Subsequently he was chosen for England for the next three years, scoring a try in the 1872 match and captaining the side in 1874. In the same year Alfred was called to the Bar, Middle Temple, and in 1875 he emigrated to New Zealand where he met and married Maude Snow, also an English emigrant. He was soon involved in Rugby again there and, in the shadow of a threat of takeover by Australian Rules Football, the clubs held a meeting in 1879. The intention was to form a New Zealand Rugby Union but this proposal was dropped due to communication difficulties and the Canterbury Rugby Union was formed instead, with Alfred one of two Vice Presidents elected at that initial meeting. In 1888 the Hamersleys moved on, this time for Vancouver in Canada where Alfred became a legal adviser to the Canadian Pacific Railway, and the City's First Solicitor. Again Alfred became involved in Rugby Union, joining the Vancouver Football (Rugby) Club, and this led to an inaugural meeting, in 1889, of the British Columbia Rugby Union where Alfred became the first President. So, apart from anything else, Alfred's pedigree of forming and supporting new sporting ventures was first class and when he retired back to Oxfordshire, England in 1905 he was the ideal person to be in on the start of a new club in Oxford.

The meeting went well and a proposal to form the new club was eagerly agreed, the name of which would be 'The Oxfordshire Nomads Rugby Union Football Club'. An organizing committee was formed that included JRF Turner, who had played for the old Oxford City club in the 1880s, CC Lynham, BH Blackwell, of Blackwell's Bookshop fame, and RW Poulton, a young student at Balliol College with an interest in boys clubs. Later in the year

*The South Canterbury "Town" team in New Zealand on 15<sup>th</sup> May 1875 included Alfred Hamersley, still wearing his England shirt.*

Ronnie Poulton won the first of three rugby 'Blues' and scored five tries in doing so, still a 'Varsity match record today. In 1914, under the surname Poulton-Palmer, he won his seventeenth cap for England, playing against France in Paris, and scored four tries, the last of which was the last try scored by England in the last International before the First World War. Sadly, Poulton-Palmer lost his life when he was shot by a sniper while supervising a trench digging party at Anton's Farm near Ploegsteert, Belgium, in 1915.

A General Meeting of the Club took place in the Clarendon Hotel in September 1909, where the organising committee's proposals were accepted, one of which was that the **Club colours were suggested as green, white and black, for no particular reason**. Officers were elected and the first President was Alfred Hamersley with James Eldridge naturally dropping into the slot as secretary. The first Captain of the Club was Wilfred Hearne Pearson who had started his education at the Oxford High School for Boys before moving on to Magdalen College School and finally the Leys School in Cambridge where he was introduced to the game, playing three-quarter. Wilfred qualified as a Pharmacist and returned to Oxford to take charge of one of the three Oxford Drug Company shops owned by his father and in this period took on the captaincy of the new rugby club. He was the team's goal kicker and featured prominently in the early seasons of the club before the First World War intervened. Wilfred's exempt occupation as a Pharmacist was withdrawn in March 1917 and he joined the Machine Gun Corps that was involved in heavy fighting on the Western Front in France, to the west of Arras. He lost his life in the Battle of the Canal du Nord on 29<sup>th</sup> September 1918.

The club's first ever match resulted in an encouraging 24–3 win against St Edward's School, Oxford, at their ground in the Woodstock Road, on Saturday 2<sup>nd</sup> October 1909. The players, some with experience and some without, had had no opportunity of playing together and the schoolboys gave them a fairly hard game. But, at last, the club was playing rugby, generally on a Saturday but sometimes on a Thursday. The end of season figures of having won ten games, lost twelve and drawn three were seen as indicative of a satisfactory first season. The fortunes of the Oxfordshire Nomads saw many highs and lows in the early seasons and, despite being the only club for miles around, set firm foundations which would prove invaluable in times to come. In a letter dated August 1971, Basil Blackwell recalled that James Eldridge was a safe if slow performer at full back, and a wise and good humoured captain when called upon to perform that role. "It was a delightful Club which conducted its affairs in the purest amateur spirit. I played in the first match, having never played before, with Ronnie Poulton playing at centre three-quarters. To give you some idea of our casual progress, from time to time we borrowed from the Berkshire Wanderers and they in turn borrowed from us except, that is, when we played each other. It was a delightful company that assembled on the field (very rarely in full strength) and though we played as hard as we might, most of us had forgotten the score before we got home. I have two outstanding memories of matches: one, against Stow-on-the-Wold, the team consisting largely of Brewers' Maltsters – solid fellows with a strong grasp of their opponents but no very strong grasp of the rules of the game. I still hear Cruttwell, later Principal of Halford College, turning to one of these somewhat gorilla-like players and saying 'Confound you, Sir, you wantonly obstructed me'. 'Never 'eard such language in all me born life.' I remember playing for Berkshire Wanderers against what today would be the Oxford Greyhounds, and then for the Nomads against my College, who did not know of my interest in the game (I was a wet-bob). The Nomads won at the cost of half of one of my teeth. Thereafter I played regularly for Merton and was awarded a beautiful magenta velvet cap with silver binding and silver tassel. Was I not proud! I long treasure the black, white and green striped shirts in which we played. I retain in my memory the happy impression of good humour, good fellowship, good sport, but not very good performances." The struggle, at times, in running the club paled into insignificance with the outbreak of the First World War. The mood of the country was such that the conflict was seen by many in the rugby fraternity as a huge 'away match' which would be quickly dealt with before everybody returned home. How wrong could they be? Rugby players from all across the country were seen as ideal soldiers coming, as they did, from a sport where discipline and respect were high in the list of ideals. In the awful carnage that followed, hundreds of British rugby clubs lost thousands of players. Compared to many clubs, Oxfordshire Nomads had a relatively small membership and the loss of eighteen members had a devastating effect on the club to the degree that, despite the war ending, officials saw no other option than to disband the club.

Thankfully this situation did not last for too long and enough interest was shown for a General Meeting to be held on 21st October, 1921. It was decided to revive the Oxfordshire Nomads club and the first match after the enforced break took place the very next day, Saturday 22nd October, 1921, against Pembroke College and was lost, 6–14. But the club was at least back in business.

As the country got used to living in peace time again there was increased interest in Rugby Union. By the mid 1920s the Nomads were fielding a second team and were using the Holywell Meadow as a home ground and, at the same time, had begun to use the Kings Arms Hotel in Holywell as a club headquarters. Local schools were now playing rugby which started to provide a few young players for the club when they left their educational establishments and the point was reached whereby the Nomads club had plenty of players but was struggling to provide games for them all. This lead to the formation of a new club in

June 1928, called the Oxford Exiles, founded by some former Nomads players, which grew in strength over a number of years to eventually provide some fierce local 'derbies' and much talk of amalgamation.

For all the increased interest there had been, and was being, shown in the game it was apparent that the standard of play had not increased at the same pace and 1929 saw the first mention of the formation of a County Union. This was seen as a way of providing a better class of rugby for local players while the clubs could retain their individuality. The Nomads played their home games for seven seasons at the Manor Road ground, which was part of the Holywell Meadow and prone to flooding from the River Cherwell. Then in 1930 the club announced that they would be using a pitch in Abberbury Avenue at Iffley for home games and the Tree Hotel for baths and teas afterwards.

In February 1932 the Oxfordshire Rugby Union was finally formed at a meeting called by Dr William Stobie, where nine clubs and schools were represented and support promised by four others. A Trial match was arranged and played at the Iffley Road ground where admission cost 7d and 1s from which gate takings totalled £6, and for the first ever Oxfordshire match, against Berkshire, seven Nomads were selected, almost half the team, a theme that was to run through most County team selections for many years. The game was won, 6–3.

Interest in Rugby Union continued to grow as clubs began to realise the importance of encouraging players after they had left school. Once more the Nomads were on the move and in 1933 started to play their home matches on a pitch at the Osberton Radiators ground in Woodstock Road, where changing rooms, teas and a bar were all on one site but still using The Kings Arms as the club headquarters.

No progress had been made over the suggestion of one strong Oxford side despite, in 1937, the knowledge that the County Championship was confined to Counties with strong leading clubs as an anchor, and that Oxfordshire would have to wait another three years to see whether the local standard went up. This was a blow to the hopes of people attempting to lead the way and, although the number of rugby players had increased significantly, the standard of play stagnated again.

But all of this was of secondary importance when the international situation drastically deteriorated once more at the end of the 1930s into a second world war. Rugby in Oxford changed almost overnight as many members once again joined the Forces and moved away, to be replaced with others posted locally as Oxford clubs struggled to keep going. By the end of 1940 the struggle had became too much and activities at Oxfordshire Nomads ceased for the duration of the war years.

Six members lost their lives in this hostile campaign. But, unlike the aftermath of the first war and despite the austere conditions of rationing, the club was better off and the members, with much vigour, got the club playing again, so much so that the first post war game took place at RAF Broadwell, near Burford, in September 1945. The benefit of years of experience, and an eagerness of the members to get involved once more in peacetime activity, saw the club take great strides forward and it was obvious that stronger fixtures were needed. The Oxfordshire County team was revived and seven Nomads players were included in the team to beat Oxford University, 11–8, in the first ever meeting between the two teams.

By now the club was playing at the St John's College ground again, but still using the Osberton Radiators club for changing and teas, as the width of the pitch at the Radiators had been narrowed due to the expansion of the nearby railway system.

A local boy, Bernard Gadney, with fourteen pre-war England caps to his credit, was now Oxfordshire RFU President and when Oxfordshire was suddenly admitted to the County

Championship in 1947, Gadney immediately called a meeting of club representatives. The intention was to form an Oxford rugby team, to include all the best local players, as a means of reaching a higher playing standard from which the County team could then be selected.

In the meantime, RB Cole, President of Oxfordshire Nomads, had negotiated an agreement with Wadham College for the sale of thirteen acres of land on the city side of the Oxford Southern Bypass and had paid the deposit out of his own pocket! The club was due to become part of the Oxford Sports Club, the proud owner of the ground, along with cricket, hockey, tennis, archery and motoring clubs, albeit with much work to do to prepare it for any sort of sports. This ground was now the obvious home for any Oxford Rugby Club but the Nomads had doubts with all the work that was now needed to get it up and running. At an open meeting in the Town Hall all the other local clubs were unanimously in favour of a proposition that the Oxfordshire Nomads Club should, in future, introduce a new level by using the best players from other clubs under an affiliation system, called Oxford Rugby Football Club, thus making that team representative of the city. Shortly afterwards, at a crowded meeting in The Kings Arms Hotel, Holywell, the Oxfordshire Nomads club decided to accept the invitation and change the club name to Oxford RFC, at the same time retaining the Nomads as the name of the team playing at the same level as previously.

Oxford RFC played its first game away at Welwyn, which was won comfortably enough, at, the start of the 1947–1948 season and this heralded the start of a good run of results. On the other hand, Oxfordshire were well beaten by Surrey in their County Championship debut. The club team won 17 of the 29 games played in that opening season which was not bad for such a venture in which not all was smooth behind the scenes. The new club committee had co-opted onto it a member from the Old Oxford Citizens, Old Southfieldians, Oxford Exiles, Morris Motors and Pressed Steel clubs but few of the representatives had attended selection meetings. Consequently the Oxford team was not, perhaps, as representative of the city as some thought it should be.

In 1948 another club was formed locally in Oxford and called Oxford Marathon RFC while the Oxford club, with a stronger fixture list, continued to make progress and even went on tour for the first time, at the end of the season to Bournemouth.

At the Southern Bypass site appeals had been made, work had been done and the ground was due to be ready for play with a cricket match in the summer of 1950. The rugby club had not been able to sustain the cost of the ground provision by itself and so an alliance with Oxford City Cricket Club and the City of Oxford Hockey Club had been formed, called Oxford Sports Club, under which those clubs would share the facilities. The ground was duly opened on time, albeit with temporary buildings, by the Mayor of Oxford on Whit Monday, 29th May 1950, and was described as a landmark in City sport.

The first rugby match at the new ground followed and was against Streatham, drawn 3–3, on Saturday 30th September 1950, and it coincided with what was to become a golden

*How the clubhouse might have looked. An architect's impression in the 1948 plan.*

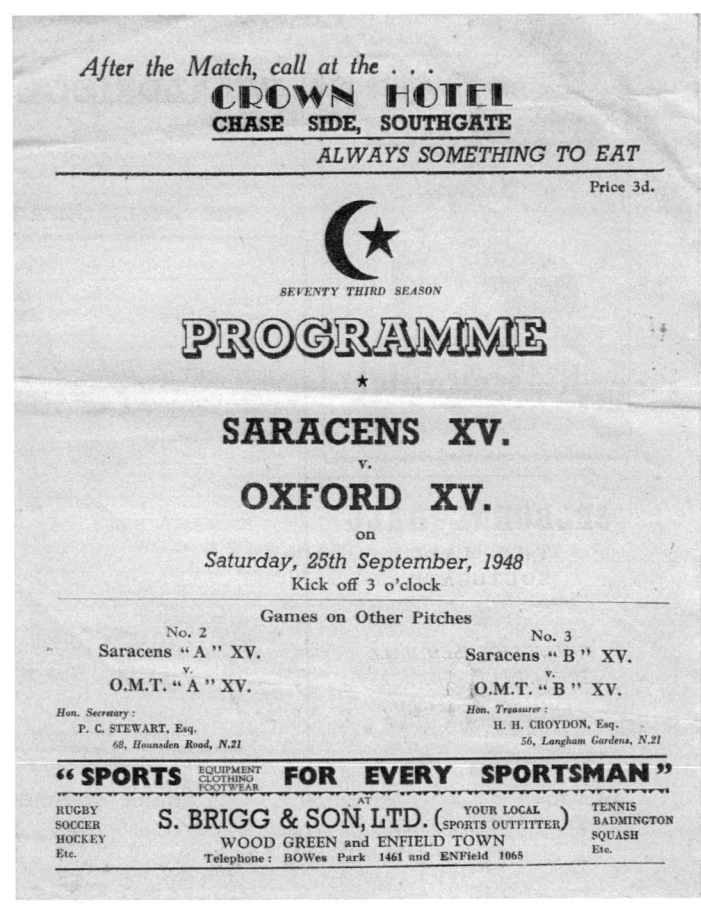

*Wow! How times have changed.*

era for the club. The new Captain, Chris Price, following Howard Darcus and George Cawkwell, both of whom had done much to lay the groundwork for such a future, was large in character and did much to set a fine spirit amongst the team with his leadership while the fixture list continued to grow in strength. At the same time the Oxfordshire team gained its first points in four seasons of County Championship rugby with a 6–6 draw against Notts, Lincs & Derbyshire at Chesterfield followed by a 3–3 draw at home to North Midlands. After a successful season Oxford won the Oxfordshire Seven-a-side Tournament and with it, the Oxford Times Cup, for the first time in 1951, and again in 1952 when the side also played in the Middlesex Sevens at Twickenham for the first time. Price was, by now, also Captain of Oxfordshire and well supported by Oxford players guided the side at last to some winning games in the Championship. In the background discussions over the pros and cons of affiliation to Oxford RFC rumbled on while the Oxford Exiles club was struggling for players.

At the end of 1953–1954 season Oxford won the Sevens Cup for the third time and again qualified for the Middlesex Sevens at Twickenham, while the 'swan song' for Chris Price came when he captained Oxfordshire to their first win over Oxford University RFC since 1946. The Oxford team had lost just two of its fixtures and this was undoubtedly the best season yet, at which point Price was to resign the captaincy and leave the area to take up employment in North Devon.

It was a hard act to follow but Ted Walters, a local lad who had learnt to play rugby at Magdalen College School in Oxford and was already a County player, stepped up to the plate to lead the club but, with several changes in personnel, a season of consolidation was in store. The following season Frank Webb took over and he was to stay and lead the club forward from that platform for the next three seasons, culminating in the Oxfordshire team which he, like Price before him, now captained, making its first appearance in a County Championship quarter final away against Devon. After three years at the helm Frank stepped down and, again like Price, left the area for employment in Devon midway through the 1958–1959 season.

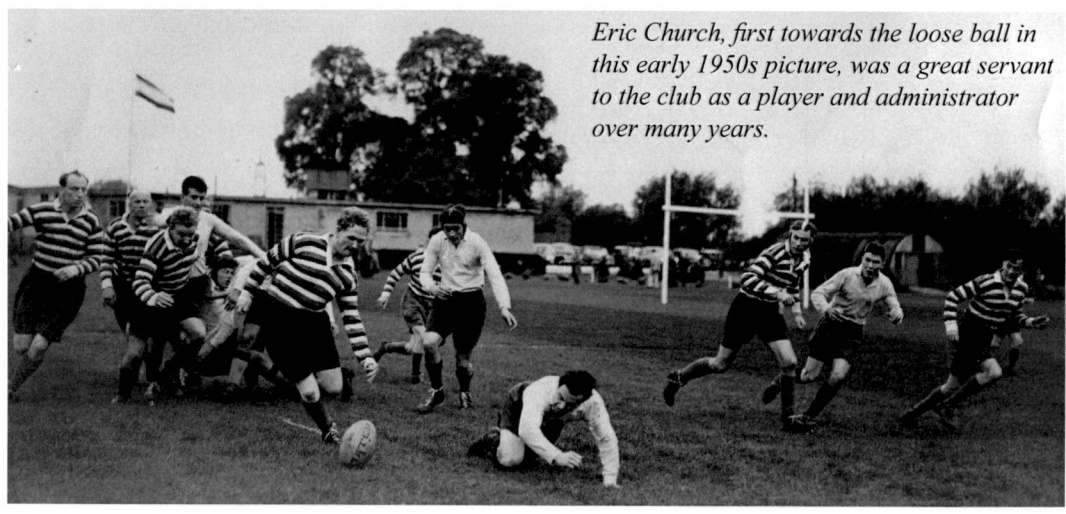

*Eric Church, first towards the loose ball in this early 1950s picture, was a great servant to the club as a player and administrator over many years.*

By now the club had a thriving Colts section formed through an alliance with an Oxford Youth side which, for some years, had been run by Gilbert Beesley, a pre war County player, who had seen the benefits of joining with Oxford RFC. At this stage some of the older players had retired whilst others moved on and the new Captain, Thom Cooper, had the job of trying to blend the club's youthful talent with the experienced players remaining. This, of course, took time and results were varied but by the time the Jubilee Dinner came round in October 1959 the club had re-focused and future prospects, hopefully for another fifty years and beyond, now looked extremely promising once again.

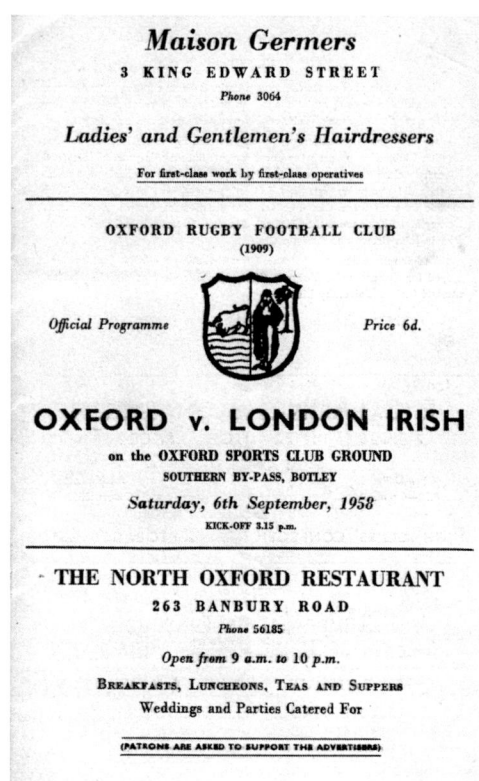

*The programme from the Oxford v London Irish match in 1958.*

*Keith Jenkins and Ken Morgan collide under a high ball in the same match.*

# Chapter 2 – Swing low!
## Season 1960–1961

In his third season as captain it fell to Physical Education teacher Thom Cooper to lead the club beyond the first fifty years. The results and performances from the previous season had been pretty even with 16 games won, 12 lost with 5 drawn and 9 points more scored at 249 than the 240 against. The Colts Fifteen had enjoyed an unprecedented season winning all their games to remain unbeaten and, with all this in mind members could be forgiven for thinking that future prospects were good with the First Fifteen being based mainly on the previous year's lineup, although Peter Pringle was a newcomer.

Pre-season training, during which David Bagnall was seen to have fully recovered from the serious illness he had suffered at the end of the season past, and the trials, the last one of which began with a talk by Andy Mulligan the Ireland Captain, led to the new season with a midweek match on the pitch at the top of South Park in Headington against a Combined Old Boys side and, in adverse weather conditions, Oxford won 11–0. This was a satisfying enough result with the Old Boys putting their toes into the water with a view to the future when Old Oxford Citizens and Old Southfieldians would be joining together in the wake of the Oxford High and Southfield schools amalgamation. The Oxford club committee had earlier declined the suggestion of a First Fifteen fixture against the proposed new club from the start of the 1962–1963 season but was happy to continue the current arrangement of an early season mid week match and, depending on results, would decide future policy. Eric Church, now the Fixture Secretary, was asked to reply tactfully and at the same time give the venture as much encouragement as possible.

It was also noted that the Oxfordshire Union, possibly in anticipation of using the Bypass ground for some of its future home matches, had made a gift to the club of £100 which enabled the final payment of the cost of erecting the stand to be made.

The first four Saturday fixtures were away from home, which always conveniently avoided a clash with the closing cricket season at the Bypass ground, and an Oxford team minus Gordon Acaster, who had an afternoon appointment with the Vicar, of: R Salter; J Cruickshank, R Hazeldine, M Jones, P Pringle; K Morgan, R Livesey; J Goodger, J Roberts, D Ranger, M Rogers, T Cooper, P West, D Howard, D Flook, found the Bridgwater & Albion club a tough nut to crack in heat wave conditions in Somerset. After an even first half Oxford found themselves 0–8 behind at the break and Bridgwater got on top in the second half to double that score. But, with six minutes left, Oxford staged a fight back and Cruickshank scored a good try which Livesey, after three unsuccessful penalty attempts, converted with a superb kick from the touchline and, five minutes later, landed his one penalty kick in the 8–16 opening defeat. Back in the West Country the next week, this time at Bristol against Clifton, Oxford scored first with a Livesey penalty and the visitors did as much, if not more, of the attacking yet it was Clifton, snapping up Oxford errors, who piled on the points. There was barely any sign of teamwork or plan although, individually, there were some good Oxford performances. Rogers shone in the lineouts and Roberts hooked magnificently, but a second penalty from Livesey was all they could muster in the 6–26 defeat, the heaviest in nine matches with Clifton.

Another undistinguished performance saw Oxford beaten again, 9–14, at Aldershot Services. Once more there were good individual efforts, but it was quite apparent that unless the team applied some method and organisation to the play it would struggle. With some unity this match could have been won and, again, Oxford took an early lead when Skates

*Charlie Ede ran the very successful Oxford Thursday Nomads, an invitation team which catered for players who had to work on Saturdays. This lineup beat Old Southfieldians 29–6 on 12th September: SC Coles, HR Moore, T Cracknell, GB Skates, ET Walters, D Barrett, MR Rhymes, A Harrington. Front row: J Buckland, K Bye, CT Ede (Capt), T Reddington, P West, K Morgan, D O'Brien.*

kicked a penalty goal but it was left to Jackson, with the only incisive run of the game, to equalise with a try after two Aldershot scores. Again Oxford went behind and it was left to Skates with his second penalty kick for any consolation.

It had been a bad start to the season and it was obvious that there was work to be done. Fortunately the team played much better away at Sutton the next week and the side had its first win of the season, 12–0, on the last Saturday in September. The much improved performance was more convincing than the score suggested and Oxford made a bright start with a pushover try touched down by Buckland, after a strike against the head, before Skates kicked a penalty and Livesey two more to close the score. Oxford also broke with unwanted tradition with this match when the team arrived at Sutton early, having gone straight to the ground with guidance from Ron Livesey and directions given by Thom Cooper!

The club received a further boost when Jack Cameron, formerly with London Scottish and a Berkshire County wing forward, joined the playing ranks along with Russell Harrington, a former Oxfordshire quarter mile sprint champion. Russell had been playing for Bicester and had joined for three games "to see how things go" in a higher class of rugby.

The result at Sutton gave the players some much needed confidence although everybody knew that Oxford's first home game was going to be a tough one. The annual midweek match against the University Captain's Fifteen on Thursday was due to be followed by another club match on Saturday. J Glover's XV included England International Richard Sharp, who'd won a Blue the previous season at fly half and newcomer Joe McPartlin, a current two cap Scottish International in the centre. Sharp, with four caps already to his credit, was in superb form scoring two tries and making two others to steal the show. Future England full back, John Willcox, added 14 points with 4 conversions and 2 penalties but although the club side was beaten 6–29, it was far from disgraced. Gordon Skates was outstanding for Oxford, probably the best forward on the field, while Cooper and Gordon Acaster also did a great amount of work. Ron Salter made some good tackles at full back but, generally, Oxford's backs lacked pace and the skills to make an impact. Skates kicked a penalty from the halfway line and Mike Stephenson added another in the second half.

There was also an interest on the University wing where American Peter Dawkins, a former 'grid iron' player, brought the innovation of a torpedo throw to the game. Although it is common place today at the lineout, at that time its use in the game was seen as a means to switch attack with a long throw infield from the wing. Unfortunately the rugby ball has bigger dimensions than its North American cousin and the move was not generally effective.

Two days later the Oxford team was at home again, this time to Old Cranleighans. In contrast to the sunshine of the previous two weeks, Oxford kicked off into heavy, driving rain and, with the advantage of a Livesey penalty goal lead, set up constant offensive in the second half. With handling a lottery, Skates touched down a pushover try. Livesey converted from the touchline and then added a second penalty before Morgan slipped his man to put Mark Jones over for a try. Again Acaster was the pick of a splendid forward effort. Another tough match followed, this time with Moseley the visitors to the Bypass ground. Although outweighted the Oxford forwards played with a fighting spirit and stubborn resistance in a hard, gruelling struggle but the team lost 0–8 after missing with three penalty attempts. It is worth noting that on the same afternoon a total of forty eight matches involving club, college and school teams in the Oxford area were due to be played.

The former Oxford RFC player, Peter Sibley, became Oxfordshire County Captain and celebrated this by leading the team to victory over Dorset & Wiltshire, 8–3, in the Southern Group of the County Championship. The team had included five Oxford players, M Jones, AD Maxton, CT Ede, J Buckland, and GB Skates in the lineup. It was an ex Oxford player, Frank Webb, now at Okehampton, who helped to break the deadlock with a strong, bustling run before slipping to Buckland to crash over and Skates kicked a conversion and a penalty goal. Soon after this it was announced that Sibley had been picked to play for the Southern Counties team against South Africa at Brighton on 22$^{nd}$ October, the only Oxfordshire player selected. The next game was away to Hertfordshire and was due to be played on the same day as the touring South Africans were due to play Oxford University at Iffley Road.

Next up for the club team were the Oxford University Greyhounds who did most of the attacking but good defending, especially by Ron Salter at full back, was one of the reasons for Oxford's 8–0 win, played on a midweek Wednesday afternoon, and the good form continued into the next Saturday at Streatham. The Oxford players were popular visitors and it was said that the match was the best at the ground thus far in the season. Streatham had won seven of their nine games but only made the game safe with a try in the last minute to edge home 9–3. Once again the pack worked hard with Livesey and Salter defending well outside.

The County match at Hertfordshire was played in impossible conditions and Oxfordshire, 0–8 at the break, looked like getting a hammering but Charlie Ede, a real warrior, led the forwards to a tremendous revival in the second half and the score remained the same at the end. On the same afternoon Roy Tapper was playing for Berkshire against Sussex and, despite the heavy rain, 7000 people crammed into Iffley Road to see the touring South Africans beat Oxford University, 24–5.

The Oxford club was not renowned for cancelling fixtures due to pitch conditions but local heavy rain over a period of time caused acre upon acre of flooded meadow land in the Botley area, caused by the overflowing of Potts Stream, and two home fixtures, against Nottingham and St Thomas's Hospital, were lost to the weather when the ground was waterlogged.

The rain eventually eased enough for Oxfordshire beat Buckinghamshire 14–11 in a 'friendly' fixture at Wycombe. Harrington made his mark with two tries with another from Maxton but it was touch and go at the end after Skates, a tireless worker, had left the field with a back injury.

Normal service resumed on Saturday 12th November for Oxford RFC with a third visit to Bedford, where Ken Morgan was available again after a broken nose, but they never looked like being lucky enough for a first win. Roberts in the tight, and Cooper and Acaster in the lineout ensured the team won their fair share of the ball but the attack was almost non existent with the mid-field backs being caught in possession too easily by Budge Rogers, Bedford's English flanker. Despite hectic defence, Oxford lost 3–18.

Loughborough College's main pitch was deemed unplayable and the second pitch was not much better for Oxford's visit, but the struggle for the clammy, sodden ball produced an extremely hard game. Despite Skates and Cameron returning after injury it was not a memorable occasion for Graham Barrett's debut on the wing and in a test of fitness both packs were barely recognizable at the end with Oxford losing again, 6–11.

Reflecting on the County group, Oxfordshire had to win at Eastbourne against Sussex to keep their championship hopes alive and the Oxford connection provided six players, Maxton, Harrington, Acaster, Cooper, Buckland and Skates, but the team went down 0–6 after a gallant fight.

Once more Oxford travelled, on 26th November, this time to Birmingham to be greeted again with mud and rain. The home side scored early and hardly ever looked dangerous again whilst the Oxford players, struggling to keep upright, could not get back into it and suffered a fourth successive defeat, 0–3.

Returning home to play on the Bypass ground for the first time in two months, against Bridgwater & Albion, it was difficult to appreciate why the side had gone all that time without a win. It was a gruelling struggle, again in atrocious conditions, where Oxford more than held their opponents and had charge of the game for most of the second half. Brian Morgan, an RAF outside half now stationed at RAF Abingdon, made a promising club debut and it was obvious that the team that scored first would win the match but no score came and the match ended 0–0.

The onset of the winter months with attendant rain, mud and dark evenings had heralded a miserable period for both Oxford RFC and Oxfordshire. This seemed also to affect Ron Grimshaw who, in his weekly *Sports Mail* column, questioned the validity of the new £1000 stand opened during the Jubilee season. "The last thing to be said of this stand is that it gives shelter from the elements. It is particularly useless for the purpose for which it was intended though, to be fair, the top half of the body may be protected from the rain – by standing on the back seat!" Ron went on to suggest that the club's Diamond Jubilee in 1969 be marked by the removal of the Golden Jubilee stand and replaced with something useful. He had obviously not enjoyed his visit for the Bridgwater match!

Oxfordshire's last Southern Group match was at home against Berkshire at Banbury, and both Gerry Howells and Roy Tapper were playing for Berkshire who had not lost in this season's matches. Oxfordshire, however, were at full strength for the first time and included Geoffrey Windsor-Lewis, a Welsh international and Cambridge 'Blue', making his debut at fly half in place of Nigel Townsend, an Old Southfieldian, and an 8–0 win deprived Berkshire of the group title and saw Oxfordshire avoid the 'wooden spoon'.

There was worse to come from the weather the following week when the home match with Stroud was cancelled due to the conditions, providing as it did a slight respite for the players, but there was a sufficient improvement for Reading to be entertained on 17th December. It was not an inspiring match although there was much effort from the players and one in particular, Ron Livesey, scored all Oxford's points in an 11–3 win with a try, two penalties and a conversion.

Oxford lost by a point at Nuneaton, 8–9, before a New Years Eve match saw the year out with a much deserved home win against Weston-super-Mare. For Oxford it was a 'holiday' selection with Steve Coles making a surprise return at scrum half, local schoolboy Ian Moffatt in at fly half and Rex Hazeldine in the centre. In a bitterly cold wind Oxford were worth more than their 8–0 win, which was just one of five victories recorded by the team in the first half of the season, having lost more than ever before at this stage. The three games cancelled bore witness to one the wettest seasons for many a year but the main trouble was not being able to field the strongest team as selected in consecutive weeks.

Oxford began 1961 with good intentions and a morning kick off in Croydon, against Old Whitgiftians, which enabled the party to go on to Twickenham to see England against South Africa. Learning from previous like ventures the team left Oxford in moonlight to arrive at the ground at 9.30am, leaving an hour to spare. They soon found that the pitch was hard and icy, and had to face a low, blinding sun in the first half. Apart from that the team played as badly as at any time during the season and it was no surprise that they found themselves fourteen points down early in the second half. But far from being the end this was the signal for an all out effort to save the game and Old Whitgiftians went to pieces the face of the onslaught. Russell Harrington ran in two tries, and then cross kicked for Thom Cooper to score a third. But Skates, already with a penalty and a conversion to his credit, sent the vital kick to the left of the posts and the game was drawn 14–14. This was Mike Stephenson's last match before leaving the Air Force for a job in Aden, and Ian Parsons, who had been posted away from the Oxford area, had won a place in Saracens First XV.

Another Harrington try, with a run from inside his own half, was the highlight of Oxford's home match with Lydney and it was left to Ron Livesey with three second half penalty goals, each one better than the one before, to give his side a 14–9 win. But, in the second of a sequence of five home games, the side could not complain at a 6–16 defeat at the hands of London Hospital. Although Cooper and Acaster dominated the lineout possession it was the visitors who took their second half chances and Oxford never recovered.

A creditable 3–3 draw with Nuneaton in heavy conditions helped to lift the spirits on 28th January and, a week later, the team edged clear of Clifton by 6–3. Due to a misunderstanding over the kick-off time Clifton arrived late and Ron Livesey used this time to get his eye in with a few kicks in the tricky, cold wind. This paid dividends as his two penalty goals provided the winning margin although this would have been bigger had Oxford brought their two potential match winners, wingers Maxton and Harrington, into play.

A strong end-to-end wind made a big impact on the following week's match and the spoiling tactics of Old Rutlishians, playing against it in the first half, completely upset the Oxford side. Skates tried to break from a scrum but, as he was held, the ball went loose and Tapper gathered to dive over for a try that Livesey converted. Soon after Don Ranger went over from a maul for Livesey to convert again. Cooper marshalled his defence well in the second period and the Old Boys side were limited to a try in a 10–3 win that was really no advert for rugby.

The Oxford side were saved from a trip to Birmingham on 18th February when Old Edwardians cancelled the scheduled match due to the poor state of the ground and Roy Tapper took the opportunity to retain the Chris Price Kicking Cup with Thom Cooper second and Ron Salter third. Off the field wing forward John Buckland had taken an appointment in Cheltenham and was leaving the club, Tony Walters had been presented with a daughter and his brother Ted, after forty games for Oxfordshire and two club appearances in the Middlesex Sevens at Twickenham, was following Buckland out of the door but to Birmingham.

Although heavy rain had left the pitch saturated and with puddles the small break from play paid dividends for Oxford who overcame the atrocious conditions in their morning start at Cobham against Westminster Hospital. Three of Oxford's youngest members, fly half Ian Moffatt, winger Graham Barrett and hooker George Webb were in grand form and, at one point, Barrett was crash tackled into a corner flag which broke in half! But he did get his own back by scoring one of the four tries in Oxford's 16–0 win.

Few victories had been more deserved than Oxford's win over Old Haberdashers but they did leave it very late. Despite having 80 per cent of the play the team found themselves in arrears after a number of defensive lapses and, following a try from Stuart Cameron after a break from Skates into the corner and a penalty from Livesey, it was left to Ian Moffatt to neatly drop a goal for the 9–8 win. But the next week, and two days after eight Oxford club players (Salter, Stone, Moffatt, Coles, Cooper, Acaster, Livesey and Skates) played

---

## O.U.R.F.C. v. OXFORDSHIRE

### Iffley Road Ground, Oxford, Thursday, 9 March 1961

### Kick-off 2.30 p.m.

| O.U.R.F.C. | OXFORDSHIRE |
|---|---|
| 1. †J. G. WILCOX (Ratcliffe & Worcester) (Captain) | 1. G. R. SALTER (Oxford) |
| 2. M. A. WARE (Bec & St. Edmund Hall) | 2. P. J. STONE (Oxford) |
| 3. †J. J. MCPARTLIN (Wimbledon College & S.E.H.) | 3. P. C. SIBLEY (Blackheath) |
| 4. P. M. W. STAFFORD (Birkenhead & Corpus Christi) | 4. †*G. WINDSOR-LEWIS (Richmond) |
| 5. J. G. ROBERTS (Newport H.S. & University) | 5. M. S. SIMMIE (Magdalen College School) |
| 6. †R. A. W. SHARP (Blundells & Balliol) | 6. I. MOFFATT (Oxford) |
| 7. T. CASS (Q.E.G.S., Wakefield, & St. Edmund Hall) | 7. †S. C. COLES (Oxford) |
| 8. J. A. COLLINGWOOD (St. Mary's & St. Edmund Hall) | 8. F. WEBB (Okehampton) |
| 9. C. S. WATES (Stowe & Brasenose) | 9. R. J. CLOKE (Cheltenham) |
| 10. J. A. H. CURRY (K.C.S., Wimbledon, & St. Edmund Hall) | 10. J. W. WOOD (Cheltenham) |
| 11. P. K. STAGG (St. Paul's & St. Peter's Hall) | 11. T. R. COOPER (Oxford) |
| 12. J. R. L. ADCOCK (Radley & Trinity) | 12. G. ACASTER (Oxford) |
| 13. N. SILK (Lewes G.S. & Merton) | 13. R. J. D. LIVESEY (Oxford) |
| 14. G. W. HINES (Christ's Hospital & Trinity) | 14. G. B. SKATES (Oxford) |
| 15. P. W. SUTCLIFFE (Workington G.S. & Queen's) | 15. R. A. HERBERTSON (Magdalen College School) |

\* International  † Blue

Touch judge: C. J. ACKFORD (Oxon Society)

*The Oxford University v Oxfordshire match card. All the county players were either playing, had played or would play, for Oxford RFC.*

in a losing Oxfordshire side against a strong Oxford University, Oxford slumped to a 0–11 home defeat to Cheltenham. The blame for defeat was laid, again, at the door of the midfield trio who were said to be slow of thought and deed with repeated mistakes in handling and tactics, and general bungling. Ron Grimshaw, in the *Oxford Mail*, mused that the club were not alone in their problems with almost every club in the country suffering from a lack of thrustful centres, and even suggested that Oxford's young outside half, Ian Moffatt, should add another yard to his speed to achieve anything in senior rugby.

The club's annual dinner took place at the Southern Bypass ground on the evening of Oxfordshire's match with the University. Mr SA Miller, President of the County Union, replying to John Willcox, England International and University Captain, said that Oxford RFC was "the backbone of the county" not just from the playing point of view but from the support of club members on the County committee, "We in the county regard this club as one of the best" he said.

It was at this time that Frank Webb announced his withdrawal from the County side, after a distinguished playing career at that level, the travel to and from Oakhampton in Devon finally proving too much although he did intend to continue playing at his club. At the other end of the scale, Brian Beale, a pupil at Headington Secondary Modern School, became the twelfth Oxfordshire schoolboy to be capped at national level since the Second World War, with his school pal, Vince Pidgeley, named as a travelling reserve.

It was a much improved Oxford side that gave a spirited display the following week, 18$^{th}$ March, to beat Taunton 10–6, and Russell Harrington returning from injury was the match winner with two tries. The pack was in splendid form with hooker George Webb taking four strikes against the head and Gordon Acaster dominating the lineouts. Moffatt was better and Ken Morgan added some thrust in the centre. The good form continued into the next week when Oxford won 11–8 at Esher with, once again, the forwards leading the way to give the team a good send off for the West Country Tour during the forthcoming Easter holiday.

Typically, having decided to tour, Oxford had arranged a tough and rigorous weekend. Perhaps at their best in the first match against Stroud on Good Friday, in which two evenly matched sides fought out an 8–8 draw, both scoring a goal and a try before the party moved on to Weston-super-Mare the next day. Oxford impressed from the start with Cooper and Don Barrett to the fore and Roy Tapper intercepted a pass to race away before kicking ahead for Malcolm Phipps to follow up and score. Ian Moffatt kicked a penalty, but the team faded badly in the second half and Weston got top to take the game 8–6 with a touchline conversion. After a days rest it was on to Barnstable for Easter Monday and another tight affair, but this time Barnstable mistakes let Oxford in with Moffatt kicking a penalty. With ten minutes left Harrington touched down a loose ball the home defence had failed to clear and Moffatt, declared man of the match for his intelligent marshalling of the team, added the goal points. It all made for memorable trip with one lost, one drawn and one won!

The tour did leave a legacy, however, and, for the first time this season the team would be playing without Captain Thom Cooper, who had broken a finger against Barnstaple and Roy Tapper was due to captain the side at home against Old Alleynians. Also injured was Russell Harrington with a re-occurrence of his hamstring injury in the same match, and Ron Livesey with a thigh muscle badly damaged against Stroud. It did mean that Malcolm Phipps, who'd had a good tour, kept his place as did 'Mossy' Bath at full back. To no avail, though, as Oxford tried hard but slipped to a narrow 10–11 loss, while a similar fate awaited the team at Lydney in the last match of the season. The players battled hard and weren't helped when Peter Stone was helped from the field just before half time with concussion, the side finally losing 0–11.

*There was a good attendance at the Players Meeting at the end of the season: standing, left to right – G Barrett, M Phipps, J Goodger, J Barcham, M Drinkwater, J Scott, D Barrett, J Rowell, G Acaster, D Eaton, G Skates, M Bath, J Maxton, R Lorrain-Smith, G Wright, M Rhymes, P West, E Church; seated – J Higgins (trainer), G Strutt, G Webb, G Savage, GR Salter, T Cooper (retiring captain), RJ Tapper, C Ede, M Jones, A Maxton, R Harrington, D Ranger, H Lodge.*

Sevens rugby was very much on the agenda this season and the club team had mixed fortunes in the competitions they had entered. But, once again, the big one was the Middlesex Sevens and Oxford did extremely well to win through a very tough Preliminary Round to reach the Twickenham Finals. Still missing Harrington and Cooper, a team of M Simmie, RJ Tapper, P Hazeldine, D Bagnall, G Skates, G Webb and D Ranger, undaunted by the 30,000 crowd, were leading against Richmond at half time in the First Round. But it didn't last and the team went on to lose 8–11.

Oxford's record for the season showed 13 wins with 15 games lost and 4 drawn. An idea of the problems with which the club had faced was shown in the fact that 45 players had appeared for the first XV – what chance of team building with this constant change? The club had had its worst first half of the season ever, but this had improved significantly with some consistency in the second part and it was a pity that Thom Cooper was handing over the captaincy after three years at the helm. No one had worked harder for the success and well being of the club.

In comparison to the previous season when the side was unbeaten, the Oxford Colts team appeared to have had a disastrous campaign, winning only 6 of the 23 games played and only two players had remained from that memorable year. For most of the boys it was their first season out of school and most would be available for the next season. Manager Gilbert Beesley was unperturbed, however, saying "The real test of Colts Rugby, apart from keeping the boys in the game, is the supply to senior XVs. In this respect the club can be well satisfied. In four years of the Colts, 10 boys have played for the First XV and 5 of them in their first season in senior rugby." There was no question that the Colts had been a valuable attribute to the club.

Elsewhere in the area, the Old Oxford Citizens had taken advantage of a dearth of local rugby on Easter Monday to celebrate their Silver Jubilee with a match at South Park between themselves and a team labeled 'Citizens Exiles'. The club had been formed on

Wednesday 1st April 1936, two years after rugby had officially taken over from football at the City of Oxford High School for Boys – the last local grammar school to make the change. The club had supported Oxford RFC on its foundation by affiliating to it for the first seven years and providing some players. But, after one of their poorest seasons, the Citizens display in the Jubilee match was uninspired and gave the impression that they were just holding on for that amalgamation with Old Southfieldians. Oxford Marathons had suffered one of their worst seasons although a reasonable Colts team was giving them some hope for the future, while Gosford All Blacks, in their fifth year, had enjoyed the most successful season to date.

## Season 1961–1962

Rugby Union had been going well at the local schools in which it was being played, thus providing clubs in the area with a number of players, to the degree that anxiety had been felt by members of clubs in the Hellenic Football League. At their annual dinner in May 1962, Mr CW Rogers, the league's Vice Chairman said "We in our small sphere wonder sometimes just where we are heading when we see our opponents on the rugby field gaining so much in the schools as it has been doing in the past year or two." In reply, Mr Maurice Love, member of the Football Association Council, said that the fault was not so much with the FA as with the headmasters.

There was a reported crisis over at Bicester where it was said that the rugby club had reached a critical point and may have to cease functioning. The reason for this alarm was that only eleven members had attended the annual meeting in June and that this was not enough to fill all the necessary offices within the club. Those gathered decided to call an Emergency General Meeting to discuss the matter further which, when held, attracted far more members than the first attempt and the 'crisis' was averted.

At Oxford RFC a period of consolidation and experiment was reported at the annual meeting, also in June. There was a profit of £84 compared to the £9 from the previous season, probably as a result of the club's decision to reorganize its travelling arrangements, often using cars instead of coaches. Travel and transport had cost £198 compared with £342 in the 1959–1960 season. In addition the final account of £45 was paid on the new stand. 17 players had played for Oxfordshire in the past season, and County Caps were awarded to John Buckland and Russell Harrington, with badges to Gordon Acaster, Gordon Skates and Thom Cooper. With so many young players having graduated from the junior teams, established First XV players would have to look to their laurels in the coming months. Gordon Skates, who had been at the club since 1954 and had just been awarded his County badge for twelve or more appearances, was elected as Captain with Roy Tapper his Vice Captain, for the new campaign ahead.

Pre season trials revealed a glut of new faces but few looked like immediate 1st team material, with the exception of Welsh International and Oxford 'Blue', Robin Davies, who had been out of the game for a year after a knee operation. Second row Mike Rogers would be out of the country until November, while Ian Moffatt and George Webb were still playing cricket.

On the first Saturday in September, Gordon Skates took advantage of a cancelled Trial match to marry Pat Dive, daughter of Club Secretary Vernon Dive, and missed the opening game of the season, away at Blackheath the following Wednesday. The team selected, on form in the trials and fitness, of: MC Bath; AR Harrington, RJ Tapper, MR Jones, AD Maxton; N Townsend, DF Bagnall; J Head, CT Ede, D Ranger, GR Acaster, TR Cooper, R Herbertson, D Curtis and I Patterson, lost 0–6 but experienced prop Don Ranger did not make the match. Playing for Oxford in the Abingdon Sevens four days earlier, he came onto the pitch during the Final, by permission of the other finalists, RAF Abingdon, who won 11–9, to replace the injured Russell Harrington and, with thirty seconds left to play in the match broke his leg! In another midweek game, a team labeled 'The Rest of Oxford' was dispatched 19–11 in a depressing match with several unhappy incidents, both sides being intent on beating each other, and the event now seemed to have limited value as a Trial match for either club or county.

For the first Saturday match of the season, Oxford, with Mike Simmie on one wing and David Bagnall at scrum half, faced tough opposition away at Clifton and were lucky to be only four points in arrears at the end, losing 10–14. Served well by the pack the team led twice but lacked consistency. Peter West and Robert Hertbertson scored tries with Roy Tapper, who enjoyed a good game, converting both. Thom Cooper was also prominent and it was later known that he would be leaving the Oxford area to begin a new job as a brewery representative in Manchester. Aged 28 years, he was on a training course in London and hoped to be available until Christmas.

Gordon Skates captained the Oxford side for the first time the following Saturday and played a prominent part in a fighting display. Oxford played with urgency in a hard game which brought a deserved 8–6 win at Nottingham, and George Webb scored the only try, Roy Tapper a penalty with Skates getting on the scoreboard with a conversion.

There was some disturbing news from India where Neil Coombes, who had captained the Nomads side in 1958, had received some information about an intended raid on a tea warehouse in Upper Assam. With other men he succeeded in foiling the raid but at a personal cost to himself when one of the intruders struck him with a sword. Eighteen stitches were needed in a gash to his neck and a bone was also splintered. In happier moments in Weymouth, John Roberts, a hooker with Oxford until this season and now playing for Dorchester, was married.

Oxford ended September with an uninspiring defeat at Aldershot Services, 11–12. Having scored the only try the team led three times but succumbed to four penalty goals, the last in the closing minutes for a scrum offence.

But there was far worse to come in October when what was described, at the time, as Oxford's "darkest hour" resulted in a new milestone being reached in the club's history. A 0–51 drubbing away at Bedford by six goals and six tries, three scored by England International Budge Rogers, and a penalty, was the heaviest defeat since the club had been renamed in 1948. The explanation was brutally simple – Oxford, slow in thought and deed, were well out of their class. There were no signs of an immediate dawn, with suitable replacements for injured players just not available, and the outlook was bleak, but perhaps the greatest weakness was that the club was unable to get the players together for mid-week training, team practice and coaching. Bedford, though, was a good team and it was thought that Oxford could benefit considerably if the lessons were learnt.

It was a tough few days for the club and its players. The University Captain, John Willcox, had announced he would bring a strong team, barring accidents on a Cornish Tour, to the Bypass ground the following Thursday. Whereas this annual match was usually the first in the University team's winter programme, this time they would have the advantage of playing together twice before they got there. There was the added pressure of an Oxford win to level the balance in the series which, at that time, stood at 4–3 to the University teams.

But the day before the match with Willcox's XV, Harrington, Moffatt, Eaton, Webb, Butler and Skates played in Oxfordshire's opening Championship match with Berkshire at Newbury.

A feature of the forward play was Webb's striking of the ball in the tight, while Skates played extremely well in the middle of the back row doing the work of two men, the eventual reward being a penalty, the last kick of the match, which earned a 9–9 draw for Oxfordshire.

Charlie Ede was recalled for the Thursday match but at prop not hooker and was an inspired selection as he had a splendid game against the University Captain's XV. But Oxford went down fighting to another heavy defeat, this time 0–40, with Richard Sharp again stamping his mark on the match.

Gordon Skates was due to miss Oxford's fifth consecutive Saturday away game, to Old Cranleighans, this time to attend the wedding of his sister-in-law, Judith Dive, to Ron Salter. Robert Herbertson took his place, his last match before going 'up' to Oxford University, and Gordon Acaster returned from an ankle injury although this was 'one in, one out' as Thom Cooper was now working in Manchester. Cranleighans, though, had only won once in the season so far and there were hopes that Oxford could reverse the recent trend. But the saga continued as two of the cars carrying players got stuck in heavy traffic en route to the ground and the game was delayed by an hour. A quick change and out onto the pitch with no warm-up was no way to prepare and the side slumped to another defeat, this time 3–11. There was a lack of direction and method in Oxford's play and although Peter West scored a good try through quick backing up, the defensive weaknesses that had shipped 102 points in three games were still in evidence.

*Thom Cooper, seen here winning yet another lineout, was due to leave the area and would be missed.*

Generally the club was in good spirit despite the constant setbacks which must have nibbled away at the players' confidence. Another club with a poor record at that time was the Oxford Marathons where the club spirit was also said to be in good heart. Using the Coach and Horses pub in St Clements, their spiritual home area, as a headquarters the club had started a ground fund. All their club teams were now wearing similiar shirts and the last vestiges of the Oxford Exiles had been consigned to the past as the shirts of that club, having been worn by the 'A' XV, were now 'retired'.

At last Oxford was due to play a first home Saturday fixture on 21st October when the visitors were Streatham. Although there was an improvement, the side promised much but produced little and seemed to have developed an inferiority complex. Bagnall was energetic but there was no zip or sparkle in the play as Oxford lost to a try conceded in the second half, 0–3. There was even more improvement the next week against Oxford University Greyhounds, who faded in the second period, but Oxford couldn't find the impetus to cross the line and lost again, 0–6.

Sandwiched between these two games was Oxfordshire's Championship match at Salisbury against Dorset & Wiltshire where the county team, with Skates once more to the fore, disappointed again in a 3–3 draw.

Continuing into November, Oxford gathered an unwanted record as they equaled the club's longest losing run of seven games in the last fifteen years when the team lost 3–6 at St Thomas's Hospital. Roy Tapper's drop goal was the only score where the forwards were said to be neither fit nor fast enough, with the backs lacking skill and striking power to use the opportunities presented to them. The club had used more than 32 players in the First XV already this season mainly due to injuries, probably a reason why it was in the doldrums, and being unable to field a consistent team. Bemoaning the fact, Ron Grimshaw recalled "At the time of its (Oxford RFC) formation the officials were warned that in all probability the club would be most unpopular locally for the first twenty years. 'At least some of the local clubs will be enjoying our present losses'. Unfortunately there is more than a grain of truth in this belief, yet a really strong club representative of the whole city whose name it bears should remain the objective. All concerned, particularly the county, would benefit."

On a lighter note Mike Rogers, the second row forward having returned home from the continent, was having a quiet lunchtime drink in his 'local' the previous Saturday when a 'raiding party' led by Dixie Deane descended. Mike was whisked away to make up the 'A' side at Shrivenham. He started playing in plimsoles but ended in stockinged feet and a pair of shorts from the opposition and, using parts of three shirts "we managed to cover him completely" said Dixie. Was the pointless 0–0 draw worth the trouble? Of course it was!

Oxfordshire went one better than two draws to beat Hertfordshire 11–6 in a hard game where an overpowering finish saw them home for the vital two points. The Oxford players concerned might have welcomed the brief respite brought by the cancellation of the match with Charing Cross Hospital the following weekend. The team, having scored just a try and a drop goal in the past six games, were able to 'gather themselves' to end their losing run when they beat Birmingham University, 17–0, at the Bypass ground. A Royal Air Force winger, Arthur Johnson, made an impressive debut, spurring the other players on, and Eaton, Tapper and Thrussell scored tries, with Curtis adding two penalties and a conversion. But the real bonus was that the side prevented the visitors from scoring. This win was extended to 'two on the trot' when Oxford beat Birmingham the following weekend, 13–6, with tries

*Oxfordshire 1961–1962, Southern Group County Champions.*
*Back row, l to r: GB Worrall (Saracens), B Butler (Oxford), J Buckland (Cheltenham), TR Cooper (Sale), F Webb (Oakhampton), IB Moffatt (Oxford), JW Wood (Cheltenham), MC Bath (Oxford).*
*Front, l to r: RJ Cloke (Cheltenham), A Johnson (Oxford), G Windsor-Lewis (Richmond), PC Sibley (Blackheath)(Capt), DCA Eaton (Oxford), GB Skates (Oxford), MS Palmer (Bedford).*

from Johnson and Dick Fogden both converted by David Curtis, who went on to win the Chris Price Kicking Cup the next day amidst thick fog and hoary frost.

But all local rugby interest was now focused on Oxfordshire's match with Sussex at Banbury in the middle of the week. Hanging on this game was the Southern group title for the winning side and it was also noted that in 1957, when the Quarter Final was played in Exeter, the Oxfordshire Union received £200 for its efforts. In the event Ian Moffatt scored a first half try for Oxfordshire in a tough match and, in the second, Frank Webb followed up a penalty kick to touch down near the posts for a try that Moffatt converted. And to put the matter beyond doubt Johnson intercepted deep in his '25' and sprinted the length of the field for a try to give the unbeaten county side an 11–0 victory and the group Championship!

Oxfordshire were now drawn at home to play Cornwall in only their second ever Quarter Final tie and negotiations for the match quickly took

*Oxfordshire v Cornwall Quarter Final match programme, January 1962.*

place. It was announced that the county had declined an offer to play in Cornwall, choosing to forego a possible large profit by playing the match in Oxfordshire, and would be incurring heavy expenses as the Cornwall party would be travelling up on the Friday before Saturday 13th January and hotel accommodation would have to be provided. Spokesman Sam Miller said "We considered it was our duty to be hosts and to give Oxfordshire people the chance of seeing their county play in the Quarter Final. We want to win this match." Commendable sentiments indeed!

Full back Maurice Bath gave an impressive display of accurate touch kicking, and defence work of equally high order in Oxford's 3–3 draw at Esher on 2nd December where both sides scored a try each. The players were good individually but the team work was poor with little coordination although this improved seven days later when the team beat the late arriving London University 6–3 at the Bypass ground. Phipps made a break in the centre and Johnson had two good runs before scoring a try from Skates' punt, and Curtis added a penalty. Bad weather then descended over the area as Christmas approached, with snow, frost and ice putting paid to many sporting fixtures. Although Oxford did get a match in away at Rugby on 23rd December, where on a hard ground and in a bitingly cold wind the team lost 3–11. This was to be the only rugby action for the club's players until well into January 1962 and gave ample time to reflect on what had gone on before.

In a direct contrast with the county side, Oxford had equaled at this point their worst ever comparative period in winning only four of the fourteen games played. The situation was not as bad as it had seemed, however, with a heavy crop of injuries playing a great part in a seven week losing sequence and once the side had become more settled it had embarked on an unbeaten run for a month. On the other hand the Oxfordshire side was unbeaten with all focus on the impending Quarter Final and, in spite of the club's poor record, Oxford provided seven players in the county side to face Cornwall on 13th January. Unfortunately

*Oxfordshire v Cornwall, January 1962. The teacher (Richard Sharp) and the pupil (Ian Moffatt).*

one of those, full back Maurice Bath, was suffering from influenza and had to withdraw to be replaced by former Oxford player Tony Pickering, now playing for Richmond. The players had been training individually due to the lack of game time and were due to get together for team practice on the Friday evening and Saturday morning. Despite the recent weather the Iffley Road pitch was reported to be in fine condition and the Oxfordshire team, all of whom were playing, or had played for, Oxford, ran out as: AD Pickering (Richmond); AB Johnson (RAF & Oxford), PC Sibley (Blackheath) (Capt), IB Moffatt (Southfield School & Oxford), DCA Eaton (Oxford); G Windsor-Lewis (Richmond), MS Palmer (Bedford); F Webb (Oakhampton), RJ Cloke (Cheltenham), J Head (Oxford), B Butler (Oxford), TR Cooper (Sale), JT Buckland (Cheltenham), GB Skates (Oxford), GB Worrall (Oxford).

Up to 3,000 spectators, rallying to Sam Miller's call, were reported to be in the ground to see the Oxfordshire forwards put up a splendid fight. Cornwall were much too strong, however, and the home team was beaten by pace and ideas in the backs where Richard Sharp had a great game with a hand in all five of his side's tries. With the last move of the game Windsor-Lewis chipped the ball to the corner and Peter Sibley ran through to touch down for Oxfordshire's only score in the 3–27 defeat.

Still in the county, Old Henliensiens announced that they were now an 'open' club and hoped that the Nomads would find a space for them in the fixture lists. Conditions improved sufficiently for Oxford to visit Old Haberdashers on 20th January for a morning kick off, the first club game for four weeks, before another visit to Twickenham to see England play Wales. The weather had left its mark with a treacherous pitch of heavy, clinging mud, inches deep, which covered most of the pitch. Gordon Skates was out with an injured shin after the Cornwall game and Bath was still missing. Oxford's lighter backs simply could not get going in such conditions, although David Bagnall was man of the match in a match the team should have won. The only Oxford score came when Peter West, returning at blind side wing forward, was backing up on the inside to take a scoring pass to equalize at 3–3. Moffatt's conversion was just wide. It was a similar story the next week with a trip to face Nuneaton where Oxford held a lead before fading to hang on for a 6–6 draw with two Gordon Skates penalties. The team had to travel without their flying winger Arthur Johnson, a Parachute Instructor at RAF Abingdon, who was up in a practice balloon when the winching gear stuck. He was unable to get down or send a message and by the time it had been fixed and he had returned to earth it was too late. True to form for this game there were many infringements and incidents, and much finger wagging from the referee, but the gloom was partially lifted with the Colts team beating Banbury Colts 19–7, and the Nomads beating Oxford Marathons, 14–0.

At last, after an eight week spell, Oxford were due to play at home on 3rd February, against Esher with the following team: D Shaw; R Harrington, IB Moffatt, R Hazeldene, AB Johnson; RJ Tapper, DF Bagnall; B Butler, G Webb, T Wilson, R Fogden, I Hill, I Patterson, GB Skates (Capt), B Morgan. In what was becoming a familiar story Oxford held an eight point lead before going down 8–11 in the second half, another game the team should have won. But things changed dramatically the next Saturday with a 21–0 win at Westminster Hospital, a score that did not flatter Oxford, before they reverted to another 6–6 draw, this time at home to Old Askeans. It was said that Ian Moffatt kicked too much although it was this that gained the result with a penalty and a drop goal!

Loughborough Colleges were due at the Bypass ground but cancelled the game because it was half term at college and the club was fortunate to arrange a late fixture with Newbold-on-Avon. Or unfortunate, as the case may be! Johnson and Bagnall scored tries and Skates a conversion but the visitors were better organized and although Oxford were good for a couple of short periods a penalty in front of their posts gave Newbold the match, 8–9.

Oxfordshire, who had given a poor performance in losing an earlier match against Lincolnshire at Banbury, 0–20, were even worse in a 3–44 defeat against Oxford University on the day of the annual Oxford RFC Dinner where Captain Gordon Skates emphasized the importance of Colts rugby at the club. He said that the club was having its worst ever season mainly because they had been giving opportunities to so many young players. "I think we are now out of the rut we were in during the early season" he said. He paid tribute to Gilbert Beesley, saying "Last season the record was enough to make anyone jump in the river, but this year he has got a side together which, after a disastrous start, has a record showing real improvement." In reply Leslie Plummer, representing the county union, emphasized that the strength of Oxfordshire teams had depended largely on Oxford RFC, which in turn, depended on individual workers such as President Arthur Archer, Secretary Vernon Dive, Ralph Westall, Harold Phillips and 'Bunny' Cole. Later, at the Oxfordshire Referees Society Dinner, Plummer suggested keeping wing forwards down in the scrum until the ball was out – does that sound familiar?

Poor finishing cost Oxford the home match with Reading, 8–15, where Ken Morgan was preferred to David Bagnall at scrum half. Morgan went on to give a good service but the forwards were rarely together and there was a general ineptitude in the team's performance with an apparent mistrust by the centres to give the ball to the wingers. Arthur Johnson returned to the side for the match at Birmingham, having been stranded at Weston-super-Mare the previous week, as did Gordon Skates. Oxford played well enough but ran out of steam towards the end and mistakes in defence were costly in the 5–9 defeat. At Taunton on

17th March, Oxford had agreed to a 5pm kick off, so both teams could watch the televised Calcutta Cup match from Edinburgh, and when the team got onto the pitch it still failed to give the wingers a chance and with the pack flagging, again lost, 0–14.

There was some dismay locally when the Rugby Union announced the decision to restrict the dates when seven-a-side tournaments could be played, to the first half of September and the whole of April, the reason being that it was thought that the growth of seven-a-side rugby could ultimately be to the detriment of Rugby Football. So big had the Oxfordshire Tournament grown that it was now held over two consecutive Sundays with the Preliminary Rounds held at various grounds around the county on the first, with the Finals held at Iffley Road the following week. It was now the biggest tournament in the country but local circumstances dictated that it be held in the first two weeks of March and there were doubts as to whether it could continue.

Oxford made changes for the home match with Nuneaton, one of which saw the First Fifteen debut of young winger Duncan Kilgour who replaced Peter Stone. With Graham Barrett playing on the other wing this made five ex Magdalen College Schoolboys in the team. Once more Oxford were out of luck with some spells of first class rugby, then quite the opposite as Dave Curtis kicked two penalties in the 6–9 defeat. But Oxford weren't the only club enduring a poor season. At the Banbury club dinner, captain John Phillips referred to lazy, idle and inconsiderate players who did not let the club know until Friday that they couldn't play, while training numbers were down to six which bore out a dismal playing record.

Suddenly there was a change of fortune. Oxford kept the ball moving in a cold wind at Old Rutlishians on 31st March in a very pleasing first half and the team finished with a good 17–0 win away from home. Hazeldine scored two tries, with Paterson and Kilgour adding one each. But the real impact was made by Robert Herbertson, who had improved tremendously since playing with Oxford University, and it was his speed to the breakdown as well as adding a try that turned the game to Oxford's favour. Skates kicked one conversion in the tricky wind.

Buoyed by this success Oxford travelled in hope to Weston-super-Mare but flattered only to deceive and looked very tired in the second half, suffering an 8–11 loss.

For the third successive Saturday Oxford travelled, this time to Cheltenham where the home team included former Oxford players John 'Chippo' Wood and Cloke in the front row. It was a pretty drab match and Oxford, without an apparent plan or any cohesion, lacked sparkle. Tapper charged down a kick for a try and Skates added a penalty, but Cheltenham won the match, 8–6, their first win in ten games!

Easter was late on the calendar in 1962 and, rugby wise, it was due to be a quiet one in Oxford. The club had a scheduled fixture at home with Stroud arranged for Good Friday but with some players on a tour and others unavailable, Stroud could not raise a team and asked to be released from the fixture. After one of Oxford's worst seasons there were few regrets! The team had played twenty seven fixtures after several had been cancelled, winning only six with seventeen lost and four drawn. Some additional playing strength was badly needed but the picture was better when the Colts record was included, they having won sixteen with nine losses.

Speaking at the Oxford Old Boys Dinner at the end of April, Peter Sibley said "The old jibe that the Oxford club was really the County had been completely disproved, for while Oxford had a very bad year, the County did well." He thought that there should be some liaison between local clubs and Oxford which would be to the benefit of everyone and urged the clubs not to be selfish by standing in the way of their better players. "This is where we have gone wrong in Oxford in the last few years. You should at least give them the chance" he urged.

At the Annual Meeting in June, Harold Phillips was elected as a Life Vice President and Club President Arthur Archer had the pleasant task of presenting him with a silver salver on his impending retirement from the Kings Arms Hotel, and Oxford. At the same time Wadham College, who owned the building, had submitted a proposal to retain only the bars as a public house whilst closing the hotel and adapting the rooms to student lodgings. Harold and his wife, who were due to retire to Brighton, had run the hotel as a private company, she having had connections with it since her parents had taken it over in 1919. It had served as a headquarters for the Oxfordshire Nomads and, latterly, Oxford RFC for many years. Coming from a rugby family his grandfather had taken his family to South Wales in the 1870s and is believed to have been among the first to introduce the handling game to the Principality, captaining the Newport Football and Athletic Club from 1879–1882. Arriving in Oxford in 1921 Harold had helped to revive the club and then played at scrum half until 1932, continuing to serve on the club committee. He had also served in two World Wars. Harold was overwhelmed at the presentation and invited all present to partake in a final gesture of beer, bread and cheese with him at the end of the meeting. A note in the club minutes says that, at the close, "there was a general stampede for our new Life Vice President's free beer, bread and cheese!"

## Season 1962–1963

Following on from such a poor season on the field, there were great hopes in the autumn of 1962 that things would be different. In the lead up to the season forty players were training at the club in the hope of turning the playing record around. It was thought that George Webb would be joining Leicester and Mike Rhymes tore knee ligaments but otherwise it was all systems go.

With a glut of seven-a-side tournaments in the offing, the club issued a policy on selection saying that if the club entered a 'seven' it would have first call on any member, and if the successful Oxford Thursday Nomads also entered a 'seven', the club would have no objection.

But disaster struck before a ball had even been passed in anger when Gordon Skates, who had been elected as Captain for a second term in office, was reported to have slipped a disc and would not be able to play until at least Christmas time. He had, in fact, injured his back during the match at Taunton in March but had played on until the end of that season. In more recent weeks the pain had increased and he was now in a plaster jacket! In his absence the team was due to be led by the Vice Captain, Ian Paterson.

Members of the youngest club in the county, Gosford All Blacks, were due to use a recently donated hut that they had transformed into a clubhouse in Langford Lane, Kidlington, at a cost of £1000 with the concrete base and plumbing installed by volunteer members. The Old Oxford Citizens club had met at the Victoria Arms, Walton Street, and decided to amalgamate with Old Southfieldians at a time to be arranged by mutual agreement, prior to the merging of the two Oxford schools. Bill Wheal predicted that the amalgamated club could grow to a size comparable to the Oxford Sports Club and to a status comparable with any Old Boys club in the country. There would be a two year interim period, vital to raise money, attract new players and look for a new ground, while there were eight fixtures this season with the amalgamated team.

Oxford's match against 'The Rest', which in the past had been a useful trial match for

*David Bagnall prepares to field a lobbed pass out of the lineout from Gerry Howells as Peter West, Derek Howard and Charlie Ede try to hold back the Cheltenham forwards.*

**WEDNESDAY, SEPTEMBER 12th, 1962**

# WASPS v OXFORD

Kick-off 6.30 p.m.

| WASPS<br>BLACK AND YELLOW | OXFORD<br>GREEN, BLACK AND SILVER |
| --- | --- |
| 1. P. V. CROOKS | 1. I. MOFFATT |
| 2. J. COKER | 5. D. KILGOUR |
| 3. R. TAPPER | 4. R. J. TAPPER |
| 4. D. W. A. ROSSER | 3. R. HAZELDINE |
| 5. A. C. B. HURST* (Capt.) | 2. R. HARRINGTON |
| 6. F. E. J. HAWKINS | 6. D. LLOYD |
| 7. R. C. ASHBY | 7. D. F. BAGNALL |
| 8. G. J. BENDON* | 8. R. HANCE |
| 9. W. TREADWELL | 9. C. T. EDE |
| 10. G. S. TAYLOR | 10. G. HOWELLS |
| 11. G. JANES | 11. R. FOGDEN |
| 12. M. J. CUTTER | 12. D. RICHMOND |
| 13. P. REDRUP | 13. I. PATERSON |
| 14. D. WILLS | 14. D. CURTIS |
| 15. J. E. WOODWARD* | 15. R. A. HERBERTSON |

*International   Referee: T. W. Meale, Esq.,   (London Society)

**NEXT HOME GAME**

WASPS v STREATHAM

SATURDAY, SEPTEMBER 15th, 1962

Kick-off 3 p.m.

both club and county, had been dropped from the fixture list as it had not recently produced the best rugby or improved relationships between the clubs, a little bit of rivalry having set in. This was due to be replaced by a match against the Club President's XV but changed again in favour of a midweek evening match against Wasps at Sudbury.

There was a further setback when Clive Oakley, formerly with Cambridge University, who had hoped to play for the club this season, broke his leg playing for the Oxford Thursday team as the Abingdon Sevens 'jinx' struck again.

In the first game of the new season Oxford gave an excellent account of themselves in fighting back with great spirit on Wednesday 12th September at Wasps, who scored early in the game while the visitors were still settling down. Andy Hurst

*Wasps v Oxford RFC team sheet 1962.*

made a typical bullocking run and was brought down by David Bagnall just short of the line but Bendon, a prop, was on hand to collect for a try, the only score of the match. The team carried this form forward to their next match at Clifton on the Saturday where Ian Moffatt gave an outstanding display in the 6–0 win.

The topical feature of Oxford's next match was that the team fielded an American on either wing. Dan Sachs studying at Worcester College, and Hewes Agnew a medical student from Baltimore working at the Radcliffe Infirmary, were both put into the inferno that is an away match at Nuneaton. Oxford were beaten 6–16 and, with Ian Moffatt having gone 'up' to Cambridge University, lacked a place kicker as three easy kicks were missed. The team also seemed to lack some leadership to pull the players together. The same day saw George Savage, a regular scrum half with the 'A' Fifteen, play his last game for the club against Gosford All Blacks before leaving to take up an appointment in Edinburgh.

But every cloud has a silver lining and, at a time when the club was due to lose Ian Moffatt to Cambridge and Robert Herbertson to Oxford University, two other players had arrived. Ray Hance, a prop forward, had studied at Aberdeen University for four years and was now working at the Weed Research Centre at Yarnton, while Lynn Evans had been at St Luke's College, Exeter, and was now teaching at Littlemore Grammar School. More news of former club members revealed that Ron Livesey was now a Barrister in Liverpool and playing for Waterloo, and hooker John Roberts was playing for Dorchester.

On the down side Drummond Maxton was still at home confined to bed after breaking a leg in a county match against Leicestershire where he had scored a try in the 6–3 win before his accident, and then having to have it broken and reset again. Meanwhile Bert Butler did not expect to be fit to play until the New Year following a summer cartilage operation, and Gordon Skates wasn't expected on the field again until after Christmas.

The RFU President, Bernard Gadney, was due to visit the Oxford club on the evening of the club's game with Aldershot Services on 29th September. He had been born in Oxford and was educated at the Dragon School before moving on, and would be watching St Edward's School against the Old Dragonians in the afternoon. Had he been on the Bypass ground instead, he would have seen an impressive 32–3 victory for the home side in a fast and exciting match which gave much hope for the future. But this hope was short lived when the team was late arriving at Sutton the following week. In the recent years the club had improved in this area but the effort was seemingly being sabotaged by one or two players, the result of the late departure causing a breathless and unsettling rush onto the field where they lost, 6–9, in a match they should have won at a canter.

It was a busy time for some Oxford players. Oxfordshire opened the Championship campaign with a great 14–0 win against Sussex at Eastbourne, the team's biggest championship win since 1956! The next day JJ McPartlin's XV arrived at the club for the annual match with the University Captain's team. Oxford fought hard all the way but couldn't match the visitors' superior strength, speed and skills which brought the expected result, 0–29. It was obvious that two hard games in forty eight hours had proved too much and the team next lost 3–13 at home to Cheltenham. Despite a good start the players were jaded and two charged down kicks led to easy Cheltenham tries.

The home match with Old Cranleighans saw a return to form to win an entertaining match 19–6 and, with Charlie Ede to the fore, showed what could be done with leadership and a settled side. The same didn't apply to Oxfordshire's match with Berkshire at Henley, the first time a Championship match had been played at that ground, where the county team gave a poor display and what should have been a comfortable win became a fight for survival in the 14–14 draw.

*Oxford RFC 1962–1963. Back row, left to right: B Piepenstock, R Palmer, I Paterson, GB Skates (Captain), R Fogden, G Howells, C Oatley, IB Moffatt. Front row: RJ Tapper, R Hazeldine, D Bagnall, D Kilgour, D Barrett, R Hance, R Herbertson.*

The training environment at the Bypass ground was enhanced with improved floodlighting which had been switched on by RC Ellis, the Manager of the Canadian Touring Team that had lost 0–56 to Oxford University the same afternoon of Tuesday 30th October. But signs that the season was entering November were becoming apparent with a decline in the weather conditions and Oxford's fortunes seemed to be going the same way! Against the University Greyhounds the team ignored the wingers and Duncan Kilgour didn't see the ball until midway through the second half, while the Greyhounds took their chances to win 9–6. The home match with St Thomas's Hospital was a dour struggle played in heavy rain. Roy Tapper kicked an 'up and under' for Lynn Evans to gather for a try and the lead, but the Hospital equalized for a 3–3 draw. At Old Askeans, Oxford played with fourteen men for most of the match in muddy, depressing and difficult conditions, as Bryan Morgan arrived late and then Ian Patterson went off with a broken finger, and lost 0–8.

The injured Gordon Skates had, by now, been advised by his doctor that it was doubtful if he would be available to play for the First Fifteen again this season and, in the circumstances, he felt it was only proper to offer his resignation as Captain. But the Committee held the unanimous opinion that he should continue to act in that role.

Oxfordshire had given themselves a good chance to win the Southern Group title with an 11–11 draw against Dorset & Wilts, and named Geoffrey Windsor-Lewis from the Richmond club, a Cambridge Blue and Welsh International, as Captain for the important away match with Hertfordshire. In the lead up to the match Tony Pickering announced his retirement from County rugby as teaching duties at Bloxham School prevented him from playing regularly. In the event the pack was outweighed but fought like demons. Ron Livesey returned to claim 'man of the match' with a try, two penalties and a conversion as the team won 16–6 to claim the title for the second season running and an away Quarter Final tie with the South West Group winners. In contrast Oxford's poor run continued and the team gave one of its worst displays of the season in losing at home to Birmingham University, 3–5, at the weekend.

Lynn Evans returned home to Wales to get married but, in his absence, Oxford won 17–0 at London University where the pack was in dominant mood and Brian Butler landed three kicks in his return to the side following a summer knee operation. Duncan Kilgour also got married, but six days later on a Friday, which meant he could still play the next day against Loughborough Colleges. A late switch saw the game played on higher ground at Westminster College away from the fog bound Bypass pitch but, with the fog creeping up the hill, 'hostilities' were restricted to thirty minutes each way. The formidable Colleges side were made to work for the 3–11 win and Oxford, although beaten, were by no means disgraced.

Drummond Maxton, still suffering the effects of a broken leg, didn't expect to play again in this season, and the Oxfordshire Union got a temporary reprieve with a special dispensation from the Rugby Union which meant that the Seven a Side Tournament could still be held in March.

Another defeat followed, this time at Lydney where the score flattered the home side. Lydney created four scoring opportunities and scored from all of them and although Bagnall gave good service to see Kilgour stride over in the corner, a hard forward battle ensued and Oxford couldn't score again to lose 3–14.

After winning just one of their last eight games, there were signs of a recovery and the Oxford team was unlucky not to win at Esher, where Ray Tapper kicked ahead and Lynn Evans raced through to gather and score with Butler adding the conversion. But shortly

*Oxfordshire Colts v Oxfordshire Schools at the Bypass, Saturday 22$^{nd}$ December 1962, the last weekend before the ten week 'freeze': back row, left to right: R Vernede (Oxford Colts), T Jarman (Oxford Old Grammarian Colts), M Laverty (OOG), R Tyrrell (OOG), P Richmond (Banbury Colts), B Lewis (B), R Sabin (B), P Webb (Ox). Front row: R Mills (Ox), V Pidgeley (Ox), M Clark (Ox), M Galloway (OOG), B Beale (Ox), A Lees (B), P Rivers (B).*

Oxford Mail *front page for December 27th. The bespectacled boy in the picture is Neville Worsfold who, many years later, became the club groundsman.*

after Evans was robbed of the ball and Esher players ran fifty yards for a try and conversion. Evans made amends with a drop goal to equalize the score at 8–8 as the Oxford team was left to rue two costly mistakes.

There was every hope of a happy holiday when, four days before Christmas Day, Oxford beat Woodford at the Bypass ground, 12–5. The front row of Ray Hance, Charlie Ede and Gerry Howells were playing together for the fourteenth time in the seventeen games so far played, while Lynn Evans was an unlikely Father Christmas in scoring all of his side's points with three penalties and a drop goal as Oxford deservedly returned to winning form.

The club was looking forward to renewed rivalry with old friends from the north of the county, Banbury, in a match arranged for Boxing Day thus resuming the fixture after a seven year break. But then something happened that was not planned by the respective fixture secretaries – it started to snow!

The blanket of snow that covered at least the southern half of England wiped out all games on Boxing Day, and was quickly followed by hard frost which ensured the snow would be around for some time. The away match with Metropolitan Police, due on the 29th December 1962, was another early casualty which gave an opportune moment to review the season so far. Oxford had won just five of the games played with two drawn and ten lost and had not enjoyed the best of luck. In different circumstances another six games might have been won although this was a slight improvement on recent seasons.

While the severe frost continued the players had resorted to training twice a week in the comparative warmth of the Alfred Street gymnasium in Oxford. Maurice Bath decided to accept medical advice to stop playing due to strained and wrenched nerves in his left shoulder, sustained whilst playing for the Nomads in November. With eighteen appearances for Oxfordshire to his credit, his experience at full back would be missed in the club.

By the end of January, with the freeze continuing, the Rugby Union circulated its decision not to extend the season despite several lost weekends. Out of the gloom came the news that another new club had been formed, this time in the village of Chinnor, near Thame. The club was making an application to use a section of the sports field in Station Road and the Chairman, Frank Angel, was hoping that the first game could be played in March.

In early February, 1963, it was reported that January had been the coldest in Oxford since 1815 with an average temperature of -3°C, and by now training had moved to the Littlemore Grammar School gymnasium with an extra session on Saturday afternoons – would the freeze ever end?

The County Union had to get permission from the Oxfordshire County Council before introducing a new badge as the Union's crest was a reproduction of the central portion of the County coat of arms. On an azure blue background the wavy diagonal lines, representative of the ford, were in silver and an ox's head in red was centred with an oak tree and a sheath of corn in opposite corners. The badge was to be awarded to those who had played twelve games and to others for services to rugby in the county.

At long last the Oxford team was able to come out of cold storage with an away game against the unbeaten London Scottish Extra 1st at Richmond. The home players busied themselves by clearing thick ice patches from the rough, undulating ground but they needn't have rushed as one Oxford driver lost his way and so three players were late. But Derek Howard didn't arrive at all and Gordon Skates was pressed into an earlier return to the game than he had anticipated. Rex Hazeldine scored a try in the Artic-like conditions, which Lynn Evans converted to equalize the score at that time but Oxford went on to lose 5–13. More weather disruption led to the cancellation of the morning kick off in London against Old Rutlishians which did nothing to help team continuity, with the anticipated loss of players to Oxfordshire the following week, March 2nd.

The club was honoured with the company of Cyril Gadney, a former member of the Oxfordshire Nomads some thirty years previously, now the Rugby Union President, together with his brother Bernard Gadney, a former scrum half who had fourteen England caps to his credit and who had played a major part in the process of the club becoming Oxford RFC in 1949. Both originated from Oxford and attended as guests at the Annual Club Dinner on Thursday 28th February.

Five Oxford players, Ian Moffatt, Rex Hazeldine, Ray Hance, Derek Howard and Clive Oatley had been named in the Oxfordshire team to play in the much delayed Quarter Final against Gloucestershire at Bristol, with David Bagnall named as reserve. Ian Parsons (Saracens), Peter Sibley (Blackheath), Ron Livesey (Waterloo) and John Buckland (Aylesbury), all former Oxford players, were also included in the selected team. Once again, Oxfordshire found competition at this level very hot but put up a very gallant performance. Geoffrey Windsor-Lewis pounced on a loose ball for a try that opened the scoring and then, after a hack through followed by a scrum, Derek Howard picked up at Number 8 and went round the scrum for his team's second try, which Ian Moffatt converted, and after half an hour Oxfordshire led 8–3. But it was not to last and Gloucestershire steadied themselves before fighting back with a vengeance to finally record their biggest win since the War, 8–42, a score line that did not reflect the credit due to the visiting side.

Back at the Southern Bypass on the same day, pitches were still unfit for play and Oxford's scheduled home game with Esher was switched to the Esher ground in London. Ron Salter had a good game at full back, and Derek Head and Don Barrett were prominent but missing almost half of the regular team was just too much and Oxford lost 0–6 when a draw would have been more of a fair result.

Most of the snow and ice had now melted away but gave way to standing water in many areas and it was this that was to play a big part in the farcical situation of Oxford's away match with Birmingham the next week on 9$^{th}$ March. A convoy of cars left the club headquarters in good time but one broke down on the way and had to be abandoned with reserve players in the other cars being drafted into the lineup. Arriving at Birmingham's ground at Northfield twenty five minutes after the scheduled start time, the party found that the ground was unplayable due to large parts of it being under water. The match had been switched to another ground nearly four miles away and some Oxford players, having changed, got lost again between grounds. The game eventually kicked off at 4.25pm just as it should have been ending! The mud was inches deep with pools of standing water which produced a grueling 0–0 slog – was it all worth it?

Another down side to the conditions was revealed when the President of the Oxford Sports Club, RB Cole, reported that there had been a £300 loss of much needed bar and catering income because of weeks of bad weather and he made an appeal to members to help make ends meet.

Oxford's fortunes did not change much in the following weeks. The pack didn't play particularly well in a 0–6 home defeat to Taunton and seemed to lack match fitness – not surprising, really – before they squandered a half time lead to eventually lose 3–17 to St Bartholomew's Hospital. All this did not augur well for the visit to Bedford where Evans was unavailable and Gordon Skates returned after the injury that had kept him out of the team for the first five months of the season. It was a strange paradox that Oxford played much better in this match than on many occasions earlier, even when they had won, but again they lacked the stamina to match Bedford's play and lost 3–25. Oxford's only score was a try which came when Ian Patterson picked up the ball from a line out to give Don Barrett a scoring pass. It was reported that Drummond Maxton had taken part in his first training session since breaking his leg playing for Oxfordshire in September, 1962.

The postponed Christmas holiday match with Banbury re-emerged as a midweek game on 3$^{rd}$ April and provided Oxford with their first win of 1963! Tries from Hazeldine (2), Kilgour, Herbertson and Roy Tapper, added to a Tapper drop goal and Moffatt's penalty and conversion, gave Oxford a lift with the season end in sight. But hope receded with an away defeat, this time to Reading 6–9, a poor quality match played in a bitingly cold wind.

*Oxford RFC Irish Tour 1963 v Clontarf: Back row, left to right: R Hazeldine, B Deane, R Hance, R Salter, B Piepenstock, C Ede, J Wood, D Paterson, driver, R Fogden, RJ Tapper, C Oatley, L Davies, M Simmie, G Howells, T Last, I Patterson, J Mawle. Middle row: K Morgan, D Barrett, G Skates (Captain), G Barrett, R Palmer. Front row: A Lisle, D Bagnall, L Evans, B Perkins, B Tomlinson.*

*A trip to Ireland is never complete without a tour around the Guiness Brewery in Dublin: Back row, left to right: I Paterson, R Hance, D Barrett, R Salter J Mawle, B Deane, E Church, K Morgan, driver, L Evans, A Lisle. Middle row: B Perkins, G Barrett, L Davies, J Scott, B Tomlinson, C Ede, R Palmer, M Simmie. Front row: T Last, B Piepenstock, R Hazeldine, D Bagnall, J Wood, D Paterson, G Skates, C Oatley.*

*... and, of course, the compulsory tasting of the product! Standing: J Scott, R Salter, D Barrett, I Paterson, J Mawle, B Tomlinson. Front: R Hance, D Bagnall, D Paterson.*

The next day at Iffley Road, Bedford won the Oxfordshire Sevens Tournament with Oxford going out at the Quarter Final stage to Bath, having beaten Sutton and Hartlepool Rovers along the way.

All of this led to what was undoubtedly the highlight of the season – the Easter Tour to Ireland! The party had planned to fly on a chartered thirty two seater aeroplane from RAF Abingdon but had to change these plans at the last minute due to Customs formalities, and left from Bristol Airport on Easter Saturday morning. Based at the Central Hotel in Dublin, the team faced Clontarf in the afternoon and the match was played in atrocious conditions, pouring rain and a very heavy hailstorm, and lost 0–11. The party was out to watch the Easter Day parade in O'Connell Street on the Sunday morning and then moved on to the next match in the afternoon against Old Belvedere where, in a thrilling match, Oxford won it's first game on Irish soil. Rex Hazeldine scored the first try which was converted by Gordon Skates, before Skates touched down after the scrum had pushed over. Then Hazeldine settled the issue late in the game with a fine try to give Oxford an excellent win, 11–9. The group was up early on Easter Monday for a one hundred mile trip to Wexford where Don Barrett scored from another pushover and Hazeldine scored again for Ray Hance to kick the conversion, for another Oxford win, this time 8–5. Another late party was enjoyed by all, including a Welsh team at Wexford that was also on tour, and the party stayed overnight before an early start back to Dublin on the Tuesday. On the way back the coach developed mechanical trouble but still managed to get to Dublin in time for an official lunch at the St James's Gate Guinness Brewery followed by a tour of the factory.

It was a fitting tribute to the group's hosts that some of the party drank bottled Guinness at breakfast after a 6am start on Wednesday morning! They would need the added strength, however, as on the way to the airport the coach eventually did what it had threatened to do, and broke down. There was no time to get a replacement, indeed there was none available due to a 'bus drivers strike, and so there was nothing to do except to get out and push! To their credit the party did get to the airport in time and arrived back at Oxford in time for lunch. It goes without saying that the hospitality in Ireland was first class and very enjoyable providing, as it did, memories of a great tour that would last for many years to come. The club owed a big debt of thanks to Desmond O'Brien, an Irish International, who was the Guinness Representative for the Oxford area and who gave great assistance in the tour arrangements.

*The new Fixture Secretary, Roy Tapper, forged the way into South Wales.*

Back at the club over the Easter weekend some of the players who did not tour played against Old Ignatians, themselves on tour. Losing on Easter Saturday by 6–11, Oxford played the visitors again on Easter Monday when their scheduled match against Abingdon was cancelled, and this time won 13–8 to square the 'rubber'.

Only one match remained, that against Cambridge at the Bypass ground. Over the course of the season there had been all the usual injuries to which players are prone, cars had broken down or got lost in strange cities and trains had been missed in distant parts of Britain, all of which had contributed to a very unsettled season for the Oxford club. Finally it was circumstances again that determined the Oxford team to play the last match against a visiting team that included England scrum half, Dickie Jeeps. Not surprisingly it was Cambridge who were much the better side and this showed in the 3–19 Oxford defeat.

There was much comment on the events of the past season in which Oxford had played twenty nine matches, winning eight, losing eighteen with three drawn. The Nomads, 'A' and Colts Fifteens had all won more than they had lost, the exception being the Extra 'A's. It had been fifteen years since the club had become 'Oxford RFC' and it was now well known with a good name and reputation. In that time it remained the club's objective to break into first class rugby but, in 1963, entry to the top class was obviously not imminent. There had been little success in recent seasons and, therefore, the club did not present an attractive proposition to better class players and needed to move up a level.

In addition the club had been unable to keep fixtures with the likes of Bedford, Coventry, Wasps and Northampton. However the enthusiasm of Roy Tapper, who had taken over as Fixture Secretary from Eric Church, had envisaged progress along a different path through games with Welsh clubs and both Pontypool and Cross Keys, together with the Cambridge University LX Club had been added to an impressive list for the following season.

Reflecting on past events in his report to the Annual Meeting in June the retiring captain, Gordon Skates, placed responsibility on the players and said "Once again the club has tried to play attractive rugby but unless there is an improvement in the general spirit of most players, Oxford RFC has a difficult time ahead. Too many players give of their best on a Saturday afternoon but do little else for the rest of the week. In spite of the dismal First Fifteen record there were many games lost which, with a little more effort and determination, should have been won. The team has come under much criticism this season for lack of enthusiasm and the majority of this is deserved, but more criticism could be levelled at the extremely poor attendance at training sessions."

Neither Old Oxford Citizens nor Old Southfieldians had been particularly successful, while the Oxford Marathons had won three more games than they'd lost. At their final Annual Meeting, members of the Old Southfieldians were anxious that the proposed title of the new amalgamated club – Oxford Old Boys – would not lead to confusion with Oxford RFC. Alan Brunsdon, retiring captain of Old Oxford Citizens, said that members could look forward to a first class season. "We are at the crossroads and have a great chance to improve our status. Some of us will find ourselves in the $2^{nd}$ or $3^{rd}$ teams but we have got be as keen as ever" he said.

# Chapter 3 – Second Coming?

The traditional name of 'Old Henliensiens' had been consigned to the past and the club, no longer restricted to former pupils of Henley Grammar School, had become simply 'Henley RFC', which was a logical step for an open club with ambitions. The Oxford Club Committee would not agree to a request from Henley for a fixture at Nomads level but kept the door open by saying it would reconsider in the future, while over at the newly formed Chinnor RFC progress was encouraging and twenty six matches had been arranged after an inaugural game at the end of the previous season.Oxford Sports Club's grounds man, Jim Charlett, had resigned after sterling service since 1952 and that after sixteen years at Christ Church, with Dick Barley taking over.

## Season 1963–1964

The new club President was Vernon Dive who had joined the club as a player in 1927 but who, far more recently, had spent eleven years in the role of Honorary Secretary before his 'promotion' at the Annual Meeting.

The club hoped to have the majority of the last season's team available for the new campaign and although Brian Piepenstock and Clive Oatley were now working in London, there was some joy with the return of hooker George Webb. Don Barrett, another old Magdalen College Schoolboy, had been elected as the new Captain and was well versed in the role having captained the Nomads team for the previous two seasons, with Ray Hance as his Vice Captain. Oxford's first game of the season saw a renewal of 'hostilities' with Hinckley, the first match between the clubs since 1958. Two players from the Harwell club who had done well in pre-season, centre Peter Bradley and winger Robin Morgan, were included in the lineup which was: R Palmer; D Kilgour, A Tanner, P Bradley, R Morgan; L Evans, K Morgan; R Hance, G Webb, J Head, J Mawle, R Fogden, D Barrett (Captain), D Howard, I Patterson.

*Relaxing at the club after pre- season training in August 1963 are: A Boulter, P West, R Hance, G Howells, J Mawle, J Higgins (Trainer), G Kitt, R Morgan.*

Steady rain on the day turned the game into a dour, tough battle between the two packs of forwards and Webb's excellent hooking was paramount. Shortly after half time Hance gave his side the lead with a forty yards penalty and the team held on as Hinckley fought back. Barrett urged his pack to a final effort and Ken Morgan dummied an opening in the Hinckley twenty five area for Evans to run and score a try under the posts. With three minutes left Hance converted to put the side clear at 8–0.

The opening season form continued with a midweek away win at Worcester, 14–3, where Oxford were on top for most of a hard and fast game with the speedy backs well supported by the open side wing forward, Don Barrett. But this trend was reversed in the next match, again away, at Old Cranleighans where the home team had the edge with their more penetrating backs. Ray Hance had an off day with his kicking, missing two conversions, and not much was seen of Oxford's backs with Lynn Evans at fly half often kicking the ball. But Peter Bradley provided a highlight with a fifty yard run for a try against the run of play in a 9–17 defeat.

The busy start to the season continued with County Trials mid-week at the club ground, which was now free of cricket commitments, and in the first two weeks many of Oxford's players had already taken part in four serious outings. This led to Oxford's first home game of the season, a new fixture with the renowned Welsh club side, Pontypool. In front of a good crowd Oxford were stubborn in defence but, after twenty minutes, the effort wilted and the team fell away to be outclassed by the fast moving Welsh players. The pace was simply too hot and Oxford had only a penalty from Ray Hance to show for their efforts.

Towards the end of September Mr RB Cole announced that the Oxford Sports Club would be exploring the possibility of developing the central part of the pavilion at the ground into a double storey block. This was in accordance with the original plans when the club was first started. Since the ground had been opened there had been a steady expansion of premises and activities. Now, in addition to a good cricket square, there were two rugby pitches, two hockey pitches, six hard courts for tennis, sections for archery and motoring, two blocks of changing rooms, a large dining room and separate large bar, committee room, two groundsman's houses, large well appointed kitchen and car park. Improvement to the approach road would be needed and new suggestions were for a swimming pool, squash courts, bowls green and indoor rifle range. An immeasurable debt was owed by the club to its voluntary helpers over the years, but "…it is becoming difficult to get this voluntary labour and it becomes necessary to think of having permanent staff such as a steward and a stewardess who would live on the premises" said Mr Cole.

The Oxford players bounced back from their 'Welsh' defeat with a 17–6 win at Aldershot Services. The pack gave a fine performance which complimented a new half back pairing of Bagnall and Ken Morgan and the only downside was a leg injury suffered by Harrington. His replacement for the game with Sutton was the young Mike Simmie, like Harrington a County sprinter, but the Oxford team was unlucky to lose again, this time 3–8. Sutton found two gaps in the home defence for an 8–0 half time lead in heavy rain. The Oxford pack dominated the second half but the team had only one try to show for their efforts when Kilgour kicked ahead and then touched down, and Oxford were unable to press home their advantage.

All of this, however, led to the annual match with the University Captain's Fifteen played on Thursday afternoon 10th October 1963. Nick Silk, whose England international career was to be cut short in 1966 by a severe knee injury after just four caps all gained in 1965, brought a strong team to the club which included three of the five Blues available to him at that time. But the Oxford players chose this match to give their finest display of the season to date and, in the first half, outplayed the visitor's pack with Ian Moffatt's penalty kick

*John Mawle contests a lineout against N Silk's XV while Ray Hance and Don Barrett await the outcome.*

from 15 yards giving them a 3–0 lead. A stern pep talk at the break brought more out of the men in blue and the score was equalized when Oxford's defence was finally beaten by a try in the corner before a rare mistake from Ray Palmer at full back gave NR Phelps, formerly of St Edward's School, a gift try. All seemed lost but, on the stroke of time, Moffatt set off on a magnificent forty yard jinking run to pass to Roy Tapper whose cross kick was gathered by Kilgour for a try in the corner. With Ray Hance's conversion just off target a 6–6 draw seemed a just result, with Oxford's back row of Barrett, Howard and Peter Sutcliffe, himself a former Oxford 'Blue', giving tireless performances. With the after effects of Thursday's battle and a very heavy pitch taking a toll, it took Oxford until the second half to demonstrate their undoubted superiority away at Old Haberdashers two days later where Moffatt again played a big part with two penalties and a conversion, as well as providing a strong and powerful presence in midfield.

The players were quickly brought down to earth with a 3–31 home defeat at the hands of Oxford University Greyhounds the following week. Out run, out tackled and out scored, the side looked tired and dispirited when leaving the field with only a Moffatt penalty to their credit. It was Moffatt's last game for a while as he was now off to teacher training at St Luke's College, Exeter, and Malcolm Phipps was due to take his place in the away game at Loughborough College seven days later. This was a better performance in which Oxford refused to concede defeat thus keeping some life in a game where the side had a good opening spell but couldn't score and lost 0–27.

Sandwiched in between these games, a lot of local rugby interest centred around the Iffley Road ground where New Zealand were due to open their 1963–64 tour with a match against Oxford University. In front of a crowd estimated at 9,000 spectators it was the University side that took the honours for the magnificent way in which they held the heavier New Zealand forwards in a 3–19 defeat. Four days later the tourists continued their winning ways with a 32–3 win against Southern Counties, who included the Oxfordshire players Kyle Mulligan, Peter Sibley and Geoff Windsor-Lewis, who captained the side, at Brighton.

This was a reminder that the County Championship was just around the corner and Oxfordshire's team included four Oxford RFC players and seven more with past Oxford connections for the home match in familiar surroundings at the Bypass Ground against Sussex. Two of the selectors, Jim O'Connell and Colin Pickford, had travelled a round trip of 308 miles to study the form of former Oxford Captain, Thom Cooper, playing for Broughton Park against Liverpool! The team was: KR Jenkins (Oxford City & County Police); IJ Parsons (Saracens), RJ Hazeldine (Moseley), IB Moffatt (St Luke's, Exeter), PC Sibley (Blackheath); G Windsor-Lewis (Richmond) (Capt), RD Livesey (Waterloo); RJ Hance (Oxford), G Webb (Oxford), A Mears (Oxford City & County Police), SK Mulligan (London Irish), TR Cooper (Broughton Park), DWG Barrett (Oxford), DW Howard (Oxford), GB Worrall (Saracens). The side was galvanized by the late arrival of the Sussex team, after their coach had broken down at Crowmarsh, and when the match started some thirty minutes late the visitors found Don Barrett in tremendous form at blindside wing forward. With Windsor-Lewis playing his first game thus far for Oxfordshire, Sussex was a well beaten side at 20–5 in what was to be the last meeting of the two teams in the championship for many years.

Back on the club scene Oxford overcame greasy conditions for a 12–3 success at home against Cheltenham, which was more than welcome after two heavy defeats. The side was more penetrative then their opponents which resulted in tries for Roy Tapper, Bagnall and Sutcliffe, and a Hance penalty. At Cobham the next week the side had to work hard to follow this up with a 12–6 win against St Thomas' Hospital and a wet, greasy ball didn't prevent a try from Howard, two Hance penalties and a Lynn Evans drop goal.

The side wasn't without its selection problems. Peter Sutcliffe had been away playing for Cumberland & Westmoreland and then suffered a slipped disc in his neck, lock John Tyack had a slipped disc in his back, Ken Morgan had torn a hamstring and Dick Fogden

*Oxfordshire 1963–1964, Runners up, County Championship Southern Group.*
*Back row, l to r: RJ Hance, M Simmie, J Mawle, MJ Parsons, DW Howard, G Windsor-Lewis (Capt), G Webb, L Evans, A Mears. Front row, l to r: IJ Parsons, R Herbertson, KR Jenkins, DWG Barrett, DF Bagnall, RJ Hazeldine.*

was moving to Bristol. On the plus side it was reported that the two local policemen, Keith Jenkins and Tony Mears, would be playing for Oxford RFC in the future.

It wasn't a surprise that Oxfordshire made no changes for the next County match where they were able to lay the Berkshire 'bogy' with a 6–0 win at Newbury. The Berkshire defence was good but couldn't prevent a Moffatt penalty and a Ron Livesey try putting Oxfordshire in a strong position in the Southern Group table.

Flood water in the Oxford area had started to subside but this didn't affect the club players too much anyway as their next encounter was away at Esher where the Oxford team were slightly surprised to take an early two try lead through Evans and John Mawle. Esher came back strongly in the second half to score a converted pushover try but Oxford's steadfast tackling deservedly won them the match at 6–5. It was back to the Bypass ground the following week to meet Kenilworth, the first meeting for several seasons between the two clubs, and Oxford's 16–0 win was not as easy as the score might suggest. David Lloyd was back to fly half to take the place of the unavailable Evans and Oxford made heavy weather of the match, coming good in the latter stages to win with four tries.

It was reported that former Blue and Oxford club player WDK 'Digger' Stobie had returned to England after several years of farming in Rhodesia and had taken on a smaller farm near Chalfont St Giles, which had given him the opportunity to join the Buckinghamshire Referees Society.

Locally, Chinnor were not downhearted despite not having won any of their nine games in the season so far. Enjoying good support in the village, they were hopeful that the six tin baths used after matches in the neighbouring Reading Room would be replaced when the sports field was fully developed. Even more locally, neither was there any despondency at the newly formed Oxford Old Boys club who had suffered five defeats in their first eight games.

Oxfordshire's third Championship game was away at Salisbury against Dorset & Wiltshire, who had played an extra game to lead the group with two wins and a draw, and they had only themselves to blame when their title chances ended in a dismal defeat. In the opening period of the game it looked as if the visitors would win by a big score as Oxfordshire crossed the line twice but were not given the scores, with players pulled back twice and pushed out of play in the corners. But somehow the home team weathered the storm, being reduced to breakaway attacks. It was from one such attack that a try was scored and, wasting every chance that came their way, Oxfordshire lost 0–3, suffering the first defeat since November 1960 in Eastbourne.The very next day the Oxford club side played host to Cambridge University LX club, the equivalent of Oxford University's Greyhounds side, and with seven changes to the side did well to draw 9–9. Lynn Evans returned to the side for the home match with old rivals Nuneaton on 30th November and spurred Oxford on with a drop goal against the run of play. Hance kicked a penalty and, in the mud, Roy Tapper scored the only try of the match for Hance to convert. Despite a strong comeback, Nuneaton couldn't score and Oxford recorded a creditable 11–0 win.

Comments in the local *Sports Mail* attributed to Mr Tony Francis, the new Secretary of the Oxford Schools Football Association, caused something of a stir when he said "I now teach soccer instead of rugby as I sincerely believe that the majority of Secondary Modern boys are, on leaving school, more likely to get a game with the larger number of junior clubs than they will with the smaller number of rugby clubs and so more profitably use their leisure time. I do not teach both games as I feel that with a limited number of boys it is better to succeed at one rather than always be mediocre at two." Mr Brian Poxon,

Secretary of the Oxfordshire Schools Rugby Union and whose work with local players was almost legendary, soon replied saying "I am surprised that one who has played rugby himself should not see the obvious merits of teaching both games in a school, thus providing games for boys who have not the particular skills required by soccer. Such a boy may well have the talents and courage to make a fine rugby player yet his whole sporting life must stagnate because the school cannot supply him with the opportunity to display those talents. To say that both games cannot be taught together without lowering the standard of one or the other is nonsense. My own school of Headington Secondary Modern proves this. Our boys play both games happily".

The young players Mike Simmie and Robert Hertbertson, now playing midweek for the University Greyhounds side, replaced Sibley and Worrall in the Oxfordshire team that recouped some credibility with a 6–0 win in the last championship match at home to Hertfordshire where, once again, the forwards were to the fore and the team finished as runners up in the group.

Hertbertson replaced 'flu victim Don Barrett in the back row and Ray Hance led the side as Oxford crushed the visiting Charing Cross Hospital with six tries in a new fixture, 31–8. But the 9–0 home win against Streatham was not an impressive performance with two Ray Hance penalties and a Roy Tapper drop goal making the winning scores. Captain Don Barrett, fit again, said afterwards "It was as well to get it out of our system". County President Jim O'Connell had travelled to the ground to watch the match but didn't even get out of the car before the 'A' team captain came over to ask "Can you ref?" Jim obtained a whistle and obliged in civvies on the Stanley Park pitch for the match against Newbury 'B'. Later he said "I stayed in midfield and asserted myself in the first few minutes!"

A 12 noon kick off was planned at Cheltenham so that players could watch the televised Wales v New Zealand match afterwards. With the Christmas holiday on the horizon once again Ray Palmer and Lynn Evans had already gone home. In at full back was Grainger Kitt who had only joined the club this season and who had worked his way up through the ranks from the 'A' XV. Both Simmie and Moffatt were named in the side but the match was cancelled due to a frozen pitch which at least gave the players a clear run into Christmas.

The next action took place on Boxing Day when a home game with Banbury renewed old rivalries and the Oxford players emerged from the morass of the second team pitch at the Bypass worthy 6–3 winners. Gerry Howells went off with a cut eye and Oxford had to play the last thirty minutes with fourteen players, this being long before replacements were allowed in the game. In an often heated and muddy battle, Ian Moffatt kicked two penalty goals and Oxford were by far the more dangerous side although Banbury gained some consolation with a try in the closing moments. Two days later Oxford ended the year with a 3–14 defeat at Old Whitgiftians to end an unbeaten sequence of nine games since 2nd November. It was a disappointing game where Oxford showed their zeal far too late to make any difference to the result.

In this sequence the side had scored 106 points and conceded only 31 and, with the other results added in, contributed to the best first half-season's record since 1956. It was an impressive turn round in the club's fortunes following, as it did, the worst two seasons in the club's history. It was somewhat unfair to lay the blame for that at Gordon Skates' door when he was absent through injury for long periods during those seasons and, in comparison, Don Barrett's splendid leadership and playing example had been paramount. He had also enjoyed the invaluable experience in the front row, and assistance, of Vice Captain Ray Hance. Explaining how the change had come about Don said "When we thought things over before the season started, we realized we had not been playing to any pattern. We were playing

*Oxford RFC 1963–1964. Back row, left to right: G Webb, M Parsons, G Windsor-Lewis, D Howard, I Paterson, G Howells, L Evans, R Castle. Front row: R Hance, D Bagnall, D Barrett (Captain), R Harrington, RJ Tapper, V O'Connell. Missing (in the toilet!): R Herbertson.*

as fifteen individuals doing our best with no plan and an emphasis on playing too much schoolboy type rugby. This year Ray Hance and I thought we should try and have a set basic formula and we decided to build up a good pack, drive the ball into good attacking positions and score from there: not to try and attack from our own goal-line.

"The front row has scrummaged really hard and the whole pack is now playing extremely well. We try to score not so much from the set pieces but from broken play. This meant building up our rucking and loose play to get possession and score from there. Sometimes people said we kick too much but the basic idea is to get ourselves into advantageous positions.

"We found in the first few games that the backs moaned a bit about not having the ball but when we started to win games they realized the plan was working and everyone was happy."

Fitness had improved and this had shown particularly in defensive covering where Roy Tapper's tackling in the centre was the best it had been for four seasons. Celebrating the arrival of 1964 was a bit of a trial when the club's New Year's Eve Dance was suddenly plunged into darkness. The two volunteer bar men, Ken Morgan and David Patterson, kept the revelers happy by two torch power and the occasional match and as far as it was known nobody was served with a pint of whisky although there was a pretty high casualty rate amongst the bar mugs. With the dance floor in total darkness public spirited John Rowell drove his car up to the open bar door, while Don Barrett led a party to Wytham to fetch hurricane lamps and a emergency generator, but with perfect timing, just as the 'relief' expedition returned the lights came on again!

Oxford's first game of 1964 at Nuneaton was arranged with an early kick off so that both teams could then watch England v New Zealand on the television. Travelling by car four players were late causing a delayed kick off, and the unsettling effect of this saw the side start the new year in the same way as they had ended the old – in defeat, this time 3–11 with Simmie scoring Oxford's only try. Worse was to follow. The players did not see as much of the international as they would have liked – by the time they had bathed, changed and got into the clubhouse, they found that the front row of chairs were all occupied by young ladies with the 'beehive' style hair-do's that were all the rage at the time!

But Oxford got back to winning ways with the visit of Old Askeans, 24–3, with the back row of Barrett, Herbertson and Ian Patterson in fine form but lost the opportunity to add to this when the match at Rugby was cancelled due to a hard frost the next week. The club had accepted an extra fixture in the following midweek not a hundred miles away from there, at Stratford for an evening kick off. The attraction was the chance to play under floodlights for the first time which was seen as novel preparation for the club's first match on the arranged Easter Tour to South Wales, at Cross Keys. This was a relative success with a 14–3 win.

Back in the groove, so to speak, Oxford enjoyed a hard fought win to reverse the previous result against Oxford University Greyhounds. Played at Stanley Park as the Iffley Road ground was ruled unfit for play, defences were to the fore but Lynn Evans opened the score in the second half when he beat five players in a ten yard space for a try, before David Bagnall went over from a scrum under the posts. Hance converted both for a 10–3 win. But Lydney proved again to be Oxford's 'bogey' where Hance gave his side an early penalty lead before the home side showed the punch in attack that Oxford lacked, to win 11–3.

A weeks respite due to a frost cancellation at Westminster Hospital gave the players a chance to regroup but they were made to work hard to beat Old Rutlishians 26–13 at the Bypass. Close marking and hard tackling kept Oxford at bay before a defensive collapse saw five tries for the home team including two for the captain, Barrett, two for Kilgour and one from Evans. Hance had his kicking boots on with four conversions and a penalty. This win put the team in good heart for the visit of Clifton the following week where the great attacking form gave Oxford a convincing 19–0 win with winger Russell Harrington adding a 'hat-trick' of three tries to the total.

It seemed quite a coup when, at much the same time, it was reported that Geoffrey Windsor-Lewis had left the London club Richmond and joined Oxford, his debut being imminent. This would be a huge plus for the club bringing with him as he would his experience as a Welsh International and a former Captain of Cambridge University. But any joy at this news was soon quashed when Oxford lost at home to Birmingham 3–9, being hustled out of the game by a light, lively and superbly fit pack of forwards.

There was a record attendance at the Annual Dinner on Thursday 5th March, held the day after Oxfordshire had beaten Oxford University 6–3, to hear Don Barrett say that a great feature of the club this season had been the co-operation of all members. He stressed the importance of having strength in depth in the playing side to meet fresh challenges that the good results, and Fixture Secretary Roy Tapper, had attracted and noted that the Nomads, having won seventeen games, had a similar playing record to the First Fifteen. Sam Miller, the Oxfordshire representative on the RFU Committee, thanked the club for its co-operation in releasing players to play for the county and said "We are very proud in this county of our record, and our success is based on this club."

With renewed enthusiasm Oxford had a convincing 14–3 win over Birmingham University who had scored first. David Bagnall replied by picking up from a scrum and racing thirty five yards for a try near the posts but Hance missed the conversion. Robert Herbertson, with a great game in attack and defence, burst through to pass to Evans, who passed on to Tyack for a try under the posts which David Castle, making an impressive debut at full back, having moved from Headingley, converted. Then Bagnall caught a drop out and got nearly to the line before passing to Malcolm Phipps for a try and, finally, Barrett scored in the corner. A fifth successive home game was played in squelching mud and incessant rain against Old Edwardians and Oxford tried to run the ball but had real difficulties in doing so before settling for a draw, 0–0.

The team was then beaten, 0–5, by a breakaway try and conversion at Taunton and this was not a good send off for a testing Easter Tour in South Wales. Staying at the Tredegar Hotel in Newport, Oxford's first game was under the floodlights at Cross Keys on Good Friday, not quite a new experience after the earlier visit to Stratford. The *Oxford Mail* headline summed it up by saying 'Friday was not so good for Oxford RFC' as the match resulted in a resounding defeat, 3–27, which Oxford's play never deserved. But passing was erratic and they conceded seven tries and worse, Lynn Evans, whose home was in Risca just a mile down the valley, broke an ankle – hardly the best way to celebrate the birth of his second daughter the previous week! The very next afternoon Oxford showed much greater spirit against Pontypool, who included the current Welsh Captain and scrum half Clive Rowlands. The programme notes for the match said "The pleasant Oxford ground is situated a few miles outside Oxford town, in country near a motorway. They have their own clubhouse, good ground and stand, together with car parks, it is surely one of the most pleasant grounds in England." The match may well have been drawn had Hance or Webb converted two of the four penalties missed. Kilgour was brought down just short of the line and Webb was over but called back. Ray Tapper, playing at fly half, kept the home side at bay with his probing punt kicks and despite having some chances, Oxford lost Peter West with a knee injury and the match 0–6 to a try and a penalty. Finally, on Easter Monday the party crossed to Somerset and again, in the match against Weston-super-Mare, Oxford had their scoring chances but very little went right in the 0–11 defeat. Once more the side finished with fourteen players as Malcolm Phipps, who had only been available for the Monday game and had travelled especially for it, dislocated his shoulder after ten minutes.

*Easter Tour 1964, programme from Cross Keys v Oxford.*

Although the team had scored only three points in three games on the tour, a magnificent forty yard penalty kick from George Webb at Cross Keys, there was a definite benefit from the experience shown by the team in the run in to the end of the season. The players gave a much improved display to beat Old Alleynians 12–3 at the Bypass where drop goals from Ray Tapper and Windsor-Lewis, and tries from Kilgour and Bagnall, saw the side home. The team then recorded their biggest ever win over Esher, 21–3, with increased power play and speed to the loose ball being a clear result of playing in Wales, with five tries scored. The following day Oxford lost to the eventual winners, Coventry, in the quarter final of the Oxfordshire Sevens Tournament having already beaten Banbury and Barkers Butts in the earlier rounds.

But the best form was yet to come! Oxford had rarely played better and gave a great display to record one of their best victories on record in beating Cross Keys 16–8 at the Bypass, quite a turnaround from the tour match. The key to this was the powerful, purposeful play of the forwards who were more than a match for the Welsh eight and this gave the backs chances they gleefully accepted. This was not a lucky win, six of the Cross Keys players were in the combined team with Pontypool which lost to the All Blacks in November, and was a day to remember in the club's history, in every way a first class performance. It was only fitting that a great victory should be celebrated in style and the party and dance which followed was so successful that the majority of the Cross Keys team stayed the night and set off for home some time on Sunday!

In the final match of the season on Saturday 25th April Oxford played in front of two dignitaries, with the Lord Mayor of Oxford, Alderman Alec Parker, and the Mayor of Cambridge present at the Bypass ground to support their respective teams. Alderman Parker had entertained his Cambridge counterpart, and both sets of club officials, at the Oxford Town Hall before the game and must have been the happiest of the two when 'his' team showed tremendous form. Cambridge, having lost just two matches in the season and scoring a total of 762 points in the process, took an early lead when former England scrum half, Dickie Jeeps, kicked an easy penalty. The turning point for Oxford came when Bagnall made a break up the middle with Howard in support who found Barrett for a try. O'Connell scored another and Oxford, inspired by the return of Barrett from injury, worked up field again and Barrett found Tapper who added a third for a very creditable 9–3 success to end a great playing season.

At the Oxford Old Boys dinner, captain Alan Brunsdon said 'negotiations were continuing' and that the club had a good chance of getting its own ground 'very soon'. Results in the first season had been quite satisfactory with nineteen wins, two draws and thirteen lost. At Oxford Marathons, their most successful side had been the 'A' XV who'd had their best season since formation in 1948.

Oxford's record for the season showed that, of the thirty nine games played twenty two had been won, the first time since the 1956–1957 season that the twenty game win barrier had been broken, with three draws and fourteen losses. Ron Grimshaw wrote in the *Sports Mail* "After their initial success and progress, Oxford in recent years have been 'marking time' indeterminately between good second class rugby and the fringe of the first class game. Both on and off the field Oxford RFC's stature has grown immeasurably and if they have not exactly 'arrived' they are certainly on the threshold." There was one outstanding factor behind the success of the season, after a period of immobility and two of the worst seasons in the clubs history, and that was the captaincy and fine leadership of Don Barrett. Younger members had made great strides as players, among them David Bagnall, who had won praise from Dickie Jeeps, Duncan Kilgour on the wing and hooker George Webb, while second row Jim Parsons had been a great fighter in the loose.

Prior to the club's annual meeting in June it became known that Don Barrett was to stand down as Captain 'owing to business pressures'. At the meeting the President, Vernon Dive, congratulated Don Barrett on leading the club first team to one of their best seasons ever, and for the magnificent example he set both on the field and off it. "I am sorry" he said "that Don will not be able to stand again". Don's last act was to propose Ray Hance as the new Captain for the new season, and he was unanimously elected. Ray had a message for his players – "We have a tremendous amount to do next season to live up to our improved fixture list with, in particular, games against Abertillery both home and away. I would like to make an old familiar complaint, let's have plenty of training."

## Season 1964–1965

> Sing, Heavenly Muse, our hero who is
> Called by the name of *Windsor-Lewis,*
> Who led to Gloucestershire his men
> And, victors, marched them home again.
> Sing also *Hazeldine, Kilgour,*
> Pounding along in godlike power,
> And give a burst to headlong *Hurst*
> Who broke the scoring barrier first
> Confounding all the prophecies.
> O, Gloucester what a fall was this!
> Well may you tremble and repine
> At *Parsons* leaping in the line,
> Or quail where *Palmer* (minus thumb)
> Thunders around behind the scrum,
> Whipping his passes out to *Evans*
> Till you're at sixes and at sevens
> And crack before the stern advance
> Of weed-deracinating *Hance.*
> More, never more will Gloucester scoff at
> The deep-laid ruse of Drop-Kick *Moffatt,*
> Gloucester, the proud and mighty high lot,
> Shot down by *Mulligan* the Pilot
> And by the weaving *Webb* outsmarted,
> By *Roberts, Sutcliffe* apple-carted.
> *Fairbrothers* all: O happy day!
> Weave, weave the laurel, twine the bay,
> And as Oxford trumpets play
> Let gold of four and twenty carat
> Crown the bald pat of whiskered *Barrett.*

The main rugby news at the start of the 1964–1965 season centred round the revision of the Laws of the Game that were implemented on 1st September. Major alterations included allowing any front row players being able to play the ball after it had touched the ground in the scrum, and an offside line in line with the back foot of loose or set scrums for players except the scrum half. In the lineout there had to now be a clear space between opposing lines of forwards, the length of which was determined by the team throwing in. In addition, players not involved were not allowed to encroach across a line ten yards behind the line of touch until the ball had left a lineout. This created a twenty yard space between opposing backs every time the ball went out of the playing area.

The revisions were seen as a way to speed up play and open up space thus giving greater freedom of movement to the players, possibly bringing an end to forward power play and reviving back play. One area not addressed was that of constant touch kicking in open play, a major bug bear of the game at that time.

The death of James Harold Abraham, who had been a founder member of the Oxfordshire Nomads club and Captain in the 1920s, was reported. He'd had the distinction of leading the Nomads in their first ever game against Oxford University Greyhounds whose team on that occasion had included A Valentine, the first American to win a Blue at Oxford.

Training at the club had started in the last week of July under Oxford United trainer, Sam Gill, as the players heeded Ray Hance's plea, although there were some absentees. Dick Fogden was now living in Bristol and Robert Herbertson was about to move to Sheffield, while Charlie Ede had badly strained thigh ligaments in a summer swimming pool accident. Young Chris Jones, a promising 2$^{nd}$ row forward, had been advised not to play whilst convalescing after a severe attack of whooping cough, and Malcolm Phipps still hadn't recovered from the shoulder dislocated at Weston-super-Mare on Easter Monday.

Oxford named David Crossley, a centre who had joined from Fylde, for their first match, at home against Hinckley. The team started the season in impressive style on a rock hard ground and although many of the players wore plimsolls the exchanges were hard. With more method and better finishing the 24–3 score could have been doubled, instead two Don Barrett tries, with one each from Bradley, Evans and Crossley, on his debut, with Hance

*Oxford Thursday team that beat Oxford Old Boys 21–3, September 1964. Back row, l to r: J Mawle, MJ Parsons, RJ Tapper, R Palmer, IC Jones, G Windsor-Lewis, B Butler, IB Moffatt, NT Moffatt. Front row, l to r: G Howells, D Paterson, D Thomas, CT Ede (Capt), S Marsh, KR Morgan.*

kicking three conversions and a penalty sufficed. It was a particularly pleasing start to the season as all four Oxford teams, and the Colts fifteen, got off to a flying start by all winning their respective matches.

The Fixture Secretary had been busy and, with the players keen to show their fitness, an intense week of games took place very early in the season. Another good home win, this time against Old Cranleighans by a similar 24–3 score, was again tempered by the hard playing surface which took its toll in sore and blistered feet with grazed knees and sore elbows. The defence had not really been tested in the first two games but came under the spotlight in London, away at Richmond. The side paid dearly for early mistakes and was put off its stride by Richmond's speed to man and ball. Finding themselves 3–19 in arrears early in the second half Oxford steadied and, with superior fitness and stamina, took the game right back. Mike Simmie intercepted to take the ball up field where Jim Parsons crashed over for a try that Moffatt converted. Moffatt added a forty five yard penalty, his second of the match, and Oxford were right back in the game. The best score of the match came in the dying minutes when Moffatt made the extra man in the line which gave Kilgour a thirty yard sprint for the Richmond line. Moffatt converted with the last kick of an eventful match where the Richmond pack was well beaten and thankful for the final whistle. The Oxford team that had come through its first real test with honours was: IB Moffatt; MS Simmie, G Windsor-Lewis, RJ Tapper, DS Kilgour; LR Evans, DF Bagnall; RJ Hance (Capt), G Webb, G Howells, D Green, MJ Parsons, DWG Barrett, I Paterson, D Paterson. But there was no time for celebration. Forty hours later the team kicked off again, in a new fixture at home to United Services, Portsmouth. Once more the Oxford players found themselves in arrears, this time 6–13, at half time. But a 'pep' talk from the captain and the wind at their backs saw the side pile on the pressure to win 25–16. Not surprisingly, it was a tired group of players that made its way to Dulwich for the away match with Old Alleynians. There was a late departure from the city and, subsequently, a delayed kick off after a 'phone call from

*Oxford RFC 1964–1965. Back row, l to r: AM Rowland, G Webb, G Howells, PW Sutcliffe, AJ Tyack, DWG Barrett, MJ Parsons, DW Howard, JRM Higgins (Trainer). Front row: DJ Castle, VR O'Connell, RJ Hance (Captain), DF Bagnall, DS Kilgour, G Windsor-Lewis, FC Inglis.*

Peter Bradley to say his car had broken down in Cowley. After a fruitless wait a replacement player was drafted in but, when the team arrived in London, they found Bradley waiting. His car had not broken down and he had not made a telephone call! The Oxford team, having used much of its' energy in the previous week, led 11–0 at half time and were lucky to scrape home, 11–8, in a tight finish. With motor cars in the news both Ray Hance and David Patterson had theirs stolen in this week. David's was found forty eight hours later but it was a week before Ray Hance's red MG Sports Midget turned up near Aylesbury, minus three wheels, spot and fog lamps, hood and radio!

Over at Oxford Old Boys, Alan Brunsdon had stood down from the captaincy to be replaced by a former University Greyhound, Alan Heard. The club announced that they would have a new ground for the following season after successful negotiations with St John's College had realized a twenty one year lease on some ground adjoining the school field in Marston Ferry Road. The site was formerly used for allotments and would take £1000 to clear and a further £1000 for a new clubhouse. Significantly, Oxford's second team, the Nomads, had beaten Oxford Old Boys on the Bypass ground, 17–6, while the club team was playing in Dulwich.

With a week's break behind them, Oxford had little trouble in keeping to their winning form. In the home match with Aldershot Services they were soon nineteen points up and then eased off into an unimpressive second half, winning the match 25–6. The players would have benefitted from the formation of a Ladies Committee at the club to organize after match teas, amongst other things, and the club was generous in its thanks, arranging a dinner for them at the Kings Arms.

October arrived and more car problems preceded the away match at Sutton when three players got lost in the Surrey countryside en route, and three Nomads gained immediate promotion into a team that maintained its form in winning 14–9.

The Oxfordshire RFU selectors announced a team that included a debut for Duncan Kilgour on the wing for the midweek match against Hertfordshire at Croxley Green. The team made its intentions clear with a terrific 29–5 win which was Oxfordshire's biggest ever win in the Championship, although Lynn Evans had some early difficulty with Maurice Palmer's service from the base of the scrum. Once this had been sorted out the team 'clicked', and the players were looking forward to the next match.

The Oxford team was now facing a difficult period of matches beginning with the home fixture against Loughborough Colleges, who included Colin McFadyean, Derek Prout and David Rollitt, all future England Internationals. The side was never really in the contest and was beaten by superior pace and fitness although Hance kicked a penalty goal and Windsor-Lewis scored a consolation try near the end of a 6–14 defeat. Five days later Oxford entertained RH Lamb's XV and the players faced with the strongest University side available at the time, containing eight Blues and an Irish International. The team had learnt lessons from the weekend's fixture and was a trifle unlucky to lose a hard match, 5–11. In the last ten minutes bounces of the ball cost them two great scoring opportunities and the side was far from disgraced in defeat. But it all changed again on the Saturday when Oxford suffered their heaviest defeat of the season, 0–21, against Oxford University Greyhounds at Iffley Road. It was the fourth year running that Oxford had failed to beat the University second string and, outfought from the start, could not complain this time either. Another midweek fixture beckoned, this time on a Tuesday evening away under floodlights, still a novelty for Oxford, against Coventry Nighthawks and, again, the side was well beaten, 8–32. Oxford more than held their own in the tight but were beaten for speed outside the scrum.

Henley RFC had been granted a sixty year lease on their Dry Leas ground, while the plans announced a year ago by RB Cole for the development of the Sports Club ground were reported to be proceeding. Added to the ambitious plans, which included a two-storied central block in the club's pavilion, there was now also a scheme being discussed to develop the second team pitch into a first team pitch. This would involve having the top pitch leveled with drainage being put in, and the stand being moved to the bypass side of the pitch. The cost of this change was estimated at £3000 but, once completed, would give the rugby club its own pitch all the year round without interference from the other sports sections. "Bunny" Cole was the only senior officer who had been at the Oxford Sports Club since the start and, in proposing him as President for another year, Vernon Dive said "The Oxford Sports Club without Bunny Cole would be rather like a guardsman without his bearskin."

Subtle first team changes had seen Vic O'Connell, a teacher at Gosford Hill School and no relation to the County President, prise Lynn Evans out of the fly half shirt and Peter West had kept his place in the back row for a period at the expense of Don Barrett. But injury to West was to see Barrett reinstated for the club trip to Stroud along with the debut on the wing of former Cambridge Blue, Fred Inglis. Tries from Kilgour and Peter Sutcliffe and two penalties from Hance saw the team home, 12–9, but it should have been more than that with Parsons and Green dominating the lineouts. This theme continued the next week when the club travelled again, to Grange Road, Cambridge, to meet that Univesity's second team, the LX Club. Leaving their familiar shirts in the clubhouse Oxford had to borrow a set and turned out in maroon. The team spent most of the game in attack but lacked scoring ideas close to the Cambridge line and, instead, conceded a try in the last minute of the game to lose 0–3.

Malcolm Phipps' bad luck continued – his return to the game in the 'A' fifteen lasted ten minutes when he broke an arm which lead to another long time out of the game and eventually down the refereeing path.

Oxfordshire's next match was also away again, at the beginning of November, at High Wycombe. Buckinghamshire, well represented with several players from London clubs in the lineup, had at last been admitted to the Championship and had taken the place of Sussex in the Southern group, while Sussex had moved to join the South Eastern group. Oxfordshire won a hard match fashioned by the forwards who were splendidly led by Don Barrett. George Webb won five 'strikes against the head' while Parsons and Peter Roberts dominated the lineouts to provide possession for the likes of Peter Sutcliffe to score a solitary try in a modest 11–3 win which saw the side lead the table with two home games to come.

With County success reflecting back into the club's Saturday fixtures, Green and Parsons were again in dominant form in the pack and the backs showed their best play of the season as Oxford beat the London Hospital Champions, St Thomas' Hospital, 31–3, at the Bypass. It was the best win of the season so far. This carried on into the West Country the following Saturday where the players faced former Oxford club man Dick Fogden in the Clifton second row. Once again Jim Parsons showed impressive form and the team missed the two unavailable Cambridge Blues, Windsor-Lewis and Inglis, in the 18–9 win. It was a happy coach that travelled back to Oxford, the Nomads having also beaten Clifton II, 16–5!

Sitting at the top of the Southern Group table, Oxfordshire had yet to play at 'home' and when they did the supporters were not disappointed with a 9–5 win over Berkshire. This was different, though, and the home pack more than met its match against the Berkshire eight but held the aces in the backs. Oxfordshire made hard work of it and, in the end, were a trifle lucky to win but win they did and were ensured of a play-off even in the event of defeat in the final group match. Lynn Evans and Derrick Howard were try scorers with Moffatt adding a penalty goal.

Travelling for three hours to play St Batholomew's Hospital at Chistlehurst in Kent, it was as well that Parsons and Green again dominated the lineout, Webb the set scrums, while Barrett foraged well in the loose and Bagnall gave a quick and efficient service at scrum half. All this came together for Oxford's third successive win, this time 16–6.

Fixtures with the Nuneaton club had started in 1949 and the twenty eighth such match loomed at the end of November. It was always going to be a tough game and Oxford had to fight back in the last minute when Inglis burst through to give Sutcliffe an easy try. Supporters held their breath as Evans came up to take the kick but it sailed through for a 14–14 draw, the eighth in the series.

There was much anticipation as Oxfordshire's match with Dorset & Wilts drew near. The team had only to draw to become Southern Group Champions for the third time in four seasons and hopes were high. The selectors did not hesitate in changing a winning Oxfordshire side and two players made their County debuts. Colin Fairbrother, a prop from Banbury, replaced Brian Butler while in the second row the in-form Oxford RFC lock, David Green, an Oxford City Policeman, took the place of Kyle Mulligan who dropped back to take Derek Howard's place in the back row of the scrum. The Oxfordshire team was always good enough to win and the players knew it, which led to an unconvincing performance where the forwards played well throughout to win plenty of possession. But the backs met stern defence, although Moffatt at full back enhanced his reputation, and it wasn't until the final moments that Windsor-Lewis was able to use his strength to break through. The side played the last twenty minutes with fourteen men after Vic O'Connell was stretchered off with a groin injury but still won by 16–0 to become champions again. The 'reward' was an away quarter final match with Gloucestershire to be played in the New Year!

After a November which had seen the club side win three and draw one of its matches the players, especially those who had been involved with the County side, perhaps deserved the break that Saturday 5th December provided with no fixture. The team had been due to visit Weston-super-Mare but the first England Trial, held on Weston's ground, saw the match cancelled after three Oxford club home games made a switch of grounds impossible. The respite lasted a week before the side was back on the road again, this time away at Old Paulines where the winning run continued with a 17–0 win. After a slow start the backs settled to give a fine display and there were tries for Inglis, Windsor-Lewis, Kilgour and Howard, with an Evans drop goal and, finally, a conversion.

As the dark days of winter took away even more sunlight the club faced its first match of the season with Welsh opposition away at Maesteg. This was a tough fixture and, in cold conditions on a frozen pitch, Oxford again started too slowly only coming to life in the second half. This wasn't good enough against such opposition and, with penalty kicks also missed, the team lost 9–12.

Next up were the Christmas holiday games with Oxford at Banbury and the Nomads facing Oxford Old Boys at South Park on Boxing Day, and Esher at home on 28th December. Lynn Evans, who had scored a lot of Oxford's points in the last six matches, had a wrist injury and would miss both allowing him the chance to recover at home in Wales over the holiday period. Ian Moffatt was drafted in to take his place and Ian's brother, Tom, was also included in the centre for the Banbury match. At this point Ian had played only two first team games for Oxford in the season so far but had accumulated twenty points, while George Webb hoped to recover from a knee injury to continue his 100% season record as hooker. In the event it was all academic as, by then, the country was in the grip of Artic weather and both games were cancelled. The night of Tuesday 29th December 1964 was reported as being one of the coldest for twenty five years, reaching a low of -10°C, and the River Thames was frozen over at Oxford and at Eynsham, where the ice was two inches thick!

Once again an enforced break gave the opportunity to reflect on a season of strengthened fixtures so far and, having played nineteen, eleven had been won, one drawn and seven lost, reflecting favourably on previous times. The team had seemed to start some games with an inferiority complex and there was a weakness in reserve strength in some positions, but it had shown a readiness for better class fixtures and there was little doubt that the success of Oxfordshire was closely linked to Oxford RFC.

Despite the weather, preparations for Oxfordshire's match at Gloucester on 13th January continued with the team announcement. Vic O'Connell was still injured from the last match and Lynn Evans was named to continue as fly half in his place. Evans had shown his versatility by playing all the group matches on the wing but was more familiar with Number 10. In his place the selectors had chosen Andy Hurst who had played previously for Oxfordshire in 1958–59 and 1959–60. Hurst had been at Oxford University but had not gained a 'Blue' although later, in 1962, played once for England. Gloucestershire, on the other hand, named the England full back, Don Rutherford, in their side and had conceded only eleven points in winning the South West Group title.

Although neither side had played for a fortnight an unrelenting battle between two evenly matched teams was witnessed when Old Whitgiftians visited on 2nd January 1965. Oxford looked safe with tries from Webb and Kilgour but the Old Boys side fought back with a penalty and a late try for a 6–6 draw, and the match was a good warm up for those involved the following week.

The real focus at this time was, of course, on the Quarter Final match at Gloucester on 11th January. This was a re-match of Oxfordshire's game two years ago when Gloucestershire had won decisively, 8–42, and most people gave the team no chance at all against a pack containing three internationals and two more in the ascendency. Eight Oxford players, Kilgour, Windsor-Lewis, Evans, Hance, Webb, Parsons, Barrett and Sutcliffe, had been named in the lineup and telegrams of good wishes for the team were received from the other counties in the Southern Group. Lynn Evans, chosen in the pivotal role at fly half, was ill and had no sleep on the Friday night. Still pale and drawn he had nothing to eat or drink before the kick off but, in the event, played a blinder as Oxfordshire took the game to their renowned opponents. Although beaten in the tight scrums the back row of Barrett, Mulligan and Sutcliffe was terrific and Barrett, the man of the match, was stupendous in his harrying with great support from a mobile front row. Oxford's physio, Jim Higgins, was able to quickly put Maurice Palmer's dislocated thumb back without him leaving the field before Palmer kicked for the corner. Collins, the Bristol winger, gathered at the line but Andy Hurst charged down his kick and recovered quickly to pick up the ball and go over for a try. Moffatt's kick hung in the wind in front of the goal but Oxfordshire had a precious half time lead. Gloucestershire applied pressure in the second half and Hampton, a big powerful winger from Rosslyn Park, set off for the line evading tackles until crashing over the line taking two defenders with him. At 3–3 the game balanced on a

*If you had one of these you were in for an exciting afternoon's rugby!*

knife edge as play see-sawed from end to end. With five minutes remaining Moffatt asked to change places with Evans at fly half and, standing well back, took a long pass from a lineout on the right hand side of the home "25" and drop kicked a goal with his left foot to give his team the lead again. It was time for cool heads in front of a baying Kingsholm crowd of 5000 but the team hung on for a well-deserved 6–3 victory.

Oxfordshire, inspired by a pre-match pep talk from the Captain, Geoffrey Windsor-Lewis, had made history by making it to the last four of the Championship, the first time a Southern Group team had reached the Semi Final. The win was no fluke and Peter Ford, the Gloucestershire Captain, admitted in his post-match speech that "There are no excuses, we were beaten by a better side". The result was also something of a surprise. Gloucestershire had already made tentative hotel bookings for the next match, against Durham in Hartlepool, arrangements which Stan Oswin, the Oxfordshire Team Secretary, was happy to help Gloucestershire with by taking them over!

Also a surprise were events on the same afternoon taking place quite a distance from Kingsholm, in Kent where a much depleted Oxford RFC met Old Askeans, reputedly one of the stronger London Old Boys sides. With eight players on County duty, two down with 'flu and one injured a makeshift side of: R Palmer; ER Rowland, NT Moffatt, RJ Tapper, FC Inglis; DJ Castle (Captain), DF Bagnall; J Head, K Withers, B Beale, B Butler, T Tyack, JP West, M Bond and D Paterson played exactly the right game in heavy conditions. The forwards were dominant from the start with West and Patterson in good form and the pace and power of Beale and Butler creating all sorts of problems in the loose. This laid the foundation for an 18–3 win, just the fourth defeat suffered by Askeans at that point of the season.

*Programme from Durham v Oxfordshire 1965.*

A sign of the times saw only four of those players retained for the next match, at home to Lydney. One was John Head who held his place in the front row at the expense of Gerry Howells. Howells had been ill the previous week which effectively ended his run of thirty seven consecutive appearances in the Oxford team, while David Green was recalled into the second row after missing the last five matches. It was a tough match, as games with Lydney usually were, but Oxford with Inglis scoring two tries just about deserved to win 11–8. More worryingly, on the next pitch, Peter West playing for the Nomads against Reading University was taken from the field with a broken jaw which required an operation the following Tuesday.

Oxford faced a real test in a new fixture against Welsh club Abertillery, who contained in their lineup two seasoned internationals in Alun Pask and Haydon Morgan. The team had to start short when David Green failed to arrive and was not in the best frame of mind. Robin Crutch,

*Oxfordshire team v Durham. Back row, l to r: L Lamb (Referee), J Higgins (Trainer), R Hazeldene (Oxford), I Moffatt (Richmond), C Fairbrother (Banbury), G Webb (Oxford), TN Roberts (Northampton), MJ Parsons (Oxford), M Simmie (Oxford University), P Sutcliffe (Oxford), L Evans (Oxford), A Tucker (Touch Judge). Front row, l to r: R Hance (Oxford), K Mulligan (RAF), G Windsor-Lewis (Oxford), J O'Connell (President), D Barrett (Oxford), AB Hurst (Wasps), M Palmer (Saracens).*

normally a fourth team player, was drafted in as the Nomads were away at Bicester, but Green was badly missed in the second row. Nonetheless Oxford led twice in a fast, thrilling game and were just 9–12 down with twenty minutes left only to crack under steady pressure to finally lose 9–21. Oxford won 11–6 in what had become an annual midweek match under Stratford's floodlights, and then took no chances in their selection for the next home match, against Westminster Hospital, with Bert Butler replacing Green. But this match was cancelled when the Hospital failed to raise a side after several injuries in Hospital Cup games.

Once again there was much interest in Oxfordshire's County Championship match, at Hartlepool against Durham. The County Selectors, never afraid to make changes, replaced Duncan Kilgour on the wing with Mike Simmie, presumably to strengthen the defence while Durham included four English Internationals, three of whom were British Lions, in John Dee, Mike Weston, Stan Hodgson and Tom Peart. An added bonus, in the days before Twickenham Finals, was that the winning team in the tie would host the Final in its own county. In light of the match and player involvement, Oxford cancelled its scheduled match in London with the Metropolitan Police.

Ray Hance passed a strenuous fitness test prior to the match, following a knee injury sustained in the game with Abertillery, to take his place in the team. A small army of volunteers started work at 7.30 in the morning of the match to clear the ten tons of straw from the pitch that had been laid to protect the surface from the elements. There was a nervous start before Weston kicked a penalty after both teams had missed kicks. The game ebbed and flowed and, just before half time, Oxfordshire reached the Durham line but could not cross as Evans was adjudged to be narrowly wide with a drop kick as the ball passed over the top of the posts. The visitors restarted full of purpose and fire to score a

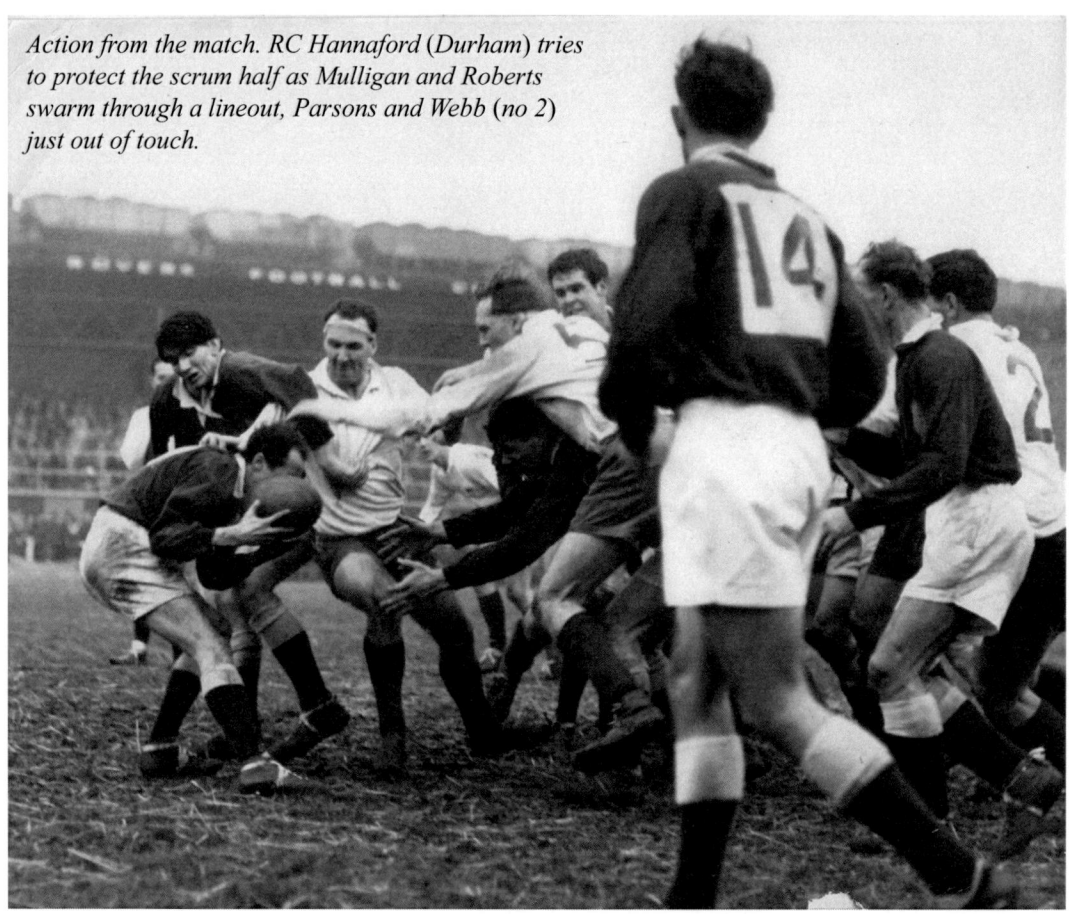

*Action from the match. RC Hannaford (Durham) tries to protect the scrum half as Mulligan and Roberts swarm through a lineout, Parsons and Webb (no 2) just out of touch.*

well-deserved try. Windsor-Lewis made a half break and then kicked to the corner where Simmie, chasing through, gathered to turn back in to the line, was held by his shirt but managed to slip the ball to Evans to score. Durham hit back and Parsons was offside, and Durham's kicker scored the winning points as gallant Oxfordshire lost 3–6. At the post match dinner the Durham captain, Mike Weston, told Oxfordshire "You certainly gave us a fright," while Geoffrey Windsor-Lewis, in reply, said "We are extremely grateful to Gloucestershire for organizing this weekend for us." Oxfordshire supporters, including Chris Price and Frank Webb who had travelled the furthest from Devon, were able to go home with their heads high, but Durham lost the Final at the same venue to Warwickshire, 9–15.

For Oxford it was a case of 'after the Lord Mayor's Show' and the side struggled to beat London University, 6–5, at the Bypass being made to fight all the way for the win. Don Barrett touched down a pushover try and Hance kicked a penalty before the students came back with a converted try in a match that saw Windsor-Lewis break a finger in his right hand, leading to an enforced break for the player. But a win it was and that heralded an unbeaten run of five matches and Streatham (8–3), Birmingham (6–0) and Cambridge (13–6) were all beaten away from the Bypass in close, hard fought games with Birmingham University (6–3) even closer at home.

Vic O'Connell had been passed fit and was playing again but David Bagnall had torn shoulder ligaments against Cambridge and was going in the opposite direction. Oxford Colts hooker, Martin Ponty, had been selected for England Youth against Wales, to be played at

Neath. Former Oxford lock forward Neil Russell was reported as playing for Dover and, sadly, one of the oldest members of the Oxfordshire Nomads, Harold Quelch, collapsed and died in his garden at Yarnells Hill, aged 69 years.

At the club dinner on March 4th the Oxfordshire President, Jim O'Connell, said that the County team had come very close to its target of the County Championship Final and that they "could not have achieved what they did without the support and playing strength of the Oxford club".

Oxford now faced a hard set of fixtures and this started with a great fight in Wales at Abertillery who had, in January, beaten Oxford by 12 points scoring seven tries into the bargain. The heavy ground produced a touch kicking contest and a rugged slog between the two packs, but Oxford had more of the match and a great move saw Kilgour brought down a yard from the line before Hance kicked a thirty yard penalty for the lead. There was more of the slog to come before Abertillery equalised with a penalty with eleven minutes left on the clock. The result was a big surprise for the home side and its supporters, and the first time that Oxford had come away unbeaten in Wales for many years. The Nomads had travelled geographically in the opposite direction to London, for a morning kick off before going on to Twickenham to watch England v Scotland (Hancock's match), with fourteen players to meet Old Rutlishians 'A' but still won 31–6. The team got back home in reasonable time but not so the 1st Fifteen who arrived back at 4am and that included the extra hour for summer time!

Oxford followed this by having to play with fourteen men, having lost Lynn Evans with a leg injury in the first five minutes, at home to Old Edwardians from Birmingham. In a scrappy match the visitors scored against the run of play which livened things up a bit before Bagnall fed Inglis for a try converted by Hance. The winning score came when, from a short penalty, Windsor-Lewis was tackled but got the ball away to George Webb who forced over. Unfortunately Hance's conversion attempt missed which left him on 99 points, one short of a century for the season.

Into April and another test came along in the form of Rhymney. Although there was an improvement in Oxford's play the side was still not at its best, but

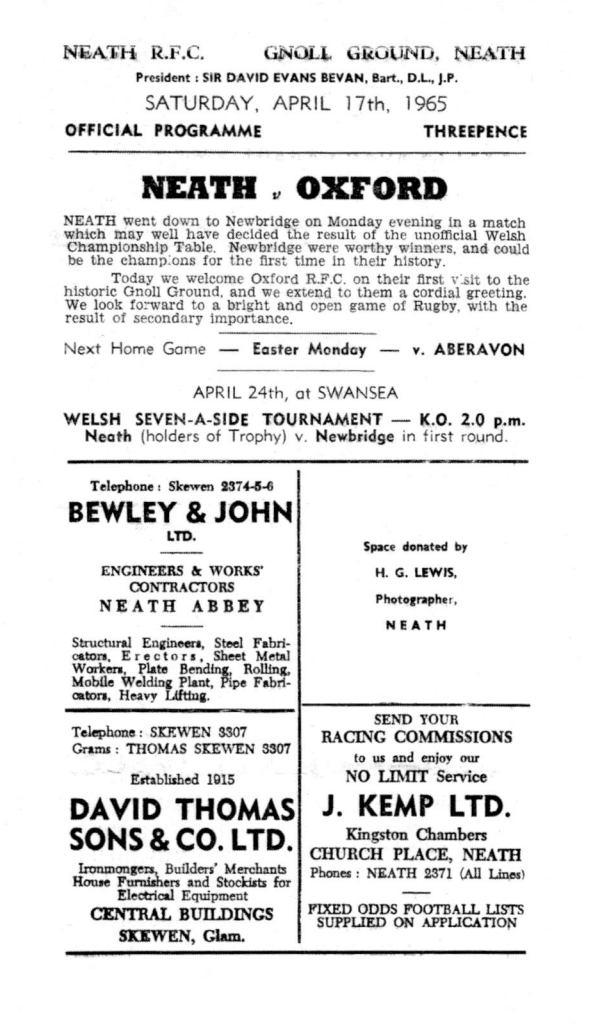

*Programme from the Neath v Oxford Match.*

good enough to overcome their Welsh visitors 17–13 and Ray Hance, at last, made it past the hundred points mark.

An away match with London Irish saw the start to an end of season flourish and the team was playing well to deserve a 9–3 half time lead. But an uncharacteristic second half collapse saw the Irish tear through Oxford's paper like defence to score five tries which did not augur well for the forthcoming Easter Tour to Wales. The following day an Oxford Seven lost to Coventry in the Oxfordshire Sevens Tournament while an Oxford Thursday team lost to Bedford in Quarter Final extra time.

The Easter weekend began with a Good Friday morning kick off at home to Worcester and the Oxford side included Mike Simmie and Peter Sibley, both home for the holiday period. The side romped home with eight tries before packing their bags and heading off to Wales. In a first meeting with Neath, Oxford's pack gave the reputable Neath forwards a good run but found that playing attractive rugby does not always bring rewards and the side failed to score in a 0–10 defeat. After a day's break the party moved on to a return with Rhymney on Easter Monday and deserved a draw, if only for the supreme effort in the final twenty minutes. But the home side held on to win 11–8 despite a penalty from Bond and a try from Beale converted by Hance.

The Welsh trip was considered to be success and many friends were made. It is interesting to note that, in a sign of the times, the tour cost each player £6–10s and that there would be little change from £10 with spending money, a fact that caused one or two players to miss the trip! As if this wasn't enough, two days later Oxford travelled to play at Cheltenham in an evening kick off where the team, perhaps not surprisingly, slumped to a dismal 0–13 defeat. It had been a long season and it was hoped that this defeat might jolt the team back to form for the last match away to Manchester where the home side had won just five of over thirty matches. In yet another new fixture Oxford's weakened team held a 9–3 lead but Manchester made a storming finish to score two tries and a 9–9 draw, a fair result.

Speaking at the Oxford Old Boys dinner, Jim O'Connell repeated his thanks for the assistance given to the county team by the Oxford club especially for the county captain, Geoff Windsor-Lewis whom, he said "was a wonderful example both on and off the field to everyone, and to whose efforts the success of the county this season has been so largely due".

The club had enjoyed a very good season with a final record not far off that of 1956–1957, and the side had scored a record number of 453 points but had conceded more than ever in 342 in winning twenty two of the thirty eight games played, with four drawn.
The team had been virtually unchanged and the continuity was valuable but there were a number of lessons to be learnt if the club was to realise its ambitions. In his seasonal report Ray Hance said that "County matches were a great strain and there was little left for the club matches afterwards. We managed to keep on winning but only just, and didn't play particularly good football." Commenting on the stronger fixtures that had been included in the list, Hance spoke of the need to acquire a 'killer instinct' saying "If we did not have the relatively soft fixtures intervening we should do even better in the strong area. When we have to switch from one to the other it takes us twenty minutes to raise the pace of our game for the stronger fixtures."

# Season 1965–1966

Pre-season news revealed that the club would be looking for a new fly half as Vic O'Connell was due to take up a teaching post in Canberra, Australia, while Ian Moffatt had married in August and was moving too, to teach in London where he would be joining Richmond. Another absentee would be Fred Inglis, a Lecturer in English at Southampton University, who with the onset of fatherhood had decided that travelling backwards and forwards to Oxford would now be too much. Against those departures there were newcomers in ex London Irish prop, Val McCarthy, and Howard Rhys Davies, a fly half, while Ray Tapper was still undecided about joining the club. Jim Parsons needed another two weeks for the harvest and David Green would continue to play midweek for the Police. It was said at this time that Green had a natural ability, physique and potential and was capable of an England cap if he chose to play regularly in a good class of rugby. Ray Hance had the daunting task of steering the team through the forty fixtures on the card as Captain again, while Charlie Ede, described as the 'Peter Pan' of local rugby, would again lead the Oxford Thursday side.

For all that there didn't seem to be much change in the Oxford team that opened the season in grand style by beating London Welsh at the Bypass ground, coming from behind in the second half to do so. The home side was slightly fortunate to lead by a Mark Bond penalty goal after an untidy first half and the Welsh went ahead after the break with a converted try. But Oxford fought back and Lynn Evans kicked ahead for Duncan Kilgour to gather and dive over for a try, and it was Evans who hit a winning drop goal for a splendid 9–5 win. Evans gave Oxford a lead with another dropped goal in a hard fought 11–11 draw at Hinckley on the Saturday where sound defensive work was to the fore after the euphoric midweek win against the Welsh. And then, in another midweek clash, the side was well beaten 3–26 at Richmond.

There was talk of a plan which would see the club level and enclose the top pitch and also remove the stand there, parallel with the Bypass, but this was tied up with the complicated future development of the ground. The changing facilities, which were good for the club as it was in 1948, also came under the spotlight and it was felt that the club needed something better.

The Oxford Old Boys club continued to search for a new ground and nine possible sites had been looked at without any definite conclusion. The £5000 appeal for a ground and clubhouse in Marston Ferry Road, next to the City of Oxford School playing fields, was still a possibility and fund raising continued.

A much improved performance by Oxford's pack laid the foundations for a 14–0 win against Old Cranleighans in the club's third of four away fixtures, and this was most welcome in heavy and wet conditions at Thames Ditton. The front row was more settled so Webb's hooking was more effective while Jim Parsons was a tower of strength. In the back row Don Barrett had another storming game with Asquith and Bond also prominent. But the half back display from Bagnall and Evans needed work on some 'understanding' although it was still early days in the season. A third midweek match, this time at US Portsmouth, saw Oxford record a convincing 16–3 win.

After the great success of the Oxfordshire County team in the previous season there was now much speculation with another Championship season drawing near. In discussing prospects for the Oxford RFC season, captain Ray Hance felt that the club team ought to do better than they did last, which was one of the club's best. Local scribe, Ron Grimshaw, wrote that "If he is right, and Ray is not a man given either to wasting words or rash predictions, then Oxfordshire must have a very good chance of repeating last season's historic performance in the County Championship. Let there be no misunderstanding, the one thing is closely connected with the other. You have only to look at the composition of the county team for reassurance on that point."

Oxford, with the Tapper brothers Roy and Ray playing together in the centre, continued to win with a 12–0 success against Old Haberdashers but were something of an enigma, looking good in much of their work but with promise remaining unfulfilled. Despite the low score there was only one team in it and Bagnall opened the score when he dived onto a bouncing ball for a try after a lineout, followed by a Bond penalty. Ray Tapper jinked inside his man and straightened up for the line and a try before Bond kicked his second penalty. But club and county prospects took a huge blow when the game was marred by a serious injury to Oxford's blindside wing forward, Don Barrett, who was stretchered off the field and to hospital with a dislocated hip. Don remembered laying in hospital at the time when a nurse came by and, looking down, said "Silly old bugger!" He was never to wear an Oxford shirt in anger again.

Peter West's luck also took a dip on the Friday night when his house in Abingdon was subject of a burglary while he slept. His wife's handbag was emptied on the bedroom floor and his trousers searched, all for a few pounds. "He wasted his talents on us", Peter later said.

Don Barrett was well enough to attend the County Trial at the club ground midweek which saw the reappearance of David Green, who had been keeping his hand in playing for Gosford All Blacks on a Saturday and Oxford City & County Police on a Wednesday, and it was announced that Geoffrey Windsor-Lewis had been reappointed as captain of Oxfordshire RFU.

The club gave one if its best displays in winning 20–6 at Aldershot Services in the worst of conditions. The start of the match was delayed while the rain changed from a torrent to a steady downpour and the running track round the pitch at the Military Stadium was under inches of water. Oxford slithered and squelched to 6–6 at halftime, all kicks, but tightened up and took control in the second half.

When David Bagnall was injured playing Sevens for the Oxford Thursday team at Streatham, the Oxford side was forced into a change at scrum half for the home match with Old Askeans. This produced one of those quirks of sporting interest when Mike Tanner, a school boy at Littlemore Grammar School, later to become Peers School, was promoted from the Nomads in his place. His partner at fly half would be Lynn Evans who had taught him the game at school! And what a remarkable debut! Tanner, who was due to 'go up' to St Edmund Hall a week later, scored three tries in the first half in Oxford's 33–3 win, the club's biggest win since 1954.

It was the start of that busy period which always seemed to come round at this time of year for some of the club's players. Five took part in a county trial match when a weakened Oxfordshire team lost 6–16 against a North Midlands side at Moseley on Tuesday 5th October, and then there was the annual match with the University Captain's team on Thursday afternoon. It had been several seasons since Oxford had won this one and the side got off to a bad start when both props, Ray Hance and Gerry Howells, had to call off with influenza. Veteran John Head got a late call and John Milner was called over from the adjoining pitch where the Oxford Thursday side were due to play. Despite this disruption it was the pack that laid the foundation for a notable 17–11 victory. With the back row of Asquith, Bond and Patterson working tirelessly Oxford's backs were lively while the Dark Blue side had Nigel Starmer-Smith to thank for tidying up at the back of the University scrum. Two days later Oxford, not surprisingly, made a lethargic start against Sutton at home but came alive in the second half, when Bagnall made some useful breaks, to scrape home 17–14 thus increasing their unbeaten run to seven games.

Oxfordshire's selection for the first defence of the Southern Group title included eight Oxford players, Kilgour, Windsor-Lewis, Simmie, Evans, Hance, Webb, Parsons and Sutcliffe who joined former members, Moffatt, Green, Herbertson and Jenkins, called in at the last moment, in the side. A new Number 8 had also been found after County Selector, Jim O'Connell, made a 400 mile round trip to Devon to watch a certain Tony Hallett playing for the Royal Navy College, Dartmouth against Brixham. As a result Hallett, who was to come to prominence again many years later as an administrator when Rugby Union became professional, made his debut for Oxfordshire.

Oxfordshire certainly hit the ground running and the 28–3 win against Dorset & Wiltshire at Marlborough was the team's biggest ever win at that time. Ian Moffatt's place kicking was immaculate and he converted all five of Oxfordshire's tries, two of which he scored himself, and a penalty for a personal triumph of nineteen points.

Back at the club it had become known that Jim Parsons was leaving to rejoin Northampton. This was the club he had first joined on leaving Kings School, Canterbury but had later come to Oxford RFC in 1964. Jim had come into contact with Northampton again when playing for the Thursdays in the Streatham Sevens. He was due to make a quick return to Oxford having been called into the Saints team for their away match against Oxford University the following Saturday!

The next club game was a difficult one, at home to the Oxford University Greyhounds and, whilst regretting Parsons' departure, the club promoted John Mawle from the Nomads to take his place and with his partner, the lofty Chris Jones, felt confident that they shouldn't fare badly in the line outs. The students played some good rugby inspired by Starmer-Smith at scrum half and in contrast the Oxford pack was slow in support. At the end of a hard and fast game the club side was relieved to hold on to the unbeaten run with a 6–6 draw.

There was sad news from Don Barrett who made it known that he had given up playing rugby. The pelvic injury he had sustained against Old Haberdashers on September 18th had healed well but had left certain weaknesses and he had accepted medical advice not to play for fear of more permanent damage. Aged just 28 years, Don had taken over the captaincy of the club after two of its worst seasons, in 1961–1963, and had led the team to one of its best seasons. As a junior player he had captained the Magdalen College School Under 15 side, a team that won all its games in 1951, and probably his greatest senior game was that for Oxfordshire against Gloucestershire the previous season. Don said "I certainly do not intend to drop out of the game but, as yet, have not quite decided which department to devote my energies."

On the plus side the club announced that Oxford City Policeman David Green had rejoined the club to fill the gap left by Parsons. Green, if anything, was thought to be a better lineout forward and a strong and tireless worker in loose play, and he went straight into Oxford's team for the next home game with Old Alleynians. But it was a scrappy affair which ended with Oxford on top at 16–0.

In the midweek Oxfordshire won again, this time 12–0, against Hertfordshire. The visitors showed little energy in attack and frustrated Oxfordshire with a very tight defence, to three Moffatt penalties and a Windsor-Lewis drop goal. But a win was a win!

With Oxford's away game against one of the best club sides in the country at that time looming, there was a crisis at scrum half where David Bagnall was unavailable being due to attend his brother's wedding the same day. Negotiations with St Edmund Hall saw Mike Tanner released to the side to play Bedford, a club that in four meetings, Oxford had yet to beat. In the event the Oxford players gave a good account of themselves and took the lead after twenty minutes when Windsor-Lewis scored. But this was a poor reward for some fine rugby before Bedford burst into life with two quick tries to put paid to Oxford hopes. The home side seemed to rely on luck and Oxford mistakes rather than skill but deserved the 16–3 success which brought, at last, an end to Oxford's great unbeaten run. With the bubble burst the club side unexpectedly produced its worst display of the season on 6th November, losing 3–26 to the St Mary's Hospital side. This was not helped when Ray Tapper's car broke down en route just before Henley and several of the team did not arrive until just before the kick off. In addition John Mawle injured a knee in the first minute and was only able to hobble until half time after which the side played with a man short.

In London again the following week Oxford featured in another one sided match but this time in their favour with a 24–0 win over St Thomas' Hospital, while a formidable test was looming on the horizon, that of Loughborough Colleges, again away from home. There was substance in this forecast and the Oxford team fell to its heaviest defeat of the season so far in losing 0–30. Despite the scoreline, the sum of six converted tries, this was by no means a one sided contest but Oxford had no answer to the speedy home backs who gave lessons in how chances should be taken. It was only the eighth occasion in eighteen years that a team had scored thirty or more points against the club.

This 'see-saw' form seemed to have little effect on Oxford's county players and Oxfordshire gave a fine display in beating Buckinghamshire, 15–6, with tries from Kilgour and Windsor-Lewis while Moffatt added a drop goal and two penalties. The result meant that the side had only to draw with Berkshire to win the title for the fourth time in five seasons.

Locally, Oxford Colts player Martin Ponty was presented with an England Schools Cap by Minister for Sport, Dennis Howell, at the Headington Secondary school prize giving ceremony, having played against the Welsh Schools, and there was much joy at Magdalen College School from where two former pupils, Mike Simmie and Nigel Starmer-Smith, were both named in the Oxford University side to meet Cambridge at Twickenham. This situation had happened on two previous occasions, in 1954 and 1956, the players being Steven Coles and Bill Lawrence, but was still a rare occasion. Locally, Simmie was playing at Oxford but Starmer-Smith had played only periodically at Gosford.

There was considered to be something of a rugby 'boom' at this time with over 500 people playing the game in Oxfordshire. Oxford RFC were fielding 5 senior sides and 2 Colts, Oxford Old Boys 4 senior sides and 2 Colts, Oxford Marathon 4 senior sides, Henley 5 senior sides and a Colts team, Banbury 2 seniors and 1 Colts, Gosford All Blacks 2 senior sides, Didcot 2 senior sides, Chinnor 1 senior side, Smiths of Witney 1 senior side and Oxford City and County Police 1 senior side, all of which was seen as a natural result of an increase of rugby activity in schools in recent years.

After what seemed a long spell on the road Oxford RFC were due to return to the Bypass ground with a home match at the end of November against the powerful Welsh club, Maesteg, and this brought a welcome return to form as Oxford won 21–6 with a heartening display. December brought with it typical winter weather and Oxford's game with Reading was notable for the incessant rain, mud, cold and wind, and the white shirts worn because of the clash with Reading's green and white hoops, did not stay white for very long. The whole thing was a stalemate except for a Lynn Evans drop goal, conjured from in front of the posts, which gave Oxford a 3–0 win. On the same afternoon speculation over the makeup of the England Trial teams was ended when former Oxford players, Ian Moffatt and Bob Herbertson, played at Gosforth but there was no place for David Green who was left to endure the Bypass mud. Moffatt was selected again to play for the Possibles against the a penalty try when Moffatt was adjudged to have made a dangerous high tackle 2 yards from the line before Starmer-Smith went off injured. The reshuffle saw Evans at scrum half and Patterson on the wing, positions neither had played before while Hurst, now in the centre, was able to hack on 70 yards a dropped ball for a try which, again, Moffatt converted for a 16–8 win and a much

*Ian Moffatt tackles David Duckham in an England Trial.*

coveted place in the semi-final once again. Writing in the *Oxford Mail,* Ron Grimshaw asked "Is there still anyone who thinks that Oxfordshire's victory over Gloucestershire in the quarter final last year was a fluke?"

Despite the absence of the ten County players Oxford RFC honoured their away fixture with London Hospital on the same afternoon. There was a sense of injustice as the team held the upper hand for most of the game but was caught twice with quick breakaways when the Hospital side equalized then passed Mark Bond's penalty goal.

Clifton agreed to travel for an early kick off on 15th January so that both teams could watch England play Wales on the television in the clubhouse afterwards. Oxford members had hoped to see Ian Moffatt, after three good trials, win his first cap for England but, sadly for him, Don Rutherford was preferred at full back in the national team. In the event heavy frost made the pitch rock hard causing Oxford's match to be cancelled. The cold weather continued and the home match with St Bartholomew's Hospital seven days later suffered the same fate, Oxford's bar profits being hit accordingly!

Although there were no games locally for two weeks, rugby was kept to the forefront of local sports pages when the Oxfordshire Union announced the team to meet Middlesex at Richmond on 5th February. The big news was that, after 24 appearances in the side, hooker George Webb had not been selected! Instead, Colin Fairbrother, a wing forward at Banbury RFC but who had been propping for county, was moved across to hook while the new prop was Ed Gould, formerly of St Edward's School and who had played for Oxford University in the three most recent 'Varsity matches. This selection caused all sorts of innuendo, that George, a local car factory worker was playing in a team of school teachers and solicitors etc and that his face didn't fit, hardly likely given his county record, that he was too feisty in loose play, and even that the County RFU Representative, Sam Miller, was from Banbury and that his club should be represented. There was, of course, no explanation from the selectors and everybody hoped they had got it right. An *Oxford Mail* comment was that "If Oxfordshire are ever to win the County Championship or even reach the final – this is the year!"

## RUGBY FOOTBALL UNION COUNTY CHAMPIONSHIP

 SEMI-FINAL

### MIDDLESEX
*versus*
### OXFORDSHIRE

THE ATHLETIC GROUND · RICHMOND
(by kind permission of the Board of Directors and the Tenant Clubs)

Saturday, 5th February, 1966

Kick-Off 2.45 p.m.

PRICE 1/-

*Middlesex v Oxfordshire match programme.*

News from the west of the county was that Witney Rugby Club had been reformed after a lapse of thirteen years. Formed again in 1935, it had been forced to fold in 1953 due to a lack of players but new industry in the area, Smith's Industries and a switch from soccer to rugby at Witney Grammar School had brought a resurgence of interest. Members of the West Oxfordshire Technical College and Smith's Industries had agreed to help form the new club, the colours of which would be a combination of the two constituent teams, black with a blue band. It would, however, be impossible to undertake a full fixture list until 1967–1968 owing to the long term commitments of both clubs. Oxford made a shaky start to their game at Worcester on 29th January but hit back to coast home 14–3. There was impressive form from George Webb who seemed determined to confound the county selectors and it was from his foot rush that Kilgour picked up to score his second and Oxford's third try in the match.

Despite having played only once in the previous four weeks, Oxford asked to be relieved of the club match at home to Stroud so that players and officials could travel to Richmond to support the Oxfordshire team in the Championship semi-final. In the event, it was a forlorn gesture as the County side could not find the same forward power as before and was never in the game with any chance of winning. It soon became apparent that there had been a major blunder in dropping George Webb and his deputy, Colin Fairbrother, consistently lost the ball on Oxfordshire's put-in to the scrum so the backs were starved of any decent possession. Added to that, the normally reliable Ian Moffatt, at full back, had a poor game by his standards and missed three kickable penalties, although the first was so close as to leave one Touch judge undecided. With the team under pressure Nigel Starmer-Smith, running behind the goal line, flipped a pass to Windsor-Lewis who had little chance to take it and Thorburn, the Middlesex flanker, dived to get one hand on it for a try which was converted. Soon afterwards Oxfordshire lost a put-in to a scrum, Thomas at fly half dropped a goal and all that had gone before was lost in a 0–8 defeat.

On reflection the team had played with little spirit and their game never got off the ground. There was sympathy for Fairbrother but recriminations over his selection with still no word from the Selection Committee, and discussions were to rumble on for weeks. But worst hit must have been Moffatt, and his chances of an England cap must surely have taken a knock with his penalty misses.

Disappointed, the Oxford players returned to the club the following week for the start of a tough fixture schedule ahead including six matches with Welsh opposition. The first was an 11am kick off in London with Guys Hospital so that the players could visit Twickenham afterwards to support England against Ireland. It was not a good day. Disrupted by an arrival at the ground 30 minutes late the match was restricted to 30 minutes each half and Oxford, taking too long to get organized, lost 0–11, while England could only draw 6–6.

Ken Morgan, at scrum half, was the only player in Oxford's backs, selected to meet Streatham at the Bypass ground, who was not playing at County level at the time. But Oxford failed to play as a team and left it until late in the second half to slip into top gear, by which time it was too late and Streatham were able to hang on to win 6–8. Flanker Mark Bond scored in his last game for the club before leaving to live and work in London having made a great contribution with 65 points in the 23 games he had played in the season. Oxford's problems mounted further when Kilgour left the field with five minutes to go, having broken an arm in three places, and Windsor-Lewis was unavailable, due to business commitments, for the daunting trip to Abertillery.

The Welsh club side was traditionally strong and this time included scrum half Alan Lewis, with Alan Pask and Hadyn Morgan in the back row, all current Internationals. It was little wonder that the Oxford players found themselves under constant pressure and the game was lost 3–22 although the visitors won unstinted praise from the crowd.

The following week saw Ed Gould play against Oxfordshire in the annual match with Oxford University which the county side lost 3–14.

But it was not all bad news. At the Annual Dinner in the Eastgate Hotel on Thursday 3rd March, Captain Ray Hance said that the time was coming when the club, with five Senior

*Oxfordshire's Nigel Starmer-Smith and Ian Patterson move to cover Trevor Wintle's blind side break.*

## O.U.R.F.C. v. OXFORDSHIRE

Iffley Road Ground, Oxford, Thursday, 3 March, 1966

Kick-off 2.30 p.m.

| O.U.R.F.C. | | OXFORDSHIRE | |
|---|---|---|---|
| 15 | J. R. CROKER (Birkenhead Pk. & St. Cath's.) | 15 | I. B. MOFFAT (Richmond) |
| 14 | C. HOLROYD (Wyggeston G.S. & Exeter) | 14 | A. C. B. HURST* (Wasps) |
| 13 | A. C. BARKER (Leighton Park & S.E.H.) | 13 | G. WINDSOR-LEWIS* (Oxford) (Captain) |
| 12 | J. R. GABITASS* (Plymouth College & St. John's) | 12 | R. J. HAZELDINE (Moseley) |
| 11 | P. R. E. McFARLAND (Ampleforth & S.E.H.) | 11 | M. F. DOUCH (Lord Williams, Thame) |
| 10 | R. H. PHILLIPS (King Henry VIII, Abergavenny & Corpus) | 10 | R. P. TAPPER (Oxford) |
| 9 | N. S. STARMER-SMITH* (M.C.S. & University) | 9 | M. R. TANNER (St. Edmund Hall & Oxford) |
| 1 | E. J. H. GOULD* (St. Edward's, Oxford, & S.E.H.) | 1 | R. J. HANCE (Oxford) |
| 2 | E. A. LLOYD* (Hilton College, S.A., & C.C.C.) | 2 | G. WEBB (Oxford) |
| 3 | C. M. JONES (Pontypridd High School & S.E.H.) | 3 | C. FAIRBROTHER (Banbury) |
| 4 | O. C. WALDRON*† (St. Nessans, Cork, & Merton) | 4 | M. J. PARSONS (Northampton) |
| 5 | W. J. HALSTEAD (Glenalmond & Lincoln) | 5 | D. GREEN (City & County Police & Oxford) |
| 6 | A. L. BUCKNALL* (Ampleforth & S.E.H.) | 6 | I. C. PATERSON (Oxford) |
| 8 | T. P. BEDFORD*† (C.B.S. Kimberley, S.A., & S.E.H.) (Captain) | 8 | T. COOKSEY (Oxford Old Boys) |
| 7 | W. G. HADMAN* (Marlborough & St. John's) | 7 | R. A. HERBERTSON (Sheffield) |
| | †Internationals    *Blues | | *Internationals |

HOLYWELL PRESS LTD., ALFRED STREET, OXFORD

*George Webb got his place back in the County team.*

and two Colts teams, would have to consider limiting playing membership. Heady times indeed! Guest speaker Tommy Bedford, a South Africa International with 23 caps who had become resident at Oxford University, made interesting comments in his speech saying that he was convinced that too much rugby was played in England. "In South Africa", he said "they train twice a week to keep fit and play about twenty three games, whereas Oxford RFC play as many as forty four games in a season. The players here may not get physically stale but might tend to get mentally stale."

Lynn Evans went off to the Lake District for a two week mountaineering holiday and Ian Parsons was selected for the RAF as Oxford lost again 3–16 at Nuneaton, and 0–6 in a midweek match at home to Birmingham University.

Suddenly the club side was enduring a barren period having scored only one try and three penalties in a sequence of five defeats. The attack and defence had gone to pieces and despite the number of playing members, a lack of reserve strength was harshly highlighted. This dismal run ended with a 9–3 home win over Cambridge, all penalties from Ray Hance, but still no tries.

Away from the pitch, much needed repairs to the lane leading to the clubhouse were remedied by a working party led by RB Cole and Arthur Archer. And, for the first time in many years, there was more than one nominee for the post of Oxfordshire County Representative at Twickenham. The club committee, possibly still smarting from the perceived poor treatment of George Webb surrounding the Championship semi-final, nominated the much respected Eric Church seconded by the Gosford All Blacks club. But the vote was lost and Sam Miller, from Banbury, continued in the role.

Geoffrey Windsor-Lewis' business commitments would prevent him from playing in any of Oxford's remaining fixtures. Morgan and Webb were both injured and Lynn Evans was now on tour in Wales with his Littlemore Grammar School team, although a 20–6 midweek win against London University and a 3–3 draw with Old Edwardians helped to temper the mood.

Suffering from the ravages of a long season, Oxford players again faced a busy and bruising period. A Wednesday evening game at Rugby was lost 3–6, and a particularly bad playing day saw the side lose 6–9 at home to Pontypool where two tries were given away through lack of concentration. There was another midweek game, another loss at home to Neath 3–8, before Oxford set off for an Easter trip to South Wales and more defeats, 3–14

*The Oxford Thursday team that won the 'Oxford Times Cup' at the Oxfordshire Sevens Tournament, 1966. L to r: MJ Parsons, WS Wakelin, IB Moffatt, DF Bagnall, RP Tapper, DS Kilgour, MS Simmie.*

*David Bagnall receives the 'Oxford Times Cup' from County President's wife, Mrs Norman.*

at Glynneath and 0–3 at Cross Keys. With all this rugby it did seem that the club were gluttons for punishment and it was back home again for an Easter Monday defeat, 3–18, to Manchester. At least the remaining fixtures were now at home and a 6–6 draw with Esher finally brought to an end another sequence, this time of six defeats. The home return with Cross Keys saw a first team debut for wing forward Ray Mills and a welcome 9–6 win in a bad tempered affair, to set up the final game of the season at home to Glynneath on Saturday 30th April.

On the penultimate Sunday there was a magnificent win for the Oxford Thursday team in the annual Oxfordshire Sevens Tournament when they beat Wasps 10–0 in the Final in front of an enthusiastic crowd at Iffley Road. It was the first time that Wasps had lost in the final in eight appearances and was particularly pleasing for Charlie Ede, who ran the Thursday team, who had played in Oxford's win over Esher in the 1954 Final. Already the team had won the Abingdon, Gosford, Streatham and Berkshire Sevens Tournaments, but Ede said "This was the one we wanted and planned to win for five years". The team of MS Simmie, DS Kilgour, RP Tapper, DF Bagnall, MJ Parsons, WS Wakelin and IB Moffatt, beat Lichfield 15–0, Cambridge 14–6, Richmond 8–5 and Griffins, who were really London Welsh in disguise, 6–3, before meeting Wasps in that memorable Final.

With the summer break now clearly in view, Oxford finished the season with a great flourish to beat Glynneath 32–3. Scoring six tries in the last 25 minutes as the Welsh side tired, was some recompense for a few previous tough trips across the border.

Ray Hance was married the next weekend, out of season of course, before presenting his report at the Annual Meeting. The senior team had played 40 games, winning 19, losing 17 and drawing 2, with 389 points scored against 347. Hance said "Everyone has heard *ad nauseum* that a strong Oxford RFC means a strong County XV and part of this is undeniable. But this year's County success had repercussions on the club and its regular record" he said. Summing up a somewhat disappointing season after a good start, "the side played well up to Christmas", he continued, "but suffered an anti-climax after the County Championship semi-final and lost a couple of games to the weather. As a result the side lost its rhythm then suffered a spate of injuries, the outcome being that in the latter part of March and beginning of April it lost the appetite for playing." It was noted that the backs were generally better than the forwards for a change!

The seeds of club v county? Surely not?

Probables in the second trial, at Torquay, where his rival on the other side was Don Rutherford, but Herbertson was not included.

Oxford University drew 5–5 with Cambridge at Twickenham in a dour match and Tommy Bedford, a South African back row International, was then elected as Captain for the Blues new season. Two days later, on the Thursday, the gloom was lifted when Oxfordshire completed a clean sweep of the Southern Group in beating Berkshire 14–3 at Windsor to take their fourth group title in five years. It was a confident and competent victory firmly founded in the excellent work of the forward pack and the intelligent play of the backs where two well placed cross kicks from Ray Tapper led to two of the three tries scored by Evans, Windsor-Lewis and Kilgour, while Moffatt added a penalty and a conversion. The 'reward' was a home quarter final against Gloucestershire to be scheduled for early in the New Year.

In the run-in to Christmas the Oxford side was dominant in London against the Metropolitan Police but failed to take most of its chances and lost 6–14 before renewing acquaintances with Bridgwater and Albion after a five year break in fixtures. The visitors might have regretted the trip, the kick off being delayed by 40 minutes minutes after 90 miles of traffic, floods and misdirections! Strong wind and rain at the Bypass did not spoil a fast and open game which was as exciting as the 5–3 score line might suggest. Oxford's score came when Windsor-Lewis grub kicked through the visitors defence for Ray Tapper to gather and score, and Bond kicked the conversion for Oxford's last points in 1965.

There was no significant rugby in Oxford over the Christmas weekend which, at least, gave the county players some valuable breathing space before the Gloucestershire encounter on 8th January.

The Nomads side was due to play Oxford Old Boys at the Bypass on Boxing Day and the team was on the crest of a wave having been unbeaten since mid-September. But this proud record fell in a close match. On the first team front it was an opportunity for Oxford to reflect on its best first half of the season record for a decade, having won thirteen and drawing two of the twenty games played.

The Oxfordshire team to face Gloucestershire was announced in this period and showed two changes from that which ended as Southern Group champions. The Magdalen boys, Mike Simmie and Nigel Starmer-Smith, replaced Duncan Kilgour and Mike Tanner but Simmie soon withdrew after being selected for a Scottish Trial due to be played on the same day, so Kilgour was quickly back in.

The Christmas break was a tonic for the Oxford team who demolished Old Rutlishians,

*Oxfordshire v Gloucestershire Quarter Final programme 1966.*

*The Oxfordshire team that beat Gloucestershire, January 1966.*
*Back row, l to r: NC Starmer-Smith (Oxford University), LR Evans (Oxford), RA Herbertson (Sheffield),*
*MJ Parsons (Northampton), D Green (Oxford City & County Police), AP Hallett (Royal NMavy),*
*IC Patterson (Oxford), RP Tapper (Oxford), JR Higgins (Trainer), A Tucker (Touch Judge).*
*Front row, l to r: DS Kilgour (Oxford) ACB Hurst (Wasps) RJ Hance (Oxford),*
*G Windsor-Lewis (Oxford) (Capt), C Fairbrother (Banbury), G Webb (Oxford), IB Moffatt (Richmond).*

24–0, on New Year's Day. The visitors were just not in the same class and Oxford's winning score should have been much greater.

The County Championship Quarter Final soon came around the following Saturday. A seat in the Iffley Road stand on the day would have cost you 10s (50p), or 5s (25p) to stand in the ground. If you couldn't get there the match was due to be broadcast live on radio with the highlights on television in the evening on one of BBC2's earlier rugby programmes. The 4000 people who did make it, the crowd being swelled by members of several local clubs who had played in the morning, filled all four sides of the ground by kick off time. The Oxfordshire team was obliged to play in a change strip of dark blue to avoid a colour clash with Gloucestershire who were to play in Oxfordshire's usual colour of white shirts. This prompted Geoffrey Windsor-Lewis, a Cambridge University 'Blue', to later say "When I arrived at the ground today I was shown into a room with 'OURFC' on the door and then had to put on a dark blue jersey. That hurt!" A short while before the game it was revealed that the white Gloucestershire shirts had not arrived and that they would revert to red but it was now too late for the home side to play in the recognized colour.

Oxfordshire produced a resounding performance and were the better side in a thrilling game. The key to it all was the home players speed to man and ball. The crash tackling of Windsor-Lewis, Evans and, later, Hurst in midfield was tremendous and, as the ball went loose in the impacts, the forwards were quickly round to mount counter attacks. So it mattered not that David Watt shaded the lineouts and Oxfordshire lost three strikes against the head in the scrum. The inspiration of Windsor-Lewis was paramount along with great performances from Fairbrother and the cool, skilful Tapper at outside half. Starmer-Smith made a half break and passed on to Windsor-Lewis who ran in from 35 yards to open the score, Moffatt converted and later kicked a penalty goal. Gloucestershire were awarded

# Chapter 4 – Broken Wings and Treading Water

By far the most interesting and exciting sporting event of a long, warm summer was the achievement of the England football team in beating West Germany, 4–2, in the World Cup Final at Wembley. It was the sort of event that people would remember where they were when it happened, the first and, to date, the only time that the tournament has been held in England. It captured the imagination of the whole country.

This was in contrast to the British Lions tour to New Zealand, which covered four and a half months from May to mid September, when the group played thirty five games in losing the four test series to the All Blacks, 0–4, but beat Australia and Canada on the same trip.

Locally the long awaited, new Oxford School, an amalgamation of the two Oxford Grammar Schools, City of Oxford High School for Boys and Southfield School, was finally set to open on the old Southfield School site at the top of Glanville Road but, to their credit, the Oxford Old Boys club was well ahead of the game in its preparations.

## Season 1966–1967

At Oxford RFC thoughts turned once again to Rugby Union. Pre season training had produced a refreshing and adventurous new spirit as the players responded to a revised, more enlightened regime under new Captain, Lynn Evans. There were increased attendances, and Evans said "People are coming down eager for training and practice. First and foremost we are trying to improve the basic skills of individuals. This, I'm sure, will lead to better individual enjoyment, better team skill, better fitness, better understanding and, eventually, a winning team."

"I want a winning side" Evans continued, "I don't want to play rugby to lose. I feel you can get fit through skills rather than through just a hard physical slog. Ultimately, of course, I want to see the club get first class status."

But, having set all this up, disaster struck when Evans fell awkwardly in the last minute of the final club trial and, dislocating his left shoulder, left the field on a stretcher. As Vice Captain, Duncan Kilgour took over as temporary Captain for the first game on 3$^{rd}$ September in South Wales against Glynneath.

It was a repeat of the last match of the previous season and Oxford found the going tough against a team out for revenge. Oliver Clark, a former England Schools centre and Harlequins Colt, scored a try on his debut but Oxford were 3–10 at half time. Oxford upped the tempo to produce excellent, fast rugby which had the Welsh players gasping and their supporters applauding, and tries from Kilgour, Hance and Michael Douch, an Oxfordshire sprinter, saw the side home to a 14–10 win, a great way to start the season.

Henley RFC celebrated the opening of the club's new £2500 changing accommodation at Dry Leas with a midweek match on 7$^{th}$ September against the County President's XV, the President being former Oxford RFC player Mike Bye, who started the game by formally kicking off. There was a sad note to the occasion when Geoffrey Windsor-Lewis, playing in the centre and who had captained Oxfordshire to two County Championship semi finals, confirmed what many people already knew in that he intended to retire from the game and that he would play once more, the following weekend for the Co-optimists before doing so. Over the summer months he had been offered, and accepted, the post of Secretary to the famous and renowned world wide Barbarians club, one of the conditions being that he didn't play regular club rugby.

*Oxford RFC 1966–1967. Back row, l to r: RJ Hance, G Webb, WS Wakelin, P Hiley, EK Moorcroft, IC Patterson, D Saunders, O Clark. Front row, l to r: RJ Tapper, DJ Castle, RP Tapper, DF Bagnall, DS Kilgour (Capt), M Douch, G Howells.*

A rampant Oxford side piled on 32 points without reply at home to London Hospital and then beat United Services, Portsmouth, 8–3 in the midweek. This game was graced with the attendance of England selector, Jeff Butterfield, who witnessed a hard fought match played in unhelpful slippery conditions due to heavy rain throughout. He was possibly checking the form of England International Mike Davis, in the US pack, but saw a thrilling last minute try when Bagnall blocked a drop kick to get away with the ball, passed to Kilgour who ran 40 yards to the fullback and then passed inside to Oliver Clark for the winning score converted by David Castle. The downside to this was that Peter Hiley in his debut, having joined from Swansea, broke a bone in his left hand.

Oxford's first defeat of the season came a little earlier than was thought might, at Sutton, something of a 'bogy' side in those recent times. Oxford was clearly the better side but could not get going with sufficient pace to beat a lively defence and lost 8–11. The team was slow and indecisive, probably due in part to a below par performance from Ray Tapper who had had his car stolen in Croydon during the morning of the match. He had to scratch about and borrow every item of his playing kit before the kick off. The car was found 48 hours later jacked up on a rubbish dump minus wheels and radio. But his rugby kit was left intact! The further outcome was that Ray had to go to London on the Monday to collect it, causing him to miss the County trial and subsequently his place in the side for the 'friendly' county warm up match, a 500 mile round trip to play Cornwall at Falmouth!

Although the club had lost the services of the much celebrated Windsor-Lewis, a natural replacement became available in Joe McPartlin, a former Oxford University Captain, who had become a Master at St Edward's School. Joe had won six International caps for Scotland between 1960 and 1962 and was a welcome addition to the ranks at Oxford RFC. It was a sporting coincidence that Joe had played for Scotland against Wales in Cardiff in 1960 when his direct opponent was Geoffrey Windsor-Lewis!

Back on the winning trail Oxford just got home, 8–6, at Reading in the mid week when Howard Firth, also a debutant, made an electrifying burst to beat three defenders for Ray Tapper to score under the posts and McPartlin to convert, and Tapper's late drop goal won the match. The annihilation of Aldershot Services, 43–0, saw newcomer David Fitzpatrick score three tries in a dream debut, having taken the place of Douch on the wing, who had left to study at Loughborough.

Much optimism was afoot at Marston Ferry Road when Charlie Ede's Invitation XV played against Oxford Old Boys to officially commemorate the opening of the 'new' ground. After a match to befit the occasion, comments such as "Now they have started they will have left behind the Oxford Club and the Bypass within five years" and "The club will get better, stronger fixtures and be supplied with a steady stream of better players from the new school. They will be better because the school will be playing all the top class schools", appeared in the local press. Ron Grimshaw, in noting the interesting theories, wrote that it would be difficult to get better fixtures, even more so to 'crash' the first class schools barrier and, in any case, Oxford School may go comprehensive in that five years. His comments resulted in him being labelled 'anti-Old Boys'.

Once again there was a club v county clash on Saturday 1st October when the County side headed off to Cornwall as Oxford themselves went west to Clifton. Only four Oxford players, Kilgour, Hance, G Webb and I Patterson, had been selected to play with John Mawle as reserve. But the real value of the warm up fixture was lost some 48 hours before kick off when five changes had to be made to the lineup. Ron Grimshaw reported in his column that at least one county player withdrew when he was told that his first team place was at stake if he took time off to play. But at least Ray Tapper was recalled to a side that was well beaten on the day. Oxfordshire's 5–3 lead ten minutes after half time stirred Cornwall into action, Oxfordshire's defence was cracked open and the match lost 5–22. This left Ron Grimshaw to question the wisdom of travelling the distance to Falmouth for a trial with much less than a full strength team.

Oxford's afternoon at Clifton didn't fare much better. The club's long running travel saga continued when one car in the convoy, with three players aboard, got lost *en route* and didn't arrive at Clifton until ten minutes before half time, and that after the game started 25 minutes late. Oxford borrowed two Clifton players and played one short until Ken Withers took the field. Already under strength, Oxford did emerge with some credit in the 0–11 defeat as Clifton struggled to press home their numerical advantage due to Oxford's defence.

Tommy Bedford, now the University Captain, brought a strong team including eight Blues to the club for midweek clash but it was the Oxford side that provided the enterprising and attacking rugby. There were no tries and Oxford paid dearly for their mistakes and were undeservedly beaten, 6–12, all the points coming from kicks at goal.

Ian Moffatt played in another England Trial at Brighton at the start of October where he missed two kicks at goal while, in the north of the county, Chipping Norton School Headmaster, Arthur Nockels, created something of a controversy when he said that soccer would not be "totally eliminated at present" but there would be no more soccer matches with other schools. Rugby Union would now be the curriculum game at his school and boys who wanted to play soccer could use the pitches on Saturday mornings. "I could not have a first Rugby fifteen and a first soccer eleven and hope to be any good" he added. The local Borough Council, having spoken to him, promised to write to the Education Department about it!

Adopting the wrong tactics in keeping the ball tight, Oxford lost again this time at Rugby. When the backs were given chances they looked dangerous but Rugby added 18 points in the last twenty five minutes to the converted try they had already scored, to beat Oxford by 23–3.

It was time again for Oxfordshire to set out on the Championship trail and the team opened with a 17–3 win, after a ragged start, against Berkshire. David Bagnall was replaced by MikeTanner, who had failed to find favour in University rugby, for Oxford's next game

*The 1966–1967 Oxfordshire team that beat Berkshire 17–3 on their way to another Southern Group title. Back row, l to r: IB Moffatt, G Webb, RA Hertbertson, JF Mawle, AP Hallett, MJ Parsons, JJ McPartlin, R Weaver, JRM Higgins (Trainer). Front row, l to r: RJ Hance, J Cooksey, MS Palmer (Capt), H Firth, DS Kilgour, C Fairbrother, JWC Ross-Jones.*

again away from home but this time still in Oxford at Iffley Road against the University Greyhounds. At last Lynn Evans was able to return and lead the side for the first time that season after injury. Oxford were let down by faulty handling and indirect running but gave the Greyhounds a hard match before allowing the home side to snatch a 14–11 win late in the game. Oxford were then able to end a run of four defeats with a 9–6 victory at Esher in an entertaining struggle where they had to rely heavily on defence to hold on for the win, and the season was turning into one of inconsistent club performances on the field.

The Oxford University club went into rugby's history book for the wrong reason on 26th October when the touring Australian side visited Iffley Road. It was the third match of the tour and the University side surprised the Australians to take the lead with a penalty, drop goal and try. In the second half the tourists came to life but it was left to Lenehan to win the match 11–9 with a great drop goal from half way. Towards the end of the match Ollie Waldron, the University's Irish International prop, left the field with a badly bleeding ear. It seemed that Waldron had been 'boring' into the Australian hooker, Russ Cullen, in the scrum and he had retaliated by biting Waldron's ear so badly that it needed several stitches. Cullen was dammed the next day when, in a statement, the Tour Manager said "I have decided that one of my players cannot be relied upon to carry out the firm decision of the Australian rugby touring team to play good clean rugby during the tour of the British Isles, and I have therefore reluctantly decided that the player, Russ Cullen, will return at once to Australia." This was an unprecedented dismissal from a touring side. Many years later Ollie Waldron was to say that when Cullen arrived home they made him 'Sportsman of the Ear'!

Ian Moffatt kicked five penalty goals, all his side's points, as Oxfordshire beat Dorset & Wiltshire 15–3 to continue the winning way in a match put back a day to avoid the Australian match, and Oxford suffered its sixth defeat of the season, 6–16, away to Bedford who were well in control in the first half. The second period saw Evans reduce the arrears with a drop goal before cross kicking for the unmarked Kilgour to gather the awkwardly bouncing ball for a try. And then, with five minutes remaining before the end of a gruelling match, Evans racing through with the ball was grabbed by the arm. The contact was enough to dislocate his shoulder again, the second time in two months and in only his third match as Captain, and it was a very disconsolate figure that gingerly left the field.

Despite the disruption the team finally played well enough to beat St Thomas' Hospital before Mawle, George Webb, Kilgour, Hance and Wakelin were called upon again for County duty in the week and a big 27–3 win in Hertfordshire. On the same day Oxford club players Oliver Clark, Roy Tapper, Gerry Howell and David Castle played for Berkshire against Buckinghamshire.

Abbey RFC, having been formed ten years earlier and playing in the Reading area, put down roots in Oxfordshire near Sonning when members cleared and prepared a ground for three pitches and a clubhouse, costing £5000. Despite the new location Abbey would continue to affiliate to the Berkshire Union.

Oxford lost to Bridgwater but just about beat Weston-super-Mare in a close game before giving the best display of the season so far in the away match with Maesteg. The team arrived late and a late change saw the Club President, Charlie Ede, at prop. This did not deter the players however, and the pack was inspired by Ede. Howard Davies' drop goal attempt was charged down but David Fitzpatrick kicked diagonally for Palmer to race and touch down in the corner. Maesteg replied to lead 5–3 before Davies was successful with a second drop kick to give Oxford a 6–5 half time lead. Roared on by an enthusiastic crowd Maesteg were on top in the second half but the Oxford defence was magnificent. With fifteen minutes left Davies intercepted and raced away for an unconverted try. Oxford had to work hard but held out until the end for a notable 9–5 win. It was noted that the traditional post match hospitality fell a bit short, triggered by Oxford's late arrival, but it was a happy group that made its way back across the border that evening!

Oxford's inconsistency, again apparent even in the 17–9 defeat of Old Edwardians, might have been excused by unusually cold weather in early December. This inconsistency, however, was in direct contrast to the Oxfordshire team which became Southern Group Champions for a record five times in six seasons, when the team beat Buckinghamshire 6–0.

The excitement of this achievement helped to eclipse a run of four away matches and Oxford lost a three win run at Metropolitan Police, 6–10, but beat Old Askeans 9–0 where McPartlin's penalty added to tries from Kilgour and Mawle. Even for a club like Oxford this was a busy period and the commitment shown by the players was tested by a match at Pontypool on Christmas Eve. There were the inevitable unavailabilities which saw a First team debut for Mike Florey, promoted from the Nomads who were due to play Oxford Old Boys in the annual Boxing Day fixture two days later. Pontypool ended a run of eleven defeats in beating Oxford 11–5 but were lucky as Oxford could have won had they taken the chances offered. David Castle completed his time in an Oxford shirt with a conversion before moving to live and work in London, while club misery was compounded when the Nomads lost to Oxford Old Boys.

The usual mid season roundup found the club side with average results, having won 11 and lost 10 games in the first part using an unusually large number of 52 players in the team to that point, and there was still a need for a big, strong, mobile and skilful lock forward. Another major bug bear was described as 'that dreadful pot holed track to the ground', supposing that the 'disgraceful condition' (of the track) may explain 28 away and only 19 home matches in this season. The remedy was swift and by 11th February it was reported that the lane had been repaired.

The death was announced of Frank Fowler, aged 86 years, the former sports correspondent to the *Oxford Mail and Times,* who had done so much, especially in the 1930s when local county rugby was in its infancy, to promote Rugby Union through the pages of those newspapers. He would have been extremely pleased at the progress made by local teams over those years since, particularly with another Quarter Final looming for Oxfordshire, this time a second trip to Redruth to play Cornwall on 14th January. But before that there was also an added bonus for local enthusiasts in that the Australians were returning to Oxford to meet the Southern Counties team at Iffley Road on New Years Eve, and four Oxford players, Webb, Mawle, Hance and Wakelin, along with former club players Parsons and Hertbertson, had been selected to meet the tourists.

These selections meant that half of Oxford's pack was missing for the away game at London Irish which ended the year, hardly the best build up for such a tough match. But Oxford led 6–3 at half time to gain much credit before falling away in the second half to lose 9–17 with Kilgour scoring a try near the end, to add to McPartlin's drop goal and Clark's try, for some consolation.

Back at Iffley Road, 15 tons of baled straw had been delivered to safeguard against an uncertain weather forecast but this was not needed as mild conditions prevailed. Before a disappointing crowd of roughly 3000 spectators the Counties team crumbled in the second half to a 6–27 defeat. The game was noted for the return to action of the Australian Phil Hawthorn, from a fractured cheekbone sustained earlier in the tour, in time for the International the following week against England.

*Southern Counties v Australia programme.*

*The Southern Counties team that lost to Australia at Iffley Road.*
*Back row, l to r: JRM Higgins (Trainer), JR Monahan (Dorset & Wilts), RA Hertbertson (Oxfordshire), AP Hallett (Oxfordshire), MJ Parsons (Oxfordshire), SJ Pilbeam (Hertfordshire), DMB Skinner (Hertfordshire), J Lancaster (Buckinghamshire), RC Ashby (Buckinghamshire). Front row, l to r: WS Wakelin (Oxfordshire), ACB Hurst (Oxfordshire), JF Mawle (Oxfordshire), IHP Laughland (Buckinghamshire) (Capt), TG Arthur (Buckinghamshire), RJ Hance (Oxfordshire).*

January 7th, the first Saturday in 1967, saw Oxford with five senior teams listed for action with the First Fifteen at home for the first time in a month, to Old Whitgiftians, the Nomads away at Nuneaton Extra 1sts, the A team at home to Gosford All Blacks, the Extra A away at Gosford All Blacks II, and a B team away at Huntercombe. The Colts were at home to Bicester Colts. But all these plans and arrangements were cancelled when heavy snow arrived after which the temperature plummeted to -9°C. The players were able to enjoy a rare Saturday off, and some watched England lose 11–23 to Australia at Twickenham, before keeping in trim with a hard session at the Littlemore Grammar School gym on the Tuesday.

Most thoughts were on the Quarter Final match and Cornwall did not select Richard Sharp and Roger Hosen following a poor England performance seven days earlier. Sharp, in particular, had been brought back from a premature retirement after a four years absence to boost England's flagging performances but, understandably, had been found somewhat wanting. The Oxfordshire team was due to travel by rail which gave the party plenty of time to ponder on Cornwall's home record of having been beaten only twice in twenty years. Leaving early on Friday morning, with lunch on the train, the party arrived before 3pm in time for a practise session before moving on to a Hotel in St Ives. Between 10,000 and 12,000 people crowded into the compact, uneven little ground on the day of the match and the atmosphere, fuelled by the St Stythians Prize Silver Band, was electric. Oxfordshire's forwards played their hearts out but the backs were given only limited opportunities, and the home defence held as the rugged Cornishmen stormed through to the Semi Final, winning 16–6. The ill-mannered behaviour of the fervent home supporters, in loudly booing and shouting when Ian Moffatt took kicks but absolute silent for Cornwall's kicker, brought an unofficial apology from the Cornwall RFU President after the match. But defensive lapses and bad luck brought about Oxfordshire's downfall, as two of Moffatt's penalties hit a post as did a drop goal attempt from Joe McPartlin. Moffatt, at full back, looked unhappy,

*Action from the match – Bill Wakelin and George Webb hold back the Aussies as John Mawle feeds the ball from a lineout.*

missing six out eight penalty attempts and a drop goal, while McPartlin's legacy was a cracked rib destined to keep him on the sidelines for two or three weeks.

Oxfordshire's defeat in the Quarter Final heralded an amazing sequence of events in the Championship. The Cornish team was now due to play at home against Surrey in the Semi Final and scored two tries in the match, but Surrey's Bob Hillier kicked two penalties to draw the match 6–6. There was similar drama in the replay at Richmond when, with the last action of the match, Roger Hosen kicked a penalty goal for Cornwall to again draw the match at 14–14 which triggered a pitch invasion by the thousands of travelling Cornish supporters. The third match, back in Redruth, was an anti-climax and Surrey won decisively 14–3 to move into the Final against Durham at Twickenham, but the excitement was yet to end, and that match was drawn, 14–14. Surrey made the long journey to Hartlepool for the team's 11$^{th}$ Championship match of the season, only to draw again, this time 0–0. After consultation with the Rugby Union it was agreed that enough was enough and that the two counties should be joint champions.

Despite County calls the Oxford club was still able to field five senior teams and a Colts but a makeshift team, missing nine players in Cornwall, responded well to the challenge of Loughborough Colleges with a determined effort before going down 9–16 at the Bypass.

David Bagnall, now with all county commitment behind him for a period, took the opportunity to get married on 21$^{st}$ January and so missed Oxford's hardest earned victory of the season to date, the match against St Bartholomew's Hospital. The team came from behind to win 8–3 with a try right at the end and Ray Hance converted the Ray Palmer try from the touchline with a magnificent kick.

Club members on the move saw Gordon Acaster off to South Africa for a three year tour with the Science Research Council in Cape Town, and Don Barrett moving to the West Country.

The new Witney Rugby Club announced that it would be starting its first full season in September with a headquarters at the Eagle Tavern, but Henley RFC, with seven senior teams, were now the biggest club player wise in Oxfordshire.

Club Captain Lynn Evans, after a three month absence, was listed to play again in the club's Extra 'A' team against Tredworth II at the end of January, the same day that the Oxford side showed that mud and rain was no obstacle to good running and handling in beating Streatham 17–6 in London with a forceful display. This didn't last, however, and two Ray Hance penalties with the wind at his back in the first half of the home game with Abertillery was not enough as Oxford crumbled to a 6–12 defeat.

A run of five games away from home on successive Saturdays fortunately coincided with a rich vein of form for the club. Nuneaton were beaten on their own ground by Oxford, 14–0, for the first time since 1956, while the odd midweek afternoon game with Birmingham University saw the welcome return of McPartlin with a 17 point haul in the 35–11 win. Old Haberdashers were dispatched 20–0, Old Rutlishians likewise 34–5 in the morning before England v France, and a great victory at Cheltenham, 12–3, saw Howard Davies launch a drop goal from 30 yards before Joe McPartlin's three penalty goals. The third, from fifty yards, hit the crossbar before rolling over, and for Davies it was his 16$^{th}$ drop goal in twenty club games!

The Rugby Union were becoming increasingly concerned about foul play in the game and the County Rep, Sam Miller, passed the message to diners at the Club Dinner on Thursday 2$^{nd}$ March, saying "I thank the Lord that in Oxfordshire this is not anything like as bad as elsewhere. We in Oxfordshire play a clean type of game. Please don't leave it to the referees, if a player is a persistent offender do something about it yourselves." Referring to the annual match between Oxford and the University Captains team, RH Phillips, the Oxford University Captain said his club was grateful to Oxford for providing his team with invaluable practice. Oxfordshire President, Mike Bye, presented John Mawle with his County Cap before Oxford Club President, Charlie Ede, presented a silver tankard to Gilbert Beesley who was retiring after thirty five years in rugby, the last fifteen of which had been given in sterling service running the club's Colts team.

Having played his way back into the game through the junior club sides, Lynn Evans returned to First team action at Cambridge on 11$^{th}$ March. It was only his fifth First team game of the season but he was able to lead the side to another win, 11–3. This was the sixth in succession thanks to a big contribution from Joe McPartlin with two penalties and a conversion, after Bagnall had pounced on a loose ball for a try having charged down a clearing kick behind the Cambridge line. Another mid-week fixture saw London University visit for the first home game for a month. Only half the team was available and the groundsman, Dick Barley, normally a third team hooker, was drafted in at the last moment to give an excellent display in the comfortable 18–5 win. The much awaited home match with Welsh club Rhymney saw the team equal a club record of eight successive wins with a splendid 20–6 victory. It was a personal triumph for scrum half David Bagnall who scored two tries early on in a game Oxford never looked like losing. He was gifted a third try and his 'hat-trick' when a loose ball was kicked straight into his arms for a try under the posts.

Visiting South Wales during the annual Easter holiday period had become something of a tradition and Oxford set out once more on another challenging Tour. Les Samuels, an RAF No 8 stationed locally joined the party, as did a Graham McKenzie who was due to play his first senior game at prop in the Monday fixture. Aged 23 years he had come to the game late and had only started playing in this season but was splendidly built for the job and had quickly progressed through the junior teams. In the event Oxford lost their win record in losing to Pontypridd 8–16, Abertillery 9–15 but drawing the last match with Cross Keys 0–0. It was no exaggeration to say that, with a little luck and consistency of effort, Oxford could have won all three and, apart from the results, the tour was deemed an unqualified success. It had been entirely self supporting and, despite the players arranging fund raising events throughout the season, the cost to each player was £10, the club not being in a position to subsidise. Even so there had been several new names in the teams on tour, necessary owing to the non availability of a few regular players who may have been unable to spare the basic £10 cost.

Getting back to winning ways a 13–8 home win against Lydney was the start of what was a fractious final month of the season for the club. Light evenings meant more rugby and two days later, on a Monday evening of all times, the club lost at home 18–32 to Maesteg in a game where all but six of the points came from kicks. In amongst eleven penalties, three drop goals and a conversion were two tries!

Oxford's attempts to break into the first class London rugby scene had been constantly frustrated by the reluctance of clubs to waver from traditional fixtures, so much so that the club had turned west and had built relations with good class Welsh clubs in an attempt to prove its worth. In doing so the club had to show a willingness to travel in the first instance and, with the rising cost of travelling to twenty nine games away from home in this season coupled with meals for visiting teams, it was no surprise that the club's finances were becoming very stretched. To help in this area it was decided that, from now onwards, the First Fifteen Match Fee would be increased to 7s 6d (37p in present day currency), with the others paying 6s 6d, and this meant that, together with a 'kitty' for entertaining guests, the players would have to find a minimum of 10s a week for the 'privilege' of playing.

How realistic this was in the circumstances and the possible effect on membership remained to be seen, with the support for a 'B' XV having already dropped off in previous weeks not entirely unusual at that time of a season.

The club was in something of a cleft stick at the Bypass ground where any profit made from the bar and fruit machine, the main sources for most rugby clubs, went to the parent body, Oxford Sports Club. The rugby club made by far the biggest and most consistent contribution of the affiliated sports clubs using the facility but was not getting any further forward, and was hampered by the lack of finance. Indeed, the club would have been in dire straits without the continued support of its Vice Presidents, of which there were two hundred and sixty one at the time, each paying 1 Guinea (£1.10p). Independence might have been the answer but the club was committed to stay at the Bypass ground.

The club did itself no favours when it scratched two hours before the start of the Preliminary Round of the 21st Oxfordshire Sevens Tournament on 2nd April, citing injuries in a very busy part of the season as the cause. This was frowned upon especially as there were two Oxford Thursday teams entered for the same competition with four Oxford first team players in the first seven. The club, however, was not alone in this action and the total number of teams that scratched totalled forty seven making the preliminary rounds, played at Oxford, Banbury and Henley, rather chaotic which prompted discussion as to the makeup of future events. Oxford Thursday II won through to the Finals while the Oxford Thursday team, as holders, were invited as guests which allowed them to retain the Berkshire Sevens at Sonning on Oxon Prelims day.

Before this though there was the 'saga' of the away game against Manchester on 8th April arranged as the return from Manchester's Easter visit the previous season. The club team saw several changes due to some players being unable to get away in time to travel, then there were late cry-offs on Friday night continuing into Saturday morning and a delayed departure after a wait in vain for two players who did not turn up. The party left Oxford with fourteen players but picked up one on the way. And then, to cap it all, the coach broke down *en route* all of which caused a fifty five minute delay after a long and tedious journey. This led to an uninspiring game in fine rain and a biting wind but, with 43 year old Danny Hughes on the wing and 40 year old David Thomas at Number 10, Oxford fought back from a 3–12 deficit to draw 12–12 with tries from Douch and Firth, a drop goal from Evans and a Hance penalty kick. John Mawle said "I've never been so embarrassed as when we arrived an hour late. But Manchester were very good about it, especially as it gave them a chance to watch the Grand National." Ron Grimshaw commented that "Some players have an odd sense of loyalty to their club. There is no point in striving for better things if the players don't support it."

The very next day saw Oxford Thursday retain The Oxford Times Cup at the Oxfordshire Sevens Tournament at Iffley Road. A nail biting Final against Moseley saw the score precariously balanced at 13–13 with moments to go and it was left to Joe McPartlin to kick a conversion to win the match, and the trophy for Oxford, 15–13 in front of a large crowd. This result was even more special as the Thursday side finished with just six players after Mike Simmie had left the field with a dislocated right hip.

Oxford lost again, 3–19, at home to Cheltenham in a mid week fixture but made up for the Manchester debacle by swamping Stroud at Stroud 22–6 in a clean, open game. Joe McPartlin's 13 points in this game took his total as leading scorer for the season to 110, well ahead of Ray Hance who had 67. Howard Davies was third in the list with 60 which

*Only six of the victorious Oxford Thursday team lineup as David Bagnall receives the 'Oxford Times Cup' from the County President's wife, Mrs Bye, followed by Bill Wakelin, Joe McPartlin, Howard Firth, Jim Parsons and Ray Tapper. Mike Simmie was on his way to Hospital!*

included a remarkable number of 17 drop goals, and the majority of all these points were from various kicks. Leading try scorer was Duncan Kilgour with 14 followed by David Fitzpatrick and Howard Firth with 10 each.

A competent Oxford side then beat Worcester 14–8 in another midweek game at home to set up to set up the season's finale. The last home game of the season with Cross Keys was keenly anticipated but a disappointing match, which should have been won comfortably, saw Oxford let slip a six point lead and then lose to a thirty yard breakaway try with five minutes left, 6–9, after several missed kicks.

Oxford needed to win the final match at Birmingham to equal the club record of wins in a season, which stood at twenty five wins from thirty eight games in the 1956–1957 campaign. But once again, with the club team on the road, it was a troubled afternoon. The team coach, having travelled to Birmingham's ground to find it being developed as a housing estate, was redirected to the University ground which the club were using until its new ground was ready. Ray Hance, following in his car, got lost and Oxford started the game half an hour late with fourteen players. This chain of events left its mark and, although the team perked up in the second half, it was too late to avoid a 14–19 loss after a ragged performance. The next day, the final day of the season, Oxford Thursday completed three notable Sevens Tournament successes when the team beat Leicester in 26–0 in the final of the Leicester Sevens competition.

The former Oxford player, Peter Sibley, was re-elected as Captain of Bath having transformed that clubs dour and often negative style of play while leading it through one of its most successful seasons to a record number of points and a record number of tries to which he, as a player, contributed the most with 21.

Another former Oxford player, Oxfordshire RFU President Mike Bye, spoke at the Oxford Old Boys Annual Dinner at the Spread Eagle Hotel in Thame, and said "As a former pupil of the old High School I had been anxious as to whether amalgamation of Old Oxford Citizens and Old Southfieldians would be successful, but it has worked exceptionally well."

The 1966–1967 season had become something of a watershed for Oxford RFC. On the field the club had played more games than ever in a season and had scored more points, but had also conceded more. Calling on more players than in previous seasons, the team was one game short of the club record of twenty five wins. None of this was a surprise in the final round up with some players having taken part in more than 60 matches including County games and others. The club was beginning to establish itself in higher echelons and no longer faced top opposition with an inferiority complex as many of the players had completed a few seasons at that level. As Captain, Lynn Evans missed many games through injury and was only moderately happy with the measured improvement saying "When we did get in front against the top sides we tended to relax and allow the opposition to assert themselves. We failed to take our chances, and the County players tended to relax after their run (in the Championship) was finished. I'd be looking for further improvement next season because I think there is something to build on."

But, off the pitch, finance continued to be a big worry. The cost of providing refreshments at the club had increased by £200 in the year past and plans were being made to reduce this figure. The biggest expenditure had been on providing labour to handle the meals instead of the voluntary arrangements of previous years, while administration in certain areas of the club was also not well organised.

Work done by school master Brian Poxon in coaching the players was praised, but Brian was a bit more forthright with his views. Too many clubs were paying lip service to coaching without taking the plunge, and Oxford was an example of this. Brian Poxon said "The club is at a crossroads. The factor most likely to influence the future is the willingness of Committee and players to accept and implement a full coaching scheme. There is an urgent need to appoint a club coach with full powers. The players must decide whether to play serious or social rugby, and if they are serious they must attend weekly training sessions." It seemed to point at a lack of enthusiasm by some players whose approach might have been questioned. Clearly the potential of the club was largely unrealised and there was a need for the club to re-assess its position of either aiming to be a top first class or a good and successful second class one.

## Season 1967–1968

Sad news over the summer months came in June when, on Sunday 18th, it was announced that one of the founder members of the club, James Eldridge, had died at his home, Wightwick, Boars Hill, at the age of 87 years. Until his retirement in 1964 he had been head of the firm of solicitors Marshall and Eldridge practising in St Michael's Street. Having founded the club as Oxfordshire Nomads RUFC with Alfred St George Hamersley in 1909, James was the club's first secretary and later became the club's first life Vice President. He maintained his interest in the club he helped to found right up to the end, though in the recent years prior to his passing ill health had made it difficult for him to get down to the Bypass ground as often as he had wished.

The Rugby Union announced that, for the next three seasons, the playing season in England would be extended to include the first Saturday in May. This was in contrast to Oxford RFC who, wisely perhaps, had cut down the number of fixtures arranged by seven to forty one before the end of April, against the forty eight arranged for the previous season. There were twenty five games at home with only sixteen away and no Easter Tour as the club attempted to juggle its financial constraints. It was good to see that the lane leading to the ground had been made up and was again quite safe for vehicles!

The new Club Captain was John Mawle, a West Oxfordshire farmer from South Leigh. John believed in 'calling a spade a spade' and, regarding the club's first fixture away at Cross Keys in Wales on 2nd September, said "I would like to state here and now that we shall be expected to sample the local hospitality and that we shall not be leaving particularly early after the game."

The club Trials were due but one player missing was David Bagnall, who had joined Northampton where he would be meeting up with Jim Parsons and another former Oxford player, Ian Moffatt, who had left Richmond to join Northampton after taking up a teaching post at Bloxham School.

Interestingly, another experiment was due to take place in some matches this season in an attempt to generally liven up the game, where no direct kicking to touch would be allowed in the opponents half except from penalty kicks.

Oxford's match at Cross Keys was a tough call for a season opener, even more so after Ray Hance had left for Vienna on behalf of the Weed Research Organisation on a United Nations assignment, and with Duncan Kilgour in London studying for his Law Finals. Against a powerful Welsh side with an on form defence, Oxford were not strong enough in a dour struggle and never looked like winning with only a Howard Davies drop goal for their efforts. The Nomads also lost, at home to Camelot, which gave some cause for concern at the club regarding the strength in depth. It seemed that the club were in for a long season although early season games were not the best to judge.

The two changes that Oxford made for the next match, at Old Cranleighans, saw Duncan Kilgour return on the wing and Ray Mills selected at wing forward, with the full team being: I Parsons; D Fitzpatrick, B Steventon, C Hill, D Kilgour; H Davies, M Bampton; J Mawle (Captain), G Webb, G McKenzie, D Saunders, M Gibbard, R Robins, R Mills and J Bartlett. In a complete change and with plenty of possession Oxford ran riot, handling well and running fast to record a big win, 3–37, with nine tries into the bargain. But there was still a need to find a place kicker and a midweek team was well and truly beaten at US Portsmouth, 6–30.

The first home match of the season saw the visit of another London Old Boys side, Old Haberdashers, that hardly provided a test of Oxford's defence as the home team romped to a 26–3 win. But the next visitors, Birmingham, turned the tables on Oxford with a vengeance. Oxford's forwards made a slow start and gradually got worse and were then very ragged, with Birmingham's first try coming from a spilt ball after which they never looked back, winning 8–24.

Back on the road again, Oxford's match at Aldershot Services was marred by an over zealous referee who constantly stopped the game, preventing any continuous flow and causing great frustration to the players and spectators alike. Added to that was Ray Mills departure from the match, at an early stage, with concussion which left Oxford to play most of the match with fourteen players. It was Clive Hill's last match before leaving for University Hall, Buckland. He had given the club sterling service in the backs but, coming the opposite way and making an excellent debut, was the tall, strong Trevor Wilde from the Cardiff Training College, who kicked three penalty goals from full back. After the misfiring start to the season he was one of three new recruits drafted in by the Selection Committee, the other two being Bernard Humphries, a wing forward formerly with Cross Keys and

Blackheath, and Chris Shinner from Cheltenham. Oxford's only try came when Davies punted ahead and Fitzpatrick gathered on the burst to score in his side's 12–3 victory and, apart from over extended mauls, this seemed to be the lengthiest piece of uninterrupted play!

The club seemed to have slipped into a loss, win, loss sequence and this continued as a faulty performance saw the side fumble to another failure in an uninteresting game when Clifton visited the Bypass. Ray Hance returned to the side to replace the injured Bob Buckingham and Oxford ran late in the game but it was too late and Clifton duly won 3–11.

The new captain of the Oxfordshire team was announced as Ian Moffatt, who had celebrated the appointment with 19 points for Northampton against the Dublin club, Bective Rangers, to complete 100 points in the first month of the season as Northampton remained the only unbeaten first class club. At the start of another championship trail the Oxfordshire team included a Scottish Trialist, Gilmore Greig, who was living in Henley. The team for the opening match against Buckinghamshire on Wednesday 11th October was named as: I Moffatt (Northampton); ACB Hurst (Wasps), LR Evans (Oxford), JWC Ross-Jones (US Portsmouth), DS Kilgour (Oxford); GR Greig (London Scottish), DF Bagnall (Northampton); JW Mawle (Oxford), G Webb (Oxford), EJH Gould (Harlequins), MJ Parsons (Northampton), AP Hallett (US Portsmouth), D Payne (Banbury), C Fairbrother (Banbury), J Cooksey (Oxford Old Boys), with Oxford RFC providing an interest in seven of those named. The team opened its account with a fine 28–5 win after outplaying and outclassing in difficult conditions, Buckinghamshire, who were regarded as their strongest opponents in the Southern Group.

It was a busy week at the club. The very next day Oxford was due to entertain RH Phillip's XV at the Bypass and Lynn Evans replaced Howard Davies at fly half. This was due to Davies' loss of form and confidence with Oxford's pack failing to produce enough 'good ball' for him to exploit his talents as an attacking player. Evans, on the other hand, was considered to be more orthodox and better able to tidy up and use to benefit the scrum service. The match was rugged and ill-tempered. Phillips lasted ten minutes and, after two hard tackles, left the field. This led to much undisciplined play from both sides all of which was pointless in a match with nothing at stake, and Oxford conceded five tries in the 9–24 defeat. On the adjoining pitch Oxford Thursday played against Leicester Thursday, all of which made for an interesting mix in the clubhouse afterwards.

Two days later the club called on the young former England Youth hooker, Martin Ponty, to make his debut at home to Rugby and Oxford defended soundly but crumbled in the second half to a 3–25 defeat. This led to more changes in the side to play Penarth the following Saturday as the club shuffled its playing personal in an endeavour to find a winning team and the tall Chris Jones, at 6′ 7″, was due to make his first appearance of the season in the second row. The changes did the trick and Oxford recorded an impressive win in muddy conditions, 13–0, the first in four games. Mills, returning from injury, worked tirelessly and the forwards outfought the visitors pack for much of the game which allowed winger David Fitzpatrick to score three tries.

There was one forced change in the Oxfordshire team to face Berkshire at Maidenhead. The selectors were indeed fortunate to have such an able deputy on hand at scrum half as Nigel Starmer-Smith, having just returned from the England tour to Canada, to replace David Bagnall who had broken his left thumb playing for Northampton against Cardiff. Oxfordshire were below form but, inspired by Moffatt, still good enough to win 17–6.

In another mid-week fixture, the next day in fact, a weakened Oxford side, fielding only half of the side that had played Penarth, were anything but disgraced by a 3–8 defeat by Oxford University Greyhounds who, themselves, were undefeated so far in that Term.

It was around this time that Oxford showed signs of having turned the corner, and the team showed tremendous courage and determination for an excellent 14–3 win over Manchester in atrocious conditions on the Bypass ground. This was Oxford's first win over the northern club and, at last, there was some promise for the future.

Mike Florey was recalled to the back row to replace Bernard Humphries who was unable to travel for the club's away match against St Thomas's Hospital at Cobham on Saturday 4th November. It was a morning kick off with the players travelling on to Twickenham in the afternoon to support England against New Zealand. Historically it had been shown that an Oxford side was rarely at its best in morning kick offs and this was an unpleasant day for rugby with wind, incessant rain and heavy mud. In the dismal conditions Oxford conceded 9 points but, after a half time 'talk' by Captain John Mawle, rallied with tries from Evans and David Savage, converted by Wilde, and it was left to Ray Mills to get a try, after a charged down kick, for a narrow 11–9 win. Moving on to Twickenham the players were unwittingly involved in the unusual occurrence of a start six minutes earlier than that advertised. This would have caught many people out, late arrivals, one last drink, toilet visits, etc. and the RFU Secretary, Robin Prescott explained that "When The Queen sits down we normally start the game. Her Majesty obviously took into consideration the fact that the players would be affected by standing around in the unpleasant weather and did not linger over the presentation. Consequently our timing was a little out." Many late comers would have missed the first try after seven minutes by the inconsiderate All Blacks, who went on to beat England 23–11.

Oxfordshire changed the entire back row for the third Championship match away at Dorset and Wiltshire on 8th November. In came Les Davies, an old Oxford High School pupil, Bernard Humphries and Bill Wakelin, formerly at Oxford but now with Wasps, and the match was given added spice when it was seen that Dorset/Wilts team included former Oxfordshire Captain, Peter Sibley, in the centre. There were two late changes to Oxfordshire's side which saw Ray Tapper, now playing at Oxford Marathons, in at fly half, and Michael Douch on the wing. The result of these changes contributed to a record Championship score as Oxfordshire, without playing to full potential, won 40–14. There were ten tries in all with Moffatt, who had scored two of them, converting five, and the side sat proudly on top of the table with one game to play. Sadly, there was a down side and Lynn Evans, who had also scored a brace of tries, fell awkwardly once more in the last quarter of the match and had to leave the field after dislocating that shoulder again. This was the third dislocation in just over a year.

A newcomer to the club was Martin Adamson who had played on the wing for South Australia in May 1966 against the British Lions. He had reputedly run 9.8 secs for the 100 yards, but could not command a place on either Oxford wing!

And more locally another new club sprang to life in Oxfordshire, as rugby's popularity grew, this time in the south where the initiative of David Cree, a sports master at Wallingford Grammar School, saw the formation of Cholsey RFC. Having been offered the use of a field in Wallingford Road by a local farmer for home matches, the club quickly became known as the 'Cholsey Moles', a name which reflected the state of the fields in which the team played! The first home game was due on 11th November against Didcot.

Some people say that life is a matter of timing. In the case of Oxford RFC this lesson was a long time in the learning when it came to some games away from home, but on the occasion of the club's visit to Weston-super-Mare in early November the matter was out of their hands. Torrential rain in the south of England had flooded many areas and some rugby fields that were just about playable were nothing more than mud heaps. The Somerset v

*Oxford RFC 1967–1968. Back row, l to r: G Howells, R Ovenall, T Wilde, C Jones, J McPartlin, N Parker, R Parker, R Stevenson. Front row, l to r: B Humphreys, G Webb, H Davies, J Mawle (Capt), R Mills, M Ponty, D Fitzpatrick.*

Gloucestershire match due to be played at Bath was in some doubt as the ground was liable to flood, but if the nearby River Avon held its banks the game would kick off at 2.30pm. How did this effect Oxford RFC? The contingency plan, should the worst come to the worst, was that the match would be switched at short notice to Weston and so the Weston club asked that Oxford arrive for a 1pm kick off so that both games could be catered for at the same ground. Oxford duly obliged, leaving the club at 9am, but all was well in Bath so the team had to wait for more than two hours as the kick off reverted to 2.30pm. The Oxford players were sluggish on the field and well below form in a dismal match. There was a good spell in the first half but then a struggle and the side was beaten long before the end, 3–11. Regarding the early arrival John Mawle said "It didn't do us any good. We played very badly, right back where we were 6 or 7 weeks ago."

There was more gloom the following Saturday when Oxford visited Loughborough Colleges. This continued to be a formidable fixture with the Colleges set up producing a string of players destined for International stardom. Oxford had won just once, in 1960, in the previous ten games and the team showed great determination to put up a gallant fight but could never match the skill of their opponents in losing 5–23.

In the same week that it was announced that former Oxford player Jim Parsons had been selected for an England Trial at Falmouth, Oxfordshire brushed aside the challenge of Hertfordshire to win a fourth consecutive clean sweep Southern Group title in winning the match at the Bypass ground. The 18–3 win saw the points aggregate pass 100 which was a Group record, and playing without the injured 'Talisman' Ian Moffatt, whose leg was in plaster, the side was well worth the win. This qualified the side for a home tie in the Quarter Final to be played in early January. Not so happy, though, was John Mawle who left the field deeply concussed after 25 minutes to spend an unscheduled night in the Radcliffe Infirmary.

Another player who was to be absent from this point was winger Duncan Kilgour whose professional commitments, while studying and working in London, prevented him travelling to matches. He wouldn't have minded missing the next match, played in steady rain, which ended in near darkness after Glynneath's late arrival due to heavy traffic. Oxford caught the unsettled visitors on the hop and scored after 4 minutes when a good three quarters move saw Oliver Clarke, deputising for Kilgour, go over in the corner. Further tries from Fitzpatrick and Mills saw Oxford home with a 16–0 win despite the inclement weather.

The club team was battling to get some consistency in the season but hopes of regained momentum from the Glynneath fixture were overshadowed by national events of a much different sort. In late October a case of Foot and Mouth Disease was reported in Oswestry and this outbreak quickly spread to reach epidemic proportions when, on 18th November, a ban was announced on the movement of farm animals covering the whole of England and Wales. With Cheshire at the centre, the outbreak stretched as far south as Cheltenham in Gloucestershire and the dry, frosty weather brought no relief as events on a national scale were effected. The International RAC Rally was called off at an estimated cost of £250,000 for fear of drivers and spectators unintentionally spreading the disease, and a ban on horse racing was to last for two months. The Irish Government issued a ban on international travel which, among lots of other things, prevented the Ireland – New Zealand match from taking place in Dublin in December thus preventing New Zealand's 'Grand Slam' attempt on their British Tour. It was to be June before the disease was brought fully under control.

Oxford's next match was due at Maesteg in South Wales on 2nd December and although Maesteg was not in an infected area the team would have to travel through infected areas to get there. Both John Mawle and Michael Gibbard were farmers and, with these circumstances in mind, Oxford cancelled the fixture. It was an unexpected respite for the players and later the following week, on Thursday evening, the weather changed to snow which put paid to Oxford's game with the Metropolitan Police in London two days later.

With three weeks away from the game Oxford were expected to beat St Bartholomew's Hospital at the Bypass but losing 3–12 to four penalty goals was a true reflection of a drab match. Then in a change of fortunes and in wet, greasy conditions the side finished as comfortable winners 19–6 at home to Stroud, which saw the return of Captain John Mawle to the side. On the international front Jim Parsons was selected to play for The Rest against England in another trial match.

There were no games over the Christmas holiday period and Joe McPartlin, now free of school commitments, became Oxford's 52nd player in this season as Oxford finished 1967 in some style with a notable victory at home to London Irish. It was easily the most spirited performance of the year in a fast and exciting match as Mawle urged his troops forward. Newcomer Nigel Parker, formerly of Eastbourne College, Kilgour and scrum half Mike Gretton were the try scorers with McPartlin, whose very presence seemed to inspire confidence, adding a conversion. There was joy elsewhere locally with the Nomads beating Bicester 25–0, the Marathons winning 12–5 at Abingdon, and Oxford Old Boys drew 3–3 with Henley.

The holiday period over Christmas and the New Year gave opportunity for reflection on the season so far when, in nineteen games, Oxford had conceded a record number of 219 points. The high number of players who had represented the club at first team level had been caused by injuries, loss of form and non-availability all of which meant that Oxford had not fielded the same team twice in succession.

Lynn Evans, also reflecting on the season so far, decided to have an operation on his troublesome left shoulder which, having been advised by a specialist, would make it "as good as new".

County rugby in the south west had been disrupted by bad weather and the Foot and Mouth epidemic as Oxfordshire awaited news as to who they would play in the Championship Quarter Final. The match was due on 13th January but Gloucestershire had yet to play Devon, then Cornwall and possibly Somerset in a play off before anybody could think of the next stage of the competition. By contrast there was great news for Oxfordshire enthusiasts when it was announced that Jim Parsons had been selected to play for England against Wales at Twickenham on 20th January.

Oxford's first test in 1968 was a home match with the Hospital Cup holders, St Mary's Hospital, but the visitors found the home side in uncompromising mood. Hooker George Webb was in superb form which helped to produce quick and early service from the useful half back partnership of Gretton and McPartlin. As a result Oxford equalled their second highest score of the season with one goal, four tries and three penalties in a 26–0 win despite the heavy conditions.

The weather was changing again and by Thursday of that week blizzards had paralysed most of the British Isles leading to the cancellation of Oxford's game at London Hospital. The conditions were short-lived, however, and Oxford selected the same team as the previous week for the trip to play Old Rutlishians in a morning kick off on 20th January. Mike Gibbard, after seven early season matches and then in and out the side, was preferred to the RAF man David Saunders in the second row of the scrum. As was usual in morning kick offs Oxford failed to produce their best but Gibbard marked the occasion with a try from a cross kick by Fitzpatrick. Mills and the rapidly improving Liam McCarthy did much good work and it was Mills who pounced onto a loose ball for Oxford's second try while, with the score balanced at 6–6, it was left to Ian Parsons to kick the winning points from a penalty in front of the posts.

With the Nomads and 'A' XV playing in morning kick offs at Wycombe it was something of a club outing as all three sides planned to meet at Twickenham to support Jim Parsons in his England debut. The national selectors were desperate for a winning side, and after November's defeat to the All Blacks, the England side had lost to 'The Rest', 5–21, in the final trial. It was Jim's performance in this match which finally sealed his selection and he was one of eight new caps in a side that showed eleven changes from the previous match. But these changes were vindicated when England let Wales off the hook in an 11–11 draw. Wales were beaten in the lineout throughout and suffered in the scrums but England's backs could not capitalise.

Oxford's winning run continued with a 5–3 success in a drab match away at Esher and the team was due to play Maesteg at the Bypass the following week, but the Welsh club called the match off citing the Foot and Mouth epidemic in a similar situation to that in December. By now the circumstances had changed somewhat and the epidemic had eased to the point that international travel between Ireland and the British mainland had resumed which had allowed the current Five Nations Championship to take place as usual. Although Maesteg's was a perfectly reasonable action some cynics at the club felt this was a 'tit for tat' call by the intended visitors. Instead the club was able to arrange an alternative fixture away against Reading where the following team was selected to represent Oxford: T Wilde; D Fitzpatrick, R Stevenson, J McPartlin, G Barrett; H Davies, M Gretton; J Mawle (Capt), G Webb, J Baird, D Ovenall, D Saunders, B Humphries, L McCarthy, N Parker.

It seems that Oxford's greatest task at Reading was in beating the bitter, cold wind and the spasmodic snow showers, and there was any amount of mishandling. But Oxford produced some good rugby in part and the players were perhaps kind in not taking all of their chances in a 24–6 win where Howard Davies kicked three drop goals.

The club team was now enjoying a good run of winning form and, with the remaining games in February due at home, it seemed quite possible that this might be extended. The match with Bridgwater and Albion proved to be a gruelling struggle where the pack ran itself into the ground, and backs support saw Oxford home 9–5 for a seventh successive win. This put the players in good spirit for the visit of Abertillery on 17th February, and the team fought magnificently against the odds after wing forward Nigel Parker was forced to leave the field suffering a deep gash over an eye with only three minutes on the clock. Joe McPartlin kicked two penalty goals and Oxford's fourteen men refused to give in as Abertillery attacked, and were able to record a first ever victory over the Welsh club, 6–0.

At last Oxfordshire's quarter final opponents were known and, once again, it would be Gloucestershire at Iffley Road on 2nd March. This was almost two months after the original date set for the match and Oxfordshire welcomed the opportunity to play against, and beat 21–6, Oxford University in the annual match. As thoughts turned towards the county match players at Oxford, with a club record in sight, were thinking in a different direction – if the team could beat Nuneaton it would be nine successive wins. The day came and Nuneaton gave Oxford some anxious moments before the home team settled to lead at half time with a Joe McPartlin penalty goal. There were tense moments as Nuneaton drew level but, late in the game, Duncan Kilgour scored twice from the left wing and McPartlin, in good kicking form, added the two conversions to see Oxford home to that elusive and well deserved record. But the team had not finished and a midweek win, 9–5, over Birmingham University made the record even more special, ten in a row!

The Rugby Union made some unusual decisions in relation to the possible result of the impending County match. If, after 80 minutes, the result was a draw then a new game would take place when changes to either lineup could be made, but that game would last for only 10 minutes each way! Should the result still be a draw the tie might then be decided on the toss of a coin but this was not certain. Perhaps the Union, which was anxious to catch up on lost time with the semi final due against Warwickshire the following week, did not think matters would last that long.

Four Oxford players were selected for Oxfordshire, Duncan Kilgour, John Mawle, George Webb and Bernard Humphries and, of course, the club side had to make changes accordingly for the home match with Cambridge. These changes seemed to upset Oxford's rhythm and confidence and the team gave what must have been the worst display of the year in losing 6–19. It was a real fall from grace after the ten match run and the first time that Cambridge had beaten Oxford in eleven matches.

A short distance away, as the crow flies, any hopes that the Oxfordshire team might beat Gloucestershire three times in a row were ended by the former England full back, Don Rutherford, who kicked five penalty goals in Gloucestershire's 18–3 win in a drab match. Ian Moffatt was the home team's sole scorer when he replied with a solitary penalty goal. At the post match dinner the visiting President, HG Smith, in thanking Oxfordshire for the game, apologised "for the delay in putting you out of your misery. We have been waiting a long time for this" he said. It didn't do them a lot of good, however, when the team lost to Warwickshire the following week!

In the week the club held its annual Vice Presidents Dinner at the Royal Oxford Hotel, where Irish International of 22 caps, Andy Mulligan, was the guest speaker, all for the princely sum of 49s 6d!

After the Cambridge setback, Oxford featured in the hardest and most closely fought game of the season so far in the home encounter with Cross Keys. In a breathless start both

*The Oxfordshire team that lost in the Quarter Final to Gloucestershire.
Back row, l to r: J Mawle, J Parsons, A Hallett, I Moffatt (Capt),
K Mulligan, W Wakelin, B Humphreys, O Waldron, J Higgins (Trainer).
Front row, l to r: M Simmie, A Hurst, J Ross-Jones, D Kilgour, N Starmer-Smith, G Greig, G Webb.*

sides scored in the first four minutes, Cross Keys after an Oxford error before McPartlin kicked a penalty goal. The same player then picked up, drew the full back and passed to send Kilgour on a 40 yard run for a try which he converted. But Cross Keys equalised, Oxford failed to take their chances and there was no more score for an 8–8 honours even draw.

The Welsh theme continued with a long journey to the valleys to play Rhymney where the Oxford players were faced with incessant rain and an icy wind, with slippery black mud underfoot. Although the home side scored in the first half Oxford fought back with relish to create several chances but could not overcome the conditions in a 0–5 defeat. It was the first time this season that Oxford had failed to score. A week later, 23rd March, similar conditions prevailed but at least the mud was a different colour with Oxford playing at the Bypass against the losing Hospital Cup finalists, Guy's Hospital. A fierce tussle took place between two sets of well drilled forwards and any effort to bring backs into play was fraught with peril! Although Guy's scored first, a pass from Webb sent Dick Ovenall over in the corner for a try before McPartlin kicked a penalty in front of the posts for a narrow victory.

Another trip to the valleys, this time to Abertillery, saw Oxford beaten 3–19. Second row forward David Saunders would recall the occasion more than most as he lost a gold tooth during the match, which was not found. Any adventurous prospector with a metal detector could well be rewarded as the tooth is probably still buried in the mud!

*Oxford RFC Annual Dinner menu card 1968.*

All these tough games put Oxford in good stead for the relatively short trip over to play Cheltenham who, themselves, had accounted for several top class clubs in the recent months. But that clubs hopes were rudely shattered by a disciplined and vigorous performance from Oxford's pack where the exchanges were fierce and relentless. Subtle touches were added by the backs and Howard Davies slid through a gap for a try converted by McPartlin. And then former Reading and Berkshire winger, Dick Goodall, evaded five tackles as he sprinted in from deep in Oxford's half for a superb try in the 8–0 victory.

A holiday period beckoned again but there was little relaxation in the camp with three fixtures over the four day Easter weekend. The club did ring the changes for each game, which brought mixed fortunes over the period, starting with a win over Reading at Oxford, 10–6, on Good Friday in a morning kick off. A much changed side then faced a long and tiresome journey north to play in a new fixture the next day, against New Brighton in The Wirral. This also marked the return to the club of Ray Tapper at fly half, his favourite position. He had left after a dispute the previous season with the club who had wanted him to play in the centre, and he'd spent much of this season at Oxford Marathon. The team was soon 9 points down but made a strong recovery when Ovenall's try was converted by McPartlin. The cause wasn't helped when wing forward Ray Mills left the field with a shoulder injury in the first half although he bravely returned to complete the second. But a late try saw the home side win, 14–5. Back home, the Monday match with Streatham saw Trevor Wilde kick a forty yard drop goal followed by a try from prop Gerry Howells before Streatham fought back to win the game with a late penalty goal, 6–8.

The end of the season was fast approaching and the familiar seven-a-side tournaments provoked some discussion at the club. Ray Tapper, Joe McPartlin and Duncan Kilgour were off to the preliminary rounds of the Middlesex Sevens with the Oxford Thursday team on the same day that Oxford were due to play at home against Pontypridd. The Thursday team failed to qualify while the fifteen-a-side team lost 6–8 to their Welsh opponents due, mainly, to missed penalty kicks. Ironically, a young Seretse Williams kicked four penalty goals for Oxford Colts in a 'curtain raiser' against Rycotewood College before the main event.

Having won the Oxfordshire Sevens for two consecutive seasons, much interest surrounded the Oxford Thursday attempt to make it three in a row. On a day of exciting rugby a Ray Tapper penalty goal gave the Oxford side a tenuous lead in the semi final against Richmond and the team then hung on with six players as Bagnall had left the field with an injury. But in the last few moments a Richmond player gathered at a lineout in the corner to plunge over for a converted try. Was the lineout throw straight? Some supporters in the corner didn't think so but, for the Thursdays, the hat trick was not to be. Richmond went on to beat the Griffins, London Welsh in disguise, 8–5, in the Final.

On the last Saturday, 27th April, Oxford lost 9–23 at Lydney when driving rain confined the game to forward play, which suited the home side, and Lydney pulled away in the second half to win.

At the end of season players meeting John Mawle announced that he would not be standing for re-election as Captain. This was a great disappointment as, under his guidance, the team had really settled down in the second part of the season, finishing with twenty games won in the thirty eight match programme including that ten match unbeaten run. It was remarkable that, in using sixty five players in those games, the club had not fielded the same side two weeks running. There was a feeling that, even in an amateur game, players still owe allegiance and loyalty to the club and, sometimes, this had not been evident and the side was rarely at full strength for those long journey away games. In the meantime John Mawle was not lost to the club and he became the club's new Fixture Secretary, taking over from Roy Tapper.

*Oxford Thursday were hoping for a third consecutive Oxfordshire Sevens title but lost in the semi-final. L to r: T Bucknall, W Wakelin, D Kilgour, D Bagnall, R Tapper, M Douch, N Parker. Who is that Policeman in the background?*

Another record worthy of mention was that claimed by the club treasurer, John Rowell, who walked from the Kings Arms in Holywell to the clubhouse at the Bypass in 31 minutes. He thought he could even improve on that time in daylight which would make it easier for him to negotiate the pot holes and puddles which had appeared again in the lane!

## Season 1968–1969

The muddy and potholed lane leading to the clubhouse and fields was an indication that all was not well within the Oxford Sports Club. At its Annual General Meeting in March the Oxford Motor Club had decided to break away from the Sports Club, after affiliation since 1950, because it was costing them too much.

In April the 135 year old Oxford City Cricket Club was forced to hold an Emergency General Meeting when the motion 'This meeting agrees that OCCC is no longer viable and therefore matches for the coming season be cancelled' was discussed. It was stated that the club had only 15 players but the President, Charles Walters, said "We have been promised more than that." Financially, a slight deficit from the previous season was cleared by generous donations from anonymous well-wishers but the club expected to face a further deficit of £130 at the end of the coming season. After much discussion the members decided to continue and attempt to recruit new players. But it did not come to much and in May the Cricket Club did, in fact, cancel the season's matches quoting a shortage of players coming through from local schools and the difficulty they found in reaching the ground.

The pressure that this placed on both the rugby club and the City of Oxford Hockey Club was only slightly eased by the re-letting of cricket facilities and the income that that brought in. Despite having made a successful reduction in catering costs and travelling expenses, and even a new record level of contributions from the Vice Presidents, Oxford RFC had made a loss of £22. A lot of this was attributed to the Saturday night dances that had all run at a loss and it had become obvious that this sort of Saturday evening activity was no longer interesting to rugby players. In these tough financial times the shortfall would be addressed by the Finance and Entertainment Committee and then with the players – "They are the ultimate source of income should all else fail." The immediate response was to raise subscriptions by 21 shillings, 50%, to 3 Guineas.

Oxford Marathons were due to celebrate the club's 21$^{st}$ season with a match against the County President's XV at the Cowley Marsh ground in late September. Having had fixture cards printed and circulated with those details therein the club received a letter from the Parks Superintendent, Mr A Walby, to say that they couldn't use the changing rooms at the ground. The changing rooms were to be used as a contractor's site office during the establishment of the City Engineer's Department at Cowley Marsh, the loan sanction for the project having been received earlier than expected and the work had to be put in hand. The Marathons, having had no indication of the scheme or loss of the changing rooms, sought a stay of execution but were offered Cutteslowe Park as an alternative. Their suggestion that the pitch there, next to the River Cherwell, was unplayable for several weeks of the year due to flooding was dismissed by Mr Walby as "Rubbish, the pitch does not flood." It was a nasty shock for the Marathons, but the situation was resolved when the club were granted the use of changing rooms at nearby Temple Cowley School which, at least, enabled them to continue at the Marsh. But all the 'toings and froings' meant that the celebration game had to be shelved for the time being.

The innovation of a two class mail system was due to be introduced to the nation later in the year by the Postal Service. The cost of 2$^{nd}$ Class postage would be 4d, while 1$^{st}$ Class would cost 5d. The Rugby Union stated that it would use only 2$^{nd}$ Class in the future unless in exceptional circumstances, causing cynics to wonder if this would cause further delay in getting a reply from that source.

Also introduced at this time was a change in the Laws of the Game which banned kicking directly to touch between the two 25 yard lines, after an experiment during the previous season. This, of course, meant that there should be more running with the ball and the players would need to be fitter than ever before. This coincided at Oxford with a break in tradition and a tough start to the season with a short two game tour of Cornwall, where the side to face Camborne on the Friday evening contained four Colts from the previous season. Liam McCarthy scored a try crafted by Martin Bampton and Duncan Kilgour, and Ray Tapper, who later added a drop goal, converted, but

*The new Oxford RFC Captain is seen here exchanging notes with the new Nomads Captain, Roy Tapper.*

the side lost a hard opening game, 8–14. The next day Oxford's lively, attacking play kept Penryn, the champion club of Cornwall, at bay and the side was 45 seconds from a notable victory when Penryn scored a second try to equalise David Fitzpatrick's try and Tapper's conversion and penalty. The Penryn conversion gave the home side the match, 10–8, after a bad fright!

Oxford's return home on 14th September to play Old Cranleighans was marred by an unfortunate incident which held the game up for 15 minutes. John Thompson, the renowned Warwickshire referee in charge of the match, suffered a small stroke just after the start of the second half and was taken to the Radcliffe Infirmary. Luckily club member Malcolm Phipps, also a referee with the Oxfordshire Society, was on the ground and took charge of the game. Torrential rain made handling difficult but Oxford mastered the wet conditions and a George Webb try settled the matter after Tapper's first half penalty, for a 6–0 win.

Suddenly, so early in the season, the club team found that it had a 'day off' when Rugby discovered it had double booked its intended fixture with Oxford on Saturday 21st September. The club did not seek a replacement match as the team was due to travel and play Cheltenham on the Monday evening. But Cheltenham contacted and asked for the match to be moved to the Thursday, and then contacted again and cancelled as the team was due to leave on a tour on Friday morning!

During a lengthy period of off field activity in rugby union, both locally and nationally, clubs in Bedfordshire and Northamptonshire had proposed changes to the County Championship set-up which were discussed at the Rugby Union AGM in the summer months. The suggestion was for a streamlined eight regional team competition run on a knockout basis with a competition for first round losers, the object of which, it was said, would improve the standard of play at international level. Oxfordshire's representative at the Rugby Union had been adamant – "If this happens Oxfordshire would disappear. We would lapse back into just club rugby and we want to carry on playing in the County Championship. Oxfordshire would be grouped with East Midlands, Leicestershire and Hertfordshire. What chance would Oxfordshire players get?" After considerable deliberation by a special RFU sub-committee and then lengthy discussion at the AGM, where the current system was described as "outdated" and "a dead duck", it was decided that the Championship would be retained in it's the current form.

With this in mind and in an attempt to improve their lot the Oxfordshire Union dispensed with the trial match system which, in recent times, had been poorly supported and, instead, arranged two 'pre-season' friendly matches, the first of which was against Staffordshire to be played at Banbury on Wednesday 25th September. On a wet and squelching evening the county team was lucky, after spending three quarters of the match in desperate defence, to grind out a 13–9 win.

Most of Oxford's players had enjoyed an unexpected two week break but were champing at the bit when Aldershot Services visited the Bypass. The 48–0 result was a crushing blow for the visitors who conceded eleven tries, six of which were scored by winger David Fitzpatrick in setting a new club record for tries in one match, beating the four scored by Mike Bye in October 1949. In the second of three games in a week, against the University Captain's XV, Oxford took the opportunity of introducing Mike Spicer, ex Northampton and the previous season's Old Towcestrians Captain, at prop, wing forward David Payne from RAF Bicester, who had played the week before against Staffordshire, and Roger Lewis, formerly at St Edward's School, another prop. Spicer was also a reliable place kicker. The University Captain, Bob Phillips, was enjoying a very rare second term in the role but

*Duncan Kilgour skilfully evades the Aldershot Services defence and the touch line as Club Treasurer, John Rowell, keeps a close eye on events.*

was on his way back from Argentina, where he'd played for the Welsh XV in the second unofficial 'Test', and only arrived at the ground with barely fifteen minutes left on the clock. It was just in time to see his side lose 11–19 to a revitalised Oxford side which was now playing with a quiet confidence, determination and spirit. These factors were in the forefront of Oxford's second win in forty eight hours, against Pontypridd 17–10, at the Bypass where Bob Stevenson, in the centre, seemed to be enjoying a new lease of life. The pack was in good form for another notable victory, Payne had a promising first game, Spicer had kicked 18 points in two games and Bagnall was very sharp at the base of the scrum, clearly benefiting from his spell in first class rugby.

In the second County 'warm up' match Oxfordshire were soundly beaten by Notts, Lincs & Derbyshire at Beeston, 6–15, with what was described as a third rate performance, the worst for many seasons, which did not auger well for the up-coming Championship games.

Oxford's game at Nuneaton in mid October was also a dull affair, in contrast to previous matches between the clubs, but it certainly came to life in the final few moments when the team hit back to wipe out an 8 point deficit to draw 11–11.

Early views on the 'non kicking' law were very favourable with Oxford's wingers, Kilgour and Fitzpatrick, far more involved than previously with the centres looking to create lots more opportunities. Discreet kicks through the defence lines and down the flanks were paying dividends, and between them the wingers responded to far outscore the other team members.

Off the field, Club Chairman Derek Howard, in his third term of office, found it necessary to resign due to a promotion at work and his successor was Eric Church, always in demand on Saturdays due to his refereeing duties. After his playing career ended Eric, a solicitor with the local firm Cole and Cole, had worked his way through the administrative ranks of the club, continuing to play a full part in rugby union.

In other places former Oxford player Howard Firth had signed for the Rugby League club Hull, as if to prove that it wasn't only Welshmen that 'went north', where he was described as "an exciting flaxen haired flyer" going on to score over 50 tries in his four years at that club.

The club's history with Loughborough Colleges had seen some sound beatings since the first fixture in 1952 with Thom Cooper's team recording the only win in 1960, so the team was due a victory. So it was when the students visited and Oxford won for the second time, 13–6. Spicer's place kicking was a feature but the result was based on good forward play supported well by the backs.

Oxfordshire's latest Championship trail started at Aylesbury against Buckinghamshire. The team began at a pace to score two quick tries through Nigel Starmer-Smith and Duncan Kilgour but then endured a grim fight to hold on to the lead to win 6–3 in an uninspiring performance.

The following day at Iffley Road, in a rare midweek Thursday afternoon fixture, Oxford completed a fine 'University Double' when the side beat Oxford University Greyhounds, 31–11, after an 11–3 half time lead. The pace was fast and furious and the Oxford players suffered two days later but survived a cliff hanger when the Guy's Hospital team ran them close in London. It needed a Spicer injury time penalty kick to square the match at 14–14 and keep that unbeaten run going.

Dave Green had returned to the club and helped the side to a muddy, slippery 12–0 win over St Thomas' Hospital on the Bypass ground, before Oxfordshire ground out another 6–3 win in similar conditions on the same pitch against Berkshire four days later. Once more it was an unimpressive display, needing Ian Moffatt to kick two penalty goals before a hard fight was endured to hold Berkshire out. This was in direct contrast to the Saturday game at home to Weston-super-Mare when high morale showed in the Oxford side. Chasing hard and fighting for every ball, Oxford came back from an early six point deficit to soundly beat the visitors, 20–9.

But Oxford's bubble burst on 16th November with an away 3–6 defeat at United Services, Portsmouth, when the side were forced to play one man short as David Green failed to turn up. This brought to an end the ten match undefeated run in this season, and the gloom stretched for another few weeks in an intermittent run in to the end of the year. Midweek, Oxfordshire notched up the team's best win of the campaign so far. Conceding two early penalties to Dorset & Wilts, the side crossed over at 6–6 to completely dominate the second half for a splendid 26–9 win which set up a group decider away at Hertfordshire who, like Oxfordshire, were also unbeaten after three group matches.

Complacency was the cause of Oxford's 9–14 home defeat to Abertillery. After a Spicer penalty and Tapper drop goal had given the side a lead it was the turn of the visitors, inspired by Welsh international scrum half Alun Lewis, to fight back and, despite a second Spicer penalty, it was too late to breach the Abertillery defence. This was followed by a thoroughly forgettable visit to Maesteg, where the pitch was a soggy morass after a week's rain, ankle deep in mud and water, and with the match being played in rain and a biting wind it was little wonder Oxford lost in the inhospitable conditions, 3–6.

To make matters worse Oxfordshire's reign as Southern Group Champions came to an end when the team lost at Hertfordshire in the final match, 0–6. Two penalty goals did for them and although Moffatt was off target with three long range attempts, it was another lethargic performance and the team's first group defeat since November 1963 which, none-the-less, was a remarkable record that would take some beating.

Oxford made hard work of a 17–3 home win against Reading on December 7th, while snow and ice on a frosty ground put paid to the match at Stroud giving the players some respite before the match at Sunbury with London Irish. Oxford rode their luck in this fixture, having to start with fourteen men as David Green again failed to appear and playing against two Irish Internationals in the front row, Ollie Waldron and Ken Kennedy. Bob Stevenson scored an early try which Spicer converted before Mick Doyle missed five kicks at goal, only for Tapper to seal an 8–0 win with a drop goal. A local Irish supporter was quoted as saying "Only an Irish team could do all that and still lose!" But this was a timely Christmas present for Oxford and a win deserved by better team work. The club was hopeful of a London double with the holiday game at Wasps to come but frost was the reason the match was cancelled.

Having reached the half way point in the season Oxford were looking good with ten matches won and two drawn with just five losses recorded. Some of the performances were of high merit and much of this was due to a new 'professional' approach and attitude to the game. There had also been some big improvements in personal performances. Centre Bob Stevenson was a player transformed and was quoted as being "the very essence of enthusiasm and inspiration" and his knowledge and experience had been invaluable. Ray Tapper had settled to something like his true ability at fly half with his kicking "on a sixpence" resulting in the wingers scoring over half the teams try total at that stage. Young lock forward Mike Gibbard was a vastly improved player and No 8 Liam McCarthy was also coming along nicely. John Mawle had been playing better than he did when captain the previous season, and George Webb was still one of the most under rated hookers in the South and Midlands.

It was around this time that the first mention of competitive rugby, away from the County Championship, came to light. The Surrey RFU had suggested two ten club leagues with promotion and relegation, and had invited Oxford RFC to take part! At the same time there were similar discussions in the North and Midlands, and there was obviously much to talk about behind the scenes. But, by the end of January 1969, the Rugby Football Union had met and rejected the idea of competition rugby and big business sponsorship.

A former club member from the 1920s, who had left to help found the old Oxford Exiles RFC, Tommy Warnock, celebrating his 21st year as Treasurer to Oxfordshire RFU, was stated as the finest example of putting something back into the game, while Oxford Sports Club made an appeal for £1000 for urgent repairs to the clubhouse and water system, and the pot hole ridden track leading to the club car park.

Lynn Evans played his first game, for the 'A' XV, since his shoulder dislocation fourteen months previously, and Jim Parsons was testing his right knee in the same team.

The club had finally lost patience with lock forward David Green who had failed to appear for three club games in this season. This was a great shame as Green had talent and much unrealised potential with the possibility of greater things beckoning but appeared to have problems away from the game. In his place came Dick Ovenall who had played in five of Oxford's games before going back to Oxford University in an attempt to win a 'Blue'. Although Dick didn't make the team he had played for the Greyhounds against Cambridge and was considered a worthy replacement for Green.

Oxford opened the New Year in fine style in beating Old Whitgiftians, a side that had lost just once previously, 19–3, then London Hospital, the holders of the Hospital's Cup, 18–0, before a 6–6 draw with Cheltenham, a muddy struggle in almost impossible conditions when the team conceded a converted penalty in the last minute of the game. All this led to one of the best performances of the season, a 26–3 win at Esher where the home side was stunned by Oxford's play. Jim Wilson, an Oxford 'Blue' at wing and full back, scored seventeen points from the centre with a try, two penalties and four conversions, Bagnall added two tries and Tapper one as the team enjoyed themselves immensely.

There were team changes for the home match with Maesteg and Colin Evans switched to the Number 8 position in place of Liam McCarthy, who had been an ever present to that point, not through any loss of form but the club wanted to see Evans in that position. Airman Bob Souter was selected at wing forward. In a bitingly cold cross wind Oxford's forwards lacked fire and gave the worst display of the season as the team went down 6–14 with only two Jim Wilson penalties to credit. It was the first defeat since November when the team lost to – Maesteg.

The weather suddenly turned for the worse with snow and ice saving the club an away trip to Bridgwater. Blizzards and snow drifts that cut off some villages in Oxfordshire also affected bar takings at the club with the home match with Glynneath also called off. The thaw came after two weeks but was too late for any rugby in Oxford. The only club to get any rugby was the Oxford side that was off to London on the Saturday morning for a match with St Bartholomew's Hospital before going on to watch England beat France at Twickenham. The 14–6 away win was somewhat tempered in the second half when Kilgour left the field with a leg injury after which the game deteriorated into a scrappy affair.

Jim Wilson was again the star with two penalties and a great try as Oxford appeared to have the home game with Cross Keys won but tempers flared in the second period and, despite a visitor being sent from the field for late tackling Fitzpatrick, the team went right off the boil and slipped to a 9–9 draw. A second draw in succession 14–14 at home midweek with Birmingham University was only slightly better. It was obvious that the players will still suffering from the effects of the cold spell and seemed unable to produce the fire and form shown before the enforced break. An 8–3 win at Cambridge on 8th March was welcome after two disappointing draws but failed to quell the doubters as the side nearly allowed the home team to draw level. Stevenson scored a fine try before Fitzpatrick found Tapper in support, after great inter-passing, for a second but it needed Bagnall to race back in the final moments to touch down to secure the win.

Saturday morning rugby before an England International proved again to be a challenge with an early kick off at Streatham & Croydon. Hampered by injuries and late cry offs, there was also a misunderstanding about the kick off time which made a hurried journey even more urgent. The Oxford side arrived for an 11.30am kick off only to find the home team changed and ready for a 10.30am start. The teams got onto the field nearly an hour late and even then Oxford started with fourteen players with Trevor Wilde joining the side ten minutes later. With all this disruption it was no surprise that Oxford lost 6–19 to complete an unhappy morning.

Rumours had continued to circulate regarding competitive rugby and the matter raised its head again at the Freemasons Hall when Oxford RFC held its Annual Dinner on Wednesday 19th March. It was something of a surprise when Sam Miller, Oxfordshire's representative at the RFU, announced that, although the RFU had recently pronounced against it, a sub-committee was soon to meet in London to discuss sixteen different schemes and suggestions for the introduction of competitive rugby. These comments were in reply to Eric Church, the Club Chairman, who said "Competitive rugby is coming whether introduced by the RFU or commercially sponsored, and I would urge the RFU that they seriously consider again

*Club stalwarts of the time, Dick Howard, Ron Salter, Peter West, Alan Lisle, John Allen and Brian 'Dixie' Deane. Great moustache, Ron!*

competitive rugby before it overtakes them." Duncan Kilgour, the Club Captain, was far more forthright about current affairs at the club and spoke regarding questions being asked about why the club was not taken seriously by the national press. "The incident of last week at Streatham is a good example of why not" he said. "Fortunately the club itself, unlike the Oxford Sports Club HQ, is not disintegrating. Another couple of years of 'run down' policy and the premises will internally fall apart. Not that you will be able to get there to see it for, by then, the approach lane will be completely impassable." The appeal made in January had obviously not been as successful as was hoped for.

The side came very close to snatching an unexpected victory in London against the Metropolitan Police with a second half come back that shook the home side. Facing a strong wind and a fourteen point deficit the fight back was spearheaded once again with the accurate kicking of Mike Spicer with three penalties and the conversion of Tapper's try, but the match was not long enough for Oxford who lost 14–17.

Travelling further in the opposite direction the next week Oxford paid the penalty for taking a weak team to Wales to play Penarth and, once again, the problems started before the match. Lots of changes in the team and positions on the Friday evening saw a light and relatively inexperienced pack take the field which was alright in the tight play but no match in the loose. Kilgour's troublesome knee did not help as the side went down 3–14.

The run of three successive defeats did not put the team in the best of minds with a quick return to Wales on the cards for a tough Easter tour. Based in Cardiff the tour opened on Good Friday with a fast, exacting game with Abertillery. Ex Peers schoolboy Alan Jenkins fast striking provided lots of good ball, with good lineout work from Mike Gibbard, John Mawle and Bob Souter, but the team gave away five points at a crucial stage of the match and then ran out of cover in the closing minutes to lose 0–10. On to Cross Keys on the Saturday, Oxford scored three excellent tries but, for once, Spicer was off form and missed vital kicks in the 9–11 defeat while, on Easter Monday, a below strength side lost 5–20 to Pontypool. The bright spot in this game was a try from Tapper who intercepted in Oxford's '25' for a breakaway which Spicer converted.

Although Oxford had lost all three games the club was happy and well satisfied with the Welsh Tour. Defeat margins were closer than might have been expected considering team and positional changes, and the over generous side had given away points in each match. In an innovative move the club Colts side had also joined the senior team on the tour but had lost 0–19 at Cross Keys, and 3–21 at Pontypool but had learned a lesson or two?

At last Oxford were due to play at the Bypass ground against Glamorgan Wanderers but the Welsh side asked for the venue to be reversed as club members were required for stewarding duties at the Wales v England match the same day. The club was offered a morning kick off in Cardiff with the incentive of tickets so that the players could see the match in the afternoon, but the club, having travelled for the past six weeks, declined the offer, the Glamorgan side was released from the fixture and Oxford did not seek a replacement match.

The end of the season was now well in view and yet again a daunting trip to South Wales loomed, this time to Pontypridd. Many players were suffering from injuries after playing on what were now hard grounds and it was not a full strength side that made the trip. Scrum half Dennis Carter was promoted straight from the Colts and endured what was a "battering baptism in the first class game". Pontypridd's scrum half Dennis John hounded Carter into mistakes and mishandlings, and Ron Grimshaw wrote in the *Oxford Mail* "While Oxford continue to send half strength teams to Wales, or elsewhere for that matter, they will continue to collect hammerings as they did at Pontypridd." Poor Dennis was not wholly to blame for the defeat and was left to reflect on Oxford Colts 34–18 win over Newbury Colts, the first for three seasons, when the team didn't seem to miss him!

In what was turning into a 'hotch potch' end to the season Oxford once more faced a long coach journey this time to play Manchester. With a team playing in the Preliminary Rounds of the Middlesex Sevens the side selected for the trip was a weak one from the outset with Ray Tapper due to miss his first game of the season. Further cry offs resulted in Oxford cancelling the match thus saving the club a 600 mile round trip with a severely weakened team. A mid week away match with Birmingham and what would have been the final match, at home to Clifton, were called off as well as Oxford's season petered out.

There was some redemption in end of season seven a side competitions where an Oxford side lost in the quarter finals of the Oxfordshire Tournament to a side named as Griffins, a pseudonym for the London Welsh club who were otherwise not allowed to play on a Sunday, who went on to beat Penryn in the Final. And there was much joy on the same afternoon when an Oxford Colts team, led by Clive Bevan, won the Oxfordshire Colts Sevens, by beating High Wycombe, 26–13, for the second year in succession. Having qualified for the Final Rounds of the Middlesex Sevens at Twickenham an Oxford side progressed beyond the first round on the day for the first time, by beating Richmond, 15–5 but were knocked out when losing 0–18 to Loughborough Colleges in the second.

There was despondency at Oxford Old Boys when, at the Annual Dinner, President Denis Rosborough reported that the club had been disturbed at the progress of Rugby Union at the Oxford School. The Club Captain, Aubrey John, went further in saying "The sooner Oxford Old Boys become an open club the better. The sooner we do this, the sooner we get a more attractive team and the sooner we shall succeed in the rugby world." He said it was a privilege and an honour to captain the club but continued "At times I have wondered if there can possibly be any future for a club with such apathy among members and such lack of support." The team had won eighteen and lost nine but of those, seventeen had been won before Christmas. "It is absolutely pathetic how we allowed ourselves to slide into this state."

*An Oxford RFC Colts team won the Oxfordshire Colts Seven a Side Tournament at Iffley Road in April, 1969. Back row, l to r: Tony Ballsdon, Seretse Williams, Roy Davies, Britain Turnbull, Richard Flisher, Alan Davies (Manager), Front row, l to r: Richard Evans, Clive Bevan (Capt), Graham Agutter.*

These comments provoked earnest debate later at the Old Boys Annual Meeting. The proposed new Captain, John Frogley, at first refused to accept the position due to lack of support given to retiring officials but reviewed his decision after lengthy discussion. A major step was taken to disband the club's Colts team. As most pupils leaving Oxford School were 18 years or over it was decided to encourage them to find their own level of rugby within the club and therefore be less of a separate entity within the club.

Over at Oxford Marathons, the club was at last able to celebrate its 21 years of existence with a match against the President's XV at South Park. It was close game and the club

*Bob Sankey powers through a tackle in the Oxfordshire Sevens at Iffley Road.*

side lost to the representative side, 8–9, thanks to a successful penalty kick in the last minute, before the celebrations continued with dinner at the Coach & Horses public house in St Clements which had served the club well as its headquarters for most of the time. The 'Maras' also announced that, in contrast to the Old Boys club, they were to revive a Colts team after a six year absence.

Ultimately, the Oxford club side finished the season with a fairly balanced record of playing thirty five, winning fifteen and losing thirteen games with five drawn. There was a little disappointment, however, as Oxford had seemed set for a record season at the half way stage but had only won five games since January. Commenting on the season Duncan Kilgour spoke of plans being shattered by a heavy crop of injuries and the sudden difficulty experienced in raising teams at a time when the club faced a list of away games, none nearer than 100 miles. It was disappointing to have to cancel fixtures at the end of the season which was also due to players who were not prepared to continue travelling away week after week. By the end of the season players who did play in all these games were utterly exhausted but, overall, the team helped to consolidate the club's position on the fringe of first class rugby.

# Chapter 5 – Home, sweet home

The summer of 1969 was dominated by a momentous and historical event of world-wide interest and importance, the first ever manned landing on the Moon in July. Who could forget those grainy pictures from so far away and that great quote "That's one small step for man, but one giant leap for mankind," from the American astronaut, Neil Armstrong.

By this time training for the new season had already started. In an attempt to keep the previous season's talented Colts together, the majority of whom were now too old for Colts rugby, Oxford RFC had announced at the Annual General Meeting in June that it would be creating a Youth team to cater specially for them. Chairman Eric Church said "We hope this team will bridge the gap between Colts rugby and senior rugby." It was decided that the new Youth team would be called the 'Vikings' and that the captain would be the previous Colts Captain, Clive Bevan. This was indeed an innovative move which would bring benefits to the club for some time to come, and there was great enthusiasm for this team at club pre-season training.

It had become obvious that the Oxford Sports Club had fallen into financial difficulties. Two years earlier the rugby club had tried to lead the way to a revival of the Sports Club's fortunes by a proposal that the rent paid to it be substantially increased provided the other sections accepted a similar burden. This provided a respite but then various sections found the increased rent a burden which they were really unable to carry, and it began to look as if the rugby club might find itself without a ground. A report in the *Oxford Times* in late August revealed that negotiations had been taking place between the club and the Hartwell Group but had broken down. They had been discussing proposals in which the motor firm, in return for financial assistance, would have had the use of the Sports Club ground and premises for the social and sporting activities of their employees. The Club issued a short statement which read "The (Sports Club) Council has decided not to pursue negotiations with the Hartwell Group. The Secretary was instructed not to divulge any information on alternatives." It seemed that something else was in the wind – was there a Plan B? In the *Sports Mail,* Ron Grimshaw speculated that one of the "alternatives" was a takeover bid by the rugby club, it having committed some years previously to staying at the Bypass ground.

Oxfordshire RFU announced that it was to do away with trial matches but would, instead, form a thirty player squad for specialist training and team practises as a way of facing a changing future. There was a search for a new scrum half as Nigel Starmer-Smith had taken a teaching job in Epsom which created travelling difficulties for mid-week games and he was now available for Surrey. The Berkshire RFU took a different view of preparation in light of the then recent clarification from the RFU regarding competitive rugby and became one of the first counties in the country to organise a County Club Knockout Cup. This would begin almost immediately and the Selectors hoped that the early season competitive element would help towards team building for the County Championship. So it was that Henley RFC and Cholsey RFC who, for the sake of geography, were also affiliated to the Berkshire Union, became the first Oxfordshire clubs to take part in such a competition when they were drawn at home to Newbury and Windsor respectively in the First Round.

## Season 1969–1970

After setting a travelling record in the previous season, the club had curtailed it's fixture list and was now due to play 'only' forty games this season of which no fewer than twenty two were at home.

Prior to Oxford's season starting in earnest several club players represented the President's XV in a match against Gosford All Blacks to celebrate the opening of a clubhouse extension opposite the airport in Langford Lane, Kidlington. Thirteen years had now passed since Alderman Frank Wise had located the ground with the original building having been bought from the Oxford Flying Club.

Oxford opened with a midweek away game at Coventry where the side lost 5–11 in a hard fought match before returning for a home match against Nuneaton on 6th September. The visitors were mediocre but Oxford's pack failed to get any clean possession and Bagnall was penalised several times for not straight. The one exception was wing forward Ray Mills who was everywhere on the field, tackling, worrying, ready to fall on the loose ball but his enthusiasm could not make up the lethargy of the other forwards. Oxford's team was:
I Parsons; D Fitzpatrick, I Ray, R Stevenson, L Robinson; R Tapper (Captain), D Bagnall; M Spicer, G Webb, R Lewis, M Gibbard, M Orr, R Mills, R Sankey, L McCarthy.

There was an improvement at Pontypool the following week and the side did not deserve to be beaten by 8–22. The wingers, Fitzpatrick and Kilgour, both scored tries with Spicer adding a conversion, but the talking point was the unusual style of the home kicker, Jeff Lester, who slotted three penalties and two conversions, using a 'round the corner' style rarely seen before.

By late September it was revealed that the rugby club had, in fact, put forward an offer to buy all the assets of the Sports Club at a price sufficient to pay off all the debts of the Sports Club. It was thought that this figure would be in the region of £15,000 and the club set out to find ways of raising this sum. Chairman Eric Church said "The rugby club has mixed feelings about the situation which has developed. On one hand we are extremely sorry the Sports Club would have failed because without the assistance of the Sports Club in the past we could never have reached our present position in the rugby world. Unfortunately it would be impossible to allow the hockey club continued use of the ground because a condition of any loan we may be able to obtain from the RFU would be that only Rugby Union Football should be played there. On the other hand to buy the ground opens up enormous possibilities for us. We shall undoubtedly have the finest ground for miles around. We hope and expect that having our own ground will provide the incentive to the players to take the club even further. This is the start of a new era for Oxford RFC and we must make sure we grasp this opportunity with both hands."

This was described at the time as a heaven sent opportunity with an era of hope dawning for the club, the takeover coming into operation just as soon as it had raised the necessary figure to complete the deal.

There was a surprise in the first ever Berkshire Cup when Henley beat Newbury 15–14 in the first round, but disappointment for the other Oxfordshire side, Cholsey, who lost to Windsor, 11–20.

Oxford set out on a new venture on 20th September having accepted an invitation to play in the Selkirk Sevens but it too was a disappointment, as the side was summarily dismissed from the tournament during extra time in a first round match with the hosts, Selkirk. Three of the players had travelled up on an overnight sleeper train and then endured a forty five minute coach trip from Berwick to get there and compete!

Members were therefore a little surprised when, on the same day, the club side beat Old Haberdashers 12–11 to record the first win of the season. A number of old faces were brought into what was a makeshift side and there was little understanding in the backs. It was left to Lynn Evans to kick a penalty goal in the very last minute of a scrappy match to secure a welcome victory.

More changes saw the absent sevens players return but the backs still didn't gell and were guilty of wasting good possession in the home match with St Mary's Hospital. This led to an unnecessary hard struggle but two tries from both Bob Souter and David Bagnall plus one from Bob Stevenson, two of which were converted by Mike Spicer, saw the side home by 19–6.

Although this season would be memorable in the light of Oxford RFC attempting to purchase the ground on which it played, there was also much to celebrate at Iffley Road where the Oxford University club was celebrating its Centenary. Several events were planned including a special Centenary Match where a Past & Present team would be pitted against the annual opponents Major Stanley's XV which would comprise of International players. This season also coincided with a South Africa Tour to the British Isles and the first match of that tour was due against Oxford University at Iffley Road. Oxfordshire had already applied to change the impending championship match with Buckinghamshire from Wednesday 5th November, ominously Bonfire Night, to the Thursday to avoid the University's attractive fixture with the tourists.

Internationally, there was much resentment at the South Africa Republic's policy of apartheid at the time and this led to growing opposition against the University's intended match against what was an all-white South African team. After an OURFC committee meeting on October 9th, the University Vice Chancellor, Alan Bullock, made a public statement dissociating the University from the match. He was replying to a letter from the heads of five Oxford Colleges objecting to a match taking place between a side carrying the University's name and an official South African team which, they claimed, was 'overtly selected according to principals of racial discrimination and whose visit will be used for political purposes in the Republic.'

Meanwhile, the Undergraduates' Joint Action Committee Against Racial Intolerance announced plans for a peaceful demonstration if the match took place. The OURFC Senior Treasurer, Mr WG Barr, Fellow of Exeter College, whose son Andrew was to later spend many playing seasons in the front row of the scrum at Oxford RFC, explained that OURFC had a private ground at Iffley Road and was financially dependent on income from gate money. Oxford University's match against South Africa had been included by tradition in the fixture lists for touring teams from overseas. "We are just told that the touring team is coming and will play us on such and such a date" he said.

There was a 'glut' of rugby locally in the first week of October. The Oxford team started slowly and were poor in the first half of the home match against Esher but were transformed in the second to finish with seven tries and four conversions in the 29–0 win. But the midweek match against CR Laidlaw's XV was a much tougher affair. One error during an isolated second half raid by the University players cost Oxford the game when Mike Heal's penalty rebounded off a post. Bob Stevenson fumbled in front of the line and Doug Boyle swept past him to gather and score. Heal's conversion and three penalty kicks were enough to win the match for the Blues and although Ian Parsons kicked two for the club side to go with his try, other kicks were missed in the 9–14 defeat.

On the county front Oxfordshire were dealt a crushing blow in the attempt to regain the Southern Group title that was lost the previous December. In an opening 5–14 defeat by Hertfordshire, the forwards, especially the back row, were particularly ineffective and the team lacked any winning zip and sparkle.

Oxford's long morning haul north to Hull on Saturday 11th October was delayed by fog and the players had trouble in settling down against Hull and East Riding. 0–6 behind at the break, Oxford fought back and Tapper took Bagnall's pass on a timed run for a try which

*George Webb tries to prevent Mike Tanner, ex Littlemore Grammar School, from kicking the ball away as Nigel Parker rushes to assist. Peter Dixon and David Barry rally to the Laidlaw XV cause.*

Parsons converted to add to a successful penalty kick as Oxford edged into an 8–6 lead, only to be pipped 8–9 as Hull kicked a last minute penalty.

Back in Oxford opposition to the University's match with South Africa was growing with the Oxford and District Trade Council adding its support to the cause. This was reinforced during the week when officials arriving at the ground found the words "Oxford rejects Apartheid" written in weed killer on the Iffley Road pitch in letters four feet high and eighteen inches across.

It was another long trip, this time west to Wales and Abertillery the next weekend where the Oxford side was out-classed and out played to lose 3–26, although the players did go on to win the skittles match in the clubhouse during the evening! But October ended on a high note with a mid- week home win against Oxford University Greyhounds, 19–13, and, two days later a "brilliant Captain's try" from Ray Tapper who, late in the game, jinked his way through the entire immobile Guy's Hospital team, saw his team home 17–9. Continuing the trend, a return to Wales and Penarth saw Oxford win 21–15 despite having upset the referee after some dubious decisions.

The Oxford club, however, was overshadowed as the real rugby interest at the time lay in events surrounding the imminent University match. The situation was now at a stage of much indecision. The head of the local Oxford Police, Chief Superintendent Bill Chapman, had written a letter to the University club to say that he could no longer guarantee the safety of people at the match, particularly the large number of schoolboys expected to attend, in the face of expected demonstrations and without the police in attendance the match could not be played. There was some disquiet amongst the ranks as officers felt that they were being denied the opportunity to provide that safety. The decision, with perhaps a small amount of panic, was not taken lightly but what it did was to just delay the inevitable confrontation between militant protesters, of whom Oxford had seen its fair share in the past and would continue to do in the future, on one side and the police and rugby supporters on the other. This took place ten days later at Swansea while the University club was left to count the cost, having to refund tickets sold.

So, if the game could not be played at Iffley Road would it be played at all? The grounds at United Services, Portsmouth and Aldershot Services were mooted but intervention by the Prime Minister, probably for the first time in the history of the game, via the Ministry of Defence saw these venues ruled out. There was much secrecy but, on the eve of the game, the venue was announced – the match would be played at Twickenham!

On the morning of the match the University Captain, Chris Laidlaw, made a statement in which he said "I would like to make Oxford University's position perfectly clear. We have never wavered in our intention to play the game. The only reason the game is not being played at Oxford is because the police felt they could no longer guarantee the safety of persons and property, which they had hitherto guaranteed. Contrary to the expressed opinion of the Fireworks Day Committee we are not hiding behind the Rugby Football Union. The right of an independent body, such as the Rugby Club, has been undermined by the threat of disorder, but the fact remains that the right to play the game, which we intend to do, is exclusively ours."

Demonstrators who got into the match, at which only the west side of the stadium was open, kept up a barrage of booing and jeering, blowing whistles and clapping rhythmically from the 5 shilling enclosure. But they were often drowned by cheers and clapping from people in the 10 shilling seats when the crowd showed its appreciation of Oxford's play.

This appreciation was well earned as Oxford University recorded a memorable win, perhaps the greatest in their 100 year history, in beating South Africa 6–3, two Mike Heal penalties to one. It was a huge rugby upset but Oxford were the better team, well led by the experienced Laidlaw and with the back row to the fore, deserved the win. While the coveted Springbok head, presented to the first side to defeat a South African team on tour, remains to this day mounted on the wall at Vincent's Club in King Edward Street, one was left to only imagine what effect, if any, the demonstrations had on those who were, after all, sporting guests in our country.

While these events attracted headlines locally and even nationally, Oxford club rugby was still operating if on a slightly lower plain! Injuries had mounted in recent weeks and the club could have almost fielded a pretty strong team of players unable to play at the time, albeit mostly forwards, in: Mawle, Ponty, Spicer, Ovenall, Sankey, McCarthy, Mills,
A Parker, Stewart and Fitzpatrick. Bob Stevenson was due to leave on a two year RAF

*Duncan Kilgour was Oxfordshire Captain this season and here he rallies the troops at half time in the match against Berkshire at Newbury. John Mawle enjoys his orange while Mike Simmie and Tony Hallett listen intently.*

posting to Singapore and Roy Davies nearly left to start University life 'up north' in Manchester without his suitcase. Having said his goodbyes, doors closed, flags waved, Roy saw his suitcase where he left it on the platform. He swiftly nipped outside, scooped up the case and got back on the train while it was moving away!

It was reported that Oxford Marathons were running five sides and, at this stage of the season, were still unbeaten but still had no ground of their own, no clubhouse and no gymnasium. But Oxford RFC came to the rescue somewhat by allowing the club to use the Bypass ground and facilities for Thursday night training.

Oxfordshire recovered from a slow, unimpressive start to drag themselves back into contention at the Bypass ground on Thursday 6$^{th}$ November. Ian Moffatt missed four penalty kicks to leave Buckinghamshire 3–0 ahead at the interval but George Webb hooked against the head and Tapper passed to Moffatt for a try and conversion near the posts, Moffatt again joined the line with a determined run for a try in the corner and finally Tapper went in under the posts giving Moffatt an easy conversion. Oxfordshire were back in the title race!

Two days later Oxford travelled to Surrey to meet St Thomas's Hospital. The team waited until late in the game when the wind was at their backs to play and win 11–9, the feature of which was two tries from Duncan Kilgour. This was a prelude to a grim duel with US Portsmouth at Oxford in a biting diagonal wind when a try late in the game settled it in the visitors favour, 9–12. There was some consolation, however, for David Bagnall who became a father with the birth of his daughter, Sarah, on Sunday morning.

There were happier times in midweek for some busy Oxford players. Berkshire just needed to draw at Newbury to win their first group title for thirteen years but were never in the game against Oxfordshire who were yards faster and back in top form for a 25–8 success.

In contrast, Nottingham were making a first visit to the Bypass and were too robust and fast moving for Oxford. Roy Newton was making his Oxford debut in the back row and scored a try but it was not a good ending when Oxford lost 6–20. Even worse, John Mawle suffered a damaged and displaced disc in his neck which would mean some weeks away from the action.

On the same weekend, November 22$^{nd}$, Oxford Marathons suffered their first defeat of the season in their first away match of the season at REME Arborfield, 12–21, while at Marston Ferry Road Oxford Old Boys ended a run of six consecutive defeats by beating Ruislip 8–3.

The dreaded 'flu bug was doing the rounds at this time and it was hoped that the Oxford hooker, George Webb, would stay clear of it after the Oxfordshire team was announced for the group decider against Dorset & Wiltshire at Wareham. For George it would be a 50$^{th}$ appearance for the county, only the sixth player to achieve this. The others were England reserve full back Ian Moffatt, Frank Webb, David Lloyd and Ted Walters with Peter Stone leading the way with 56 appearances. All these players were, or had been, Oxford players. The selected team, prior to John Mawle's injury, was: IB Moffatt (Northampton); MS Simmie (London Scottish), PRE McFarlane (Rosslyn Park), AJ Payne (Harlequins), DS Kilgour (Oxford) (Captain); RP Tapper (Oxford), DF Bagnall (Oxford); EJH Gould (Richmond), G Webb (Oxford), JF Mawle (Oxford), DH Pitt (Oxford), RJ Ovenall (Oxford), L McCarthy (Oxford), H Sharp (Oxford), AP Hallett (US Portsmouth), from whom much was expected.

It wasn't just the 'flu bug disrupting club selections as seasonal weather conditions got a grip and Oxford's trip to play London Hospital was called off as snow, ice and then frost made conditions unplayable. There wasn't a silver lining for Oxfordshire when the team frittered away several chances to lose 14–17 at Wareham to end championship hopes for another season. Webb and Moffatt were each awarded a tankard after the match for their 50 county appearances.

Oxford University's Centenary celebrations continued when the reinforced students team lost by two points, 16–18, against the Barbarians at Iffley Road. This match, taking the place of the annual match against Major Stanley's XV, was excellent preparation for the Varsity where Cambridge University were favourites to win. The result was a 9–6 win by Oxford in a score line dominated by five penalty kicks that gave the wrong impression of an exciting match.

Bad weather also accounted for the loss of another fixture, a new one, away at Harrogate but at least the club were saved the expense of travelling. Not so the following Saturday with another trek into South Wales, this time to Tredegar. After a three week lay-off Oxford were not sharp enough, lacked method and made too many mistakes while the back row trio of Liam McCarthy, Newton and Mills were ineffective. The need for a reliable kicker also raised its head again.

In a busy season a busy Christmas period was approaching. The rugby club, in the process of taking over the sports club, had also taken over arrangements for the annual Boxing Day Ball previously a sports club commitment. This was to be held at the Randolph Hotel in Oxford where the Yankee Clippers Showband was to be the main attraction backed by cabaret artists and a buffet. Tickets were priced at £3.10s for a double and £2 a single and the club needed to sell 108 double tickets to clear any costs incurred but, by mid-December, sales had been slow. Chairman Eric Church suggested that members might 'dress up' their cars to drive around the town thus advertising the event. Jim O'Connell promised to supply a loud hailer to use from the vehicles!

On the playing front London Irish had queried the fixture against the club in Oxford on 20th December as this coincided with England's international with South Africa at Twickenham. Would the club prefer a morning kick off in London and go to the match in the afternoon? Oxford elected to stay at home with a 1pm kick off and Jim O'Connell was tasked with providing a television, preferably colour, so that both sides could watch the international match afterwards in the clubhouse. There were some incredulous looks from supporters when a chauffeur driven Mercedes arrived in the car park out of which got Tony O'Reilly, the Irish winger who had played in all four tests for the British Lions on the 1955 tour of South Africa, and the 1959 tour of New Zealand. A London Irish Committee member was quick to assure the on looking Oxford players and officials. "We don't pay for that!" he said. In what was described as one of the best games that the Bypass ground had seen Oxford beat London Irish for the third consecutive time, by 8–6. Falling behind to an early penalty the Oxford players, with O'Reilly in the centre and Irish international prop Ollie Waldron at prop against them, rallied and Dick Ovenall touched down for a try after Nigel Furley had kicked through with Ian Parsons kicking the conversion. Parsons later added a

*A great game at the Bypass to end the year! David Pitt holds on to the ball against London Irish with help on its way from Colin Evans, Ray Tapper and Lynn Evans.*

penalty to secure what was a big win for the club. It was a good day all round – England also beat South Africa 11–8.

Any Christmas warmth provided by the win against London Irish soon dissipated a few days later when a team weakened by 'flu travelled to play Bath on Boxing Day. Missing from the lineup were Liam McCarthy and Ray Tapper, a very rare absentee. Mike Florey stepped up to replace McCarthy, Lynn Evans moved to fly half and in the centre was Seretse Williams, a 17 year old Peers Schoolboy making his First team debut. It was a scrappy game in which Bath, with the dominant possession, commanded play although Oxford sparked for a short time in the second half when Bagnall passed to Furley from a five yard scrum for a try, Ian Ray kicked a drop goal and Parsons added a penalty. But all to no avail as Bath won 27–9. Back at the Bypass the Nomads entertained Oxford Old Boys who played a tight game, kicking for advantage when they could. In the second half Nigel Townsend broke and kicked ahead for Mick Honour to win the race and touch down for the Old Boys, the only score of the game.

If the alarm bells couldn't be heard at Bath they rang loud and clear at Weston-super-Mare twenty four hours later. Added to the 'flu victims were the inevitable injuries from the previous day and the Oxford team, always looking uncomfortable, suffered its heaviest defeat of the season, 9–35. If there was a bright side it was that Williams scored a try along with Alan Barraclough, another debutant, and another Peers Schoolboy, Alan Jenkins. At a Committee meeting on 30th December a question was asked regarding the Bath and Weston games which, it was said, were unfair to both players and officials alike. Roy Tapper said that the offer of a Bath fixture was too good an opportunity to miss especially as Bath had offered to pay a guarantee of £20. It was agreed that the Captain should write to Bath thanking them for the fixture, explaining selection problems and apologising for the absence of committee members due to 'flu.

On a brighter note, however, it was reported that the Boxing Day Ball had made for an excellent evening which had shown a small profit of £35 while the Christmas Draw had made £180. At this time the club was in credit to the tune of £493.

The club was about to enter the 1970s facing possibly the greatest challenge of its history. Eric Church announced that the rugby club was "now in a position to go ahead" with the takeover of the Oxford Sports Club. "We shall be buying on the basis that we discharge the sports club's liabilities and provided that the liabilities are within the bounds of the figures indicated – about £15,000 – the takeover will be on 28th February. The Rugby Club has agreed that we will pay The City of Oxford Hockey Club a sum of money of compensation for the work they have done for the club. The Tennis Section is going to take over the courts and some land and will become a separate entity. Money to take over the ground has come partly by loan from the Rugby Union, £5000 to be paid back over twenty years at 2% interest, a £500 loan from the Oxfordshire Rugby Memorial Trust Fund and with the help of well-wishers we think we can raise the necessary capital."

There was no doubt that this was a daunting task, to convert the whole undertaking into a viable concern but it was important for rugby in Oxfordshire that the club succeeded in the venture.

This also reflected on the Oxford Old Boys club whom it was thought would have to find a new ground. The club would be able to hire grounds around the city but, to maintain its status and success, would have to have a clubhouse and, with the shortage of available sites,

*Ollie Waldron is held by George Webb. David Pitt, Colin Evans, Roy Newton and Dick Ovenall get ready to pile in.*

the question of amalgamation with Oxford RFC being the wisest course ahead briefly raised its head.

By the time the club played its first game of the seventies on January 3rd the 'flu bug was on the wane which meant that selection was from strength. The result was a great 17–11 home win over Cross Keys with some spirited and imaginative rugby to come from behind twice. Seretse Williams scored the last of three tries for Oxford in only his third senior game, while a return to Wales to meet Maesteg the following week was cancelled due to bad weather conditions.

The President of the City of Oxford Hockey Club, which had previously been concerned about its future in having to move from its erstwhile home, announced that "owing to the uncertainty created by the takeover of the Oxford Sports Club by the Oxford Rugby Club, which necessitated the removal of the Hockey Club from the Bypass ground under the rules of the Rugby Union, the club announce that they have arranged for two pitches to be available at Horspath Road next season. Changing and appropriate tea rooms are available made possible by the willing cooperation of the Parks Superintendent. A new pitch will be laid in the centre of the running track in addition."

The fit and energetic students of Loughborough College were too much for Oxford who suffered a 3–21 defeat away from home. There was slight improvement the next week when Oxford played some good attacking rugby but paid dearly for defensive weaknesses in another defeat, this time 9–22 against St Bartholomew's Hospital. This weekend also marked the occasion of Oxford Old Boys first win of the season, 12–6 over Eton Manor, and Gosford All Blacks became the first club in the country to entertain and play against HMP Springhill, near Aylesbury. After permission from the Home Office the game, on a Sunday, was won 27–15 the day after the club had beaten Oxford Vikings 6–3.

On the injury front it was revealed that John Mawle had been forced to give up the game on medical advice. Following his neck injury in November he had been warned of the risk of permanent injury if he continued playing.

There was some good news with the selection of David Bagnall and George Webb as substitutes for the Southern Counties team to play South Africa at Gloucester. In the days before replacements were allowed during a match this meant that substitutes covered for the team against injury or illness during the build-up but then sat in the stand if not required. That is just what happened to Bagnall and Webb and was particularly disappointing for Webb as the selected hooker, Oxford Blue David Barry, had not played county rugby for two seasons. The Springboks played badly in front of a 12,000 crowd but, despite the inclusion of Moffatt and Simmie in the Counties team, won 13–0.

The final game of the South Africa Tour took place at Twickenham, the traditional match against the Barbarians, on Saturday 31st January. The Oxford club had arranged another of those morning kick offs to coincide this time against Wasps and, as often happened with Oxford, when faced with a hard task they excelled themselves. Sankey, Newton and Sharp were an effective back row but Oxford's best player was Ray Tapper, no doubt inspired by the surroundings of his former club. Despite continued concern over the lack of a recognised place kicker, Tapper sent over two penalties, missed one late in the game and was just wide with a drop goal in a very creditable 6–6 draw. The vogue continued with a 14–14 result at home to Bridgwater & Albion in a bad tempered affair after what had started as a good game.

Ron Salter, now a hard working Committee man, brought a proposal to the table which would see the club field transformed into a golf driving range, something he had seen at another club. The Committee were enthusiastic, agreed to go ahead with the idea and this venture was to bring some much needed revenue to the club at a financially sensitive time.

One of the club's Saturday night dances had been arranged for 14th February after the Abertillery game. It was not uncommon for the visitors coach to go empty to the Nurses home in Headington to collect those who had responded to the club's invitation. In this case time was short and it was noted that "Nurses are needed but if not available Committee members are invited to attend and make conversation."

Further afield, thirty two clubs were meeting to hammer out details of a new league system which was not an entirely new idea but, this time, the Rugby Union were believed to be sympathetic to the scheme.

The club had more strong fixtures lined up in the following two months but poor weather put paid to the visit of Abertillery. Maesteg were the next visitors to Oxford and a mistake by Martin Bampton at scrum half cost his side the game in which they at least deserved a draw. John Hopkins, understudy to the great Gareth Edwards in the Welsh set up, charged down Bampton's clearance kick, gathered and ran through to score and equal Furley's penalty and Stewart's try. The conversion kick saw Maesteg home 6–8. At home again an excellent display saw Kilgour score twice, both converted by Tapper, and Roy Newton added a try to the 13–3 win over Streatham. Oxford lost their grip on this match which was puzzling when it seemed they could take on some of the better sides and match them quite happily.

Although contracts still had to be signed, the long awaited takeover of the Oxford Sports Club took place, as predicted, at the end of February. There was no ceremony, just a handing over of the keys. There followed some strong words from Eric Church at the Annual Dinner, held on Thursday 5th March, when he said "Once the club has succeeded in acquiring the assets of the Oxford Sports Club they would be facing an annual deficit of nearly £1000. That has to be made up by hard labour by the rugby club. Unless we do that we shall be faced with becoming the Oxfordshire Nomads again and with an Oxfordshire Nomads fixture list." Oxfordshire RFU President Stan Oswin, himself a former Oxford RFC player, said "Quite frankly it is vitally important for rugby in this county that this club does not fail. It is important that this club should succeed and every member should be prepared to work hard not just for the season, but throughout the year. It has to become a centre where people will come instead of going to the local pub." One of the first actions of the new Bar Committee was to reduce the cost of a pint of beer!

The end of the winter was in sight but bad weather had always been just around the corner. The blizzards that had hit Oxfordshire during the week of the dinner had caused chaos locally and, despite the best efforts of committee and players who spent the Saturday morning of 7th March trying to clear the pitch of snow, the home match with Cambridge had to be called off which led to an impromptu game of football!

The run of home games continued with a 0–6 defeat against Pontypool, a 13–8 mid-week win against Birmingham University and, after being 0–6 behind Penarth, made a great come back to win 14–6. Ian Ray had one of his finest games for Oxford so far in this match, scoring all his sides points.

This was one of those years where Easter came early in the calendar and the club, always searching for better fixtures to improve its status and reputation, had arranged three hard games in South Wales. Based at the Queens Hotel in Cardiff, the team set out on Good Friday for a 6pm kick off with Glamorgan Wanderers where a lot of good chances were wasted in the 6–14 defeat. The following day the side travelled 'up the valley' to meet

*The long arm of the law! Or former long arm as Bob Sankey, having just left Thames Valley Police, reaches out to prevent an attack in the Oxfordshire Sevens against Loughborough Colleges.*

Pontypridd and, once more, Oxford were far too generous to the hosts. The home players showed a greater determination and were quicker thinking which brought another defeat, 8–18. Added to that, David Bagnall left the field with a badly torn hamstring. After a Sunday respite, Oxford gave a woefully inept display to lose the final match against Cross Keys, 9–12. Lynn Evans had given the side a two try lead but, once more, the side threw away golden chances. George Webb's absence had seen a late reshuffle of the Oxford pack and the injured Ray Mills was recalled to the back row. After the match his injuries were diagnosed as two broken ribs and he would miss the remainder of the season.

One of the social highlights of the tour was Treasurer John Rowell's dip in the sea at Porthcawl! It started over a lunchtime glass of beer at the Esplanade Hotel and, at first, it was to be a sponsored dip with a bonus for full immersion. Sometime later, having braved the bitterly cold wind to reach the deserted beach, conditions were so unpleasant that all bets were promptly called off. But John insisted and, against all advice and pressures, he stripped to his pants and sprinted fifty yards to the water for one of the briefest and bravest dips on record! After coffee, a drive back to Cardiff and a couple of hours in bed John was none the worse for his experience!

The Oxford team's performances on tour did little to help the club's ambitions and, back at home, matters were not improved when Henley received a letter from the club cancelling the match with Oxford Nomads due for Easter Monday. This had left no time for the home club to arrange another fixture and Tony Cooke, the Henley Press Officer asked "Have Oxford no use for the telephone? Henley are keen to play the Oxford club and the game would have been well supported. We feel that links between county clubs should be strengthened but the late cancellation is hardly the right way to go about things."

But rising above the despondency was the success of the Oxford Colts tour to Cornwall. The Colts players had raised funds by their own efforts through the season, including a

15 mile sponsored walk from the Gosford club in Kidlington to the Oxford clubhouse, to finance the approximate cost of £120 including £80 for a coach. The team, captained by Dick Surman and on the crest of a wave losing only four of their games in the season to that point, returned home unbeaten after games against Penryn, 28–26, Hayle, 26–8, and Camborne, 16–3. Surman also had the distinction of scoring the last try of the tour, against Camborne, which was well received.

The Oxford senior side was much changed through illness and injury, and frustration reigned when the team held Clifton to a nine point lead at the Bypass but with the wind at their backs could only score once in the second half, this a try after great interchange in the backs that saw Evans go over with Ian Ray converting. But penalties were given away, chances were wasted, and the side lost 5–9.

Despite summer months on the horizon April showers hit with a vengeance in what made for a very wet month. A churned up pitch in Manchester added little to place kicking and the home side hit Oxford hard in the first twenty minutes when the damage was done as the visitors found their feet in a 6–11 loss. Oxford made another poor start on another quagmire pitch, this time in London, against the Metropolitan Police. At 0–6 down Ian Ray made a brilliant break before passing to Tapper who kicked on for Roy Davies to gather up and score. Ray and Evans both kicked penalties but Oxford lost again, this time 9–16.

Finally, on 25th April, Oxford hosted the Cornish club Penryn, who also had a side in the Oxfordshire Sevens the following day. The date clashed with Oxford's appearance in the final rounds of the Middlesex Sevens, destined to effect selection of the club team. There had been a suggestion that the Penryn match be played on Friday evening with Penryn visiting Banbury on the Saturday but this did not materialise. On the day the Seven's team lost at Twickenham in the first round of matches when, slow off the mark, the side conceded fifteen points against St Luke's College, Exeter, and then pulled back ten which was not enough. At Oxford, in driving rain and on yet another quagmire pitch, the side gave a poor performance in losing 0–13 to Penryn in what developed into a forward battle.

This long, testing and historic season ground to an end with quarter final defeat against Loughborough Colleges in the Oxfordshire Sevens. The tournament was won by The Griffins who were really London Welsh in disguise, Welsh players not being allowed to play officially on a Sunday at that time.

At the Oxford Old Boys RFC Dinner which soon followed, President Denis Rosborough scotched rumours of any amalgamation with local clubs, saying "There has been talk of the Old Boys merging with Oxford. Our present policy is to stay as we are and to strengthen our financial position."

At the Annual Meeting in June, Eric Church acknowledged the closure of Oxford Sports Club in saying "It was unfortunate that the noble ideas, and spirit of self-help, which led to the formation of the Sports Club diminished with the passing of the years and in changing social conditions, so that in particular it had become difficult to find sufficient people to devote enough time to the Sports Club to make it a financial success." He went on to say that, having taken over the facility "already an encouraging revival of spirit in the Club is obvious."

A Golf Driving Range had been set up and a Groundsman had been employed to help run it as part of his duties. A number of ladies had spontaneously formed a Ladies Sub Committee, a Gala Day had been held at the club the previous summer and the £5 Draw continued to flourish under Jim O'Connell. The successful Club Dinner, Vice Presidents Dinner and the Christmas Draw had all been organised by David Bagnall's Sub Committee, and all these events brought income to the club.

John Rowell, Oxford's Treasurer, reported in June that the club still did not know the final settlement figure in taking the premises over and, although there was an excess of income over expenditure, warned "This club has to raise a lot of money in the next few years, not only to pay its way but to go ahead and improve facilities." Subscriptions were raised to 3 Guineas whilst the Vice President fee was a minimum of 1 Guinea.

Ray Tapper noted a disappointing end to the season from the Easter Tour onwards before which the season had been fairly satisfactory. There had been a lack of a reliable place kicker otherwise another eight or nine victories could have come the club's way despite the loss of a number of established players, but this had given opportunities to other players and the future looked bright. The worst performances had been saved for the Easter Tour which, he said, epitomised the attitude of certain playing members. A very cheap tour was made possible by the efforts of the usual club minded players and officials but was received with little gratitude by those players who consistently expected everything to be done for them, while the usual story of late cry offs had been a difficulty throughout the season.

The club was at a cross roads in its already long history and a united effort, both on and off the field, was very much needed if it was to establish itself as a top class rugby club. It did seem that there was much to look forward to!

# Chapter 6 – Up for the Cup!

The rugby community in the Oxford area and beyond were looking forward to celebrating the Centenary of the Rugby Football Union in the forthcoming season in what could only be a 'one-off' occasion. A number of events were planned and there was much anticipation with a Centenary Dinner for Oxfordshire clubs to be held in Christ Church Great Hall in December, the visit of two foreign rugby dignitaries from Ceylon and Spain, and a visit from the touring Fiji side to play Oxford University at Iffley Road amongst many other things on a much wider scale.

A very successful Gala had been held by the club on Spring Bank Holiday which had made £200 and thanks, in particular, were due to David Bagnall and Ray Mills.

## Season 1970–1971

Oxford's fixtures for the season had been reduced to a slightly more acceptable 35 in accordance with recently pronounced RFU policy and the First XV were due to play 17 home games with 18 away from home.

Lynn Evans was the new Oxford RFC Captain having been elected for a second time after a break of four years. Now aged 31 years Lynn had played for Cross Keys, Risca, the Royal Air Force and St Luke's College, Exeter before coming to Oxford in 1961. Lynn's previous season as Captain, in 1966–1967, had been an unlucky one for him with a pre-season injury and more in the season but he was now raring to go again. Asked what he felt was the biggest single factor in this very important year for the club, he said "For the players to accept the principle of team training. They must want to come along to these sessions because they can see and appreciate the value of them. We have had to lay down the principle that 1st and Nomad players must attend Thursday evening training sessions, but really the players should not feel that this is obligatory – they should feel it is worthwhile coming along because they want to improve team and unit skills. It is going to take time, a long time perhaps". He went on to say that the biggest aim was to beat the Welsh clubs at home and "down there". "The players are feeling that they are giving something to a rugby club which was not possible before because they were just part of a sports club" concluded Evans.

The coaching team was to consist of Lynn Evans, Vice Captain Martin Deighton, who would bring with him the experience of a year in New Zealand provincial rugby, with Emrys Harris mainly responsible for the Colts.

An innovation from the Oxfordshire RFU was the introduction of a Knockout Cup competition. Former County President Sam Miller was responsible for the arrangements and also for obtaining the cup, which was donated anonymously. At the Oxford RFC Committee in August it transpired that not all of the players wished to participate but all affiliated clubs in the county agreed to enter. This official competition was the first of its kind and would be a real step into the dark for local rugby clubs. At least Lynn Evans showed enthusiasm when he said "Obviously we would like to do well in the new Oxfordshire Knockout Cup, which I think is a good idea – and become the first winners."

Another innovation, this time brought to the club by Lynn Evans, was the introduction of Team Managers whose main duties would be to help with the behind-the-scenes administration. There would be two First XV Managers in John Deanes and Alun Davies,

*This Oxford RFC 7s team took part in the Abingdon RFC Tournament at the beginning of the season. Back row, l to r: R Newton, P MacFarlane, M Cook, R Sankey. Kneeling at front: R Mills, M Bampton, G Hand.*

the Nomads Manager would be John Gray, the Vikings, Danny Hughes and the Extra 'A', Charlie Ede. Dick Barley would manage the Colts.

There was much enthusiasm in the hard exchanges of a three period trial match before the opening fixture on 5th September, a home match with Stroud, where the club team made a sound start to the season with a 14–3 victory. The backs benefitted from good service from the forwards who outplayed their opponents and particularly outstanding was Roy Davies who scored two tries. What came in the next match, at Lydney, was something of a surprise – an 11–34 defeat, the heaviest in three years. The team did not arrive very early then found there were only thirteen shirts in the bag, had no time for a team talk and consequently made a bad start. There was hope for the future, however, in a fight back period in the second half when those 11 points were scored. Tackling, or lack of it, was a problem and there was still no place kicker. There was further dismay at County level when Oxfordshire entertained North Midlands in a 'warm-up' match, only to lose 3–44, which didn't bode well for the team's immediate future.

The draw for the first ever Oxfordshire Cup competition had given Oxford a trip to play against age old rivals, Banbury, on a Monday evening of all times two days after the Lydney match. Oxford officials were concerned that the date for the second round, should they reach it, had been fixed for a Monday again, 5th October. This was the usual busy time in Oxford's card with four possible matches in an eight day period and a fifth would hardly be consistent with the RFU's request to constituent bodies not to make too heavy a demand on players at the start of a season. Banbury did not now feature regularly on Oxford's list and relished the chance to meet old adversaries on equal terms but a revitalised Oxford, still smarting from the humiliating defeat two days earlier, turned on a splendid display of non-stop attacking rugby to defeat the gallant home side 19–3. Having held Oxford to 3 points in the first half Banbury wilted and conceded four tries in the second half, the best scoring chances coming from breaks by Ray Tapper.

On 26th September the Oxford club entertained guests who were delegates to the RFU Centenary Congress both before, with a tour of the City and lunch at the club, and after the home match with Aldershot Services. The match was a non-event and Oxford scored fifteen tries in a 55–3 romp that did not do either side much good.

*The club's first ever Oxfordshire Cup match was away against Banbury. Here, Dick Ovenall wins the lineout ball as George Webb, Ray Hance and David Fitzgerald-Lombard bind in watched by John Harwood (left) and Banbury's Colin Fairbrother and Richard Court.*

Five days later the team travelled the short distance to play another evening County Cup match, this time against Bicester in the Second Round. The home side played hard and never gave up, and Oxford had to match this enthusiasm, but steady pressure brought another eleven tries in another big score, this time 46–6, as the club progressed to the semi-finals due in a few months' time! With the return of Ray Hance the side seemed to have solved the place kicking problem with Hance adding five conversions and a penalty to those scored in previous games.

After the high scoring games reality came home to roost with the return of regular fixtures and the visit of Pontypridd on 3rd October. It was a see-saw struggle in an exciting game where both sides held the lead and Duncan Kilgour's try should have won it for Oxford but the home side dropped back and in the final five minutes Pontypridd scored twice to win 12–19.

There was no let up for some of the players and Oxfordshire, still smarting from defeat at the hands of North Midlands, suffered its heaviest loss in the Championship, 3–19, at home to Dorset & Wiltshire. Some Oxford players had difficulty in getting time off to play in the annual midweek against the Peter Carroll's XV, the University team in disguise, the following day and of those that did four had played the county the previous day. But, crucially, it was a new recruit making a dream debut for the club that turned a hard match in Oxford's favour. Brian Williamson had played for Pontypridd on Oxford's Easter Tour in March but was now stationed at the Royal Air Force base in Abingdon. He was truly a 'flying winger' scoring two tries, the second in injury time, which added to a Lynn Evans penalty goal, sealed a hard fought 9–8 victory and a great boost for the club.

Despite encouraging progress in the wins and losses column several factors led to inconsistency in club selection and hardly ever did the team selected early in the week take the field at the weekend. The club had attracted a handful of experienced players from local RAF stations but these players were often unavailable due to Command team matches both in this country and Germany. Injuries played a key part, as always, and the club was also operating a 'no train, no play' policy to improve and raise team spirit which, by and large, concentrated the attention of most players, although one or two fell foul, and was admirable where and when practicable.

A regular front row had materialised however with John Harwood and Roger Powell propping George Webb and even this was disrupted when Webb was selected for the South in the 10–8 defeat of the touring Fiji at Bournemouth on 11th November. For George this was quite an honour. The Fijians were making only their second European Tour, the first being to Wales and France in 1964, and this was part of the Rugby Union Centenary celebrations while, many miles away, Fiji was celebrating its independence. But nothing was sacrosanct and a month later even Webb was dropped for failing to train prior to the home game with Cross Keys. His replacement, 'Tug' Wilson from RAF Abingdon had a most unhappy afternoon and hardly won any scrummage ball, which contributed to a home 12–19 defeat against what was generally acknowledged to be the worst team in Wales at that time. This promoted debate in a situation where the club would be judged on results and not adherence to domestic discipline.

Added to this the club was attempting to find the best second row combination with three players, Dick Ovenall, Mike Gibbard and David Pitt all vying for two places, while at scrum half David Bagnall's attack of Lumbago saw Alan Barraclough promoted from the Nomads on a number of occasions.

In many respects the club was fortunate to have a good standard Colts team to fall back on and it was an advantage to be able to 'blood' some of them in the circumstances. Seretse Williams was a prime example of this and he found himself in the same back division as Lynn Evans, his Sports Master at Peers School, when scoring the winning try against St Mary's Hospital in London, and this after playing for his school team in the morning! But there was also a cloud on the horizon in this respect when it became known that Headington Secondary School had no fixtures arranged this year and would no longer be playing rugby. This was a sad change by a school that had produced three England Under 15 Internationals in George Webb, Martin Ponty and Brian Beale in recent years. Some other schools were set to follow and much of this was put down to the 'phenomenal rise' of soccer after the success of Oxford United who were presently in Division Two of the Football League. Other

*Oxford RFC 1970–1971. Back row, l to r: RJ Hance, M Deighton, G Webb, R Ovenall, RF Newton, M Grant, RGA Sankey, T Lombard, J Deans (Team Manager). Front row, l to r: NCW Furley, A Stewart, RP Tapper, LR Evans (Capt), DF Bagnall, J Thomas, DS Kilgour.*

considerations came from the rumblings of industrial dispute within the Teachers Union over pay and conditions which would have far reaching implications when the more militant members were to withdraw their support for school rugby teams, amongst other after school activities, training and playing after school hours. Many of these schools had traditionally provided many readymade players to local clubs over a long period of time and the clubs would be left with the dilemma of who was going to teach local youths to play the game into the future!

The Oxfordshire County team had failed to reach the knockout stages of the Championship for the third season in succession and had used 42 players in the six games played, which included two 'warm ups'. The playing record of 1 game won, 2 drawn and 4 lost brought a comment from Ron Grimshaw in the *Sports Mail*: "There are players about (who might represent the County in the next few years) but while they languish in the low/middle class rugby of Banbury, Chinnor, Marathons and Old Boys they will never speed or sharpen up to County Championship standard."

The Oxford club team was not having things its own way in attempting to maintain standards in their higher grade of rugby. There did seem to be a difference between the Hospital sides and the more resilient Welsh clubs that had appeared on the fixture list but this wasn't so apparent when the strong Abertillery visited in December. The players gave their most spirited display of the season so far to spring a big surprise with a 20–14 win after finding themselves five points behind at half time. This deserved win was down to consistent forward drive and power where Martin Deighton's aggressive leadership paid off, coupled with relentless covering and tackling in defence. It was a different story, however, the following week when Oxford crashed to an 8–42 defeat at Metropolitan Police, remarkable in the fact that the side showed only two changes from the Abertillery victory, one of those being pack leader Deighton who had failed to train in the week. The team was a shadow of that from the previous week. This did not bode well for the run-in to Christmas and another away match, this time at Sunbury against London Irish. Oxford, although showing

*Graham Barrett robs a Cross Keys opponent, with Seretse Williams in support, in the 12–19 home defeat.*

*Dick Ovenall, Seretse Williams, John Thomas, Dave Pitt and Colin Evans close in around the fallen Cross Keys player.*

improvement, failed in a bid for their fourth successive win over the exiles, who scored their twelfth win in a row, by 13–27. But this did leave the club with respectable mid-season figures of having won nine and lost seven games to date, excluding the two county cup matches.

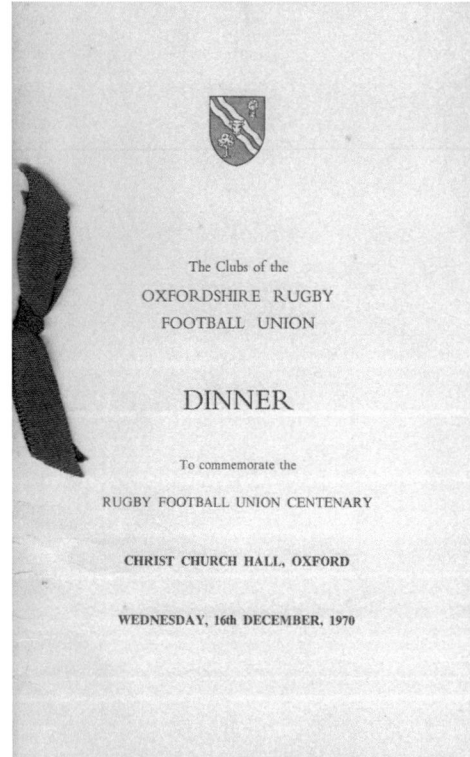

A highlight in December was the dinner held in the regal surroundings of the Great Hall of Christ Church to celebrate the Rugby Football Union Centenary and was attended by over 300 representatives of clubs affiliated to the Oxfordshire Rugby Union. Described as a perfect setting, the tables were individually lit and bore attractive hand painted club and county shields and diners heard the President of the RFU, Mr WC Ramsey, say that the RFU "had an obligation to the world, particularly if we want our outlook of amateurism to survive." There was, however, some ribald behaviour, and some of the shields disappeared during the evening. Bruce Moffatt, the County President, was later to say how bitter and hurt he was "that a certain section made such pigs of themselves. It was a poor show for these people to have marred the evening for so many others." Efforts to get the shields returned proved unsuccessful.

*The Menu Card from Oxfordshire's RFU Centenary Dinner 1970.*

On the home front the hall at the club ground, dull, scarred and faded for some years with paint flaking from the walls and ceiling, was completely redecorated in six days by a working party of volunteers. This was completed in time for the clubs Christmas Carol evening and there was an open invitation for people to 'come and see', without danger of damage to motor vehicles as the approach road had also been repaired!

The club bar, now run by voluntary staff, was open every evening including Sundays and Sunday lunch times. This now helped to provide valuable income for the club and the price of Light Ale and Brown Ale was reduced from 1/6d to 1/4d (7p!) per bottle. Another innovation was that of a Ladies Committee who, amongst other things, took responsibility for ordering and maintaining crockery, the production of flags and curtains and even ran a popular lingerie party.

England remained well down the pecking order on the international scene and the late 1960s and 1970s were particularly bleak for the national side. Added to what is now seen as a haphazard, almost senseless selection policy, there was no internal structure, apart from the County Championship, to bring players through to the required standard having been raised on what might be seen as meaningless friendly fixtures, were there such a thing as a friendly fixture! The overseers of the game were steadfast in the belief that any move to competition rugby at any level would lead to the fall of amateurism. Following discussions with the thirty seven leading clubs, the Rugby Football Union ignored the views and opinions before them and decided to go ahead with plans for a national knockout competition in the 1971–1972 season. At a local level this gave added incentive to the four clubs left in the Oxfordshire competition as the winners would go forward to play off with other county winners in the Southern Group for a place in the national qualifying round in November.

Although there seemed to be a tougher half season fixture list waiting, Oxford made a good start to 1971 with wins against Rhymney and Esher in contrasting fortunes. The team made hard work in beating Rhymney, down to fourteen players after an injury to Captain Russell Shurmer, 18–14 in a frustrating display but gave the exact opposite performance away at Hersham against Esher. All the forwards joined in fast handling movements with astonishing pace and there were six tries most, as usual, initiated by Ray Tapper at fly half.

Loughborough Colleges exposed hesitancy in Oxford's defence and although the home team did not play badly there were too many basic errors and Martin Bampton's slow service with a greasy ball did nothing for Tapper, already hampered with a strapped right thigh, in the 6–22 loss.

But it all came good with a fine all round 15–13 game against St Bartholomew's Hospital, the current Hospital's Cup holders, in London when the side was able to resist a late recovery. The front row of Harwood, Webb and Deighton were well to the fore in the wind and rain. The club planned on selecting the same team for the away match at Bridgwater & Albion on 30th January which meant that the Nomads, due to play at the same venue, would also be strong with several experienced players trying to get back into the team. The First XV selected for the trip was: NCW Furley; DS Kilgour, LR Evans (Capt), JS Sempill, SA Williams; RP Tapper, MJH Bampton; JS Harwood, G Webb, ME Deighton, MJ Gibbard, DH Pitt, PM Long, JD Heydon, RF Newton, while the Nomads team was: A Stewart; GFG Barrett, RJ Tapper, PRE McFarland, P Ladkin; B Richardson, A Barraclough (Capt); JF Mawle, P Webb, R Powell, RJ Ovenall, R McCarthy, RGA Sankey, M Florey, P Dedrick. But these games were cancelled due to the Somerset pitches being unfit.

The week off was more of a hindrance than a help to the Oxford team which suffered a surprise 16–25 defeat at Birmingham after an inconsistent performance in heavy conditions.

There was a boost for the team that travelled to old opponents Nuneaton with the return of John Mawle to the front row. The tough forward pack leader had retired from playing on medical advice with a neck injury a year previously but had started playing again through the Oxford Thursday team and then the lower sides at the club. The players were to claim 'daylight robbery' in the 8–10 defeat when two groundings were disallowed in another game they could have clearly won.

Another boost came when David Bagnall was named in the team to meet Maesteg at the Bypass after a twelve game absence due to an injury received against Maesteg in November. He replaced Martin Bampton, while Phil Dedrick was recalled to the flank. The biggest crowd of the season braved the rain lashed ground to see Oxford meet one of the most successful clubs in Wales. There was despair when mistakes and a badly missed tackle cost the game, 0–6, and victory escaped once again. It was a different story the following week however. Never at their best in morning kick offs, Oxford were unimpressive in losing 6–17 at Streatham before the party moved on to see England draw 14–14 with France at Twickenham.

Oxford was now fielding its biggest, strongest pack in years but the power and potential was not being realised. The players lacked cohesion and were not 'ball hungry' in the rucks and mauls, while one or two didn't tackle and this posed the question as to whether they were too big and too heavy? Another defeat came at Cambridge, this time 6–14, and Oxford made changes in an attempt to end the five game sequence of defeats. Bagnall was moved to full back, Bampton was reinstated at scrum half with Mike Gibbard returning to the second row and these changes seemed to do the trick as Oxford beat Clifton at home 15–0, thanks to four Evans penalties and a Bampton try.

Lynn Evans missed his first game of the season and there were several other changes for the mid- week match at home to Birmingham University and the club team was badly exposed by the students after two excellent tries from Sempill and Kilgour, in a surprise

*Oxford RFC Nomads 1970–1971. Back row, l to r: J Gray (Team Manager), J Ward, R Powell, M Gibbard, J Harwood, R McCarthy, P Dyson, R Thornthwaite, K Hillyer. Front row, l to r: M Hughes, RJ Tapper, C James, A Barraclough (Capt), R Flisher, G Hand, H Sharp.*

11–22 defeat. This was followed by two trips to Wales at the end of March where Oxford lost on consecutive Saturdays, to Penarth and Cross Keys, before beating Old Haberdashers 33–11 in a welcome home win.

On 20th March came the news that Oxford RFC had completed the purchase of the ground and buildings at the Bypass for a figure approaching £15,000. This was made possible by a loans of £5000 from the RFU (£2000 in excess of the usual maximum loan), £1500 from the brewers, and £500 from the Oxfordshire RFU Memorial Trust Fund. The club had helped themselves by selling the Oxford Sports Tennis Club their courts and land for a pavilion at the bargain price of £1250. The final figure also included £500 compensation to the City of Oxford Hockey Club while the club was also awaiting news of an application for a Government grant to improve existing buildings.

*Club Chairman Eric Church was still active on the field. Here he prepares to Referee the Oxford Thursday XV (Ray Tapper) against Abingdon (John Eyre).*

This heralded the Easter Tour where Oxford broke with tradition and ventured west to Cornwall for the first time. The journey to the party's accommodation in Camborne took up most of Good Friday and one and a half hours after booking in the team ran out to play Penryn, ten miles away. At least half of both teams were county players and Penryn had been regarded as unofficial Cornish Champions for several previous seasons. Oxford gave an excellent display but travel fatigue told in the closing stages. Evans scored Oxford's only try to add to Alan Barraclough's long range drop goal, and seven kicks at goal were missed as Oxford went down 6–8 in a fast game. Easter Saturday dawned in brilliant spring sunshine as the party made the short journey to Falmouth. Playing open running rugby Oxford scored four tries through Roy Davies, Martin Deighton, Nigel Furley and Ray Tapper to give the side its first win on the road, 12–8. This was Oxford's first win on any tour since 1963 in Ireland, the year that Captain Lynn Evans joined the club. Falmouth made a come-back but not enough to trouble the tourists whose lack of a kicker was again exposed. Duncan Kilgour's overhead catch from Seretse Williams' cross kick, and sprint for the line was the highlight of Oxford's 14–5 win over Camborne. This added to tries from Roy Davies and Hugh Sharp before the party headed for home after its successful trip to the Duchy.

The tour results instilled a great spirit in the party and only two enforced changes were made for the visit of St Helen's on 17th April. The Oxford team was inspired by 19 points from the boot of Lynn Evans and played some excellent rugby to win 28–11 but there was sadness when the side was reduced to fourteen players after David Bagnall had to leave the field with a broken left arm.

At a time when the players would perhaps be dusting their boots down and thinking of the beach, there was unfinished business in the shape of the Oxfordshire Cup. Very much in its infancy the various rounds had been stuck into the season where they could be. On the grounds of neutrality the first semi-final, between Chinnor and Henley, took place at the Bypass with a relatively comfortable 16–3 win for Henley. The following evening, Thursday 21st April, at Marston Ferry Road, Oxford played well with sense and control for fifteen minutes against Oxford Marathon but this was enough to put them through to the final. It was touch and go in an exciting finish to a close and hard game where the Marathon forwards gave a good display with speed and drive to harass Oxford into errors. Oxford, ten points clear with as many minutes to go, relaxed almost fatally but another penalty from Mick Groom and a Fred Bannister try at the final whistle was not enough for the Maras.

And so dawned the first ever Oxfordshire County Cup Final – a Thursday evening actually, with a 6.30pm kick off on 28th April at the University ground in Iffley Road. Oxford fielded a big, mobile pack but the star of the game was Ray Tapper with three tries as the side eventually ran away with the game. It was not a great final but there was plenty of excitement with Roy Tapper, Alan Barraclough and Nigel Furley also adding a try each in the 28–6 win. Henley scored a consolation try through Steve Gough. The Oxford team on this historic rugby occasion was: A Barraclough; NCW Furley, RJ Tapper, LR Evans (Capt), DS Kilgour; RP Tapper, MJH Bampton; JF Mawle, G Webb, R Powell, JS Harwood, DJ Heydon, B Sharp, R Davies, RF Newton.

*Victorious Captain Lynn Evans leads the singing back at the clubhouse.*

*Oxford RFC became the first winners of the Oxfordshire Cup when they beat Henley, 28–6. The players in celebratory mood are: back row, l to r: J Mawle, R Newton, R Davies, J Higgins (President), A Barraclough, J Deans (Team Manager), R Powell, RP Tapper (waving the cup!), LR Evans, J Harwood, D Kilgour, RJ Tapper, G Webb. Front row, l to r: H Sharp, N Furley, M Bampton, D Heydon.*

The general feeling was that the cup competition had provided fresh stimulus, interest and support for the game in Oxfordshire. A Marathon forward was quoted as saying: "At least we have proved we are the only club in the County capable of giving Oxford a game and a much better one than a lot of clubs on their fixture list", while another said "What a good thing it would be for the county team if all clubs co-operated to loan players to Oxford so that the best talent in the county would have the opportunity of regularly playing together in good class football". This, of course, was where we came in twenty two years previously and was one of the prime objectives behind the formation of the Oxford club but, as local affiliations and loyalties ran high, the whole scheme quickly went sour largely through misunderstanding of the basic idea.

As the dust settled a club team lost in the Preliminary Rounds of the Middlesex Sevens having earlier made no progress beyond the second round of the Oxfordshire Sevens, celebrating twenty five years, on 17th April.

During the season Oxford had taken the momentous step of becoming a rugby club in its own right. It had led the way locally with moderate success and in winning 21 games had scored a record 606 points while, in losing 17 games, had conceded 507, also a record. Missing just one game Captain Lynn Evans topped the scorers chart with 160 points in 37 appearances to show how much the club was indebted to him both on and off the field. Ray Tapper made one appearance less giving excellent service to the club and all this laid a firm base for a successful future in what had been a very full and memorable RFU centenary season.

## Season 1971–1972

There was little respite for the followers of the great game in the summer of 1971. At the end of the previous season attention quickly turned to the imminent British Lions Tour of New Zealand from which much was expected. Wales had won a 'Grand Slam' and provided the party with the majority from the Home Unions. John Dawes, the Captain, was also Welsh and had imposed his own style of running and counter attacking from broken play on both the national side and his club side, London Welsh. The Assistant Manager/Coach was the visionary Carwyn James and these two led a team of keen and willing 'disciples' to a 2–1 Test series win against the All Blacks, the first time this had been achieved by the Lions touring side.

By the time the Fourth Test had been played, to a 14–14 draw, on 14th August, Oxford club players had been training under the wings of Oxford United Trainer Ken Fish on Tuesday evenings and former Richmond wing forward Paul Charteris on Thursday evenings, for some weeks. After such a promising season in 1970–71 Oxford had a lot to look forward to. Having helped to lay a strong base both on and off the field from which to look ahead Lynn Evans resigned the captaincy due to his being away on a course for the first part of the season. The new captain was David Bagnall who joined in the pre-season training despite not having fully recovered from breaking his arm in April. Lock forward David Pitt was named as Vice Captain.

The club had further strengthened its fixture list with matches against Preston Grasshoppers and Liverpool while Old Merchant Taylors and Taunton were back on the list after several years absence. As County Champions, Oxford had a match with Aylesbury in early October to aim at. This was to be the first of several regional knock out matches to determine who would go through to play in the newly conceived National Knock Out Cup. As a result of these protracted matches, where Oxford might make progress, the club was exempted from the early rounds of the Oxfordshire Cup through to the semi-final. This was a temporary arrangement and all county cup games would be played on Sundays.

Another important feature of the new season was that the value of scoring a try had been increased from three points to four in an attempt to encourage and reward attacking rugby, and Oxford featured in the game where the first four point try in the country was scored when they accepted to play away at Coventry on Wednesday 1$^{st}$ September. Unfortunately the try was against them as they went down to a 3–44 defeat against a club side that contained six current and past England internationals. Playing on the evening that followed hard club trials, Oxford were no way prepared both physically or psychologically for such a tough fixture with some of the players just returned from holiday at the weekend, while Coventry had trained together for two months. It wasn't all doom however as the Coventry club presented Oxford with a cheque worth £30 for 'expenses'.

The disappointment continued three days later with a home defeat, 4–27, to Nuneaton where Oxford's only try was scored by Bob Stevenson, recently returned from his Singapore posting, after an opening from Roy Davies. Matters weren't much better at Stroud the following week in a 12–47 defeat, where Oxford's lack of fitness was leading to some awful defensive weaknesses.

Oxford had shipped 118 points in losing the first three games of the campaign, albeit against pretty formidable opposition, and the player's general fitness had been questioned. There was hope of better things with the return of Coach, Paul Chateris from holiday, which was expected to make a difference together with the return of Captain David Bagnall. Other players were due to return to the fold although some present incumbents were due to leave for University in October.

The next game, away at Old Merchant Taylors, proved to be something of a turning point although the hosts were not as strong as had been expected. Oxford made six changes bringing Mike Florey, Phil Dedrick and Mike Gibbard into the pack while Kit Brownless, a former Oxford University player who had joined the club only the previous week, came in for his debut on the wing. Ray Tapper captained the side again in the absence of David Pitt who was missing with an ear infection. In a much improved performance Oxford scored seven tries with the dominant pack giving the backs many chances to excel in the 35–7 win, a result that gave much encouragement. Hooker Alan Jenkins, another product of Peers School rugby, scored a try and Brownless scored four on his debut after which he was promptly named, along with six other Oxford players, in the losing Oxfordshire team that played North Midlands in a pre-Championship trial at Moseley.

Oxford continued in the Military Stadium against Aldershot Services where the side held on to an early lead to win 24–14. On field rugby was rapidly improving and a 30–13 win came when Tredegar were on the receiving end of Oxford's biggest and best win to that point against Welsh opposition in a fast moving game. More good news came in that David Bagnall made his seasonal debut, in the Vikings side against Culham College, his first game since injury in April.

And so, on the very next day, came a moment of reckoning for Oxford. The first of a series of qualifying matches in the National Knockout Cup at Aylesbury, against whom the club would not have normally considered a First XV fixture, now had a great deal at stake. Preparation was not good with the team, showing just one change from that which had faced Tredegar, having played an exhausting match the previous day with no recovery time for the players. It was little surprise that Oxford struggled and only got the upper hand in the last part of a match where frustration and anxiety were to the fore. Trailing 4–7, Lynn Evans made a crucial break through when he gathered up a loose ball to score, and fullback Alan Stewart added the try that took Oxford clear, Nigel Furley having scored earlier, for the 14–7 win.

This was the last match for full back Alan Stewart, who left the club having taken a position in Nottingham, so Bagnall's return to action in the 13–10 Vikings win at Culham was timely, and he found himself in the vacant full back position for the mid-week match against Owen Jones' University Captains XV. There was another significant change in that hooker Alan Jenkins had also left the club in a bid to win a Blue and he, having played twice for Oxford in the weekend previous, now found himself facing his former team mates three days later! Martin Ponty, a former England schoolboy international, was drafted into Oxford's front row for his first senior game for two seasons, mainly due to injury. Lynn Evans was also missing having started a course in London. These disruptions had an effect on the side whose run of success came to an end in a 3–39 defeat where the University side denied Oxford any great possession in the loose and lineouts although Ponty gave a good account of himself in the scrums. Another defeat followed, 6–28, this time at home to Bridgwater a few days later.

A quickly convened players meeting agreed to relax the 'no train – no play' rule to allow Lynn Evans, who was now away from Oxford during the week on a course, to play at the weekends. This was a strange turn of events as it was Lynn who had had to enforce the rule the previous season when he was Captain!

As if Oxford players weren't getting enough rugby, six were selected for the opening County Championship match against Berkshire in midweek. Nigel Furley, John Harwood, Dick Ovenall, Phil Dedrick, George Webb – after only two games in Oxford's lower sides, and Lynn Evans with a special dispensation, featured in a dramatic win by a try to nil at Newbury where Dedrick forced himself over in the corner, with four minutes left to play in the rain and mud.

The Oxford team was lifted with news of John Mawle's return to the side for the home match with Glamorgan Wanderers on 16th October. Tapper intercepted, in the incessant biting rain, to give his side a 4–0 half time lead and Evans landed two penalty goals in the 10–0 win but it was not a happy return for Mawle who was stretchered off to hospital near the end with an ugly head wound.

The team showed three changes for the next qualifying round of the National Cup in Hertfordshire against Old Verulamians the next day. Two penalties and a drop goal from Evans gave Oxford a lead but it was not easy against a determined home side that fought back. Dedrick's try off the back row against his old club gave some comfort before Evans chipped ahead for Furley to touch down and Oxford eventually won 17–13 to progress in the competition.

Guy's Hospital proved to be spirited opponents on their visit to the Bypass ground but lost an absorbing contest 14–16 as Evans and Tapper scored all of Oxford's points. This time seven Oxford players were selected for Oxfordshire in the midweek clash with Dorset & Wiltshire. Of those seven there were three, Duncan Kilgour the Captain just returning from a six week injury after playing sevens, George Webb playing in Oxford's lower sides, and Dick Ovenall, who disliked Sunday rugby and had lost his place, who were not currently playing in the First XV. Powell, Fox, Dedrick and Harwood were those expected to continue top form. In the event Oxfordshire had an easy victory over the present champions, 33–14.

There was much heated discussion in the clubhouse during the ensuing week. Two wins in the regional qualifying rounds had seen Oxford reach the Southern Area Final, due to

*Spot the ball! An absorbing lineout picture with, l to r, Phil Dedrick, John Harwood, Dyson Heydon, Nigel Fox, Mike Gibbard, Garth Lewis, Dick Ovenall and Martin Ponty about to spring into action while scrum half Alan Barraclough awaits the outcome.*

be played at the Bypass on Sunday 31st October, against REME Arborfield. Just a year previously the Rugby Football Union had been under pressure to introduce league rugby but had, instead, introduced a cup competition the reception of which had been luke warm. However, in that time it had been surprising just how much interest was generated and some clubs were now cancelling Saturday fixtures or fielding weakened sides in an attempt to keep players fresh for Sunday cup games. This practise was seen as not being in keeping with the spirit of rugby but, against that, there were now financial considerations to think about depending on how far a club progressed. It was known that the winners of the regional final would play away against London Welsh in the First Round proper and this provided a big dilemma for Oxford officials. It was accepted that Oxford's fixture list, strengthened over many years, was the best in the area and yet a fixture against REME Arborfield, another club that Oxford would not normally have entertained on their list, could cause just such a conflict with a fixture against old and valued rivals, Lydney. And yet this was the situation for the coming weekend. Finally, after a selection meeting that lasted for over two hours, club officials decided to withdraw the First XV from the trip to Lydney in preparation for the Sunday cup match and sent a strong Nomads side to fulfil the Saturday fixture. There was no question of Oxford cancelling the match and the Lydney club, who declined Oxford's suggestion of a midweek match later in the season, were made aware of the circumstances.

The weakened side gave a good account of themselves and, although outgunned, scored two tries in a 10–36 defeat while the club's cup team trained at the home ground. Despite the preparation, Sunday's cup match was a desperately close affair. The Army side was a fit bunch of players obviously intent on making a name for themselves. Oxford monopolised possession in the first half but had only a penalty goal from Nigel Furley to show for it. REME sensed the chance to go ahead and, inspired by their Berkshire scrum half David Spawforth, took the lead with a try from close in after a short penalty. Oxford were made to chase the game and, three minutes before the final whistle, the Oxford pack won the

*Nigel Furley kicks his side ahead with a penalty against REME Arborfield watched by John Mawle, David Bagnall, David Pitt, Nigel Fox, Jeff Thomas and Garth Lewis.*

ball against the head for the seventh time, Bagnall threw a long pass to Tapper who kicked diagonally for Duncan Kilgour to fractionally beat the defence to the touch down the match winning try. There was much relief in the clubhouse after the match, Oxford having reached the last thirty two clubs in the National Cup and a plum away draw to arguably the best club side in the country at that time, London Welsh.

The Oxford side was in great spirit after the cup win, especially the forwards who hoped to reproduce some of the same form against Maesteg at home but, despite a late rally were beaten 17–21 in a keen, fluctuating struggle. Nine Oxford players helped the county team to entertain Hertfordshire in the midweek in what was 'billed' as a Championship decider but, with both teams having won their previous two outings, it was Oxfordshire who made mistakes and the side went down by 6–19.

Oxford followed this with two wins, against St Thomas' Hospital, 20–3, and US Portsmouth, 17–12, with varying displays of form while, once again, there was some drama as the cup weekend approached. The club fully intended to play the scheduled home Saturday fixture against London Hospital and selected a side where all but two had played in the first string in this season. Teams were also announced for the Nomads, Vikings and 'A' teams. The team selected to play against London Welsh, whom Oxford had beaten 9–5 the last time the teams had met in 1965, was to meet on the Saturday morning for a final training session. Late in the week, however, London Hospital called to say that they were not prepared to travel to play an Oxford reserve side. Further, they would lodge an official protest with the Rugby Football Union.

In reality Oxford had no chance of defeating London Welsh who named twelve Internationals in their side, six of them members of the recent best-ever British Lions tourists. The club, determined to do well, were looking beyond the match knowing that a good performance would give them a lever when trying to raise standards and improve the fixture list. David Bagnall, Captain, said "We're working hard to persuade smaller clubs in

*London Welsh v Oxford match programme.*

the County to send on promising players to us on the basis that Coventry, Bristol and Gloucester work. That way Oxford could become a club of genuine first class ranking one day. If the players don't make the grade with us they would still return to their junior clubs as better footballers."

There was a change after Tuesday night's training when David Pitt, who had been selected, did not appear and was replaced by Mike Gibbard. Young prop forward Nigel Fox who, three times a week persuaded his parents to drive him from Brackley to Oxford for training and games, faced a 'bitter-sweet' decision. He choose to face London Welsh with Oxford and, as Captain of the Oxfordshire Youth team due to meet Middlesex in a Championship match on the Saturday, lost his place in the team and the captaincy.

The match attracted a lot of interest locally and four coaches were booked to take supporters to the game as well as many others making their own way. 25 shillings (£1.25) was the cost of the trip which included travel both ways, a ticket into the ground, stand, and clubhouse afterwards, and a 'doggy-bag' lunch and rosette in club colours

*David Bagnall gets the ball away despite being hassled by London Welsh scrum half, Willie Hullin.*

prepared by the club's Ladies Committee.

It was a first, too, for London Welsh who were required to obtain special dispensation from the Welsh Rugby Union to play on a Sunday, the first 'Welsh' club to do so.

Not surprisingly Oxford made a nervous start in front of a reported crowd of 3,500, the largest gathering most of the team would have encountered, and the team conceded two early tries before slick play from the Welsh took then to a 26–0 half time lead. It did seem that the plucky visitors were in for a hiding but an outstanding second half display won

*Great Holiday entertainment was provided by the visit of the South African 'Proteas' to play Oxfordshire. Lynn Evans (Oxford) collects an offload from the fallen Micheal Douch (Bedford).*

Oxford many friends. While the side were never going to recoup the deficit Lynn Evans clawed back three points with a 35 yard penalty goal and Ray Tapper added a drop goal. Oxford camped in the London Welsh half for twenty minutes and nearly scored twice. Evans kicked through for Duncan Kilgour to chase and touch down but his attempt was disallowed by the unsighted referee before Evans, again, was hunted down by Gerald Davies and his inside pass was slightly knocked on by the supporting Ray Tapper in the act of diving over the line. London Welsh had the last word when Merv 'The Swerve' Davies scored the sixth and final try. Oxford took great pride in having won the second half 6–4 and the club received a cheque for £478 as half of the gate receipts.

The same Oxford team travelled to Pontypool the following week to face a team captained by the erstwhile Wales captain, Terry Cobner, fresh back from injury. For Oxford it was a case of 'after The Lord Mayor's Show' and the 0–27 defeat reflected that. But confidence was restored and a 22–10 home win over St Mary's Hospital put the players in good spirits for the visit of London Irish on 18th December. It was a tough match as the forwards squared up to each other but Lynn Evans was the hero with a try, two penalties and two conversions while Oxford, as a team, showed some quality to deserve their fourth win, 18–6, in the last five meetings between the two clubs.

The club had no games over the Christmas period, which fell over a weekend, but club members were well catered for when the Nomads entertained and beat Oxford Old Boys, 21–9, on Boxing Day morning. Attention was then centred on Iffley Road where eight Oxford players had been selected for the Oxfordshire team that was to take on the South Africa Rugby Federation side known as 'The Proteas' in the afternoon. The Proteas were on a ground breaking six match tour in England, being the first Cape Coloured team to do so, and they went on to delight the fair sized crowd with six tries in their 35–20 win. The Africans were much sharper and quicker on to the loose ball and there was little doubt about

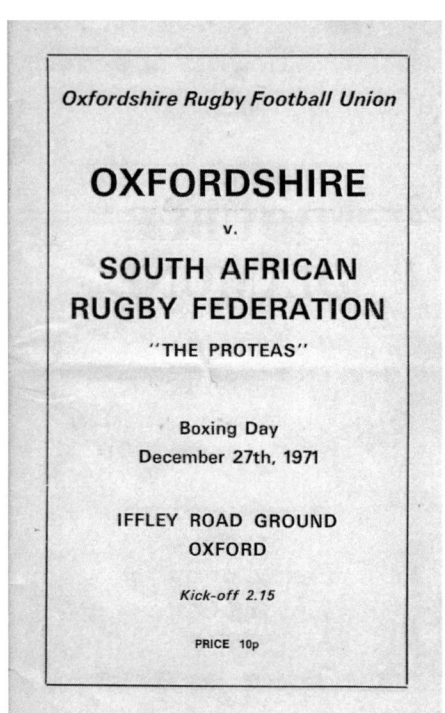

*Oxfordshire v South African Rugby Federation match programme 1971.*

the result once they had taken the lead despite four Oxfordshire tries in reply. Although the Proteas won just two of their tour fixtures there was little doubt that this historic occasion played a small part in helping to break down barriers back home. The players would have learnt a great deal from the experience and one of them, Errol Tobias, went on to win six caps for South Africa when the country was still following a policy of apartheid.

Oxford ended 1971, the half way stage in this season, having won 12 games and losing 9 with a high total of points against accounted for, in part, by the increased value of a try. After the disastrous start to the season when 118 points had been conceded in losing the first three games, the side recovered well to reach the first round of the National Cup and then defeated London Irish.

To describe Oxford's start to 1972 as unlucky would be something of an understatement. Lock forward Mike Gibbard had broken his nose in Oxfordshire's December defeat against Buckinghamshire which, incidentally, had ended that team's Championship hopes once again. With one nostril completely closed he had played again for the club but, not surprisingly, found breathing to be difficult and had been advised by his doctor not to play again. Liam McCarthy's 'on-off' affair with London Irish was back on again and, despite an on-going shoulder injury, elected to take the road to the Capital once again. Against all this Ray Tapper's leg was now out of plaster and he was now able to resume light training.

Oxford began the year with the long journey of over 100 miles to Cross Keys in South Wales to enter a debate as to whether the proposed game should take place or not on the muddy and water logged pitch. An earlier decision could have saved the trip! This led to a much delayed start and a 'game' under inadequate floodlights. In the circumstances Oxford adapted themselves commendably in the atrocious conditions but lost by the odd point, 7–8.

A tough away match against a fit and fast running Loughborough Colleges side was the last thing that Oxford needed the day before the club's Oxfordshire Cup game against Henley, but that was Oxford's lot on 15th January. With Lynn Evans missing, Alan Barraclough was the team place kicker and he missed chances before the home side broke away in the last fifteen minutes to win 14–3. Oxford, as the cup holders, were expected to do well against Henley and were boosted by the return from injury of Ray Tapper and Duncan Kilgour. But disaster struck once again and the side was reduced to fourteen players when centre Ian Ray left the field after five minutes with a hamstring injury, although Oxford's eventual demise came from disorganised, disjointed forward play, a faltering half back combination and bad tactics. Henley, to their credit, made the most of the chances that came their way and Oxford were hustled and bustled out of the competition, losing 6–17. In the other semi-final Oxford Old Boys won 16–6 at Bicester to set up an Oxford Old Boys v Henley final.

There was much gloom after this result when it was realised that the club would have to wait at least two years before entertaining the hope of another occasion like that of the previous November's match at London Welsh. In the inevitable fallout David Bagnall was

*Oxford RFC 1971–1972. Back row, l to r: J Deans (Trainer), PRE McFarlane, PJS Dedrick, R Ovenall, M Gibbard, D Heydon, J Harwood, N Fox, N Furley, E Hacker (Team Manager). Front row, l to r: L Evans, I McDougall, A Barraclough, RP Tapper, DF Bagnall (Capt), N Ponty, G Lewis, DS Kilgour.*

dropped after a run of poor form with David Pitt taking over the captaincy. Also left out were prop Nigel Fox and Dick Ovenall while a young Ray McCarthy was given an outing on the flank for the home game with Esher. In the event Oxford ended a dismal losing sequence by beating Esher 16–12 and turned towards youth even more for the next match by including debuts for Eugene Gratwohl and Clive Bevan in the 20–4 home win against Preston Grasshoppers.

This, however, proved to be a false dawn and there were further losses against Taunton, Abertillery and Maesteg before a welcome win against Cambridge. The defeat at Maesteg, albeit by a controversial try, was likely to be the last between the clubs as Maesteg were now saying that it was far too far to travel to Oxford even after the opening of a new stretch of motorway. Maybe the club would be paying the price for being unable to always take their strongest team?

On the social front the Club Dinner took place at the Emperor Ballroom at Pressed Steel Fisher and an attraction for the 169 diners, who paid £2 each for the pleasure, was a guest list that included Carwyn James, the recent British Lions coach, Dr Tom Kemp, President of the Rugby Football Union, Peter Dixon, ex Oxford Blue and now England Captain, and Owen Jones, Oxford University Captain. There was silence when Carwyn James stood up to say that "The most important factor about the British Lions touring

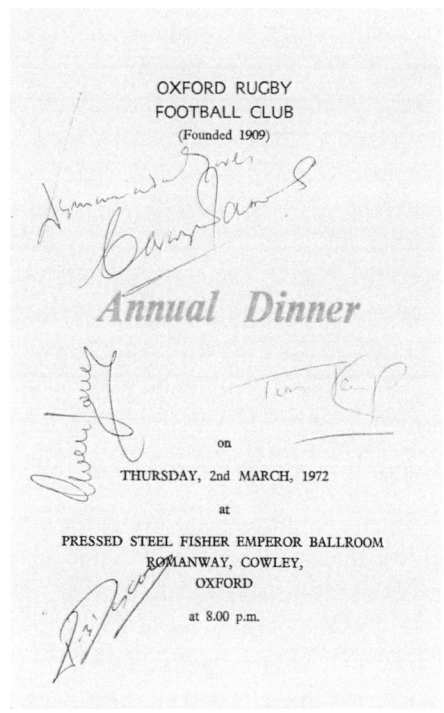

*Oxford RFC 1972 Dinner Menu.*

team that beat New Zealand was their total belief in themselves. To succeed any side must believe in their own capabilities. Success brought enjoyment into the game so let us spend the hours well but we must play every game to win. The difference between winning and losing is the difference between bloody hell and bloody good. In the last resort you are only appreciated if you win." So attentive were the audience that time was temporarily forgotten and it was only when the speeches ended at 10.50pm was it realised that there had been no bar extension applied for and 'last orders' were called for 11pm!

David Bagnall had regained his First team place, but this time in the centre, having replaced Jeff Thomas against Maesteg, and thus resumed the captaincy but was to preside over a less than desirable run in to the end of the season. Failing to heed the words of the great Carwyn James the team conceded three tries at home to Streatham & Croydon despite playing with a freezing gale force wind at their backs. The conditions deteriorated to blinding sleet and snow in the second half and it was no surprise the match was abandoned with Oxford 3–15 in arrears.

Having beaten Henley 11–7 in the Oxfordshire Cup Final, Oxford Old Boys were only able to draw 0–0 at home with Marlow in a Southern Group preliminary tie which allowed Marlow to progress as the away team. Marlow went on to lose 4–42 in the First Round proper away to Rosslyn Park in the following season. The Old Boys were facing an inquiry, for whatever sanction that could have brought, into circumstances behind the cancellation of their match with Old Windsorians the day before they beat Henley. Oxford might have thought that had they not played Loughborough Colleges with a full team the day before, they might have beaten Henley to qualify for that Final.

Oxford's attacking play had lost its potency with only goal kicks to show on the board in successive defeats away against Clifton and Manchester and home with the Metropolitan Police. But there was the Easter Tour to look forward to, this time to the north-west at the end of March. The club announced separate team selections from the twenty four players before the partry travelled, and John Harwood was due to play in all three! Once more Oxford scored just a penalty goal against New Brighton, a game played in continuous rain, and lost 3–18 before moving on to the next day to lose 4–24 at St Helen's. A young Roy Calver notched Oxford's try, only the second since 26$^{th}$ February, a reward for following up a charged down kick, whilst the leaky defence did not improve. As if stung into action Oxford gave their most purposeful performance for several weeks in the final match against Liverpool. The hosts had recovered from Barraclough's early penalty as Tapper slipped the ball to Ian McDougal for a try but Barraclough missed the conversion and then an easy penalty before Liverpool went on to win 7–19. The Committee were later to hear that the tour had been an excellent social success, particularly New Brighton's entertainment, if not so good on the field with the exception of the Liverpool match.

This left one game to be played, at home to Birmingham on 8$^{th}$ April, and a try from Eugene Gratwohl, who dribbled the ball clear to touch down near the posts, was little respite in a match where, again, weak midfield defence cost dearly in the 6–25 defeat.

The following weeks were concerned with seven-a-side rugby and a club team of: Seretse Williams, Ian Ray, Ray Tapper, David Bagnall, John Harwood, Roy Davies and Phil Dedrick played through the Preliminary Rounds of the Oxfordshire Seven-a-Side Tournament against Richmond II, Broad Street and Swindon without conceding a point whilst scoring eighty points in the process. Oh, that this could be transferred to the fifteen-a-side team! In the Iffley Road Finals the same team played poorly but beat Oxford Old Boys 8–6 before improving in confidence to beat Saracens 30–16, Bristol 20–6, and then Northampton 14–10 to reach the Tournament Final for the first time since 1955. It was there that any fortune ran out in a 10–34 defeat by Bedford. But the team had given its supporters something to cheer about in an otherwise dismal end to the season.

The club's policy of not playing after the Easter holiday meant that the regular season had finished relatively early giving plenty of time to reflect on what had gone wrong. There had been a poor start to the season but the team had soon recovered. The Knockout Cup provided a real stimulus and all the players had worked hard through to the London Welsh game. Perhaps it was to be expected that the side did not rise to that level afterwards and the second half of the season record was one of the worst recorded. One bright point was the selection of Nigel Fox for the England Youth team that drew with their Welsh counterparts at Pontypool in March. The one record the team did set, albeit unwanted, was of the longest losing sequence, eight games, in the club's history with final statistics of: played 39, won 15, lost 24, points for 417, against 675.

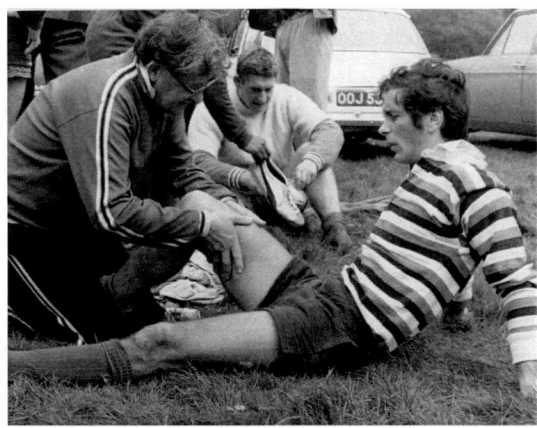

*John Deans gives Ray Tapper a much needed massage as John Harwood awaits his turn during the Oxfordshire Sevens.*

## Season 1972–1973

The summer of 1972 was eventful for several reasons, not the least of which saw yours truly married in June, an event that attracted the attention of a small group of club players as they passed the church in Cowley, the result of which saw the same group rush home, change clothes and gate crash the reception wearing button holes picked *en route*!

The New Zealand team was due to tour the British Isles in the coming season and would

*Tubby gets married! At the reception: Best Man Ray Mills, Ray McCarthy, David Pitt and Ian McDougall.*

be playing against Southern Counties at Iffley Road on Wednesday 20th December. In making the arrangements for this the Oxfordshire Union asked the club for the use of its ground on Monday 18th with a Dance in the evening afterwards. The Southern Counties group would train at the ground on the Tuesday, and there was to be a public Dance at the Town Hall on the evening of the match when the bar would be run and staffed by members of local clubs. Later, at a meeting of the clubs, it was decided on a vote that Oxford RFC should not be allowed to participate as the clubs probably thought that Oxford RFC had had a big enough 'bite of the cherry', and the club was not given the chance to help with the organisation during the mercenary procedure. Only the Henley club voted in favour of Oxford's inclusion. Gosford, Marathons, Henley, Witney, Oxford Old Boys, Bicester and Wheatley would share the proceeds. There were rumblings of ill feeling – what chance was there of getting an Oxford Championship side together? Local scribe Ron Grimshaw observed that "although Oxford Old Boys are County Champions it is an unpalatable fact to some that any aspiring young player could only look to one club in Oxford for better fixtures."

There was good news in July when the club received a letter in reply to a request made shortly after the purchase of the ground, now two years ago, from the Ministry of the Environment offering a grant of £6450 for refurbishment of the club buildings. This sum went together well with the £281 received as a portion of the share out after the first RFU Knockout Cup Competition.

The Rugby Football Union reported that cup rugby had 'made a favourable impression'. In the wake of this came news that there had been alterations to the County Cup competition as the organisers tried to get it right, in that cup games would be played on designated Saturdays, this following the problems that clubs faced previously when expected to play Sunday matches, the day after regular Saturday fixtures. The club voiced an opinion not to take part as it was not in the interest of the club to cancel Saturday fixtures of obvious better standard but, after County amendments, decided to enter again not least because of the chance to receive money from the financial pot.

The previous season's captain, David Bagnall, had undergone a successful operation for a back injury and was advised by a specialist not to play rugby again.

Former club player Peter West, now back in the area, was appointed as the club's first official coach and he would be helped by the Club Captain, Ray Tapper, and Lynn Evans, all of whom attended a high powered Lions coaching course, the content of which was later published in book form 'The Lions Speak'.

Oxford started the season with a convincing home win over Weston-super-Mare, 25–12, with a team of: P Raybould; I McDougall, LR Evans, ROP Jones, SA Williams; RP Tapper, MJH Bampton; C Bevan, G Webb, N Fox, JS Harwood, R Powell, DM Blake, R McCarthy and PJS Dedrick. There was much relief as all the pre-season training, planning and hard work came to fruition. The previous season's Oxford University Captain, Owen Jones, scored a try on his club debut as did Vice Captain Phil Dedrick and winger Seretse Williams while the now fit again full back Phil Raybould added three penalties and two conversions.

Two cancelled fixtures against Tredegar and Cross Keys, due to Welsh Cup involvement, led to two 'fill in' matches with Newbury and Witney, won 41–3 and 58–0, and suddenly Oxford had played three games and scored 124 points which was good for early season morale.

There followed a sixteen hour road trip of over 350 miles for a first visit to Preston Grasshoppers. It was very much back to reality in the 12–27 defeat with a shoddy performance, but the team then eked out an 11–9 win at home with Sidcup. After a first half pounding by the visitors the side settled to come back before another big win 56–6 against a weak St Bartholomew's Hospital side when Phil Dedrick and Roy Davies were again in splendid form despite the loss of Seretse Williams to Hull University and Nigel Fox to Northampton Agricultural College.

The Sunday date for Oxford's knockout cup match with Wheatley had been moved twice to fit in with County squad training sessions which involved several Oxford players. Another was announced for the morning of Oxford's Wheatley match, the day following the Hospital game, and the club agreed that their players could train in the morning and play in the afternoon. Signs of another crowded season! In the event, and after all that, Wheatley, the youngest club in the county, called off with only nine fit players giving Oxford a bye to the next round.

On the same afternoon Oxford Old Boys, the cup holders, went out of the competition on a technicality following a 0–0 home draw with Henley, a rematch of the previous seasons final, Henley, being the away side in such a situation, went through to the next round to be drawn away to Oxford!

Club Captaincy passed, for one game only, to centre Owen Jones for the Thursday 12th October game against Tim Seymour's XV. This was in recognition of him being the immediate past OURFC Captain and he led the club team to a good 21–6 win. The players were beginning to gell, showed fortitude and stuck well to the task in hand. Forty eight hours later the side was on the road to Cardiff where Oxford came back from 9–17 down at half time to beat Glamorgan Wanderers 27–23. This was a great win, especially in Wales, with Roger Powell, the most improved player in the club, leading from the front in a magnificent forward performance.

The home 24–4 win against London Hospital was notable for the debut of winger Bob Reynolds who scored three tries. A welcome addition to the club Bob was a teacher at Lord William's School in Thame and a player with blistering pace who was unfortunate, through injury, not to get a 'Blue' at Oxford the previous season. Phil Raybould kicked the other twelve points and it was noted that he had scored in every game in which he had played to date in the season.

In the away match at Guy's Hospital the Oxford side was hampered by the loss of centre Lynn Evans who was stretchered from the field after ten minutes with a dislocated shoulder, the fourth such injury he had suffered in his playing career. Roy Davies was press ganged into the backs and his loss to the forwards was crucial as Oxford lost shape and the match 13–25. In the week following Lynn, 34 years old, announced his retirement saying "I am very disappointed at leaving a winning side and being unable to finish the season with them. Things are going so well now

*Pre-season conflab. New Coach Peter West, Captain Ray Tapper, Lynn Evans and Phil Dedrick confer.*

*Oxford RFC 1972–1973. Back row, l to r: G Howells, R Davies, J Deans (Trainer), N Fox, R Powell, B Whitcombe, D Heydon, J Harwood, R McCarthy, E Littlechild, M Kerrison, B Deane (Team Manager), P West (Coach). Front row, l to r: I Ray, P Webb, P Raybould, A Barraclough, RP Tapper (Capt), D Kilgour, M Pigg, J Burnell, L Evans.*

and they are playing well, especially after such a disappointing season last year. But this is it. I've decided to call it a day. I'm not going through all this again."

John Harwood returned to the side after a lengthy spell out of the game with a knee injury for the club's second successive Saturday in London, this time to meet the Metropolitan Police. Ian Ray came in for Evans at centre as Oxford attempted to beat the 'Bobbies' for the first time, but these additions did little for the team in a match noted for its distasteful incidents during another defeat, 16–23. And then the Coventry side Caludon Old Boys filled in, when St Thomas's Hospital couldn't raise a side, to give Oxford some awkward moments before the home team returned to winning ways 34–9.

There was much focus on the Oxfordshire County team at this time. After a wobbly start and a 10–23 friendly defeat against South Warwickshire at Leamington the team, containing anything up to twelve Oxford RFC and two former club players, had started the Southern Group campaign with a good team performance and a 20–6 win against Buckinghamshire.

Duncan Kilgour's 50th County appearance coincided with a great 35–0 win over Berkshire, with Ian Ray scoring three tries, before the team overcame Dorset & Wilts 23–3. Everything hinged on the away match against Hertfordshire at Croxley Green and after a very tough encounter, Oxfordshire came away with a 10–3 win and the Southern Group Championship again, after a break of five years. In the four games the team scored 88 points with just 12 against and they now faced the South West Group winners in the New Year. County caps were awarded to Alan Barraclough, Roy Davies and Bob Sankey after the game. The midweek Hertfordshire match was sandwiched between Oxford losses at US Portsmouth, 9–18, and home to Hull & East Riding, 9–24, as the fatigue of County squad and training sessions, mostly on Sundays, club training on Tuesdays and Thursdays as well as county and club games, began to tell. In the county match period Oxford's record was won 4 lost 4.

There was a boost for the club in that four players, Owen Jones, Ian Ray, John Harwood and Alan Barraclough were selected for the Southern Group squad in preparation for the

*The Oxfordshire that beat Berkshire 35–0, a record score between the two sides: All Oxford except where noted. Back row, l to r: C Ede (Coach), R Reynolds, A Jenkins (Henley), R McCarthy, R Powell, D Heydon, R Lewis, P Raybould, M Jones (Henley), R Sankey (Wasps). Front row, l to r: RP Tapper, R Davies, D Kilgour, R Jones, I Ray, A Barraclough.*

match against New Zealand in December, while Harwood, a teacher at Redefield School in Blackbird Leys, was named as a travelling reserve for the first England Trial, North v South, at Broughton Park on 2nd December. John was later guaranteed a place in the South team, due to injuries, but was sadly to lose his chance when he went down with tonsillitis.

With County excitement temporarily behind them the Oxford team made a spirited second half rally on a rain and wind swept ground to draw 21–21 with Tredegar. This was a good result for the team where Raybould kicked five penalties and converted Kilgour's try to equal the visitors scoring rate. Coach Peter West observed that the result "did a lot to make the forwards believe in themselves again after a bad month." The form continued when Oxford beat Lydney 15–9 on December 9th and showed the best form for some weeks. The visitors included David Pitt at lock, Oxford's Vice Captain the previous season, who was now travelling to play for his former club. In a gruelling struggle Reynolds scored a try on his return from a four match lay off before leaving the field, this time with a shoulder injury. The next day Oxford showed several changes in the team to meet Banbury in the County Cup due to the Southern Counties players required for training at Henley prior to a warm up game against Gloucester in the week, and Ray Tapper's poisoned toe, but were never in any danger of losing and progressed through with a 22–3 win.

The same four players were stood down against Maesteg but Ken Saunders, a big strong running centre and already a County player, joined from Gosford All Blacks. All in vain, however, as Oxford, enduring an 'off-day', were well beaten 3–15. Perhaps all minds were focused on Southern Counties match with New Zealand in the midweek, 20th December. Although he played in the warm up match against Gloucester the previous week, where the team lost 7–29, Alan Barraclough, from the four Oxford players involved, was the unlucky omission from the final lineup against New Zealand. The All Blacks duly recorded a 26–6 win but the match was a bit of an anti-climax. In a less than expected display by the tourists, Southern Counties were brave but, with Ray an outstanding figure in the backs and Harwood giving a good account of himself, lost to the tourists overall strength.

In a Ray McCarthy versus brother Liam McCarthy sub plot, Oxford gave a ragged performance in a 6–13 defeat away to London Irish before ending 1972 in vintage form as Stroud were dismissed by 31–6 to avenge the heavy defeat in the last season.

At the halfway stage of the season a simple pattern had emerged where Oxford won seven of the first eight games before mixed fortunes. County games and various squad sessions had seen some players in playing kit up to five nights a week in some cases and there had been the inevitable problem of injuries. The club had found a new star in full back Phil Raybould who had scored in every game he had played in to date but, against this, the team had now lost Lynn Evans through injury while Owen Jones was returning home to Wales after his Oxford sojourn.

Ian Ray and Ray Tapper worked cleverly to put

*Southern Counties v New Zealand match programme.*

*Southern Counties v New Zealand. Back row, l to r: A Jones (Team Secretary), C Boulter (Berks), M Marshall (Berks), S Godfrey (Berks), J Harwood (Oxon), W Lyon (Berks), D Vivian (Berks), J Higgins (Trainer). Middle row, l to r: A Barraclough (Oxon), M Phillips (Herts), H Malins (D&W), M Hannel (D&W), J Jarrett (D&W), K Richardson (D&W), I Ray (Oxon), I Vinter (Herts). Front row, l to r: S Crabtree (Berks), D Spawforth (Berks), ROP Jones (Oxon), J Vaughan (Berks) (Capt), R Ellis-Jones (Berks), D Llewelyn (Bucks), P Cadle (Herts).*

*Boxing Day fun as Oxford Old Boys entertain Oxford Nomads. Clive Bevan, Nigel Townsend, Ray McCarthy, Martin Ponty and John Harwood are the players still standing.*

Kilgour away for a try late in Oxford's home game with Old Whitgiftians, and Raybould converted from the touchline to see the team home for a first win in 1973, 12–9.

The second weekend of the year saw twelve Oxford players plus six travelling reserves in the Oxfordshire side for the County Championship Quarter Final match at Gloucester, which left virtually a 2nd XV to face Loughborough Colleges. This at least enabled Phil Dedrick to return for his first senior game since injury in October but, inevitably, Oxford crashed to a heavy defeat, 11–52. Over in Gloucester against the County Champions, Oxfordshire were not nearly as badly beaten by Gloucestershire as a 12–39 score might suggest. Played at a sharp pace Gloucestershire made far fewer mistakes than Oxfordshire but made much more of their chances in an entertaining and exciting game.

*George Webb, Roger Powell, John Harwood, Max Kerrison and Ray McCarthy fight to keep the unbeaten Manchester players at bay, while Alan Barraclough gets ready to field the ball.*

At last Rugby Union returned to something like normal at the club. The returning players had no other distractions except to concentrate on the visit of unbeaten Manchester in the next match. The visitors travelled through fog, snow and ice to reach the Bypass ground and both teams faced a strong icy wind which drove rain across the ground. The game was decided early on before the players froze. Two tries, from Reynolds and Ted Littlechild, a Ray Tapper drop goal plus points from Raybould was enough for a 16–10 win to send the Manchester team home with their tails between their legs. The very next day Oxford faced a repeat of the previous season's cup semi-final against Henley, again at the Bypass. The Manchester game twenty four hours earlier was hardly the best preparation and the game was not to be remembered for good rugby. Henley stayed in touch for long periods but Raybould's 13 points were significantly added to tries from Ray and Kilgour in Oxford's 21–12 win. It was suggested that referees might be appointed from outside the county for matches in the latter stages of the cup as Derek Howard, a former Oxford and Oxfordshire player now turned 'whistle blower', ruled that Oxford persistently infringed without giving warning, producing a staccato game. Oxford Marathons beat Bicester 26–0 in the other semi-final over at Cowley Marsh.

Buoyed by these two weekend victories Oxford romped to a 17–3 win at Esher before a narrow 9–11 defeat at Bridgwater & Albion where the team was reduced to fourteen players after Ted Littlechild dislocated a knee. Oxford then sprung a major upset in Welsh rugby in a 23–0 win over visiting Abertillery. This was an exciting victory with the forwards proving to be a really good unit but team plaudits were well deserved and demonstrated by Ray Tapper who, in one run, performed a double dummy scissors, kicked ahead, caught his own kick and ran 30 yards to score! From that came a 6–17 defeat to a strong side at Nuneaton before the side travelled a longer, but more fruitful, distance to Cambridge where the home team was crushed in Oxford's 38–9 win.

The Oxfordshire Cup Final was designated for a Saturday, 3$^{rd}$ March, and Oxford's original opponents, Streatham & Croydon, relieved the club of the fixture without prejudice. For the match against local team Oxford Marathon, the Oxford club was afforded the luxury of being able to field the same team for the fourth week in succession. For the Mara's Fred Bannister was declared fit having spent some time in the Oxford Eye Hospital following his team's recent battle with Matson. In a keenly contested match the Maras put up a good fight in the forwards but suffered from a lack of a Plan B. Plan A was to kick the ball high into the air, their backs were seldom seen in attack and the only points scored were four penalty goals from the left foot of Mike Groom. This was trumped by Raybould who kicked five penalties and a conversion of Nigel Fox's try in Oxford 24–12 win.

It was a case of 'after the Lord Mayor's Show' the following week when Oxford visited Birmingham and slumped to a 0–19 defeat. It was the first time that Oxford had failed to score this season but, more significantly, it saw the end of Phil Raybould's amazing record of having scored in every game in which he had played. In thirty six club and county games he had amassed 348 points and established a club record to date of 294 points. On this occasion, on a heavy ground, he had missed four kicks at goal. After a week, however, he was back in the groove when his two penalties helped Oxford to a narrow 14–13 win at home to Clifton. Oxford then faced a stern test in Pontypool's visit and soon found that bravery in defence was not enough in falling to a 4–14 defeat.

Once again the Rugby Union had decreed Saturday cup rugby and Oxford lost a fixture with Taunton to accommodate a Southern Area championship match away against Aldershot Services, this a result of the club becoming Oxfordshire Champions once more. The Services were taking the match seriously and flew in the Number 8 from duty in Northern Ireland but Oxford had far too much fire power and fast running rugby to ensure a comfortable 38–13 win which brought a home tie with Aylesbury in the Area Final. Winger

*Oxford's Cup Final team on the steps at Iffley Road. Back row, l to r: P West (Coach), J Deans (Team Manager), G Webb, R Lewis, M Kerrison, D Heydon, R Powell, N Fox, D Kilgour. Front row, l to r: J Harwood, K Saunders, M Pigg, R Davies, RP Tapper (Capt), I Cornthwaite, A Barraclough, P Raybould.*

*All eyes on Marathon's Micky Groom as he kicks over the forwards once more.*

*A happy Ray Tapper, Oxford's Captain, collects the Oxfordshire Cup from the County President's wife, Mrs Boddington.*

Ted Littlechild, fit again, scored four tries and Ray McCarthy, looking much happier in his accustomed Number 8 role, added two.

St Mary's Hospital could not raise a side and cancelled the match on 7th April giving Oxford a rare weekend off which was welcome respite before the match in Wales against Maesteg. The rest obviously paid off and Oxford, with the wind at their backs, came back from a 6–10 deficit to take the lead and win 18–16. As Oxford had found previously, a win in Wales by an English club is noteworthy at any time!

Easter loomed, a late one this year, and Oxford opened a three game tour of the North East with a noteworthy 12–4 win over West Hartlepool on Good Friday. John Harwood was Oxford's try scorer while Raybould kicked the rest, but it was a different story on the Saturday and a 6–15 loss to Durham City. In the third game, against Hull & East Riding, Oxford failed to penetrate the home defence and lost 6–16 with Raybould again the points scorer.

While many other rugby folk were hanging up their boots and winter coats with thoughts of the beach, Oxford had one more game to play. In contrast to the previous season this game was due to be played on the very last day of the season, Monday 30th April, with an evening kick off and just hours to spare. The occasion was the Southern Area Final against Aylesbury and was only the second time that the clubs had met. The visitors put up a tremendous performance in a very close match and Raybould, who else, won the game with a penalty kick to bring Oxford's season to a successful close, 13–10.

This had been an excellent, and one of the most successful seasons in the Oxford club's history. The number of games won totalled 24, just one short of the club record of 25 set in the 1956–1957 season under the captaincy of Frank Webb, while there had been 24 wins also in 1966–1967 under Lynn Evans, and 1950–1951 and 1953–1954, both under Chris Price. Captain Ray Tapper, himself a proud Welshman, in extolling the memories of games won against the Welsh clubs, later said "It is common knowledge I'm afraid to say, that the Welsh are at their most generous when they have beaten you. What they are like when they lose, I'm not so sure because they very rarely stay to let you find out."

## Season 1973–1974

Money received from the Department of the Environment was being put to good use with the changing rooms revamped and car park resurfaced. Improvements were being made to the dining hall but there was a set-back in as much as it was found that the central structure was rotting. Now twenty five years old, this had been erected as a temporary structure and now needed to be completely rebuilt together with the provision of a new bar. There was a delay in this work when plans with a local contractor fell through which meant that building work extended into the start of the new season.

Towards the end of the previous season the International Rugby Board revised the lineout laws of the game in an attempt to clean up what was seen as a messy way to restart the game when the ball went off the pitch. The new laws required two lines of opposing players to be 2 feet apart and 1 yard apart either side of their team mates while no length of lineout could extend beyond 15 yards from the touchline. It was hoped that these changes would promote much more two handed catching, but one commentator suggested that referees would now need to carry a calliper and yardstick amongst their match day kit! Another thought that, with more gaps in the lineout, the scrum half would be more exposed. Should this thought become a reality Oxford's new Captain, scrum half Alan Barraclough, a teacher at Christ Church Cathedral School who had been at the club for four years, would face extra challenges.

Doubt was cast on hopes that the club could build on the previous season's successes when it was realised that the club would lose the front five players in the pack from that time. Roger Lewis and George Webb had retired, Nigel Fox and John Harwood had moved and were hoping to play for Northampton and Roger Powell had joined Swansea. Added to that Dyson Heydon had returned home to Australia, as had Max Kerrison to New Zealand while young hooker Martin Ponty was immigrating to the same destination. It was quite ironic that these players had helped the club to reach the stage where it now had a home draw in the National Knockout Cup against London Scottish in October.

On the plus side Fred Bannister joined the club from Oxford Marathons to try his luck at a higher grade. Having been at Maras for several years he also hoped that his move "may help break the horrible spirit there is in local rugby." Also joining was 'Jock' Lee, a flanker from Christchurch in New Zealand who was hoping to win a 'Blue' at Oxford in December. Another newcomer was prop Stuart Pickering, an RAF player who had been posted locally.

The start to the season was not good and was only destined to get worse. Ray McCarthy moved to the second row to partner Brian Whitcombe to accommodate the back row newcomers for the opening match, a defeat at Weston-super-Mare 16–25. The team was reduced to fourteen players for the first half due to the absence of hooker Peter Webb who, travelling to the game from Devon, was delayed when his car broke down in holiday traffic. In his absence Oxford conceded 19 points but did close the gap after his arrival. More disaster followed the next day when Ray Tapper broke his collar bone and Ian Ray suffered an ankle injury, both playing in the annual Abingdon Sevens. This certainly disrupted Oxford's early season plans and, with both injuries looking like being long term, provoked discussion as to whether the club should enter teams in early season sevens, due to the risk of injury. Should players have a sense of responsibility and respect the wishes of their club? In what is a game for players, did it all come down to priorities and what was most prestigious for the club, Abingdon sevens or winning regular 15-a-side games?

Seretse Williams wore the number 10 shirt in the midweek match at home to Richmond while newcomer Mike Hutchins, from the Waterloo club, went straight into the centre. The Oxford team was not disgraced in the 3–32 defeat and never lacked effort but there were huge gaps in defence and many tackles were missed. Players were having difficulty in adapting to the new line out laws, but Roy Davies was outstanding as the club won its first game of the season against Reading, 28–15, and then repeated the dose the following week with the club's biggest ever score, 83–0, against a very weak Old Merchant Taylors side. Ian McDougal scored 4 tries, Ian Cornthwaite and Malcolm Pigg 3 tries each, Seretse Williams 2 tries and Hutchins and Davies 1 try each. Raybould chipped in with 8 conversions and a penalty in the romp. Twenty fours later on Sunday 16th September and nobody had expected a rugby

*Jerry Smith is swallowed up by the Richmond defence as ex-England Captain Tony Bucknall homes in on the incident.*

club from America to be of any great standard but the Santa Monica team, formed just one year earlier by former Oxford player, Bob Thrussell, arrived as USA champions and provided a big challenge. The Americans had already won their first two games on the tour and also the Plate Competition in the Kent 7s. Four days earlier on the Thursday evening Oxford Old Boys were on the end of a comprehensive lesson and were crushed 0–42. The visitors were tough opponents and, with Thrussell hitting the post with two penalty kicks Oxford were eventually fortunate to scrape home 14–13, to inflict a first tour defeat on Santa Monica before the team continued to Wales.

Finally the summer weather broke and in heavy rain Oxford scored early in the home match with Preston Grasshoppers, before the ball got too wet, when, from Barraclough's pass Malcom Pigg made the break to put over Seretse Williams. Raybould's conversion failed but soon after kicked a penalty before conditions worsened but these scores were enough for a 7–3 win. Further good news was that Ray Tapper had had the stitches removed after his shoulder operation although his arm was still in a sling. Tapper's absence was still causing problems and Peter Steele from RAF Benson was tried at No. 10 for the match in Taunton where Oxford scored the best try of the match inside two minutes but then went on to lose 7–25.

The club was having a hard time with lots of players absent for various reasons and the team lost to the unofficial Welsh Champions, Pontypool, making their first visit to the Bypass ground, 6–13. A makeshift side lost to the DC Kay's XV in the annual midweek fixture 9–19, with only three penalty kicks from Barraclough to show for their efforts.

All this was not good preparation for the prestigious National Cup 1st Round match at home with London Scottish on Sunday 14th October. Fortunately the Glamorgan Wanderers club had asked to be released from the scheduled Saturday fixture, due to Welsh Cup

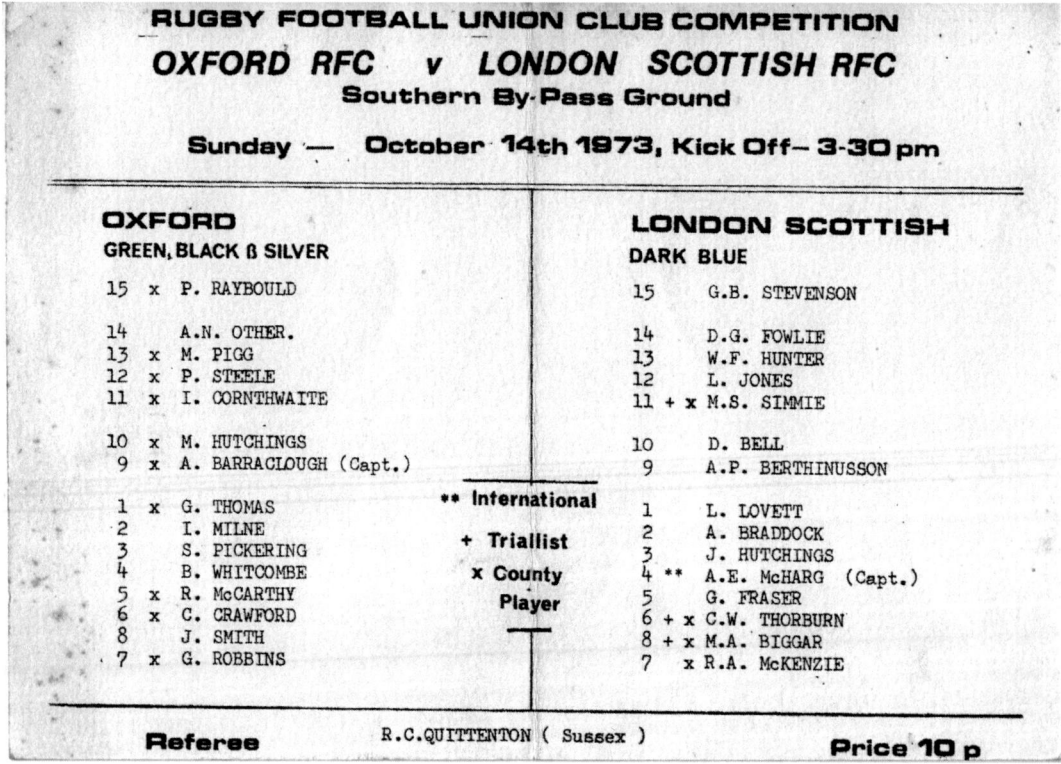

*Oxford v London Scottish match card.*

commitments, which gave Oxford a few hours breathing space. The central part of the clubhouse had been razed to the ground and did not look immediately good to the eye although there was, of course, a bright future in this direction with a new clubhouse, bar and lounge. To compensate for this a large marquee and outside bar to cater for the expected visitors was erected. Ravaged by injuries, Oxford revealed Gareth Thomas from RAF Benson at prop and Gwyn Robbins, a schools adviser, both newcomers to the club, in the team named to play. Oxford's team for the match was: P Raybould; DS Kilgour, M Pigg, K Saunders, I Cornthwaite; M Hutchings, A Barraclough (Capt); G Thomas, I Milne, S Pickering, B Whitcombe, R McCarthy, C Crawford, G Robbins, J Smith. The team defied current injury and off field challenges to play with tremendous spirit and drive, and rose to new heights in defence to lead London Scottish by 9–6 with fifteen minutes to play. But three lapses cost Oxford dearly and David Bell, the Scottish fly half, added two penalties and a drop goal to his earlier penalties and Oxford lost 9–15. Harsh comments in the national press alleged that Oxford, in providing hope for their supporters, had neither skill nor teamwork only courage and determination. In defeat it was a memorable day! London Scottish went all the way to the Twickenham final where they lost 6–26 to Coventry.

Was this defeat one of Oxford's finest hours? On the evidence of the London Scottish game the side could hold its own in the first class game if they could regularly raise their game. But as usually happens there was a come-down the following week when the club team was met with atrocious ground conditions at Cross Keys and it was little wonder that the game deteriorated into a war of attrition between two well matched packs. Oxford led at the break after Pigg had intercepted on his '25', kicked ahead into the driving rain for Cornthwaite to win the race to touch down. But Cross Keys lasted the gruelling pace better, with two tries to dispatch Oxford 6–8 with both packs hardly recognisable.

*Ray McCarthy feeds the ball to Alan Barraclough, supported by Gareth Thomas, Ian Milne and Jerry Smith against London Scottish. David Bell lurks in the background* (*second left*).

With the season now eight weeks old Ray McCarthy, having played nine club games in the second row of the scrum now decided that he only wanted to play in his favoured position of No.8. The result of this was that he now dropped down into a very strong Vikings side, with players returning from injury. In his absence Oxford returned to form to end the losing run in beating Guy's Hospital 20–10 with a competent performance. This didn't last long however when the team, under constant pressure, were never in the match in a 3–21 defeat at Tredegar.

The school teacher's dispute over pay and conditions that took place in the early 1970s was soon to have a direct influence on the playing of Rugby Union. Teachers, who had previously given up time to introduce rugby to their pupils and in many cases run inter school matches, had decided, as part of the industrial action, to work to rule. The result of this was that no longer could rugby clubs sit at the end of a conveyor belt of young ready-made rugby players anxious to continue playing. From now on it was going to be down to the clubs to make their own players and, with that, came the advent of Mini Rugby with suitably abbreviated rules for young boys who could later be fed into Colts and senior rugby. This form of rugby was given universal approval by the RFU and a twenty minute match between 12 year olds took place as a curtain-raiser at Twickenham prior to the England v Australia on 17th November. In Oxfordshire the Witney club had been drawing around 50 youngsters every Sunday morning, and Henley had been staging a similar programme. The Oxford club decided to follow suit although the organisation was left to parents of participating children, and nearly 40 children turned up at the club on 11th November when school teacher Lynn Evans, now the County Coach, took the first session.

The Oxford club was also attracting attention of a different sort at this time. Due to the increased traffic volume on the adjoining A34 the County Council closed the entrance to North Hinksey Village which bordered the club ground because the turn off was now considered dangerous. This forced all traffic visiting the club site to travel through the village and twelve residents instructed a solicitor to oppose a bar extension planned until 12.30am on 15th November due to noise made by people leaving the clubhouse and driving through the village late at night. The application for the extension was granted but the Chairman of the Magistrates said that he hoped users of the clubhouse would be reminded to have regard for the nearby residents.

After scoring three tries in his Vikings game, Ray McCarthy was soon back, through injuries, this time at No.8, as Oxford beat Guildford & Godalming 25–3. Once more this didn't last long and Raybould watched in anguish as his last minute penalty hit a post in the 9–10 home defeat to US Portsmouth. In late November discussions centred around the number of players now available and the possible need for a squad system to keep everybody happy. With competition for places hotting up Oxford hit top form to win 22–10 away at Bridgwater & Albion.

The Club Committee was asked to consider a report following a meeting between Witney Rugby Club and County officials, the gist of which revolved around the host club's concern about the lack of contact with the ordinary club player in local clubs. It was stated that there was a 'feeling of detachment from County, and players in particular must be made aware of the County.' Witney felt that it was very important that the County Committee should be seen by the average player to be operating fairly, therefore the composition of the County Committee was a major concern with over-representation of any one club. (Oxford club members held several posts within the County structure.) County trials and selection also gave some concern and two trials were suggested to give more junior clubs and players a fair showing. It was later agreed that a meeting of all club chairmen and secretaries be held to discuss the issues, while the newly formed 'Oxtails' team, a County second XV, would help alleviate any selection problems. The subsequent meeting, while not a waste of time, was not all that productive and achieved very little while there were even protests when the centrally situated Oxford club was used as a venue!

Lynn Evans was announced as the Coach of the Oxfordshire County XV but there was a poor turnout for the County trials. Phil Raybould had elected to play for Staffordshire this season and the team, with nine players making their county debuts including the Witney full back Geoff Cranville, beat South Warwickshire 14–3 at Banbury. There was a much publicised extra match in the programme, that being against Nigel Starmer-Smith's International XV in aid of the Oxfordshire Association of Boys Clubs where the county team lost 24–40. Played on a Wednesday afternoon the difference in class was clearly obvious but, perhaps more importantly, the event was very poorly supported and profits were minimal. This did nothing in the next match for the team's morale and the champions, as they were from the previous season, lost 9–19 to the previous season's bottom placed Buckinghamshire. The team was described in the national press as 'appalling', without technique, skill, plan or purpose. Seretse Williams travelled by train from college in Hull but missed a connection in Birmingham and finished the journey by taxi but arrived at the ground too late to play. In the 9–21 defeat at Berkshire the team was slightly better. Then in the next match Phil Dedrick's try and Mike Groom's kicking saw them home 15–10 at Dorset & Wilts. But this joy was short lived and in a low standard game spiritless Oxfordshire were never in contention in the home 7–28 loss to Hertfordshire. Oxford's troubles were the County's troubles which brought to mind the saying 'when Oxford have a good season so do Oxfordshire' and, of course, the reverse also applies. Ron Grimshaw wrote that "there was a lack of playing talent and skill, and players are not likely to improve much while they remain in junior clubs."

December was a poor month for the club except that, at last, the roof was on the dining hall area of the clubhouse. After the heights at Bridgwater it was back to earth at the Bypass and 11–22 defeat by a solid Solihull side and 7–18 to Pontypridd, while Ray Tapper was starting back in the Vikings. Back to South Wales where Phil Dedrick's two tries were not enough in another loss, this time 10–19 at Maesteg. The Christmas fixture on 22$^{nd}$ December with London Irish attracted much attention to the Bypass ground and more disruption as the team lost prop Richard Quinby after twelve minutes after which Oxford's fourteen men

*Four former pupils of Magdalen College School had all made their name at Oxford RFC and in Oxfordshire colours. Left to right: David Bagnall, Peter Sibley, Duncan Kilgour and Don Barrett.*

crumbled against Irish International Ken Kennedy's team by almost a record score, 3–52.

Oxford Thursday rugby at the club was coming under increasing pressure with challenges on club players to attend training sessions, County commitments and the unwritten rule that Saturday First XV players should not play on Thursdays. Originally set up to provide players who wouldn't normally be available on Saturdays through work etc, a match on a Thursday, the Oxford Thursday Nomads were ably run by the genial Charlie Ede, had become an institution over a long period of time with the team often containing International players who were 'up' at the University, and matches were of a high standard. Charlie occasionally flirted with danger and had agreed to play the touring Natal University side after an arranged match at Newport had been called off due to the lighting ban, prevalent at that time caused through industrial and international actions. The game was due not on a Thursday but a Sunday, 9th December at the Bypass ground. News of the match leaked and there were soon threats of demonstrations by anti-apartheid supporters. With bricks and planks available from the clubhouse site, fears of ground damage caused the club to cancel the match. But Natal did get a game, at a town just over 40 miles away and beat a 'pick-up' side 48–12. Charlie was quoted as saying "As far as I know, no Oxford side played Natal University last Sunday." But there were at least four Oxford players in the scratch team captained by a local player!

The Boxing Day fixture saw a strong Nomads side beat Oxford Old Boys 29–0. The Old Boys were happy though, as the club had been offered a new ground with three pitches being raised above flooding level and a new clubhouse. The other Oxford club, Oxford Marathon, had secured continued use of the Cowley Marsh ground with permission to build a clubhouse. There were thoughts of 'How things change' as this was the ground that the Oxford club had looked at obtaining after the Second World War.

The Oxford team was boosted by the return of Ray Tapper for what was only his second First[t] XV match of the season at home to Streatham & Croydon. There were more problems though when the team lost Phil Dedrick, the best forward, with ankle ligament damage after he'd scored his team's first try, and Brian Whitcombe with a broken collar bone in the last ten minutes but at least Oxford were able to end 1973 on a winning note, 20–13.

At the halfway stage of the season Oxford had won fewer games than in any half season since 1962, had suffered a new club record of 13 games lost, and the heaviest defeat of their twenty six seasons. The loss of the coach, Peter West, who had moved away with his job, had been significant and the club recalled Charlie Ede in an attempt to get back on the winning trail.

Despite the heavy, muddy going a degree of confidence returned when Oxford scored nine tries to nil with open, attacking rugby in a 40–0 win at Old Whitgiftians, but were unimpressive the following week in beating Esher 17–10 at the Bypass in a scrappy game. A determined Duncan Kilgour, on the wing, had found a new lease of life while on the other side Bob Reynolds returned with several exciting runs, but there was some concern over the forwards.

Oxford were faced with two games over the weekend of 19th January, the second of which was the Oxfordshire Cup semi-final against Henley. Maybe this was on the minds of the players in the away match at Loughborough College as the team was incredibly slack in defence in the 0–33 defeat. It was in this match that Phil Raybould lost his 'score a game' record in this season. At the Bypass on Sunday the day started with a curtain raiser demonstration of the latest thing to sweep through the game – mini rugby – with the Oxford boys playing against their Henley counterparts. Oxford lost this match 4–12 but there were some familiar surnames, Mark Francis, Ian Bye and Alan Hacker, in the side. In the main

*Ian Cornthwaite looks outside to offload to Ken Saunders against Esher.*

event, watched by a large crowd, Oxford soaked up pressure from Henley, who took an early lead, but three penalty kicks from Raybould saw the side gradually pull away with variety and enterprise, and finally Barraclough's reverse pass found Tapper who sent Reynolds away on an unopposed run to the line to secure a 12–4 win and another final appearance.

The second semi-final was a local derby with Oxford Marathons facing Oxford Old Boys at Cowley Marsh where the home team held a 3–0 lead for much of the match, only for John Carr kick a penalty in the fifth minute of injury time to draw the match which saw the Old Boys go through to the final as the away side much to the despair of the Marathons.

On the same weekend Oxford were losing 12–23 at home to Tredegar, who adapted themselves better to the difficult mud and driving rain and typical Welsh spirit saw the side twice come from behind to win the match. Seven days later and Oxford averted a second successive Welsh defeat when the team beat Penarth 12–10 albeit courtesy of Phil Raybould's four penalty kicks, the last of which went over from 45 yards! Still on the Welsh trail Oxford, having replaced the proposed fixture with Abertillery with a trip to Glamorgan Wanderers, were left with a blank weekend when the home pitch was declared unfit to play.

Ray McCarthy was suffering more than most in that the local factory where he was employed and was working a three day week as a result of nationwide industrial action. Energy was being saved across the country, because of a miner's dispute, and one of Ray's working days were some Saturdays and this saw him lose his place in the club team as a result.

After a free weekend the 25th Anniversary of matches with Nuneaton, first played in 1949, loomed at the Bypass ground. The time off gave Reynolds and Dedrick extra time to recover from injuries, and Reynolds marked his come-back with a try in the third minute. Oxford made a good start but suffered an inept collapse in the 9–23 loss.

The club was determined to keep traditional fixtures in spite of cup commitments and another two game weekend, this time with the cup final on the Sunday, and made five changes in what they saw as the starting lineup for the Saturday match against Cambridge. This was no easy game and although Oxford won 24–10 the team had to play for the victory. A feature of this game was a 'man of the match' performance from Bob Reynolds who scored four tries, But one of the players not rested was Ray Tapper and, near the end of the match, he suffered badly bruised ribs and it was a major blow when he acceded to medical advice and withdrew on the morning of the match. The Old Boys, with no game on Saturday, had no such problems and had been fortunate enough to be able to prepare, despite the lighting ban, by the light of street lights adjacent to their Marston Ferry Road ground. After all that had gone on Oxford were favourites to win the cup again, but in something of a shock result, were strangely fumbling and uncertain. Phil Raybould moved up from full back to take Tapper's place and was a disastrously inept substitute, as the Old Boys handed out a lesson in sound, basic rugby, a feature of which was Tony Tyrer taking passes on the burst to score three tries in his side's 18–6 win. Oxford Coach Charlie Ede said "I have never seen us play so badly but they thoroughly deserved to win, and there was only one team in it." Winger Duncan Kilgour, describing the painful experience said "We were awful."

Spirits were low at the club during the following week with Ray Tapper again at the centre of the inevitable discussions. Just how important was the Cambridge match in view of lost prestige and possible income to the club?

St Mary's Hospital cancelled the listed match and the Oxford team took out its frustrations in a hastily arranged replacement match with Wimborne, 64–10. Duncan Kilgour, described as a 'veteran' and having seen three tries conceded down his side of the field in the final, was replaced by Cornthwaite for the home match with Birmingham. The pack was ineffective, well beaten and was described as a 'shambles' in the 7–27 defeat. There was a slight improvement at Clifton where Oxford took a lead but Clifton came back in the second half to impose another loss, 10–18.

There was some light in the gloom when the full Italian team came to Oxford as part of a three game tour. Matched with Oxfordshire, the game was due to take place on the Iffley Road ground on Wednesday 20th March and by the time Italy arrived the team had already lost 12–28 to Middlesex and 7–16 against Sussex. Arriving on the day of the match the tourists enjoyed a sherry with the Lord Mayor in the Oxford Town Hall and were then entertained to lunch by the Oxfordshire RFU. After a brief walkabout tour of the City they had tea at Iffley Road before the match and were guests of the County at dinner in the evening at the Eastgate Hotel. Talk about a busy day! There was drama in the Oxfordshire camp before the match when selectors dropped chosen players, Roy Davies, now of Broughton Park, Liam McCarthy from London Irish and Fred Bannister who was suffering from a hamstring injury, who failed to turn up for training on the Sunday beforehand, a complete back row. They were replaced by Jim Burnell, 'Jock' Lee and Barry Mott. The halftime score of 3–3 was increased with another Italian penalty and they could have been forgiven for thinking the tour would end on a high note, but Ian Ray cut back inside for a try near the posts, Bob Reynolds scored two hard worked touchdowns and finally Rap Tapper added a fourth. Mick Groom dominated the scoreboard with four conversions and two penalties as Oxfordshire inflicted the heaviest defeat of the tour on the Italians. Who would have thought, all those years later, that Italy would regularly feature in the International Championship?

On 23rd March Oxford visibly reeled under the pace and pressure from Metropolitan Police at Imber Court to lose 9–42. A full page length report was devoted to the match in the

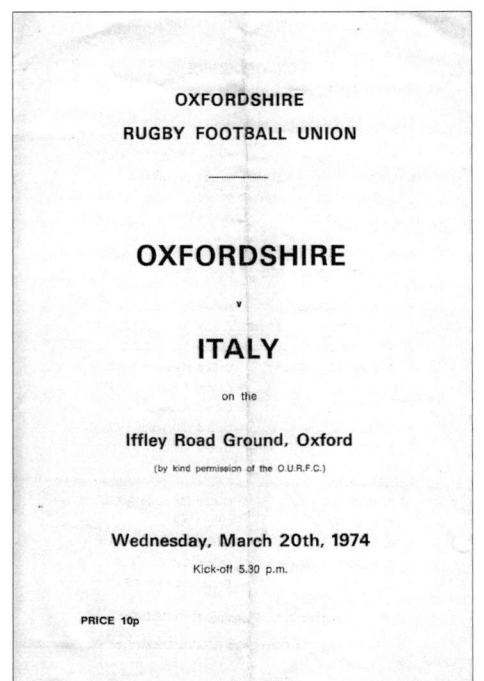 

Oxfordshire v Italy match programme.

Oxfordshire v Italy Dinner Menu. A 5.30pm kick off, 8pm Dinner, a tight schedule!

following *Police Review* but the only mention of the visitors was a line at the bottom of the page which read "Richard Tyrrell, a serving officer with Thames Valley, played for Oxford."

There was no scheduled match the next week, probably a good thing with the club dinner taking place. Affiliation was bravely revived as the prime topic amongst the guest speakers when Mike Boddington, the County President, referred to the recently published Mallaby Report. "Since the 40 major clubs would be given a much bigger say in the affairs of the game if the Mallaby Report proposals were adopted, was this not then the time for Oxford to think of becoming one of the major clubs?" he wisely asked. Ron Grimshaw suggested that the approaches and attitudes may have been wrong in the past but now surely is the time to forget, to put aside past prejudices and pettiness and take a long, hard sensible look to the future. Club Captain Alan Barraclough suggested that it would be a long time before the President's words came to fruition!

Oxford's proposed Easter Tour to Scotland was cancelled after, having already arranged games with Hawick and Gala, officials failed to find a place in one of the Sevens Tournaments due to take place that weekend, and an inter club sevens tournament was arranged for Easter Monday at the club. Only two fixtures remained and Oxford gave a sorry performance to lose 22–3 at Lydney and finally ended the season with a home defeat, 0–28, to Rugby with a much changed side on a hard ground. It was a blessed relief!

In the final few days of what had been a long season came the Oxford Old Boys match with Aylesbury in the Southern Group Final. The Old Boys, having lost all five games played since the Oxfordshire Final, played the match at Iffley Road because they preferred the bigger pitch, but this plan backfired and the team soon had problems in losing the match 9–19.

The season had been very mixed for the First XV with a few highs but too many depressions and the team had won less games, fourteen, than for a decade. Some of this

*Oxford RFC Colts 1974–1975.*
*Back row, l to r: E Harris (Coach), E Hacker (Coach), T Ward, G Penny, N Fielding, R Edwards, R Gray, M Minch, S Anderson, K Davies, P Hookham, J Gray (Manager), R Barley (Manager).*
*Middle row, l to r: B Howard, K White, R Scott (Capt), G Martin, P Wiggins, T Newbury.*
*Front row, l to r: J Smith, I Turner, D Roper, M Ralph, T Round, N Bronway, H Kershaw.*

could be attributed to the loss of the front five forwards and the team also laboured for most of the season without a regular coach, for which there was a real need. The outstanding event of the year was undoubtedly the major improvement of the clubhouse where the central part had been completely rebuilt and enlarged, the old bar had been enlarged and a new lounge bar added. All the work had been carried out under the supervision of David Bagnall with a great deal of time and effort. Whilst this had been carried out in the playing season with disruption and discomfort for the players there would surely be many future benefits.

Looking back on the season in general a former Old Oxford Citizens RFC Captain, Bill Wheal, well known in local sporting circles was compelled to say "The only way to improve the standard of Oxfordshire Rugby is by affiliation of all clubs in the new county to a main club at 1st and 2nd team level. We must face the brutal facts: Oxford RFC has a near first class fixture list but is incapable generally at competing in this class. The other foremost clubs, Oxford Old Boys, Henley, Marathons and Banbury are playing third class fixtures. The rest are playing fourth class rugby.

The main obstacle to affiliation is 'power politics' within the game locally. If Oxford want the affiliation they need so badly they must work on an equal partnership with other clubs. I suggest clubs stop acting like children and try a little 'give and take'. It's time local rugby woke up!" Food for thought over the summer period.

# Season 1974–1975

Player movement in the summer had seen Phil Raybould move to play for Northampton to replace the former Oxford fullback, Ian Moffatt, who had retired from the game. Raybould had been at Oxford for two and a half seasons and in that time had amassed 590 points. The 'flying' Bob Reynolds had gone to New Zealand after a farewell in Oxfordshire that had seen two tries against Italy in March while, after a year at Northampton, John Harwood had gone in the same direction to live for a year.

The new Club Captain was a 'no nonsense' prop forward, Stuart Pickering, a Sergeant in the Royal Air Force stationed at Brize Norton. He had learnt to play rugby in Singapore and Newark, and had already played in the Inter-Services Tournament. Making a very welcome and timely return to the club was Peter West who, once again, had taken up the coaching mantle, and he and Pickering had an important message for the players, writing to say: "We have to start from scratch with no pre-conceived ideas. We intend to religiously apply a 'no training – no selection policy' at senior level. We are in the situation of totally rebuilding the team which is prepared to work hard together for each other, necessary to meet the present circumstances. Prima Donnas who don't train, don't fit in. It will require self-discipline and dedication."

Elsewhere it was reported that Oxford Old Boys were in negotiation with the local authority regarding a new ground, thought to be at Court Farm, Marston, where £40,000 would be needed for a new clubhouse, bar and changing rooms, and £15,000 had been already raised. The lease on the Marston Ferry Road ground was due to expire in 1976 and by then the club hoped to have everything ready on the new site.

The club was pleased to be able to fill in a fixture with Westcliff after the touring side's arranged opponents cancelled. Held on a Tuesday training evening Peter West took the opportunity to see 27 of his players in action. Unlike previous seasons, when the late summer weather was warm and grounds sun baked, the season was welcomed in by a swirling wind and, at intervals, heavy rain as Oxford won 11–0 against the Southend based team.

It was still windy four days later and Weston-super-Mare took advantage of it in the opening half of the opening match to take a half time lead that Oxford could not match in the second period as the team went down 4–13. There was more excitement the next day as Oxford played a President's XV, comprised of players from Oxfordshire clubs, when the Vice President of The Rugby Football Union officially opened the new clubhouse facilities. In a game where the scratch team held the upper hand for long periods Oxford came good towards the end to win 17–15. This success continued with a good 17–4 win in perfect conditions on a first visit to Sidcup but the team came unstuck at Stroud in a 4–12 defeat. The spirit

*New Captain Stuart Pickering reads out pre-season Trial teams.*

apparent in the team was ably displayed by Malcolm Pigg who drove home to Oxford from Cornwall and then on to Stroud for the match. After a 7 hour drive he arrived 25 minutes before the kick-off to be told by coach Peter West that he'd lost his place as he could hardly be mentally and physically prepared after such a long drive. So he watched the 1st team play and then played in the Nomads match that followed, there being only one pitch at Stroud.

One of Oxford's early season needs was a regular goal kicker and Peter Ramsden, who was in the Royal Air Force at Brize Norton, was promoted from the Nomads for that purpose despite his relative inexperience as a winger, for the club's third successive away trip, this time to Preston Grasshoppers. But the distance did not seem to bother the players who played well enough for a 20–4 win in miserable conditions of wind and rain. However the trip was not without incident. The club had planned a diversion afterwards to see the Blackpool Illuminations and the party left at 7.45pm. About six miles down the road the coach broke down, conveniently outside a pub. The party was eventually advised to return to the Preston clubhouse but the coach eventually gave up this time outside a fish and chip shop. From there the players were ferried back by mini bus arriving at 11.30pm just as a disco was ending. The steward provided coffee and sandwiches and a few blankets before the players were roused at 5.15am as the relief coach arrived to take them back to Oxford where they arrived exactly 24 hours after setting off from the Bypass ground. Some away trip!

All this was put aside for the annual midweek match with Oxford University. This was the first time in the series that the Dark Blues had played as Oxford University when previously they had played as the University Captain's XV. Nigel Street, having joined from Esher, Fred Bannister and John Gunter kept their places in the back row in a very close and even tussle, and while Charles Kent kicked a drop goal for the Blues it was Street who was credited with Oxford's try after a break from Martin Bampton and points kicked by Ramsden in the 9–3 win.

Oxford won again on 5th October beating St Helens 19–10 before the mini run of victories came to an end with a disappointing display at the hands of Glamorgan Wanderers. The team conceded 13 points before tempers flared in the second half and in one skirmish giant

*Oxford University Captain Charles Kent attempts to bursts through Oxford's defence.*

lock Chris Jones was sent from the field, the first player to do so in a senior game since Tony Ginger twenty two years previously. This ended all hope of a comeback in the 0–17 defeat. The club's problems continued eight days later with the visit to South Wales. Injuries at half back saw Giles Thomas, a Radley schoolboy the season earlier, selected at scrum half while Peter Ramsden, who had been brought in primarily for his place kicking but had failed to land a single goal in the previous two games, gave way on the wing to Duncan Kilgour. Pontypool had requested a Sunday kick off so that their members could watch Wales against Tonga in Cardiff on the Saturday in which Pontypool's Terry Cobner was playing. There were heavy showers before the kick-off which restricted the attendance to around 2000 and Oxford found no sympathy for agreeing to the first Sunday match to be held in the town. But the team earned full marks from the appreciative crowd for the way in which they came back into the game despite losing 10–25.

Meanwhile, over in Reading a remarkable incident occurred when the complete Oxford 'A' team, the club's fourth side, was sent from the field near the end of the match with Reading University III. Oxford hooker George Webb was dismissed for alleged dangerous play and he walked to the touchline where he stopped to chat with a spectator. The referee would not restart the game until he had gone to the pavilion and when it was suggested to the referee that he should perhaps tell him that, he promptly blew his whistle and dismissed the remaining fourteen Oxford players! The Oxford side was losing 7–17 at the time in what was described as "the cleanest possible game." The referee was given an Oxford team list afterwards of: DF Bagnall; B Turnbull, GFG Barrett, AA Dunnill, A Parker; LR Evans, M Elias; R Quinby, G Webb, M Ralph, G Anderson, G Penny, D Paterson (Capt), D Bibby, M Roberts. There was much speculation in the following days as to what might happen. Would the whole team, which included David Bagnall, the County Match and Team Secretary, and the County Coach Lynn Evans, be summoned to appear before the County Disciplinary Committee? Any embarrassing situations were however averted when it was revealed that the referee's report stated that he did not send off the entire team and did not abandon the game although he had "ended the game early because of the players' attitude." But the club was issued with a warning as to their future conduct, and George Webb was

*Big Chris Jones gets the ball back to scrum half Martin Bampton with help from Stuart Pickering, Brian Whitcombe, Fred Bannister and John Gunter. Jock Lee looks on.*

suspended for two weeks as was Chris Jones for the incident against Glamorgan Wanderers.

Improvement continued with a 39–4 demolition of a lukewarm Guy's Hospital team but this came to a shuddering halt a week later when Oxford's forwards met their match in the form of a solid and well drilled Solihull pack which led to a 4–23 loss.

Oxford's defeat in the County Cup Final the previous season had led to a decision where the club declared the intention of fielding a strong Nomads XV prior to cup games on a Sunday. This would keep faith with the regular Saturday fixture list and, in the four years of cup competition, the club had never cancelled a First XV fixture. The club rested the First XV and sent a strong Nomads side to Guildford & Godalming which ended in a 3–13 defeat. Nigel Rose set a challenge of who would get back to the clubhouse first and was soon out of sight after leaving the Guildford ground. The following car stayed back all the way but cut across the grass verge on the bypass at the top of the lane while Nigel went on to and around Botley roundabout. The occupants quickly ordered half pints in pint mugs to look comfortable when Nigel walked in. His face was a picture! This selection policy kept other players fresh and a 28–7 win at Bicester saw the team into the cup quarter finals. On the same afternoon the cup holders, Oxford Old Boys, lost 0–11 at Chinnor.

In their sixth successive away match Oxford were again beaten up front and suffered a 6–28 loss at US Portsmouth as a result, before returning to the Bypass and better form against Lydney. Winger Clive Richardson was promoted from the Nomads after a sparkling five try performance the week before and he duly obliged with three more in the 21–9 victory. The topsy turvy form continued until the end of November when Oxford's visit to Rugby was used as an occasion to celebrate the opening of Rugby's new clubhouse. Rugby celebrated on the field also to the delight of their Vice Presidents with a decisive 34–6 win over the visitors.

Following the review of some aspects of County rugby, instigated by Witney RFC the previous season, Witney full back Gary Grant was selected for Oxfordshire team to visit Hertfordshire in the opening Championship group match but lost his place when he failed to turn up on the Sunday prior to the mid-week match on 9th October. The Witney club had played Llandaff in Cardiff the previous day. The team contained six Oxford players, Ian McDougall, Duncan Kilgour, Ray Tapper, Stuart Pickering, Chris Jones and Phil Dedrick while four others had played for the club at some time. A spirited rally allowed the team to come from a long way behind to beat Hertfordshire 19–17. Kilgour, in his 62nd County appearance, scored two tries, the second of which when he latched on to a Tapper cross kick, a play seen many times on the Bypass ground, to score in the corner late in the game. Mick Groom's conversion clinched the match for Oxfordshire. But Groom's five penalty kicks were not enough to save Oxfordshire in a 15–18 defeat by Buckinghamshire, before a split knee cap caused an enforced break in his rugby. Eighteen year old Clive Woodward, already at fly half for Harlequins and who qualified for Oxfordshire on grounds of residency as his father was serving at RAF Brize Norton, was introduced to the team at centre but the injury hit side went down 3–14 to Berkshire at Banbury where the game was switched to a smaller adjoining pitch because the main pitch was under water. Woodward was, of course, to go on and play for England and then coach the national side to World Cup glory in 2003. It was he who, when the water logged Twickenham caused the cancellation of Harlequins match with Oxford University, put his head round the Oxford clubhouse door on 16th November looking for a game. Phil Kelly, the club's 'A' fifteen captain, was beside himself in accepting the offer and the team understandably recorded a 49–0 win over Cholsey II. Woodward left his mark in his second and last appearance by helping Oxfordshire to avoid the 'wooden spoon', kicking three penalties and a conversion in a 19–8 win against Dorset & Wiltshire. The Oxford lock forward, David Jones, created history in this game by becoming Oxfordshire's first substitute in a Championship match. Substitutes were allowed for the first time in the County Championship in this season when six could be named but only two used and only then when a doctor ruled that a player was unfit to continue. Jones replaced Jerry Smith in the 68th minute of the match.

Following the defeat at Rugby the club made five changes for the visit to Tredegar when full back Mike Hughes, after fourteen consecutive appearances, Mathias Williams, Nick Forrester, Phil Dedrick and the unavailable Stuart Pickering, playing for the RAF, were all replaced. The team had only itself to blame for the 7–12 defeat after a slow start when chances lost could have made all the difference. Peter Ramsden, at full back, was the Oxford man-of-the-match by virtue of his size, strength and speed and it was he who engineered the teams' only try by Kilgour.

Experienced scrum half Phil Blake returned for the home cup match with RAF Brize Norton, as did Stuart Pickering and both he and Ramsden were due to clash with their mid-week team mates. It was Blake's first senior game since injury in September at Stroud. The club team overwhelmed the airmen 54–7 with ten tries of which seven were converted by Tapper to earn Oxford a home draw against Henley – again!

The team faced a different proposition the following week with a visit to London Irish whose team included Irish internationals Ken Kennedy and Mick Molloy. There was little Christmas joy for Oxford on a cold and blustery December afternoon with a 3–25 half time deficit. But the team drew plaudits for the determined way in which they stemmed the points flow in the second period. Richardson intercepted a Molloy pass to sprint 70 yards for a try that Tapper converted to add to his two penalty kicks which at least gave some respect to the final 12–37 score.

Oxford made an excellent start to 1975 in beating the most successful of all the London Old Boys Clubs, Old Whitgiftians, 28–3. Tapper, standing in as captain in Pickering's absence, led the way with a try, three conversions and a penalty in a splendid performance. But his lone penalty could not save the day at Esher as Oxford conceded two in a very close game to lose 3–6.

Tapper's mercurial form was again evident in the cup semi-final against Henley on the Bypass. The home team were trailing for at least an hour in a close and tense match before some magic from Tapper helped to create a try for Kilgour under the posts and Oxford hung on to win 12–6 and a place, again, in the final. This result at least gave some consolation to a farcical situation over fixtures. Both clubs had regular fixtures, Henley with Twickenham and Oxford with Loughborough Colleges on the Saturday afternoon but both agreed that the cup match should take place on Saturday when players were fresh. Loughborough agreed to play on Sunday but Twickenham did not. The stalemate was broken when the organising sub-committee ruled that the game would be played on Sunday. So, on Oxford's adjoining pitch, an Oxford XV comprising of several guest players, entertained and beat Loughborough, for whom a certain Ted Sandbach featured at full back, 18–15. There was mounting criticism of the cup competitions beyond Oxfordshire from clubs like Oxford who took the long term view that regular fixtures were very important, compounded locally by Oxford who had left 25th/26th January free should the instance of a cup match be a possibility.

This free date was quickly filled by an eager Oxford University Greyhounds side that caused Oxford to work hard for a 13–10 win. Once again Tapper was the winner with three

*Oxford RFC 1974–1975. Back row, l to r: J Deans (Trainer), J Smith, D Kemble, N Forrester, R Forsyth, S Williams, D Jones, P West (Coach). Middle row, l to r: C Richardson, W Cooke, N Bourne, C Bevan, R Parker. Front row, l to r: R Calver, D Kilgour, S Pickering (Capt), R Tapper.*

penalties while Richardson scored Oxford's only try, and it was also Tapper's drop goal that secured a 3–3 draw with Bridgwater & Albion the following week.

The club introduced Stuart Boyce, a doctor at the Radcliffe Infirmary and an Australian International with 12 caps, in the centre for the home match with Abertillery but two brief lapses cost the game, 15–18, where a draw would have been a fair result. But a 13–11 win after a hard slog in muddy conditions away at Nuneaton put the team in good stead for the forthcoming cup final a week later, it being the club's first win there since 1967.

Another local derby cup final quickly loomed, Oxford's fourth appearance in the five seasons since the competition began. Again the opponents were Oxford Marathon whom Oxford had beaten two seasons previously. Once again the Maras put up a good fight in the forwards but this was a rare day when their kicker, Mike Groom, was badly off form.

*Scrum half Richard Parker is off down the blind side in the Cup Final against Oxford Marathon.*

*Clive Richardson scoots round Andy Norman on his way to the try line.*

*Oxford RFC, the 1975 Oxfordshire Cup winners celebrate back at the club.
Along the back: Peter Ramsden, Ray Tapper, Richard Parker, John Gunter, Duncan Kilgour,
Nigel Street, Brian Whitcombe, Alan Lisle, Nick Forrester. Middle: Roy Calver, Clive Bevan,
Sid Carter, John Deans, Eric Church, Clive Richardson, Jim O'Connell, Seretse Williams,
Brian Deane. At the front: Alan Davies, Peter West, Stuart Pickering.*

The Maras backs were rarely seen and, in contrast, Clive Richardson scored three tries on Oxford's wing to add to a fourth from Peter Ramsden. Three of the tries were converted by Tapper to give Oxford a comfortable win and the title of County Champions once more. It was a fine farewell for Ramsden who was playing his final match for the club before leaving for a posting in Gibraltar.

Oxford continued with a 13–12 away win at Streatham but lost the next three games to Birmingham, Clifton and the Metropolitan Police. This brought Easter into focus, early this year at the end of March. The club had decided against touring and opted instead for a series of three home matches, all against clubs new to the fixture list. The first, against the Vale of Lune, saw a fortunate 20–18 win after Oxford had taken a 20–4 lead, when a missed conversion in the final minute would have seen a draw. It was the reverse the next day against Walsall as Oxford came back when Kilgour latched on to a Tapper cross kick, the old trick, for a try that Tapper converted for a commendable 10–6 victory. After a days' rest Oxford were back in action for the Monday match with Warrington and celebrated after a hard game with a 21–4 win. Again Richardson notched up three tries in the club's third win in four days.

The team was forced into six changes for the home game with Tredegar due to injuries after the busy Easter weekend, and unavailabilities, and both looked and played like a scratch team in losing 3–9.

The final arranged fixture for the season was an away trip to Pontypridd on 12$^{th}$ April but the club was forced to cancel this by virtue of the fact that, as county champions, an away Preliminary Round match against Havant in the National Club Championship took precedence. This was an unusual but understandable step for the club to take and Havant, likewise, cancelled a match with Old Tiffinians. Although players were due to return

*Oxford v Warrington, Easter 1975. Seretse gets his man!*

*David Kemble stumbles but stays on his feet with Clive Bevan and Stuart Pickering not far away.*

*David Jones touches down for a try against Havant after a charge down with Roger Forsyth in support. But it wasn't enough.*

for Oxford two other key figures were not available. Brian Whitcombe, after thirty two games in the second row this season, stayed at home as his wife was expecting a baby, and Stuart Boyce could not get time away from the hospital. Oxford were favourites to win and although Havant had enjoyed a good season the standard of their opposition was seen to be lower than that of Oxford's. It was a close game, as these cup games always were, and Havant shook Oxford with a penalty goal after 60 seconds. The game ebbed and flowed before David Jones charged down a clearance kick and crossed for a try that Tapper converted and Oxford looked to have won the game when Tapper kicked his fourth penalty, this one from 40 yards. But straight from the kick off Havant surged forward to score a try and win the game by the narrowest of margins, 18–19. There was little consolation for Oxford who failed to produce their best form and Stuart Pickering said afterwards "I am bitterly disappointed. We played badly all round, there was just not enough ball." Havant went on to play and beat Hemel Hempstead at home to secure a place in the next season's club championship. With the use of a crystal ball(!) we are able to say that, in a first round home tie in the 1975–1976 season, Havant played and beat Thurrock 12-4 but in another home match in the second round lost to Yorkshire based club Roundhay, later to merge with Headingley to become Leeds Carnegie, 3-24.

For Oxford it was a sad way to end the season and the club was left to reflect on what might have been. The club had won 21 of its games and lost 17 with 1 drawn. The top scorer was Ray Tapper with 155 points from 28 conversions, 26 penalties, 3 tries and 3 drop goals, followed by Clive Richardson with 76 points from 19 tries and Duncan Kilgour with 36 points from 9 tries. Tapper had also made the most appearances with 33 games. Peter West was upbeat and spoke of great spirit and determination within the team, and felt sad not to be able to see it develop as he was leaving the area to take up a job in the motor industry in the Midlands.

There had also been some success off the field and Chairman Eric Church told the Annual Meeting that hopes for increased revenue had been fulfilled due to outside bookings of the clubhouse. This meant that Bar Committee Chairman, Ray Mills, and his helpers had had to work long hours, an unacceptable burden, but finances allowed the club to employ a full time Steward and Roger Mitty took this role. The club was due to be open every evening except Monday including lunch times and this would fit well with the Golf Driving Range that would continue to provide revenue under the control of the new groundsman, Bill Mason.

## Season 1975–1976

The big news as the season approached was that Rugby Union had opened its doors to sponsorship. John Player & Sons, tobacco manufacturers from Nottingham, would give £100,000 over the following three years towards the National Club Championship, or Knockout Cup as it was known, the money to be used in the best interests of the game as decided by the RFU. Nationally the cup had its teething troubles but was now an established event. But in some counties clubs were dropping out of county cup competitions citing too much rugby and interference with normal fixtures and routine, but Oxfordshire seemed to be bucking the trend when it was revealed that the Oxford University Greyhounds and the newly formed Chipping Norton club would be entering the Oxfordshire Knockout Cup where Oxford had been drawn away to Oxford Marathon, a repeat of the last seasons' final.

On the home front Vice Presidents subscriptions were doubled from £2 to £4 as the previous sum hardly covered the cost of various communications. Treasurer John Rowell said "Without the continued support of our Vice Presidents the club cannot survive." At that time there were 370 Vice Presidents and 10 Life Vice President members of the club.

Newcomer to the club was Mick Groom while prop Graham McKenzie was returning to Oxford RFC where he had learnt the game in the late 1960s, after a period at Oxford Marathon. Both said that they wanted to play a few seasons in a higher grade of rugby. They were joined by Cambridge University Blue, Mike Hodgson, a full back, while centre Mike Hutchings returned after a two year absence. Prop Stuart Pickering was elected as Captain for a second season. His claim was that he was the oldest player ever to win an RAF cap and, coming late into the game, had to work hard to maintain standards and had proved to be an enthusiastic club member.

The Oxford team faltered badly in the first match of the season at Weston-super-Mare. The home club was celebrating its centenary season and their place kicker, Robert Hazard, his 200th appearance for the club. Oxford were hesitant and, while Phil Blake, John Gunter and Phil Dedrick caught the eye, were left with just an excellent penalty kick from Hodgson in the 3–21 defeat.

Groom was moved up from the Nomads four days later for the evening kick off with California. The American team had walloped Gosford All Blacks at the weekend but then lost to a modest Oxford 12–0. Oxford's experience was paramount against a team who admitted that the base of the tour was to learn about the game. The occasion prompted Oxford's former President, Jim O'Connell, to make a pointed statement saying that his own club had taken about twelve months to arrange a trip in their own country but California, with no clubhouse to provide bar profits, had risen to the challenge of air fares etc by menial tasks such as serving at petrol pumps. Oxford had been invited to California but first they must shrug off the apathy that often shrouded the club. "The problem we have to overcome is the old, old story – getting people to work. Even at rugby clubs people are work-shy" he said.

The trip to which Jim O'Connell referred was Oxford's early season tour to Cornwall that started at Penzance on Saturday 13th September in vicious weather conditions. Lashing rain swept on by gale force winds made rugby very difficult while the influence of England prop Brian 'Stack' Stevens was felt. Oxford dealt with the conditions best and Bob Buckingham was sturdy in the pack along with Phil Dedrick but it was Ian McDougal who latched on to a loose ball after a failed clearance kick. Tapper converted to add to his penalty goal as Oxford recorded a notable victory, 9–3. Two days later, in sunshine, the team disappointed in a 10–21 defeat against Redruth, the first time the two sides had met. Nigel Bourne scored in the corner while Groom kicked two penalties as Oxford's comeback was too late to make a difference.

The club kept faith with the team that beat Penzance & Newlyn for the following weekend's match with Stroud but the players struggled against the adventurous Stroud backs in a 3–28 defeat.

Maybe there was a hangover from the previous season's County Championship as interest in the Oxfordshire team seemed to be at a low ebb. The traditional trial match was cancelled after only 25 players turned up for squad training from the 40 who had been sent cards. Ray Tapper, the previous Captain, announced that he would not be available for county rugby this season and then, a few days later, Lynn Evans resigned as Coach to the Oxfordshire RFU citing his extreme disappointment and displeasure at the attitude of the clubs and to squad training. He said "I have become fed up with this general attitude and have no heart for the job." Nevertheless the Oxfordshire team beat South Warwickshire 16–9 in a pre-championship 'friendly'.

Further afield, the RFU frowned on the idea of an Anglo/Welsh league as not being in the best interests of the game. Instead the clubs involved planned not a league but a merit table within existing fixtures, while 'up north' leading clubs were planning the same thing. The bottom line was that there was growing interest for competition in the game.

Oxford shrugged off any apathy that remained after the Stroud defeat to beat Cheltenham 22–9 away in a win that again featured three tries from Clive Richardson. This was followed by a substantial victory over Worthing, 28–0, on 4th October. Six tries were scored and several others should have been with full back Ted Sandbach, now a teacher at Magdalen College School, often moving into the line to make an extra man in attack. Only two conversions were added which sparked a debate about goal kicking when the obvious choice, Mick Groom, was playing in the Nomads. His rival scrum half though, Phil Blake, was playing well enough to retain the position.

The club's next match, an evening kick off away to Lydney on Wednesday 8th October, was a direct clash with Oxfordshire's opening championship match with Dorset & Wilts at Salisbury. Club Fixture Secretary Roger Forsyth said "We tried all ways to find another suitable date to switch the match but Tuesday (the day before the county game) was the only alternative date that Lydney could offer." Even this clashed with a pre match get-together after a cancelled Sunday squad session. The club accepted that Oxford players would be involved but were concerned about others who might be asked to travel as substitutes and then miss out on both games. Nine Oxford players played in the county team that lost to Dorset & Wilts 15–22, the home team's first win for three years and their first over Oxfordshire in six years, after Oxfordshire let slip a 15–6 lead. At Lydney a much reduced Oxford team lost 9–12 despite a home prop being sent off for kicking an Oxford player which was equalised with David Jones later leaving the field with a broken nose.

This began a sequence of four consecutive defeats for the club, away matches at Glamorgan Wanderers, where centre Mike Hutchings was sent off after dissent, Oxford University and Esher, while a 15–26 Oxfordshire defeat against Hertfordshire at Henley in the same period compounded some Oxford players' misery. Oxfordshire's hopes for the season were now virtually over. There was a desperate need for good, big forwards as when injuries set in the team was in trouble. The question of "Isn't it time the county selectors started looking elsewhere for players other than the Oxford club?" was asked, but clubs hadn't been too keen to nominate any likely candidates.

All this made for a gloomy period at the club and there was an air of frustration after four games without a win. But the visit of the Guy's Hospital team on Saturday 25th October offered some hope and Oxford started strongly, rewarded with a Groom penalty. A long searing run from Sandbach which split the Medics defence resulted in a try for Kilgour, then Williams collected a Tapper cross kick for another. Both were converted by Groom to give the home side a healthy 15–0 lead. Oxford looked comfortable but Guy's had other ideas and attacked to reduce and then equalise the score. David Pitt touched down to restore the lead but in the heat of the forward battle players momentarily lost control and the Oxford captain, Stuart Pickering, was sent off for kicking an opponent in the scrum. The match result was a comfortable looking 28–15 win after Sandbach added Oxford's fourth try but all the post-match talk was about the sending off incident.

The very next day Oxford travelled the short distance to play Oxford Marathon on the Cowley Marsh Recreation Ground in a County Cup match. Before the match Pickering lectured his players about over-reacting and was himself warned by several people of this danger. Then, in the first scrum he alleged that two fingers were poked in his eyes, swung

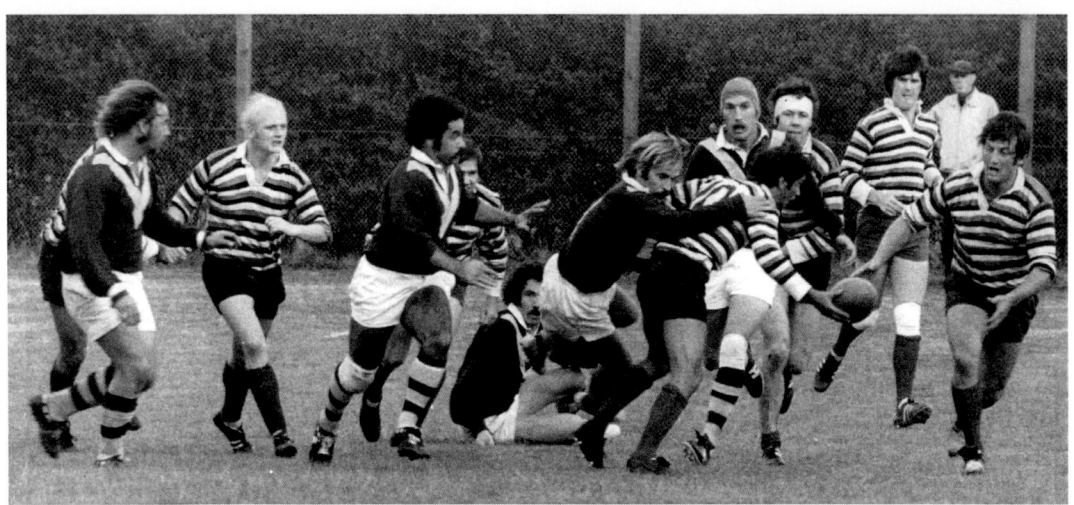
*Ray Tapper offloads to Phil Dedrick against Santa Monica, Mike Hodgson in the background.*

*Mike Hutchings on the charge with Clive Bevan and Stuart Pickering in support.*

*Ted Sandbach in typical form.*

*John Gunter drops down on the ball while Mike Groom and the McCarthy brothers watch points.*

*Mick Groom kicks against his former club Oxford Marathon, while Nick Forrester and David Pitt await the outcome.*

*Forrester and Ray McCarthy stretch in the lineout.*

a punch and was sent off for the second time within 15 minutes of actual playing time. Although reduced to fourteen players Oxford won a sour match easily enough, 27–4, but a fair amount of the match did little for the image of the game. Stuart Pickering tendered his resignation that evening which was accepted, the Committee saying that it "wishes to express its whole hearted thanks for his services to the club." His situation drew sadness from the Oxford players, one of whom said "He has led us well at a difficult time for the club. Of course he was silly but, in a cup match, we believe he was deliberately provoked."

Elsewhere on the day there were shocks when Bicester beat Henley, while the Old Boys lost at Banbury, despite having rested their First XV players by sending a 2nd XV to lose at Chiltern 0–50.

Oxford went on to lose 3–12 to Pontypool, who included four current Welsh internationals in the forwards, 8–18 at Tredegar and then 10–12 to United Services, Portsmouth in nasty conditions at the Bypass ground.

Ray Tapper was appointed as Captain for the remainder of the season, his third stint in the role and he celebrated with a 17–15 win over Sutton & Epsom after Groom's brilliant last ditch tackle in the dying moments saved the day, and then kicked a drop goal in injury time against Streatham & Croydon for the desired win, 10–9.

At last, after eighteen months deliberating, the RFU announced the decision that all rounds of the National Club Championship would be played on fixed dates. Locally, Stuart Pickering was banned from playing for 9 weeks and could resume playing on 15th January. At the same time the RFU said, in a widely publicised attempt to stamp out foul play, that it would support England selectors if they left disciplined players out of the team while hoping county and club selectors would follow suit. What this meant, of course, is that a player, having served his sentence and wiped the slate clean, could continue to pay the penalty through non selection.

Having held a 15 point lead and subsequently lost on two occasions, Oxfordshire produced a sustained performance to beat Buckinghamshire, 15–12, and then an enterprising 13–4 victory over Berkshire to finish third in the table. This was based on the forwards where Nigel Goodey won eight strikes against the head, but the chief architect was again

*In October 1975 the Club President, John Rowell, invited former Presidents to a lunch. Here they are, back row l to r: CT Ede (1966–67), JF Mawle (1972–74), VP Dive (1963–66), S Pether (1955–59), AW Archer (1961–63), JRM Higgins (1969–71). Front row l to r: HW Phillips, RB 'Bunnie' Cole (1945–49), J Rowell (1975–79), WE Ross-Harper (1954–55 & 1959–60), ET Hull (1953–54 & 1960–61), RA Ede (1971–72), CJ O'Connell (1974–75).*

Groom with safe fielding, touch kicking and 9 points. Soon afterwards it was announced that Groom and Ted Sandbach had been selected for the Southern Counties squad from which the team to face Australia at Aylesbury on 10$^{th}$ December would be chosen.

Oxford came unstuck at home to Lydney at the start of December and the side was well beaten up front in a 6–34 defeat. Best try of the match though came from Sandbach in a swerving run from the home 25 yard line to score in the corner for a Groom conversion. Maybe the players had some thought for the following day when, showing little change to personnel, Oxford beat Bicester in a county cup match comfortably enough with tries from Kilgour, Cornthwaite and Sandbach.

Mick Groom was eventually selected as scrum half for the Southern Counties to play Australia in a team that also included ex Oxford player Ian Ray in the centre. The team put up a splendid, spirited fight and Groom was very busy round the scrum in a thoroughly competent performance by him adding to the scoreline with a long range penalty kick in the 14–33 defeat.

Oxford finished the year unbeaten and Ray Tapper was to the fore in organising a fine performance in the 14–7 win at Solihull where the McCarthy brothers, Liam and Ray, made their mark in the back row. Rugby were beaten 20–15 to avenge a heavy defeat in the previous season before the team ended 1975 with a 9–9 draw at Walsall.

It had been a traumatic few months but despite all the upheavals the club finished with a creditable best first half of the season for three years. Ray Tapper had taken over the captaincy at a very difficult time and maintained, if not lifted, spirits within the club that had already won six games under his guidance.

David Pitt ensured that the club faced a new challenge at the start of 1976. The tradition of not getting married during a rugby season was broken when he announced that his wedding would take place on 3rd January in Devon! Wedding guests included Mike Hutchings, Phil Dedrick, Andy Smith, Roger Steer and Ian McDougall which meant some movement in the club's playing ranks for the away game at Old Whitgiftians was inevitable! In the event the deputies did well to keep Oxford's run of success going with a 19–13 win. The team included ever present Nigel Goodey, while scrum half Phil Blake was still keeping Mick Groom in the Nomads, and won again this time 27–10 over Esher. But it was case of down to earth with a bump in the 6–33 defeat at Loughborough Colleges when a certain Clive Woodward scored a brilliant try before tempers flared and prop Roger Steer was sent off for fighting.

With the bubble burst Oxford featured in a dour struggle at home to Sidcup which produced one of those rare results – a 0–0 draw. Matters didn't improve much the following day, at home to Chinnor in the county cup semi-final. Ray McCarthy, ever improving, ran hard down the touchline to pass inside for Andy Smith to touch down, and then beat winger Nigel Pollard to score himself for a Tapper conversion as the team edged home, 10–0.

January ended with a rare weekend off for the players as a frozen ground put paid to the visit of Stafford but this did Oxford no apparent favours in a 3–25 defeat at Bridgwater the following week. A view on tactics was that the team should play for position rather than expose the defence with running rugby. Another defeat this time 15–26 at Yorkshire club Morley was followed by a creditable win against Nuneaton, 11–10.

Cup final weekend loomed but the Oxford club was determined to honour the listed fixture at Maesteg on the Saturday. The home side, unable to find like opposition, agreed to the visit of the strongest side Oxford could send and, to this point, the Nomads had lost only three games in the season. The side included thirteen players with First XV experience but had a rude awakening as Welsh Merit Table side Maesteg won 50–15.

*Stuart Pickering made his comeback in January 1976 for RAF Brize Norton against Thames Valley Police but never again appeared at the Southern Bypass ground.*

There was some talk about the validity of a neutral venue for the cup final as the Iffley Road ground was home to Oxford's opponents, Oxford University Greyhounds, but in reality this view was insignificant. The Greyhounds, the University club's second XV, were still carrying out fitness tests an hour before kick-off to see who would play where. Oxford's prop Graham McKenzie went down with 'flu on the morning of the match which proved to be a blow as Oxford were badly beaten for technique in the front row. In a tedious match Oxford fell foul of the referee and the players became increasingly irritated. With penalty after penalty going against them the game deteriorated and the Greyhounds scored the only try of the match to add to four penalty goals scored earlier. For Oxford only Ray Tapper troubled the scoreboard with two penalty kicks in a 6–18 defeat which was later described as the poorest final to date. Oxford team was: EPL Sandbach; SA Boyce, SA Williams, AP Smith, C Richardson; RP Tapper (Capt.), PJ Blake; D Jones, N Goodey, RGB Steer, JB Whitcombe, RH Forsyth, MAA Florey, L McCarthy and RP McCarthy.

There were some long faces at the club after this defeat, not because the team was decisively beaten but because the players expected to win and the result was a shock. The next week Oxford lost a morning fixture at Streatham & Croydon and then went on to watch England lose 12–13 to Ireland at Twickenham before losing next 3–22 at home to Birmingham.

A first ever away win at Metropolitan Police at Imber Court helped to lift the gloom and the team were deserved winners with two penalties from Wallace Ewart before he returned home to Northern Ireland. But it took a try from Mike Florey with minutes to go to clinch it at 10–6.

Another home defeat followed, this time by a point, 11–12 to Weston-super-Mare before the team scraped home against Gloucestershire side Hucclecote Old Boys, 10–6. But worse was to come with a record 3–53 loss at Pontypridd on 10th April where Nigel Goodey left the field with a broken nose just before the break. Ironically the club had agreed to a switch

*McCarthy competes in the lineout against Weston-super-Mare watched by John Taylor and Phil Blake.*

of venues as the Pontypool team had returned from a continental tour the day before the match.

The Oxford club recalled George Webb to hook for the two home Easter games which marked the end of the regular season after he had 'officially retired' three seasons previously although he had been playing in the junior teams. The Easter Saturday match saw a long awaited return to form as Oxford romped home against Durham City, 32–11, for the team's biggest win of the season, and this was followed two days later with a deserved 10–6 victory over Manchester. Nigel Pollard scored the last try of the campaign and Mick Groom converted to bring his First team total to 98 points.

The overall results with 19 games won, 2 drawn and 20 lost showed a creditable enough season's rugby and considering the strength of the fixture list the position gave reasonable satisfaction in a period of recovery and rebuilding.

*Ray Tapper – fleet footed, ball in two hands, carves out another break.*

The team had shown a resilience to bounce back after the occasional adversity and with a reliable place kicker would have had a better record. Mick Groom, who spent most of the season piling up points in the Nomads, played in only 17 of the 41 First XV matches. On the other hand the Nomads, under the capable and obviously inspirational management of Keith Chapman, had lost just 4 of 33 games played.

The season was not completely over however, as a club team produced the surprise of the Oxfordshire 7's Tournament and, in beating Northampton, Richmond (the holders), and London Scottish, reached the final at Iffley Road. The team of: A Smith, SA Williams, RP Tapper, MJ Groom, D Jones, PJS Dedrick and N Street played some dazzling rugby but eventually ran out of steam to lose 12–34 to Saracens.

The club's first paid steward, Roger Mitty, left the post after ten months for work with 'Help The Aged' with some saying he could have integrated both jobs by staying where he was and, having done so much to help get the club on its feet socially, his services would be missed.

## Season 1976–1977

At the June AGM, after showing a profit of £121, playing subscriptions were increased by 50p to £5 after a proposal from the players. Chairman Eric Church, who had so ably steered the club through the difficult period following the dissolving of the Sports Club through to the then relatively strong position, stood down and was replaced by David Bagnall while, after seven years, Secretary David Fitzpatrick made way for Ron Martin.

Locally, Oxford City Planning Committee turned down an Oxford Marathon plan for a clubhouse and changing facilities at Cowley Marsh on the Chairman's casting vote while Oxford Old Boys had a similar plan in the Green Belt at Sandford rejected by the South Oxfordshire Council as both clubs sought a permanent home.

The summer of 1976 was to be known as 'The year of the drought' and no rain fell for several months causing rock hard grounds and playing havoc during much reduced pre-season training where any tackle practice was limited to kneeling. The RFU advised all clubs to proceed with the utmost caution! Ironically a new replacement law was introduced which allowed a maximum of two replacements during a match in any team at all levels but only after an injury.

Prop forward Graham McKenzie was elected as Captain for the new season and the club would rely on the old guard plus a few players from other local clubs who wanted to try their hand in a higher level. Interestingly Oxfordshire Cup match dates were published, all Sundays, but the club's fixture list was nevertheless full.

Oxford's opening match, at the Bypass, against Weston-super-Mare, was preceded by a drought breaking storm but not enough rain fell to make any difference. Mick Groom opened the teams account with a penalty after five minutes before Nigel Goodey added a try from Nigel Street's pass which was converted for a 9–3 opening success.

The club had opted for a short early season tour and a plan for a relaxing stroll on the Cornish sands was washed out by a strong cold wind and heavy driving rain which continued into the match at Redruth. Oxford's forwards outplayed the home pack but, in the conditions, did not score tries and the excellent Groom kicked three penalties in a 9–9 draw. The Redruth club lost several hundreds of pounds in gate money when a hoax telephone call, believed to have been made from Oxford, informed a national agency that the game was cancelled. Nonetheless the home club still handed over guarantee money to Oxford after the match. For the Monday game, 6 o'clock kick off, Groom, Taylor and Hodgson had to return home as they could not take more time from work and the club had to borrow a local scrum half to complete the team to meet Penzance and it was no surprise that the weakened lineup, lack of a place kicker, more injuries and the ravages of a weekend tour all proved too much and Oxford lost 4–27 in continuous drizzle.

A county trial two days later where Oxfordshire played a County Clubs XV drew in Oxford players and centre Andy Smith was a casualty. Nigel Goodey was sent off along with the Stroud Captain after an incident at the end of a game in Stroud that Oxford lost 3–16.

Returning to home ground at the end of September the team showed great resilience to come back from 3–12 to beat Burton 15–12 without Graham McKenzie who was best man at a wedding, and this form was repeated the following week with another home win, this time 34–0 against Cheltenham. Local youngster Eugene Gratwohl, another product of Peers School, scored three tries from the centre but failed to appear as selected when Oxford lost the annual midweek match with Oxford University 9–12 where Groom kicked three penalties.

Roger Jones, an ex-Marlow player, had been appointed as Coach for the season but, living in London, had found travelling too much and joined Rosslyn Park. His replacement came from within the club with the experienced Roger Forsyth taking over the role.

Oxford were to lose the next five matches against Glamorgan Wanderers, Stourbridge, Manchester, Pontypool and Upper Clapton. In Manchester the team held a healthy 13–3 half time lead with a Mike Hodgson try, two Groom penalties and a Tapper drop goal but within five minutes of the restart Hodgson collided with Nigel Goodey and both had to leave the field, Hodgson with concussion and Goodey requiring stitches. Two minutes later they were joined in the ambulance by Seretse Williams, injured in a head-on tackle. Facing a much reduced side, Manchester got on top to win 13–19. To make matters worse Roger Steer was 'sent off' after remarks made to the referee as the teams left the field. Goodey was declared fit to play the following week, also with a severe reprimand after his sending off at Stroud, as the team gathered to play at Pontypool. With the prospect of facing the famed Welsh front row of the era, in Graham Price, Bobby Windsor and Charlie Faulkner together with Welsh

*Full back Dai David in a determined pursuit against Burton with John Wynn nearby.*

back row player Terry Cobner in what could be described as the best club pack in the world, the players were possibly not in the most positive of minds. The 3–44 defeat reflected this and Windsor was reported as saying that he had "expected Oxford to put their weight and height to better advantage" and was "disappointed Oxford did not put up more of a fight".

During this period the touring Japan side trained at the Bypass ground before demolishing the Oxford University side 37–0 at Iffley Road. Oxfordshire started the Southern Group campaign with six Oxford players, Hodgson, Sandbach, Groom, McKenzie, Pitt and Taylor in the side to face Berkshire while Pollard and Goodey were named replacements. England selector Derek Morgan watched a drab battle with Oxfordshire winning 15–7 and the side went on to beat Dorset & Wiltshire 15–3 two weeks later with Groom kicking three penalties and a conversion on both occasions. Two weeks later Oxfordshire became Southern Group champions again, four years after the last success, with a 17–6 victory over Buckinghamshire at Aylesbury. Duncan Kilgour scored one of three excellent tries and Groom added a penalty and a conversion.

Disturbed by what they saw as a lack of discipline and the subsequent effects on team and club reputation, the Oxford Club Committee decided on a 'get tough' policy. In an effort to clean up the game and to eliminate a lot of dissent that seemed to be creeping in, players sent off would automatically be suspended for two weeks. Later, Oxford Marathons took a similar step in announcing a two week ban on players but this would be in addition to any imposed by the County Discipline Committee. Keith Walker, the club secretary, wrote to players saying that the lowering in standards of behaviour by members had led to three dismissals already in the season. "This puts the club in a bad light due to dissent and unnecessary violence and retaliation. The club is getting a bad reputation in the local area, is not attracting any new players and plans for a new clubhouse may be hampered."

*Pontypool v Oxford match programme.*

With county interest temporarily suspended Oxford found what some thought was their true form and splendid attacking rugby produced eight tries in the away match against Guildford & Godalming. Mick Groom amassed 27 points with 3 tries, 1 penalty and 6 conversions while David David scored 2 tries and Tapper, John Taylor and Nigel Pollard added 1 each. The following day things were not so easy as the team won at RAF Brize Norton in a difficult cup tie, and even more creditable a week later was the 9–9 draw against United Services in Portsmouth.

A club v county clash provided Oxfordshire's fly half Ian Wright, with four England caps in 1971, with a dilemma. Having guided Oxfordshire to a Southern Group title he now found that his club, Northampton, had a John Player Cup clash with Widnes on the same Saturday, 27th November, as the County Championship quarter final match against Gloucestershire. He decided to play for his club and Ray Tapper, with thirty appearances for Oxfordshire in the previous ten years, was recalled. In a rousing match Ted Sandbach gave the visitors the lead with an opportunist try and the merciless Gloucestershire side, with six Internationals, were made to fight for their 37–12 success. This match impacted on Oxford RFC, who had provided seven players and a replacement to the county team, and a home fixture with Welsh side Tredegar. An Oxford side of: David; Johnson, Price, Williams, Barrett; Fitzsimmons, Blake; Bevan, Goodey, Jones, R McCarthy, Rose, L McCarthy, Florey and McClure enjoyed another creditable and encouraging 10–3 win where the front row was particularly effective.

Lydney were beaten 15–10 but the two pre-Christmas games with Esher and Rugby, played in snow, frost and slush were both lost. The club's Oxfordshire Cup match with Oxford University Greyhounds, a rematch of the previous season's final, was postponed due to a frozen pitch and then the students cried off with the new date being out of term and they being unable to raise a side.

*Roger McClure gets close to a tussle for the ball.*

The mid-term report was of a very average season so far with more games lost than won. But talk of the town was about the club's plans to build two squash courts on the club premises at a cost of £20,600. This sum was made up from £3500 already held, a Sports Council grant of £3100, a Bank Loan over five years of £7000, a Bank Overdraft of £3000 and a National Playing Fields Association grant of £500. A loan of £3500 was to be raised from club members who would be repaid at advantageous interest rates. This project, overseen by David Bagnall, was seen as a way of securing the club's financial future by way of increased membership and it was hoped that the courts would be in use by the end of April 1977.

Also heading in the right direction was the Oxford Marathon club and the Oxford City Council had approved in principle a recommendation that the club be granted a lease of land to build a clubhouse at the Horspath Road site.

Oxford began the New Year with a great 33–3 win over visiting Old Whitgiftians at the Bypass ground. The club had created a surprise by selecting Malcolm Fitzsimmons at fly half instead of Ray Tapper in the pre-Christmas match at Rugby and he had kept his place in the team only to leave the field shortly before half time with an ankle injury. Winger Graham Barrett, whose guile and experience of many years brought tries with his first four touches of the ball, was Man of the Match.

Winger Nick Johnson scored five tries as Oxford continued the New Year form by beating Stafford 27–16. Even better was the 10–10 draw with the much vaunted Loughborough Colleges on 15th January. The performance was based on a stern defence but Oxford could have won the match had Barrett's touch down not been ruled out for a foot in touch near the end. The effort made had a definite effect after Oxford took the field 24 hours later for the Oxfordshire Cup semi-final with Henley who were the much sharper side against a jaded

*Oxford RFC 1976–1977. Back row, l to r: T Round, G Barrett, N Rose, R McCarthy, N Street, N Johnson, D David, M Hodgson, R McClure. Front row, l to r: N Pollard, RP Tapper, D Jones, G McKenzie (Capt), M Florey, N Goodey, R Forsyth (Coach).*

home team. Oxford lost 10–13 and went out of the competition leaving Henley to play Chinnor in the final. Once more the result might have been different as the normally reliable Groom missed six shots at goal while an indiscreet remark to the referee gave Irvine Gale an easy penalty for Henley, the three points being decisive.

Local scribe Ron Grimshaw wrote a week later "A point proved beyond argument is that it is asking too much of the players to turn out in two hard games on successive days." He noted that neither Henley nor Chinnor had played on the Saturday and both would be £250 better off while one would be guaranteed another £100 plus the chance of getting among the 'big' money. He went on to say "I applaud clubs brave enough not to cancel Saturday games the day before cup ties, but at the same time, in these hard financial days, I begin to wonder whether clubs can afford these admirably high moral standards."

Oxford were to lose the next two games by a similar score, 4–8, away at Sidcup and then Walsall. There was some comfort in the Midlands match as Paul Sapsford, a prop forward with immense strength who had toured Argentina with the Junior All Blacks and now a dentist in Oxford, made his debut for the club.

The club's home game with Bridgwater on 5$^{th}$ February was delayed when the coach bringing the visitors broke down on the motorway near Swindon. The hour and a half wait was not without its compensations as both players and supporters were able to watch the first half of England's match with Ireland on the television! Despite losing Sapsford with concussion at half time Oxford were good enough for a 10–0 win in a bruising encounter, before being found wanting in several departments in the 13–32 home defeat to Morley. On the same weekend Chinnor, in that club's first final, became Oxfordshire Champions when beating Henley 9–6.

In an end to end wind and on a glue pot of a pitch Oxford made a great comeback from 0–12 down to take the lead and then succumb to a late match drawing penalty, 15–15 at Nuneaton.

During the following week club officials were surprised to learn that Paul Sapsford had been selected to play for Harlequins against Headingley at The Stoop Memorial Ground after selection for Oxford against Gordon League. There had been interest in the player from several directions but officials felt that the club should have had some official notification.

Oxford went on to lose 6–13 to Gordon League but beat Streatham 9–3 at the beginning of March. Two close home defeats followed, 7–10 and 0–3 against Maesteg and Clifton during which time Mick Groom, having a poor run with his place kicking, was replaced at scrum half by Phil Blake. In a mud bath at Imber Court, Tapper's two penalties were enough to beat the Metropolitan Police 6–0 but another home defeat followed, this time 3–9 to Walsall.

The club faced a hard Easter programme with the first of three matches in four days at Bath on Good Friday. It was an uncomfortable visit for Oxford who spent most of the eighty minutes in defence held by a far superior Bath side who dominated in every department to win 0–32. Back on home soil the next day Oxford faced Pontypridd, who were looking to score over 1000 points in the season, with a much changed side due to injuries. The inevitable result was a 9–44 defeat and in probably the club's best two fixtures, a total of 76 points conceded in two days. A day's rest paid dividends as the club met Lydney on Easter Monday who, themselves, were playing their fourth match in five days. Survival played a large part in the game in which Oxford came from behind to win 22–13.

Oxford's final game of the season took place on 15$^{th}$ April when Nick Johnson scored the opening try at Birmingham. After that the home team stepped up and Oxford's defence fell to pieces in the last quarter to concede 26 points in the 7–43 defeat.

*Frank Webb, who had captained the club from 1955 to 1958, was now President of the Devon Rugby Union and presided over the Devon RFU Centenary Dinner and Ball in April 1977. With him here are DC Manley (England), RAW Sharp (England & Lions), GC Brown (Devon Hon Secretary) and REG Jeeps (RFU President, England & Lions).*

The last two weekends in April were taken up with sevens when Oxford were beaten 0–24 by Wasps in the final round of the Middlesex 7s, and by Borough Road College 18–22 after extra time in the Oxfordshire 7s quarter finals.

Thirteen wins and four draws represented the club's worst playing record since the 1963–64 season when only eight games were won. With the usual crop of injuries 45 players were used and only twice did the same team play together. A serious blow was the loss of Mick Groom's kicking form while there was the early disruption of a change of coach when Roger Forsyth took over. Off the field there was talk of new training floodlights and two new squash courts were shortly to be opened which, it was hoped, would boost club membership.

The Oxford Colts team had had a remarkable season after starting with just four players and finished as winners of the first County Colts Cup, beating Chinnor, who were hoping for a county club 'double', 11–9 with tries from Peter Mills and Martin Geddes, and a penalty from John Green. The winning team was: K Powell; N Scroggs, S Dunnill, C Charnock, J Green (Captain); M Geddes, A Griffiths; P Maton, J Bunce, A Dunbar, P Mills, N Surman, R Hixon, P Jones, S Anderson. Maton and Griffths had played in England Trials and much credit was due to Manager Ernie Hacker and Coach Emrys Harris, and several members of the team were due to play in senior rugby the following season.

The club had established a Mini Rugby section in January 1973 and the season just finished had seen another significant increase in young schoolboy activities within the club to the degree that boys having joined then were now 16 years old and ready to train with the Colts. Tom Rees, a parent helper, said "Mini Rugby is long term, but mini boys are the future of Oxford RFC especially Colts. Out of nothing, nothing is produced."

# Season 1977–1978

Following the national boundary revision of 1974 seven clubs formerly in Berkshire, Abingdon, Grove, AERE Harwell, Didcot, Cholsey, RAF Abingdon and RMCS Shrivenham had found themselves, on paper at least, in Oxfordshire and the Southern Group finally decided that the clubs would now come under the jurisdiction of the Oxfordshire RFU. This meant, of course, that former Berkshire clubs would now be included in the Oxfordshire Cup for the first time, this season.

At the Annual General Meeting in June, Lynn Evans was appointed as Club Coach to be assisted by John Gunter. Evans said "We must step it up or we are going to be left behind."

Scrum half Phil Blake had been elected as club captain for the new season but in July, after only one month, he resigned due to an on-going ankle injury which had not responded to the treatment he had been having since Christmas 1977, giving grave doubts about his future fitness. As Nomads Captain he had played in just 10 of the 27 games completed by the team in the previous season and a handful in the First XV. He was due to retain his involvement however when he was named as Nomads Team Manager. In August, flank forward Roger McLure, an Oxford University 'Blue', was announced as Blake's replacement. McLure was familiar with late call ups, his replacement of Hawksworth in the 1973 'Varsity match was so late that he was never mentioned in the programme team list or pen pictures.

One more important factor was to emerge pre-season. Following the club's defeat by Henley in the County Cup Final the club committee had decreed that the First XV would not play in Saturday fixtures prior to a county cup match on a Sunday in future. It had taken seven years for the club to reach this point!

Oxford faced a tough opener to the season with an away trip to play Weston-super-Mare and included Bob Reynolds on the wing. Reynolds had played for the club a few seasons previously after narrowly missing an Oxford 'Blue' through injury and his last appearance before emigrating to New Zealand was for Oxfordshire against Italy in 1974. His ambition was to play in whatever grade of rugby he could but this was cut short when he was involved in a road accident and he decided to return home over land. In the course of that five month trip he contracted Hepititis and needed a considerable time to recover. During this time he had been teaching at Redefield School in Blackbird Leys but was now fit and raring to go. The team that played was: D David; R Reynolds, S Seward, N Pollard, I McDougall; RP Tapper, MJ Groom; A Smith, N Goodey, G MacKenzie, F Morgan, R Rose, N Street, R McCarthy, RN McClure (Capt) and all put up a great performance in the 6–6 draw where Groom also missed four kicks at goal. There were soon injuries and McDougal was set for three months on the side lines after dislocating a shoulder.

Colts flanker Peter Mills was presented with a tankard by President John Rowell before leaving to join the Royal Navy.

The club side lost both games on a short weekend tour to Cornwall, 12–16 against Redruth and 8–25 at Penzance, where Ron Salter won the golf tournament and Ray Tapper was booked for speeding on the way down!

Home defeat followed against Stroud, 6–16, the visitors scoring when McClure was off the field getting his split boot repaired, while Nigel Street was not likely to forget his 50th First Team appearance for the club, spent partly in the treatment room having four stitches inserted to a head wound. But the only drama in another home defeat, 9–15 with Birmingham, was the fact that Oxford threw away a nine point lead!

The County v Clubs trial match revealed that Graham Warrington, playing for Witney, could more than hold his own in representative rugby, invariably outjumping and winning lineout ball against John Orwin of Gloucester fame.

Having lost all five games in September the team at last recorded its first win of the season, at Cheltenham 11–0, when it was clearly the better side with Blake and Tapper playing well behind a dominant pack. But the euphoria did not last long and the club followed by suffering two heavy defeats, 6–41 and 0–46 against Oxford University and Glamorgan Wanderers. Only a 40–3 win against Harwell in the Oxfordshire Cup and then a 10–3 home win against Manchester offered any respite before an inevitable 9–27 home defeat against Pontypool. It was noted that visiting Welsh teams always boosted profits at the club and nearly £40 was taken in the collection box while the bar takings were a record for a club match.

It seemed that Roger McClure, unfailing in personal effort or graft, was unable to motivate his largely inexperienced side. The team was lacking in physical fitness and low in spirit. As well as missing the injured McDougal along with centre Andy Smith after a knee ligament operation the club had also lost David Jones, Seretse Williams and Chris Jones to a Charlie Ede inspired recruitment drive at Oxford Old Boys, Charlie having moved his allegiance to that club.

In contrast Oxfordshire beat Buckinghamshire 18–12 with a 'Houdini' display when a last gasp goal won the game in the fourth minute of injury time, continued with a dramatic 19–15 win at Swindon against Dorset & Wiltshire where Eugene Gratwohl scored a try on his county debut, and then completed a clean sweep to retain the Southern Group Championship title with a 22–9 win in the rain at Newbury against Berkshire. This meant another Quarter Final match against old adversaries, Gloucestershire, on Saturday 12th November.

After the club's traumatic start to the season Oxford began November with the best team performance so far and a 35–9 win over Preston Grasshoppers scoring six tries in the process from Nick Johnson (2), Nigel Rose, Roger McClure, Bob Reynolds and Andy Norman. Mick Groom added four conversions to the total.

Oxford lost at home to Guildford & Godalming 6–15 but had saved all the First team players, other than those playing against Gloucestershire, for the County Cup match the

*Oxford RFC 1977–1978. Back row, l to r: J Taylor, L Evans (Coach), S Carter (Manager), K Bulley, G McKenzie, D Pitt, L McCarthy, B Whitcombe, A Dunn, A Norman, N Street, A Smith, D David, J Deans (Trainer), J Gunter (Coach). Front row, l to r: RP Tapper, N Goodey, N Johnson, R McClure (Capt), M Groom, W Powell, R Reynolds, G Lewis.*

*John Taylor tries to break past a Pontypridd visitor with support from McClure, McCarthy and McKenzie.*

*John Taylor tackles, will Bob Reynolds poach the Pontypridd back hand off load?*

following day at Bicester, an uninspiring 13–6 win. At Iffley Road Oxfordshire went out of the County Championship when losing 15–29 to neighbouring Gloucestershire, who were slightly flattered by the scoreline. Gareth Lewis, Nick Johnson, Mike Groom, Adrian Dunn and Nigel Street all featured in this match.

Lynn Evans had formed a coaching team of John Kennady, John Gunter and Andy Smith and, at last, this was having some effect, while Em Harris was doing the Colts. Evans saw the development of mini rugby as particularly important at the club and was looking for Under 14 and Under 15 teams after Christmas as an essential link into the Colts team. He said "We also have a duty at Oxford to improve our relationships with other clubs to share coaching sessions with us. Other clubs must see us as a rugby club with a first class coaching organisation".

Oxford responded on the second highest pitch in Wales, carved out of the hillside, with a splendid effort to beat Tredegar 24–13. It was the club's first win on Welsh soil for five seasons and both Bob Reynolds and Adrian Dunn scored two tries with Johnson one while Groom kicked two conversions.

A weak Oxford team lost 6–23 to Lydney the day before a competent display saw Henley defeated 21–4 in the next round of the County Cup, as if to justify the club's new policy in that direction.

The rest of December saw defeats at home to Pontypridd, always welcome opponents, and on the road to Walsall and Burton on Trent, both in the Christmas/New Year period. The only spark was an eleven try romp at home to Abingdon who had replaced Rugby at short notice due to a fixture mix-up.

As the New Year dawned Ray McCarthy announced that he would be leaving the club after 168 First Team appearances to date to take up a post in Bath where he hoped to continue playing.

Oxford's record at this stage was not a particularly good one with eight wins, one draw and twelve defeats. Forty four players had been seen in First Team colours, a reflection perhaps, of the club's cup policy and an indeterminate injury list and although the team was now settled there were some difficult games ahead.

This was not obvious with a 17–13 win at Old Whitgiftians where Oxford might easily have doubled their score, and this was followed by a confident 24–7 home win against Esher, captained by former Oxford player Peter Long. January ended with a cup semi-final away at Littlemore where a gutsy display in unrelenting defence by the home side failed to stem a 44–0 win for Oxford which saw them into Cup Final against Banbury due to be played on 12th February.

A letter published in the *Oxford Mail* from David Jeffrey, a former Didcot RFC Secretary, revived the old and controversial topic of affiliation and amalgamation. His view was that there was a need for the creation of an atmosphere of goodwill and co-operation between Oxford RFC and all local clubs which would arrest the flow of good players from the area to more senior clubs and allow any player in Oxford to be available for Oxford First XV. He suggested that Oxford RFC should be satisfied with two teams and a Colts team and making available all other players to other clubs as required. As usual the seeds fell on stony ground!!

At the beginning of February there appeared a notice in the *Oxford Mail* to say "We regret that tomorrows Sports Mail will not be published due to the effect of sanctions imposed by members of the National Union of Journalists in a dispute over a national pay agreement". The *Sports Mail,* or 'Green 'Un' as it was popularly known by local sports

*Confusion as the ball goes to ground against Esher watched by Liam McCarthy, Phil Blake, Graham McKenzie, Nigel Rose and Nigel Street.*

enthusiasts, had been published for many years on a Saturday tea time and contained regular features covering most local sports together with up to date results and reports of games played that day both locally and nationally. A pile of such newspapers were quickly bought after delivery to the Oxford RFC bar especially when the First XV had played away. It was a sad day for the newspaper because it never appeared again and a valuable line of communication, especially for rugby supporters through Ron Grimshaw's regular roundup, was lost.

Not that there was much sport to report as February was almost completely wiped out due to weather of harsh and freezing conditions. Games were cancelled due to frozen pitches but one, the County Cup Final, had to be resolved and, after two postponements, was settled for Sunday 26th February at Iffley Road. Pitch conditions were far from perfect and very muddy after the ground had been frozen rock hard but Oxford hooker Nigel Goodey was keen to get under way in his 100th club appearance.

It had been almost a month since either team had played and this resulted in a dour struggle on the heavy playing surface. Ray McCarthy led out the team in his final appearance and Oxford scored first when Ray Tapper passed to Bob Reynolds who chipped for the corner where Andy Norman tapped over the line and beat Banbury winger Eugene Gratwohl to the touch down. Banbury came back strongly and No 8 Maurice Bell scored a try after a fine move in reply to give Banbury a 7–6 lead after Ray Shaw had kicked a penalty in the second half. This stirred the Oxford side into more action and the pack drove up field to maul close to the Banbury line. Scrum half Phil Blake, on his knees, got the ball away to Tapper who appeared to fumble. The players fractionally stopped but Tapper was quickest to react, jinked and passed to Nick Johnson for Oxford's second try. It was a happy Roger McClure who lifted the trophy after the 10–7 win which also gave the club the increased sponsorship from John Player of £450.

*Littlemore's Simon Chislett is well wrapped up by Oxford players in the Knockout Cup.*

*Six injured Oxford RFC players recovering on 'sick parade', Phil Dedrick (knee), Nigel Pollard (broken ankle), Andy 'Smokey' Smith (knee), Ian McDougall (shoulder), Paul Murphy (broken leg) and Frazer Morgan (knee). Don't we just love those sheepskin coats and bell bottom trousers! In later years Paul Murphy was to become the President of the Rugby Football Union.*

Oxford's reaction to the cup success was an awful 6–28 defeat at Streatham & Croydon where three tries were conceded in the last ten minutes. But the team responded well with wins against Marlow 18–6, Clifton 19–14, Lydney 30–11, Askeans 25–7 where Ray Tapper celebrated his 365th appearance in Oxford colours with thirteen points, Stratford 23–22 and the Metropolitan Police 9–7.

Remarkably, despite an Easter Saturday home defeat to Chester, the team had turned the season around after a mediocre first half to record seven victories since the beginning of the New Year. Much of this was down to Roger McClure's leadership and, after former misgivings, the team was one win short of twenty for the season.

That one game was a home match against Havant on 27th April in the National Cup area final playoff for a place in the John Player Cup the following season. After Oxford's successful run the omens were good and some of the players stretched their legs in the Oxfordshire Sevens on the weekend prior to the match when one team went out of the competition losing to St Luke's College in the Quarter Final, and the other to eventual winners Bath. But it was not to be. On the last weekend of the season Havant trailed by two points for much of the game until a huge fifty yard plus penalty kick in the closing moments put paid to Oxford's hope of John Player Cup glory and the money that went with it. Mick Groom, who had scored in every club game he had played in, kicked two penalties but missed five others as Oxford slumped to defeat. The team on the day was: M Groom; A Norman, R Reynolds, G Lewis, N Johnson; R Tapper, W Powell; A Dunn, N Goodey, G McKenzie, B Wintcombe, D Pitt, L McCarthy, N Street, R McClure (Captain).

In what, results wise, would have been normally considered a more than average season, the Havant result was a huge disappointment as the club missed a golden opportunity to further its ambitions of first class status.

Groom's season record of 202 points from the twenty seven club games in which he'd played and 64 points from five Oxfordshire appearances was quite an achievement, while Graham McKenzie had now played in one hundred matches for Oxford.

At the club dinner in May, Roger Arneil, former Scottish international and British Lion, suggested that one result of modern coaching was an increase in dirty play. In his retiring speech Roger McClure referred to inconsistent performances along with several moments to savour during the season, and the only remedy to a declining fixture list was by good performances on the field. He hoped that under the new Captain, Adrian Dunn, the club would get nearer to the record of twenty six wins in a season.

*Bar Committee outing at a Southampton Football Club! Left to right: Phil Kelly, Ron Salter, Vic Gordge, John Bagnall, Stuart Davies with Courage rep Geoff Cattermole.*

# Chapter 7 – Let there be light.

Close season activity saw Philip Kelly awarded the Harold Phillips Cup for outstanding service to the club mainly through his work on the Bar Committee and as Fourth team Captain, while Paul Ashby was the most improved player.

The Golf Driving Range that had recently been running at a loss had been closed in April but the Squash Courts had reached optimum membership and this brought predicted funds into the club that was showing some ambition off the field.

Plans for floodlighting the First Team pitch were well advanced to a cost of £11,000 and this sum was to be made up from several sources including a Southern Sports Council grant and loans from club members. It was thought that the lights would ease problems caused by postponements of Saturday fixtures and help the club in its attempt to attain first class status.

A playing highlight of the season was the visit of the touring Argentina team that was due to play against Southern Counties at the Iffley Road ground at the end of September. Locally the Southern Counties had agreed to play against Oxford as a warm up for that match as an event to open Oxford's new floodlights.

On the club front David Jones had returned from Oxford Old Boys and Nigel Pollard, having recovered from a broken ankle that had restricted him to just seven games in the previous season, was due to play on the wing in the club's opening match against Weston-super-Mare. The new captain, Adrian Dunn, had effectively replaced Graham McKenzie in the front row and McKenzie had returned to Oxford Marathon tempted, no doubt, by the enthusiasm generated by that club's opening of a new £25,000 clubhouse at the Horspath Road ground which had been completed in seven months with 80% of the work done by club members.

## Season 1978–1979

On his first match as Oxford Captain, Adrian Dunn opened the scoring with a try in the home game with Weston-super-Mare on 2$^{nd}$ September and Mick Groom carried on from the previous season with a conversion but, with a twelve point lead, the team lost hooker Nigel Goodey with concussion. It was a strange decision to move Liam McCarthy to hook and the side, with little possession from the set piece, lost 12–32.

Adrian Dunn showed his commitment to the club the following weekend when he drove to St Ives on the Saturday morning to meet his playing colleagues prior to Oxford's short Cornish tour match at Redruth. In blustery conditions the game was much closer than the 6–18 defeat would suggest, and Dunn returned to Oxford after the game to take part in the Southern Counties squad training on Sunday. On Monday he drove again to Cornwall, this time for the evening match at Penzance & Newlyn which the team lost 9–20. Still searching for a first win of the season Oxford travelled to Stroud where dreadful defence in the second half squandered a seven point lead in the 7–34 defeat.

Despite some last minute wire connections the floodlights were declared ready for the midweek match with Southern Counties on 19$^{th}$ September. The club was to be congratulated for its enterprise being the first in the county to lead the way with pitch lighting and the teams for that historic occasion were: Oxford: M Groom; N Pollard, P Ashby, G Lewis, N Johnson; R Tapper, D Rees; A Dunn (Capt), N Goodey, K Bulley, D Pitt, M Minch, C Pittaway, N Street, J Taylor.

Southern Counties: I Gale (Henley); C Rees (London Welsh), D Course (Richmond),

*The Oxfordshire RFU President, Tony Cooke (Henley), and Oxford RFC President John Rowell prepare for the big switch on of the club's new floodlights.*

*Southern Counties v Argentina match programme.*

*The light shines down on Oxford's pack of forwards as the backs wait patiently in the first floodlit club match in Oxfordshire.*

B Reynolds (Army), K Ellis-Jones (London Welsh); I Wright (Rosslyn Park) (Capt), I George (Rosslyn Park); P Rendall (Wasps), A Jenkins (Henley), G Pearce (Northampton), J Orwin (Gloucester), J Mawle (Bedford), N Dudding (Henley), C Sharp (Richmond), A Hoon (Newbury). Oxford played with great spirit to pull back a 3–14 deficit to 11–14 but then conceded points late in the game to lose 11–32.

Mick Groom surrendered his 'score a match' record in Oxford's sixth defeat, 4–19, of the season at home to Walsall, and there was a suggestion that Ray Tapper, a loyal servant over many years, should retire but he answered his critics with a fine display and 18 points in a 34–12 win over Taunton. This was a hard won and convincing result after much work on the training field and Oxford's intention to run the ball paid handsomely with great displays from scrum half David Rose, full back David David and centre Gareth Lewis.

Away from the club Southern Counties were rather feeble and made little impression on Argentina at Iffley Road where the great Hugo Porta notched 19 points in his team's 39–9 win. The seven Oxfordshire players in the team were not deterred however as the county team, which included Oxford's Nick Johnson, Adrian Dunn, Gareth Lewis and Nigel Street with Chris Pittaway on the replacement bench, went on to beat Berkshire 32–11 at Banbury in their first title defence.

Success continued for Oxford with an 11–6 win over Cheltenham but the side was denied a worthy victory over neighbours Oxford University under the new Bypass lights when a penalty that everyone thought had gone over was denied by the referee in the 12–13 loss. Cinderford were next up in a match that replaced Glamorgan Wanderers on the fixture list due to Welsh Cup commitments and the Oxford players, in the wrong frame of mind, produced their worst performance of the season, seeming to lose interest, in the 6–4 win.

*The previous season's most improved player, Paul Ashby, brings down a Cinderford opponent.*

In another close match at Bletchley, Oxfordshire conceded possession late in the game but hung on to beat Buckinghamshire 24–21 with six Oxford players in the ranks.

Oxford's front row of Dunn, Goodey and Bulley, having played together for ten of the first eleven games of the season, was broken up when Goodey sustained a broken nose in the county cup match at Didcot which saw Oxford restricted to two Tapper penalties and a David Rose try in the 10–0 win. This was hardly ideal preparation for the next match, away at Pontypool, where the Nomads Captain Andy Smith replaced Goodey to face British Lion Bobby Windsor. Oxford led from a Tapper penalty but went on to the biggest defeat in the club's history in losing 3–69 and were outclassed in every phase of the game.

In contrast Oxfordshire won the Southern Group title for the third successive season when they beat Dorset & Wiltshire 31–7 and awaited news of who the quarter final opponents would be.

To the west Witney RFC bought a piece of land on Hailey Road for £15,000 opposite the Oxford University Farm, partly funded with an RFU loan of £6000, upon which to build a clubhouse and ground of their own, while Oxford RFC were unveiling news of a new floodlit event.

This was to be a floodlit knockout cup competition with eight games in the first round and played on consecutive Wednesday evenings involving sixteen clubs. It was to start on 8th November and the club organised a spectacular parachute drop into the floodlit arena to precede the kick off by three servicemen and a civilian of the RAF Sports Parachute Association display team, the Robins. This team, with smoke canisters attached to their boots, jumped from a Cessna 206 aircraft at 3000 feet and landed on a cross in the middle of the pitch, the first time that a jump of this nature into a floodlit arena had been attempted in the country. A local weekly newspaper, *The Oxford Star*, produced a three page pull out to celebrate the occasion supported by advertisements one of which read "The North Oxford Garage Ltd have been led to believe that players from Oxford Rugby Club perform better after dark and we now expect to see this proven." The competition was sponsored by the Courage Brewery and, in the opening match Chinnor beat Grove 13–4.

*The Didcot players look as they have been in a battle as they lineup against Oxford's Charlie Rogers, John Taylor and Nigel Street.*

Oxford gained some retribution after two costly defeats when the team beat Havant 16–6 but then lost 7–10 to Guildford & Godalming with a lethargic performance which saw the team debuts of Billy Greenhalgh and Geoff Elliott.

It was not possible for the club to enforce its policy of not playing before an important cup match when five of its players, Reynolds, Johnson, Dunn, Street and Taylor represented Oxfordshire against Gloucestershire at Cheltenham on Saturday 18th November in the County Championship Quarter Final where the team gave a good account of themselves but lost 10–25. Banbury, with one county representative in Richard Court, were due at the Bypass the next day and Oxford, who included Dunn, Johnson and Street, went on to win with a competent performance 16–3. Ray Tapper was the man of the match with two penalties and a conversion after conjuring tries for Greenhalgh and Johnson. This was followed by a 29–0 over Witney in the Floodlit Cup which saw Graham Warrington dominate the lineout for the visitors.

The club's match with Lydney was brought forward to a midweek floodlit defeat to avoid the day before the next county cup match, this time at Iffley Road against Oxford University Greyhounds. The 'Hounds, at peak form and fitness just prior to their annual match with Cambridge, scored early and then hung on. Nigel Street scored Oxford's try and Oxford had another disallowed while Tapper's penalty attempt to draw the match and go through on the away team rule, drifted agonisingly wide of the posts. The 4–7 defeat was another disappointment in a game that Oxford should have won and this reflected in the team's run in to the New Year with defeats against Tredegar, Exeter St Luke's, Burton and Birmingham with snatches of good play but no winning results until the last match of 1978, an 11–7 win in the resurrected fixture at Worcester.

It had been a very low key year so far for the club, probably the worst opening half of a season for a long time with eight games won but fifteen lost. The Playing Committee held a special meeting to look at the club's position and future policy bearing in mind the obvious deterioration in playing standards and results. The need for training by all was stressed with players expected to attend both Tuesday and Thursday sessions and failure to appear on Thursdays could result in being dropped. Coach John Gunter was unable to continue and Lynn Evans agreed to take the Thursday sessions for the rest of the season and stressed a positive attitude to the game and loyalty to the club.

The club had the benefit of an enforced break when the Bypass ground was snow bound on 6th January causing the cancellation of the match with Old Whitgiftians after which freezing conditions set in. A few days later the pitch was deemed playable by all concerned and Oxford beat Oxford Marathon 45–0 in the Floodlit Cup. Oxford's running and handling in the cold conditions brought eight tries and the Maras backs were outclassed. Loughborough Colleges came to the ground at the weekend but refused to play on a pitch that they considered was frozen too hard to the point of being dangerous despite the Oxford club and assigned match referee declaring it fit for play. Loughborough captain Clive Woodward said "The pitch is too hard and dangerous. Had we suffered injuries we would have been in trouble especially with UAU (University Athletic Union) games coming up." His team boarded the bus and left without a meal or drinks.

Oxford Old Boys used the Bypass lights to prepare for their county cup semi-final but to no avail as they lost to Oxford University Greyhounds 3–9 while Henley went through against Bicester on the away team rule in a 6–6 draw, both games plagued by fog.

With the calibre of the three quarters to select from it was no surprise, with the likes of Lewis, Tapper, Reynolds, Greenhalgh, Johnson, Norman, Asnby, David and Phil Blake at scrum half to pick from, that the club team turned to a running, passing style of play and this resulted in a run of five wins in succession, adding Sutton Coldfield, Sidcup and Bridgwater & Albion to the list. But this run came to an end in the mud at United Services Portsmouth where Ashby went off and coach Lynn Evans took to the field for his first Oxford game since November 1972!

In the County Cup Final, Henley beat Oxford University Greyhounds 9–3 in a drab game where all the points came from kicks. But Henley didn't mind that, the win being their first in four final appearances.

Tony Yendole, formerly with Wakefield but now teaching in the area, was named for his First XV debut at Nuneaton in place of the injured Ashby but snow and ice put paid to that game. When he did get on to the field he lasted just ten minutes before sustaining a shoulder injury in the 8–16 home defeat to Solihull.

Mid-week relief saw Bob Reynolds score three tries as the club beat Gosford All Blacks in the Floodlit Cup but two further defeats against Streatham & Croydon, 3–22, and Esher, 6–12, showed a disparity in the standard of games at the time. Ray Tapper was due to play his 400th game for Oxford when the team played Banbury in the first Floodlit Cup Final. Tickets were sent to all the clubs that had competed and the Courage Brewery provided free beer. It was a hard fought game up front but Banbury never looked like winning. Billy Greenhalgh was the vital link for all three tries that Oxford scored, one for Bob Reynolds in his 50th appearance and two for Andy Norman in the 14–0 win which provided some

*Oxford's Captain Adrian Dunn receives the Courage Floodlit Cup from Brewery Rep, Tony Allen, after beating Banbury in the Final.*

*After the Final, Adrian Dunn presented Ray Tapper and his wife Christine with mementos to mark Ray's 400th appearance for Oxford RFC.
L to r: Adrian de Baat, Chris Pittaway, Nick Johnson, Ray Mills, Christine Tapper, Nigel Pollard, Ray Tapper, Billy Greenhalgh, Paul Ashby, Adrian Dunn, Nigel Street.*

consolation for the Oxfordshire Cup exit. After the match Ray Tapper was presented with an inscribed ice bucket and his wife, Christine, with a pair of miniature riding boots.

Back to Saturdays and a late drop goal meant a further defeat, 16–18, at Stafford but, a week later, saw a feast of attacking rugby in what was possible the best game seen on the Bypass ground in this season. The visitors, Maesteg, were top of the Welsh Merit Table at the time and held a 9–20 lead early in the second half. But a tremendous effort by the Oxford team saw them fight back and Andy Smith's try in the last minute was converted by Greenhalgh for a 23–23 draw which club members saw as a moral victory!

Welsh opposition continued into April with a visit from Glamorgan Wanderers and Oxford's cause was not helped when Kim Bulley dived in for a loose ball from an offside position and Wanderers were awarded a penalty try. And then Reynolds was harshly disallowed a try when apparently failing to ground the ball properly in the 12–15 defeat. On such small margins!

The club entered two teams in the Oxfordshire Sevens Tournament and both failed to pass the Preliminary Round stage although the club was invited back as a guest side when other clubs withdrew and made some amends in beating London Welsh 22–6 before losing to Exeter University.

Down south in the county Henley failed to make it into the John Player Cup proper when losing 0–10 at home to Maidstone in a qualifying final.

There was no Easter Tour for Oxford but the team did travel to play Pontypridd on the Saturday but only had one lock forward available. Graham Warrington, on tour in South Wales with the Witney club, recalled meeting Oxford officials Ray Tapper and Lynn Evans in the iconic Angel Hotel in Cardiff and, impressed with the situation and surroundings, agreed to 'guest' in the match with Frazer Morgan his partner in the second row of the scrum. The 16–43 loss was not a good result but Warrington gave a good account of himself and even scored Oxford's last try in the match. Back in Oxford on Easter Monday the club team, in its last match of the season, beat Lydney 26–3, which was just reward for their efforts. Both wingers, Lewis and Norman, scored tries as did all the back row of McCarthy, Street and Pittaway.

Inspired by the undoubted success of the Floodlit Cup, which had brought together several local clubs some of whom wouldn't normally have played each other, the club decided to end the season with a Floodlit Sevens Tournament. Len and Muriel Bagnall, who had recently stood back after nearly ten years of managing and providing catering on match days at the club, were both made Life Vice Presidents for their efforts and it was they who provided 'The Bagnall Trophy' to be presented to the winners at the end of what was hoped would be an annual competition. The event, organised by Andy Smith and David Pitt, was not the hoped for money spinner due to adverse weather on the day of the tournament, sometimes a deluge, but the rugby was good. Oxford beat Northampton and then Oxford Marathon before losing to an Andy Ripley led Rosslyn Park side, the eventual winners, in the semi-final. It was a bright finish to Oxford's first season with its lights!

The appraisal which took place after Oxford's defeat to the Oxford University Greyhounds had the desired effect. The change of style had taken some time to become affective and, although the clubs record may have looked mediocre in terms of wins and losses, the team had on several occasions played attractive rugby without getting the results it deserved. Two players, Paul Ashby and Kim Bulley, played in all thirty eight games while Tapper missed only one and Dunn only two, in the fifteen wins and one drawn. Mick Groom won the club's Kicking Cup presented by Chris Price in 1954.

Speaking at the club's Annual Dinner, Nigel Starmer-Smith thought that England Rugby was not doing itself justice with lack of consistency in selection being a problem. He thought that the County Championship needed up grading or scrapped altogether and that the John Player Cup was not the answer. "Why not try leagues as in Scotland instead of Merit Tables?" he asked. A glimpse into the future perhaps?

Sadly, Jim Higgins passed away in May this year at the age of 69 years. In 1969 he became the first President of Oxford RFC not to have played for the club, but had been Trainer for the preceding ten years. His splendid moustache and military bearing were reminders of his wartime service as a Sergeant Major in the Oxfordshire Yeomanry and he went about his business patrolling the touchline in a pristine white tracksuit.

There were signs that local rugby was getting itself on an even firmer foothold with Oxford Old Boys obtaining planning permission for a £3500 extension and improvements to the clubhouse in Marston Ferry Road, where it was also proposed to turn the pitches round so that the ball would be kicked onto the road less often!

Pat Hall, the then Witney RFC Chairman, replied to a smear of 'high jinks' and 'booze ups' remarks that were made at a meeting of the West Oxfordshire District Council, which he claimed were damaging plans for the club's new ground at Hailey Road. Mr Hall said "We are responsible people who have to keep fit and we object very strongly to a distasteful label being put on us".

*Oxford RFC 1978–1979. Back row, l to r: A Dunn (Capt), N Goodey, G McKenzie, R McCarthy, N Rose, N Street, L McCarthy, R McClure. Front row, l to r: W Powell, RP Tapper, N Johnson, R Reynolds, G Lewis, A Norman, M Groom.*

# Season 1979–1980

After a summer of very changeable weather, conditions at Weston-super-Mare in early September supported the view that summer begins when the rugby season starts. Oxford's performance in the opening match suggested that some of the players were still on holiday, mentally at least. With new captain Bob Reynolds at the helm it was a poor performance in the 6–18 defeat. Nigel Street's try was the first of the season but Billy Greenhalgh's boot could have kept Oxford in contention.

Mike Groom had returned to Oxford Marathons after being asked to start the season in Oxford's 3rd XV but Oxford had the evergreen Phil Blake and Malcolm Fitzsimmons, who were joined by Geoff Rotherforth from Wheatley, to contend for the scrum half position. Graham Warrington had also joined the club but had ruptured a tendon in pre-season training which was due to keep him out of the game for a few weeks, while fellow lock forward Frazer Morgan had revived the same back injury that had kept him out of most of the previous season playing cricket.

These challenges were put behind the team when it came back from a 0–10 deficit to beat Worcester 29–10 on the same day that saw Mick Groom kick 15 points of his side's 19–0 win over the Nomads, but early promise ended in a 9–20 defeat at home to Stroud.

*The Flying Bob Reynolds was the new Club Captain.*

*Chris Pittaway leads Oxford away against Stroud, Kim Bulley, Jim Tozer and Charlie Rogers follow.*

The following week saw Paul Ashby's fiftieth appearance and Mark Churchward replacing Adrian Dunn, who was playing for the Southern Counties in the 6–6 draw against Canada at Aylesbury, in the game against Birmingham where Oxford fell 15–16 to a try in the dying moments. The need for a regular goal kicker was apparent with Tapper slotting just one of eight attempts. September ended on a bright note and a great team try. In the third minute of injury time against Guildford & Godalming Gareth Lewis picked up in the 22 area, passed to Tapper who stepped past four players before passing to Archie Young who shipped on to Nick Johnson to scorch in for Oxford's 21–18 win. It was a fitting end to Johnson's sojourn at the club prior to his returning to Nottingham. It was also Andy Smith's fiftieth appearance while Warrington was making his seasonal debut after injury.

Oxfordshire began the Southern Group title defence at Wareham against Dorset & Wiltshire with four Oxford players, Andy Norman, Gareth Lewis, Adrian Dunn and Chris Pittaway in the side – a good job they did as tries from Norman and Lewis saw the side win 8–6 in a close encounter.

The next day Oxford held a resurgent Oxford University side with a 6–4 half time lead at Iffley Road but the students changed gear, pace and handling and Oxford lost 6–38. There was improvement at Cheltenham but still a defeat, 7–11, where Andy Griffiths scored the try of the match before this run of losses was stemmed in the home, 16–14, win against Berry Hill. The Oxford team that achieved this was: Greenhalgh; Lewis, Ashby, Fitzsimmons, Norman; Griffiths, Blake; Dunn, Goodey, Bulley, Warrington, Rogers, Young, Elliott, Pittaway.

An innovative money raiser was held at the start of November when the club promoted a Boxing Dinner at Elms Court Ballroom in nearby Botley to take the place of the annual Vice Presidents Dinner. Over 200 tickets were sold and there was the surreal view of boxers in the centre ring sweating, bleeding and hitting each other while the diners, in ties and suits, sat nearby at surrounding tables eating the ample dinner. Never-the-less this was a popular and lucrative event.

Oxfordshire beat Berkshire 19–3 but Oxford joy was short lived with defeats to Abercynon, 16–18, Pontypool, 6–36, Walsall, 4–23, and Tredegar, 4–36, after a long trip to the second highest pitch in South Wales before Oxfordshire won again, this time under floodlights for the first time, at the Bypass Ground against Buckinghamshire. The 16–9 win saw the county, with Lewis, Norman, Warrington, Dunn and Street in the team, win its fourth successive Southern Group title which brought a home Quarter Final match with old opponents Gloucestershire. This game was also played on the Bypass Ground on 17th November when entry cost £1 with 50p to park the car. Bales of straw were placed along both sides of the pitch for spectators to sit on, on a 'first come first served' basis and Oxford prop Kim Bulley made his debut but late changes at full back and fly half unsettled the side and Gloucestershire were again the winners, 10–36.

After twenty six consecutive appearances, sixteen at the end of the previous season, Phil Blake was replaced at scrum half by Geoff Rotherforth and Oxford produced a 39–3 win over Didcot in the Floodlit Cup followed by a County Cup win over Royal Air Force Benson, 74–6. Despite this the club moved to stem the run of defeats in regular fixtures, the teams five wins being of no real consequence in the fifteen games played. The club had started the season with four coaches in Lynn Evans, Roy Mercer, John Gunter and Andy Smith but things hadn't been working out as planned and the club decided on a change which saw Ray Tapper taking on the coaching role while he was still, of course, in First XV contention.

Oxford's forwards were in a dominant mood and winger Reynolds showed the way with an interception and sixty yard run to the posts to open the scoring in the 24–14 win under floodlights against Lydney. This was followed by another home win in the County Cup when a superb display by winger Andy Norman brought him three tries as Oxford beat Oxford University Greyhounds 18–10 with Pittaway adding a fourth.

Rhys James, a Civil Servant who had played for both Llanelli and Swansea, had joined the Oxford club where he had been playing in the Nomads. He made his First XV debut in the away match with United Services, Portsmouth, but it was not a winning one and the big Services pack won the forwards battle and the match 3–14.

An uninspiring time for the club saw defeats against Solihull and Esher on windswept and muddy fields and morale was not helped by Billy Greenhalgh's reoccurring hamstring injury that had seen him miss the last ten games. Now the diagnosis suggested a damaged cartilage which would see him miss more games. In the match against Esher, Chris Pittaway was forced off with eight minutes to go and David Dillon, former 4th XV Captain and now regular touch judge, ran on to the pitch for a rare 1st team appearance on a bitterly cold afternoon. Finally, over the Christmas period, Oxford ended the decade by sending an understrength side, through injuries and unavailabilities, to a 6–38 defeat at Burton-on-Trent.

There was much debate over the selection of Tapper and Blake at half back for the match at Old Whitgiftians to open 1980. Both had now been at the club for many years. Was this good for the club's future and forward planning? To be fair to both players they were the best available at the time. The forwards played well but centre field was an area of weakness in this 3–7 defeat as Oxford continued where they had left off in 1979.

What a difference a week made! Virtually the same team with the exception of Lewis at full back and Ashby and James in the centre produced a fast and flowing game and a 4–0 win at Loughborough Colleges where Andy Norman scored the all-important try, the first win there for twenty eight years. This was followed by a 17–3 win midweek against Bicester in the Floodlit Cup, where Blake scored his first try for six seasons, and then Henley, 8–6, in the County Cup which saw Greenhalgh's earlier than predicted return. He had missed sixteen games.

It was reported that Oxford club officials had taken part in talks in London with a

*It must be Christmas! Rhys James battles through the snow against Esher.*

*The bare cheek of it! Kim Bulley turns his back but Frazer Morgan can't resist a look during Oxford's home defeat with Sidcup who were to become Merit Table opponents.*

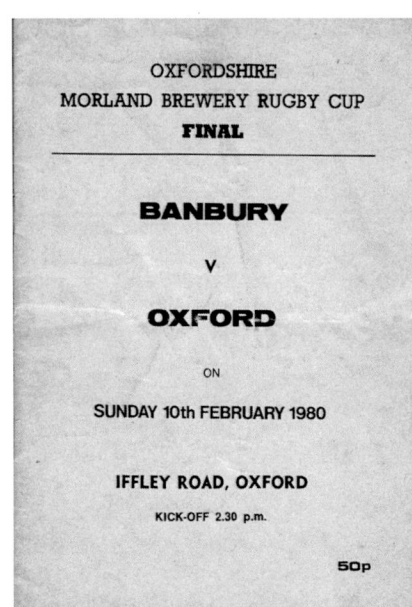

*Banbury v Oxford Cup Final programme.*

view to the formation of a Merit Table, operative from the following season if talks were successful, where 70% of club fixtures were needed to qualify. Merit Tables were generally seen as an incentive and hoped for improvement in playing standards while there was a suggestion from Grove RFC for the formation of an Oxfordshire League competition. This had been mooted previously and had drawn little interest.

In a pre-cup final boost two Greenhalgh penalty goals saw Oxford beat Bridgwater & Albion 6–3 in the rural setting of North Petherton where sheep grazed beyond a goal line. The Morland Brewery was now the sponsor of the Oxfordshire Knockout Cup competition and on a heavy and stamina sapping Iffley Road pitch the Oxford pack out scrummed, over powered and out shoved the Banbury forwards in another dour final. Ray Tapper played an integral part in the match with two drop goals and then instigated a blind side move that resulted in a Rhys James try. Greenhalgh added a penalty to make the final score 13–6. Rule changes meant that this win would see Oxford through to the national John Player Cup in the next season, the first two rounds of which would be played on a regional basis to replace the regional qualifying games at the end of a season that had taken place up to that point. The draw was due in July.

Two days later Oxford entertained the Argentinian touring side, San Patricio, in what turned out to be anything but a friendly encounter. The visitors were confrontational which resulted in a very fractious match described by one observer as the re-enactment of a wartime battle! Barry Broad, a scrum half from Banbury where he couldn't get a First XV place, kicked two penalties and scored a try while Reynolds and Florey added two more but the 21–17 Oxford win took back stage. Graham Warrington was sent from the field after a lineout melee and subsequently banned

*Phil Blake gets the ball away in the Cup Final with Banbury's Ray Shaw in close attendance.*

*Banbury flanker John Colgrave resorts to a head lock in trying to stop Billy Greenhalgh getting the ball away to Bob Reynolds.*

from playing for thirty days, and the match referee later said "The real trouble was that none of them (the Argentinians) understood my instructions. They were also deaf to the whistle when they had the adrenalin flowing".

Order was restored under Friday evening lights as a Malcolm Fitzsimmons try saw Oxford beat old rivals Nuneaton 16–13 for the third win in six days, but unsavoury tactics by visiting Havant left a sour taste in a 10–10 draw.

The club team lost for the first time in a Floodlit Cup match when Banbury ended a fifteen year wait in winning 3–27 to avenge the County Cup Final defeat. Oxford's pack was unrecognisable to that which played in the Cup Final due to injuries and un-availabilities but Banbury weren't worried about that!

Billy Greenhalgh's boot made all the difference in wins against Esher, 15–12, and Clifton, 15–10, with a total of four penalties and three successful conversions of tries from Pittaway, Tapper and Dunn.

Graham Warrington returned to dominate the lineouts in Henley's Golden Jubilee match on 15$^{th}$ March while Greenhalgh scored all of Oxford's points but Henley's good play in the first and last ten minutes of the game saw them home in a 16–22 win. Playing away again the following week, this time a much longer trip to Preston, Oxford suffered even before reaching the ground when prop Kim Bulley twisted an ankle at a motorway stop and had to pull out. A swiftly reorganised and unsettled side went on to lose to the Grasshoppers, 6–32.

At home Banbury went on to win the Oxford Floodlit Cup by beating Oxford Old Boys 18–3, while three long range penalties from Greenhalgh, who else, were enough in Oxford's 9–6 win at Taunton. This was the last hurrah however. Oxford Colts lost 0–22 to Abingdon in the County Colts Cup Final and the senior team conceded 57 points without reply over the Easter period in defeats to the Metropolitan Police and Lydney.

As usual there was still some rugby to play albeit of the seven-a-side version. In the Oxford Floodlit Sevens the club side reached the final only to lose 18–20 to Oxford University. The players stood in silent memory of Mrs Muriel Bagnall who, with her husband Len, was a joint donor of the trophy and who had passed away earlier in the week.

The sight of the following week was that of Ray Tapper, 39 years old, running a mazy forty yards for a try in the Oxfordshire 7s qualifiers. In the final Oxford University beat London Welsh, 36–6, to record a Sevens 'double'.

A long list of injuries resulted in Oxford winning only one of the last six games of the campaign which spoilt an otherwise good second half of the season. The use of 49 players in the First XV told its own story but the team did win 17 games with 1 drawn from the 40 played, winning the County Cup and being the only Oxfordshire team to qualify for the finals of the Oxfordshire 7s.

## Season 1980–1981

A British Lions side led by Englishman Bill Beaumont lost a test series to South Africa 1–3 in the summer months and it was perhaps that the attention the eighteen match tour attracted was enough to keep local players' minds away from club rugby. It had long been the way that Oxford began each season as poor starters and this season was no exception which drew comments from certain quarters querying what actually happened in pre-season training. It did seem that only competitive matches captured the attention of some players and by then, of course, it was a little late.

Former Captain Adrian Dunn had retired but Tony Staples, a prop forward from Bicester, had taken his place in the squad along with scrum half Geoff Whitfield from Grove and

Nigel Goodey had been named as the new captain. Phil Dedrick had already waited for two years for a knee operation and his hopes were raised when a letter from the Nuffield Orthopaedic Hospital dropped through his door. But this merely asked if he wanted to remain on the waiting list! Hopes dashed again!

The traditional match with Weston-super-Mare opened the season but Oxford had no fire, method or plan and only three goals from Tony Yendole to show in the 9–29 defeat. The same player kicked three more as the club side lost a mid-week match 9–12 against an Oxfordshire XV in a slightly improved performance, and were vigorous but disjointed in a 0–3 defeat at Worcester where Oxford's wingers received only six passes in the whole match!

The county team, with Lewis, James, Staples and Warrington included, were cruelly exposed by Leicestershire 3–24 in a warm up defeat while Oxford turned, once again, to Ray Tapper for inspiration and Billy Greenhalgh replaced the Nomads Captain, Yendole, the scorer of all of the club's points in this season so far, for the next match at Stroud.

All of this hardly boosted morale prior to the John Player Cup 1st Round in which the club had been drawn at home to Bournemouth. The Oxford team faced a big beefy pack and was well beaten up having played with what was described as 'amazing ineptitude'. Greenhalgh kicked a penalty goal and the team nearly scored a try near the end, which would have been embarrassing. The result was a 3–3 draw but Bournemouth went through on the away team rule while the Oxford club was left with £500 as 1st Round losers. The Oxford team that day was: W Greenhalgh; D Hoare, P Ashby, R James, A Norman; R Tapper, G Whitfield; A Staples, N Goodey (Capt), K Bulley, G Warrington, S Griffiths, N Street, K Freeman, G Elliot.

David Bagnall was now running mini rugby at the club on Sunday mornings in Under 10, 12, 14 and 16 years age groups and, nationally, discussions had begun with regard to league rugby in an attempt to revitalise the game in England.

Disappointment locally continued when Oxfordshire, after four years at the top of the Southern Group of the County Championship, were beaten 13–18 by Buckinghamshire at Marlow in a close game. I suppose it had to happen sometime but not all the players had reported to Henley for training on the Monday before the game. Maybe they were still suffering from Saturday games at a time when John Burgess and 'Budge' Rogers were leading a nation tour trying to 'sell' the creation of Divisional Merit Tables/leagues, one result of which would devalue the County Championship as no Merit Table players would be available for County teams. In the same week the fast moving Oxford University team ran riot at the Bypass ground to leave the Oxford team gasping with a 6–43 loss.

There was some light at the end of the tunnel and in the second half Oxford produced the best performance of the season so far against Cheltenham. Staples picked up a loose ball, passed to Goodey who sent Reynolds in from inside the Oxford half. Greenhalgh converted and Tapper added a drop goal but it wasn't enough in the 9–14 defeat. This was followed by a high scoring defeat at Rugby, 25–29, where Oxford squandered a 21–4 half time lead while Oxfordshire got back on the winning trail with a 26–6 win against Dorset & Wiltshire.

The improvement seen at Rugby was timely with an Oxfordshire Cup match at home to Oxford Old Boys coming up on 18th October and, at last, this saw the club's first win of the season, 15–0, in eight attempts. Rhys James pounced on the ball in the in-goal area for a try after Tapper's kick had caused confusion and Greenhalgh added the conversion and three penalty goals. The Old Boys were brave in defence and former Oxford player Ted Sandbach crossed the home line twice but was called back on both occasions after a foot in touch. This welcome success brought another local derby with Oxford Marathon due in the next round but, after five First XV games, scrum half Geoff Whitfield returned to Grove. It is worth recording that sixteen teams competed in this round showing the popularity and diversity of the game locally at this time. Apart from Oxford and Oxford Marathon the other clubs were Littlemore, Cholsey, Grove, Banbury, Bicester Garrison, Witney, RAF Benson, RMCS Shrivenham, Henley, Didcot, Chinnor, Chipping Norton, Gosford All Blacks and RAF Brize Norton. This list would have been added to by Bicester except for a misdemeanour during the previous season.

In the week Oxfordshire beat Berkshire 20–4 but the earlier defeat against Buckinghamshire had proved costly as it was that county that became the new Southern Group Champions.

Direct from local club rugby Oxford faced a daunting trip to South Wales to face Pontypool at the end of October. It was very unfortunate that the club team was greatly weakened by the absence of four second row forwards and the Number 8, all suffering from injuries, and Ray Tapper who was away on a golfing holiday. The selected team was due to meet the full might of Pontypool including current Welsh internationals Graham Price, Bobby Windsor, Charlie Faulkner, all of 'Max Boyce' fame, Terry Cobner and Jeff Squire and there was no surprise in the 10–59 defeat. This was the last occasion that the famous Welsh front row played together for Pontypool in a competitive match. Oxford filled the spaces from within the club and Peter Mack and David Hazeldine played in the second row with Stuart Davies at Number 8, and at least the team earned the respect of a large crowd with a plucky performance. Karl Freeman scored a try and Greenhalgh added two penalties in a game refereed by the former University Captain and Oxford player, ROP Jones. Later in the week Sports Reporter John O'Callaghan poured scorn on local rugby when he asked in the *Oxford Times:* "Does local rugby lack ambition? When a team is sorely depleted by injuries as Oxford RFC were when they faced Pontypool on Saturday, are they entitled to look for a helping hand from other local clubs? Judging by the response the answer is clearly 'No!' Certainly Oxford did not get such help and filled the gaps in their First XV from their own ranks. The lack of ambition among local players rather than the unhelpful attitude of some clubs is perhaps the more disturbing feature. Pontypool provide Oxford with one of their few really first class fixtures and probably their toughest test of the season. To meet the best should be the natural desire among rugby players, yet the opportunity presented to so many of them, to take the chance, possibly the chance of a lifetime, was not lost. If the Welsh fans form a poor impression of Oxford rugby who is to blame – those who tried or those that did not or would not? And will the fixture be renewed?"

Of those late call ups Stuart Davies kept his place in the side and Oxford's experience perhaps told as the team beat Sutton Coldfield 18–15, the first win of the season in ten club matches. But it was a 'one off' as Oxford went under 3–21 at the County Ground against Exeter when, again, the team was beaten in the forwards.

All of this led to the next county cup match, at home to Oxford Marathon. This was a hotly contested match which left the Maras kicking themselves in frustration. Winning the forward battle gave the visitors much possession which was not used wisely and the price was paid when Oxford scored an excellently worked try in the closing minutes to win the match 15–13, this after Groom missed a penalty kick almost on time. Oxford's reward for a hard struggle was another home draw, this time against RAF Brize Norton. In the week there was less pressure as the club easily overcame Grove 53–10 in the Floodlit Cup.

After two games with local opposition the strong and uncompromising Stroud offered sterner competition and defeat, 6–17, followed by similar results against Metropolitan Police,4–25, and Lydney, 6–21. The team was short of Greenhalgh, Reynolds, Goodey, whose ankle was now in plaster after the Pontypool match, Warrington, Rogers, Elliot and scrum half Howard Jones who was alternating with Colts rugby in an attempt to win an England cap at that level, and badly needed these players to return.

RAF Brize Norton, normally a mid-week side, were brushed aside in the Oxfordshire Cup as Lewis, Street, James, Davies, Elliot and Reynolds all enjoyed a try each while Tapper, back again, added two penalties in his 450th club appearance, and Lewis a conversion in the 32–6 win. It was one of those 'golden' weekends where all five of the Oxford club teams fielded won their matches. The confidence gained brought Oxford success at United Services, Portsmouth against a big, strong side where Tony Staples and Reynolds registered tries and, over the Christmas holiday period on Boxing Day the team won again, this time against Solihull where Yendole was conspicuous in defence and attack. This short but bright run of form ended when an unfamiliar looking Oxford side lost at Esher on 27th December, 4–18.

1981 began with the welcome return of some players from injury, the instant result of which was a 29–0 win over Old Whitgiftians. Dominant forward play produced plenty of good possession and the backs excelled with a running game. The Oxford team on that day was: A Yendole; A Norman, P Ashby, G Lewis, R Reynolds; R Tapper, P Blake; A Staples, A Smith, K Bulley, J Tozer, S Griffiths, M Florey, S Davies, G Elliot.

James, Jones and Rogers were due to return for the Loughborough Students match where Oxford's front five were retained for the sixth successive game but, despite Andy Norman's

*Oxford players Paul Ashby, Kim Bulley, Jim Tozer, Chris Pittaway, Peter Mack and Phil Blake look around as Stroud score in Oxford's defeat.*

*Stuart Davies and Gareth Lewis get to grips in the Cup with an RAF Brize Norton player as Jim Tozer and Stephan Griffiths approach.*

try from a Tapper cross kick, penalties given away were decisive and the students kicked four to win 4–12.

There were signs that the club team was beginning to emerge from a fairly bleak few months and were favourites to beat Littlemore at Peers School in the county cup semi-final. The home team was helped by incessant rain driven by a strong, cold wind and, deprived of much possession, put up a great fight in defence and tackled like demons. Peter Jones opened for Littlemore with a penalty kick but Oxford, with tries from Reynolds and Freeman, a Yendole conversion and Tapper penalty, eventually edged home 13–3. Significantly Club Captain Nigel Goodey came on to the field as a replacement with three minutes to go, his first action since the end of October. In the north of the county Henley produced a purple patch to beat Banbury 16–3 to set up another Oxford-Henley final.

Goodey was to start, as was Warrington who had been absent since 4th October, and Liam McCarthy was added to the mix as Oxford showed good form but lost at Sidcup 14–19 and then drew with Clifton in swirling fog on the Bypass while the Nomads were demonstrating the strength in depth at the time, losing just one of the last eleven games.

The RFU Playing Sub Committee, led by John Burgess, on the restructuring of the game suggested that league rugby could begin in 1985 with the County Championship downgraded to a second class competition. Premier league clubs were yet to be named and there was some opposition as club's traditional fixture lists would have to be scaled down to fit in league matches. But there was still a long way to go.

*A desperate Henley attempt to stop Oxford's scrum half Howard Jones in the Cup Final as Tony Yendole waits to see what happens.*

*Oxford RFC 1980–1981. Back row, l to r: Sid Carter (Manager), Andy Norman, Tony Yendole, Tony Staples, Geoff Elliott, Stepahn Griffiths, Graham Warrington, Rhys James, Gareth Lewis, Liam McCarthy, Bob Reynolds, Ron Martin (Scretary). Front row, l to r: Andy Smith, Howard Jones, Kim Bulley, Nigel Goodey (Capt), Ray Tapper, Karl Freeman, Billy Greenhalgh.*

Billy Greenhalgh returned to the side for his first match in three months as Oxford beat Bridgwater & Albion 23–9 with returning players making a difference as the county cup final with Henley loomed on 15th February. This was Oxford's eighth appearance in the eleven year history of the competition and conditions were due to be slippery as overnight frost thawed on the Iffley Road pitch. This did not deter Oxford's open game and Greenhalgh's two penalties gave his team the lead before Karl Freeman touched down as the Oxford pack drove across Henley's line for a half time 10–0 lead. Henley came back strongly in the second half and only a crunching tackle from Freeman on England Colts winger Russell Challis followed by Nigel Goodey's smother tackle close to the line prevented a Henley score and Oxford went on to a 10–6 win, deserved on the run of play.

Buoyed by this success Oxford's run continued with a 12–11 win at Nuneaton where the home team's backs were contained while Greenhalgh took scoring opportunities with four penalties, and then the Berry Hill team suffered its first Saturday defeat of the season to a comprehensive 23–7 Oxford win. Joy was short lived however when Henley exacted revenge for the county cup defeat by beating Oxford 6–12 in the Floodlit Cup semi-final.

Weather conditions were not good to say the least at the beginning of March and, with the first team pitch unplayable, the side was forced to play against Streatham & Croydon on pitch two. Even then the game took place with incessant rain making the pitch inches deep in mud and water. Oxford attacked into an uncharted morass of mud but had only two penalties from Tony Yendole to show as forward play was loose and the match was lost 6–9. Due to the state of the ground Oxford's home match had to be switched to Esher the following week and, in Oxford's second visit in this season, a 'see-saw' match saw the side lead 21–7 only for Esher to come back to lead by a point before Liam McCarthy touched down for Yendole to convert for a worthy 27–22 win.

Two defeats followed, the first away to a Jan Webster led Walsall, 7–22, where the ex-England scrum half guided a large pack to victory in gruelling conditions, and then an 8–20 loss at Guildford & Godalming where back row forward Stuart Davies scored two tries. The following week he lost his place in the side for the best of reasons – he was the official Dental Officer as England Colts played Wales Youth at Iffley Road. In his absence Chris Horton and ex-Oxford Colt Andy Griffiths, in for the injured Ray Tapper, provided a fresh lease of life at half back as Oxford returned to winning ways against Sutton & Epsom, 22–0, at the end of March.

There was a proposal for an Oxfordshire Merit Table and all clubs were due to be canvassed for an opinion which had to be returned by 21st April. Any implementation would have probably seen some clubs scale down and use bona fide second fifteens.

Newbury beat Henley to win the Floodlit Cup as the April sevens season began with Oxford's win in a closed tournament at Henley where Banbury and Grove were beaten before a leaping interception from Gareth Lewis brought victory in the final against Henley, 16–12. The Oxfordshire Tournament, once second only in size and stature to the famed Middlesex Sevens, had now been reduced to a one day event with twenty four entries and no local club reached the quarter finals, Loughborough Colleges beating Saracens 30–6 in the final held, on this occasion, at Oxford RFC. Oxford club teams played in the Esher Sevens and Middlesex Sevens without much success and, finally, Oxford University beat Loughborough Colleges 22–12 to retain the Bagnall Trophy in Oxford's Floodlit Sevens.

On Saturdays Oxford were proving to be consistently inconsistent and lost 7–11 at home to Wolverhampton despite Mike Florey and family travelling up from holiday in Bognor so that he could play, and then returning the same evening. And on Easter Monday a much changed Oxford team lost at home to Lydney, 19–35, to end the season.

*Nigel Goodey prepares to go head to head with Henley's Alan Jenkins propped by Kim Bulley.*

Oxford's season of 17 wins, 2 draws and 21 losses was not impressive but had been a slight improvement on the previous season although the club had achieved the stated ambition of winning the county cup.

In the background there was still no news about a proposed Oxfordshire Merit Table while the future of the County Championship was undecided, it still being under consideration after the reported down grading not being well received.

# Chapter 8 – The times they are a-changin'

The Rugby Football Union saw fit to issue a warning to its 2000 member clubs to behave whilst 'on tour' following reports of 'irresponsible and bad behaviour' having been received at Twickenham. The warning claimed that 'behaviour greatly exaggerated by an excess of alcohol' had seen many travel companies, airlines and hotels refusing to accept business from rugby clubs, and that only 'responsible officials' should organise tours.

The matter of league rugby was only very slowly gathering momentum and the RFU issued a breakdown of the proposed league structure that it was hoped would begin in two years hence. There were to be three national leagues with sixty regionalised feeder leagues but it was stressed that this was a 'practical exercise only'. Only eight Oxfordshire clubs were included in the preliminary exercise of groupings with Oxford in a South and South West Division while below them in a Southern league were Banbury and Henley, and one division down in a Bucks and Oxon league were Chinnor, Bicester, Gosford All Blacks, Oxford Marathon and Oxford Old Boys. It was known that there was considerable opposition to league rugby particularly from major clubs whose traditional fixture lists would be disrupted, and others who felt that they were placed too low. But some smaller, ambitious clubs saw the scheme as a means to climb to the higher echelons of the game and was, perhaps, another reason for some bigger clubs to complain as they saw their status under possible threat. Clubs were asked for their views, to be reported back through the County Unions before yet another report would be issued. It was noted that there was no mention of the Oxford and Cambridge Universities whose traditional programmes would be totally disrupted should league plans go ahead.

In the wider world the Third Test between New Zealand and South Africa in Auckland was marred by fighting in streets near to the ground while some anti-apartheid demonstrators chained themselves to Auckland Harbour Bridge to disrupt traffic. There was even a small aeroplane flying over the ground dropping flour bombs during play in a match won by New Zealand, 25–22.

## Season 1981–1982

In April the players had held the traditional annual meeting to discuss the election of captain for the forthcoming season which had then been put up to the club's Annual General Meeting for approval. Of the three players nominated two were hookers, Captain Nigel Goodey and Nomads Captain Andy Smith who had been Goodey's able deputy during the latter's prolonged injury absence. The first vote eliminated Goodey who then left the meeting before Smith was voted in as the player's choice. A letter was later received from Goodey stating his resignation from the club, and the Committee noted his efforts and commitment in the previous years with gratitude.

*New Club Captain Andy Smith.*

The new season also marked the Oxfordshire RFU Golden Jubilee and extra matches were planned, as part of the celebrations, against Southern Counties at Henley in November, and against an International XV at Banbury in April. Results would be important as the final placings in this season's championship groups would determine into which groups counties would be placed in the 1982–83 season in the new two tier County Championship with promotion and relegation.

Another club celebrating, this time a Silver Jubilee, was the Reading club Abbey and Oxford provided opposition under Abbey's new floodlights which also marked Gareth Lewis' 100th club appearance. But the team looked under prepared in a 6–19 defeat while several possibilities were not available for the first Saturday fixture, away at Weston-super-Mare. On a bone hard pitch this was a dress rehearsal for the John Player Cup match on the same ground on 26th September. So short was the team of suitable players that the now retired Adrian Dunn was called into the side for his first match in eighteen months. It was also his 100th appearance for the club which qualified him for an Honours Tie, although he had already received one for Services to the Club. Oxford, notorious bad starters to a season, lost 3–19. This week also saw the debut of Nigel Goodey for Oxford Old Boys in that club's 30–3 win over Oxford Marathon.

The club fielded a new fly half in the young Ian Graham for mid-week 16–21 defeat against an Oxfordshire XV and improvement was seen in a convincing 18–4 home win against Worcester on the Saturday when Bob Reynolds scored three tries in his first senior game of the season. Oxford's team was: A Yendole; E Kernaghan, R James, S Page, R Reynolds; I Graham, H Jones; P Mack, A Smith (Capt), K Bulley, C Rogers, G Warrington, C Pittaway, N Forrester, K Freeman.

The club's 13–20 home defeat to Stroud drew a 'tongue in cheek' comment in the local press "The laying on of hands is an ecclesiastical activity which has no place on the rugby field but, frankly, some of the attempted tackles were more like papal blessings." Obviously Oxford's defence needed tightening!

Oxford Old Boys celebrated the opening of a new clubhouse at Marston Ferry Road at a reputed cost of £100,000 with a match and 14–27 defeat against an Invitation XV.

*Karl Freeman (7) peels round a line out against Worcester with Andy Smith, Nick Forrester, Kim Bulley and Peter Mack hiding Graham Warrington all in the picture.*

The charismatic Charlie Ede had by now left the Oxford club after a dispute with club officials regarding the use of pitches for the Oxford Thursday team that he ran. He had been instrumental in bringing some players to the club through the mid-week invitation team that had a reputation for playing enjoyable no pressure running rugby. Charlie was also very well known for his team's success on the Sevens scene and, after a while, turned up at Oxford Old Boys. Ray Tapper, thought to be near the end of his playing career due to his age, was to follow and this continued what was to become a well-trodden path in this direction.

The Stroud match and result was not the hoped for morale booster for the John Player Cup match at Weston-super-Mare. But Oxford had a plan! The conditions at the Somerset venue were totally different from the season opener with heavy rain, thunder and hail. Research Psychologist Andy Smith planned to take the home side on up front and play them at their own game, and this brought Oxford a hard fought victory. Billy Greenhalgh put on a great performance at full back with defensive kicking and handling and, crucially, three penalties in the first half. Supported by Steve Page, a recent Cambridge University 'Blue' and now teaching at Abingdon School, in the centre, this was enough to see Oxford into the second round with a 9–6 win.

Ray Tapper, now appearing in Oxford Old Boys colours, set up his new club's 32–4 win over the Nomads in the final of the popular Gosford Sevens while only eight teams entered the Oxford Floodlit Cup. It was later explained that only eight teams had been invited as the club wished for its junior sides to also use the floodlight facility.

The team resumed a run of four successive defeats against Oxford University, 7–23, Cheshunt, 0–30, Rugby, 8–24, and Wolverhampton, 9–28, relieved by wins against Sutton Coldfield, 10–0, Swindon in the Floodlit Cup, 22–17, and Burton, 15–14 as Oxford's renowned inconsistency continued.

The lack of a goal kicker had cost Oxfordshire dearly in an 11–15 defeat in Berkshire

*Oxford centre Steve Page, a Cambridge 'Blue', tries to reach Tony Yendole (15) with the ball with Ian Graham and Chris Pittaway coming across in the home defeat against Rugby.*

and this was followed by a classic clash of fixtures when Oxford's Steve Page, Rhys James, Graham Warrington and Karl Freeman all played against Buckinghamshire in another defeat, 9–17, as the county team lost the Southern Group title. The game took place at the Bypass ground at the same time as Oxford University's attractive match with the touring Australia at Iffley Road and a crowd of 6000 saw the lion hearted student team suffer a 12–19 loss.

There was concern about some player's indifference towards county rugby. The new regulations allowed players to play for the county in which they played their club rugby. Oxfordshire suffered by losing several of the better players from clubs outside the county and were not the side they once were. Maybe these players could see no county playing progress along with the pressure of extra training sessions and games in the Jubilee year. The following season was due to present further challenges when county games would be played on Saturdays.

The Oxfordshire team was saved from the embarrassment of a 'white wash' in its final championship game when a 12–12 draw gave the host, Dorset & Wilts, the group title and Oxfordshire the 'wooden spoon' in the Jubilee season.

The club team had been playing well at times and there was a welcome 26–16 county cup win under lights against Thames Valley Police, and then six tries in the total of 31 in a satisfactory 31–15 win over Upper Clapton as a prelude to the John Player Cup 2nd Round match at home to High Wycombe on December 5th. The losers were guaranteed a sum of £725 plus a percentage of the gate money from the semis and final of the competition, while the winners could expect nearly £2000. There was an unusual clash of colours and Oxford, as the home team, was obliged to change and the team turned out in all green shirts donated by Club President John Mawle. The match was a 'nip and tuck' affair but

*Geoff Elliott evades a tackler with a swivel of the hips in the match with Sutton Coldfield.*

*Playing in green shirts Billy Greenhalgh makes a break in the John Player Cup against Wycombe with Bob Reynolds in support.*

Wycombe's pack took control at a crucial point in the second half. Oxford's last score was a great try involving Page and Reynolds which saw James go over in the corner. Greenhalgh converted from the touchline to make the score 9–10, and an injury time penalty from fifty years looked good but drifted agonisingly wide past the post as Oxford went out of the competition. Wycombe's prize was an away draw to Gloucester.

The Bicester/Henley county cup match on the same weekend was shrouded in controversy. The Henley scrum half Huw Jones was injured in the sixth minute but not replaced until the 41$^{st}$ minute by Willie Carr who went on to score 11 points, eclipsing Bicester's lead and eventual 13–23 defeat. The Bicester club protested that this player was ineligible, upheld by the County Discipline Committee and Henley were excluded from the competition, having to forfeit any income from it. A future appeal was rejected. Having lost the game on the day Bicester now went through and were due to meet the winners of the RAF Brize Norton/Oxford tie, yet to be played.

Just days later heavy overnight snow in Oxford and the south of England put the 100$^{th}$ University match at Twickenham in jeopardy. Long before the days of underground heating at the stadium, the pitch was carpeted by several inches of snow. There were no attempts to clear the pitch which drew some criticism of the RFU, but where would they have

*Tony Yendole covers the inside break as John Tilsey looks outside.*

put the cleared snow? The game went ahead and Cambridge University beat their Oxford counterparts 9–6 to take an overall lead in the series for the first time.

Oxford's John Player Cup match saw the county cup match with RAF Brize Norton postponed and this meant that the club was back to the undesirable position of playing two games in a weekend, and only Kim Bulley and Keith Fowler, who had joined from Littlemore, retained their places in the team selected to meet US Portsmouth with the Brize Norton game the next day. But the deep snow covering most of Oxfordshire was not going to go away and both matches were inevitably cancelled and postponed. This on/off situation was to continue for the next few weekends including the Christmas period where Oxford's planned match at Esher had been called off due to the home team having doubts about raising a side to play.

After a month without any rugby the Oxford team was at last able to start 1982 with the customary fixture, this time in Croydon, against Old Whitgiftians. A little bit out of touch after the long break some players got lost en route in London while Geoff Elliott was denied that pleasure when he broke down near Oxford. The team played with fourteen players until half time when Elliott appeared, skipper Andy Smith robbed the scrum half for a try and Steve Page added another converted by Greenhalgh for a 10–0 win.

Teams were selected again for a 'double' weekend on 9th January but the snow intervened once more. Over the night of January 13th Oxford was the coldest place in Britain at a temperature of -20°C while, during the same night, Moscow in Russia was warmer at -16°C!

Rugby Union came to life again on Saturday 23rd January when Oxford lost to Sidcup on the Bypass ground, 13–18, as the forwards fell away in the second half. Perhaps there was a thought for the next day and the short journey to RAF Brize Norton for the much postponed county cup match. A lot of the players were playing two days running and were still rusty after the long lay-off but the team won 20–4 after some anxious moments. Up in East Oxford the Old Boys beat Oxford Marathon 20–7 to reach that clubs first final for eight years as Mick Groom kicked one penalty in five as Maras suffered an off day.

The club held an open meeting in February and after lengthy discussion on the possible effect on the club Mike Florey proposed that the club accept the principle of league rugby as outlined by the RFU. John Deans seconded the proposal and the twenty two members present voted for with none against.

Keith Fowler returned to Littlemore after restricted First team appearances and Oxford lost 19–28 under mid-week lights at Cheltenham's new Prince of Wales stadium, with the pitch inside a running track. Oxford played its part in a fast and exciting match and two questionable tries were the difference.

Once more a 'double' weekend beckoned as Oxford caught up with fixtures and another weakened team conceded defeat at home to the Metropolitan Police, 3–12, before going over to Bicester the next day for the overdue county cup semi-final. It was a bit of a stamina test for Oxford with some of the players having played five games in nine days and the game was balanced at 6–6. But, with fifteen minutes left, Rhys James picked up a loose ball and sprinted to the line to break the deadlock. Greenhalgh converted from the touchline and then added a third penalty for Oxford's 15–6 win and a date with Oxford Old Boys in the final.

With the pressure off, the club recorded a fine 29–24 win at Bridgwater & Albion where Andy Norman marked his return with two tries in a strong wind on an extremely muddy pitch. It was just the tonic needed as a prelude to the Oxfordshire Cup Final. With the experienced Phil Blake back in the side Oxford were due to meet an Old Boys side that contained five former Oxford players, two of whom were captains in Tapper and Goodey, along with Sandbach, Ashby and Williams, that had lost just six games in the season at that point. In a frantic first half Warrington completely dominated the lineouts and Oxford's pack of forwards went on to provide a great platform. With Ian Graham off the pitch receiving attention the Old Boys scored first when Ashby made a break in the centre, passed on to Sandbach who returned the ball to Ashby who scored for Tapper to convert. Greenhalgh reduced the arrears with a penalty and, in the second half, Norman scored, with the referee playing advantage when the Old Boys collapsed a scrum lost against the head, to give Oxford a slender 7–6 lead which was held until the end. Such was the tension with the score so close that Oxford Secretary Ron Martin could not watch the last ten minutes and spent the time pacing the changing room. It was Oxford's third successive cup final win and there was little doubt that the best side won. The Old Boys, who had underestimated Oxford's tight play, were gracious in defeat and the two teams met again at Marston Ferry Road after the match. Teams: Oxford: W Greenhalgh; J Tilsey, R James, S Page, A Norman; I Graham (H Jones 21 mins), P Blake; A Staples, A Smith (Capt), P Maton, G Warrington, S Griffiths, G Elliott, C Pittaway, N Dobson. Oxford Old Boys: J Pyle; E Sandbach, P Ashby, S Williams, D Jones; R Tapper, R Nevers; A John, N Goodey, C Champion (Capt), A Cooke, A Reid, M Haines, T Haines, I Grant.

*There was no love lost in the 1982 Valentine's Day Cup Final. This is the match programme.*

Oxford lost again 3–22 to Nuneaton and made changes, some enforced, for the Floodlit Cup Final against Banbury. After playing badly the team was lucky to win 15–14 when Greenhalgh kicked a late penalty to win it before a six try success against Bournemouth well and truly 'laid the ghost' from the club's John Player Cup exit two years previously with an emphatic 33–9 win. Club secretary Ron Martin, a veritable 'jack of all trades', now acting as sponge man ran out towards an injured player with bucket of water and bag but lost his boot in the thick mud and sat on his bottom with hardly a drop spilt. Regaining his feet he ran on minus the boot only to be waved back to the touchline as the injured player had recovered without the magic sponge!

Off the field the club was suddenly hit with a cash flow problem due to the large amount of water used in the club's communal after match baths. The cost of water had risen and was now linked with a sewerage rate, and Thames Water had sent a demand for £1000, a figure that had not been budgeted for. And at the same time Customs and Excise had ruled that Value Added Tax (VAT) was payable on match fees and had also sent a demand for £500 calculated over the past two seasons, also not budgeted for. The club had suffered through very little income from bar takings as there had been no rugby over the Christmas and New Year period. To counter these set-backs the club launched a novel appeal to members and friends to donate a minimum of £5. Each unit of £5 would be linked to a draw in which 40 per cent of the takings, up to a maximum of £400, would be returned in the draw to be made at the end of March. In this draw the sum of £200 was won by former player EJ Robins while Dai David scooped £70 and Brian Deane £40. £490 was raised towards club funds this way and contributors were listed in 'Oxygen'. The club also decided to install showers as a means of reducing water costs.

Streatham & Croydon offered a morning kick off on 5th March so that all could see

# OBs have no answer to power pack

**Oxford 7pts, Oxford Old Boys 6pts**

**By RON GRIMSHAW**

THE better side won ... and Oxford are county club champions and holders of the Oxfordshire Morland Brewery Knockout Cup for a record third successive year largely due to their pack which provided the platform for victory at Iffley Road yesterday.

The Old Boys did not win a single line-out and later were well out-scrummaged — with four consecutive strikes against the head at one stage — and beaten in rucks and mauls.

Their plans to unsettle Oxford's big lock forward, Graham Warrington, who was man of the match in my book, ended at the first line-out where they were penalised for illegal play. After that Warrington completely dominated all line-out play and with a little more control in other tight play Oxford would have had a couple more tries.

Having said that a reliable place kicker on either side could have put the match out of reach of the opposition.

So often a match-winner in the past Billy Greenhalgh was successful with only one out of seven shots at goal while Ray Tapper, Paul Ashby and Mark Haines between them also missed half a dozen penalty shots at goal.

### Frantic

A typically tense, frantic first half, while full of commitment, was of extraordinarily low quality and highlighted only by a superb try by the Old Boys.

This came during a brief period while Oxford were a man short; their young fly half Ian Graham was receiving attention for concussion before leaving the field to be replaced by Howard Jones.

From a midfield scrum the Old Boys won good possession and started a rare passing movement which posed no threat until Ashby received the ball.

With great determination he accelerated through the centre leaving two defenders in his wake. As a third closed he passed out to left winger Ted Sandbach who, with remarkable dexterity, brought the ball under control as it came to him below waist height and almost behind his back.

Having gathered in he sped along the wing beating another two defenders before cutting in towards goal and when tackled he had Ashby on his right to take a return pass and crash over the line.

The conversion was made by Tapper and for a while Oxford, who had clearly not got things right in their reorganisation behind the scrum, were back on their heels and struggling.

They survived a period of concentrated pressure, even at the expense of giving away a couple of penalties, but then suffered another setback when No 8 Neill Dobson went off to have stitches inserted into a cut eyebrow.

It was in the third minute of injury time when Greenhalgh, at his fifth attempt, landed a penalty goal which brought Oxford relief and new hope.

Dobson returned for the second half which opened with Greenhalgh hitting the top of an upright with another penalty attempt.

When Oxford won a strike against the head and let out the ball to Jones on the wing, Seretse Williams tackled the little scrum half and ran him back about 20 yards.

Following a midfield break by Steve Page it seemed that Greenhalgh must score but he was held by a tight defence at the line but Oxford's pressure eventually told.

### Miscued

They made another strike against the head and the Old Boys collapsed the scrum to prevent them driving over. The referee acknowledged the offence but played the advantage law.

Oxford regained possession and Phil Blake whipped out a pass to Rhys James (who had taken over at fly half) and Greenhalgh linked again to give a not too hopeful pass out to Andy Norman on the wing.

Norman is not possessed with the keenest eyesight in the game — "if I see them long enough I can usually take the pass" — but he saw this one long ebough to bring it under control, with a little legerdemain, and go on and over. Greenhalgh missed the conversion.

The Old Boys tried again and their best chance came after 22 minutes when Tapper miscued a fairly easy penalty shot, which was not their last chance but the others by Ashby and Haines were much harder and from longer range.

Oxford came again and Page was once over the line but held up by tenacious defenders and James was in full cry when he too was held at the lne.

First class attacking positions at scrums near the line were wasted as Oxford conceded penalties for basic offences but they knew they had control of matters forward.

**Oxford:** W Greenhalgh; J Tilsey, R James, S Page, A Norman; I Graham (H Jones 21 mins), P Blake; A Staples, A P Smith (capt), P Maton, G Warrington, S Griffiths, G Elliott, C Pittaway, N Dobson.

**Oxford Old Boys:** J Pyle; E P L Sandbach, P Ashby, S A Williams, D Jones; R P Tapper, R Nevers; A John, N Goodey, C Champion (capt), A Cooke, A Reid, M Haines, T Haines, I Grant.

**Referee:** A Thompson (Gloucester — Bristol Society).

## Sporting seven

SEVEN soccer club members are planning a sponsored walk in a bid to raise £1,000 to help a man get a kidney dialysis machine.

The seven from Thame United hope to help Richard Rampling, 35, of 11 Holliers Close, Thame, who has just launched a £5,000 appeal for a new machine.

Husband and wife Rick and Rose Fairburn, Stan Eustace, Jim Edwards, Kevin Edwards, Ray Janes and Ron Eele plan to walk from Thame to Abingdon and back on February 20.

*Oxford Mail Sports Reporter, Ron Grimshaw, wrote the match report.*

England and Wales at Twickenham. This would have meant leaving at 7/7.30am and experience told that such an arrangement would be inviting problems, so the club declined and Streatham cancelled the match. When the team did take the field again it was an 'off the boil' performance but three great moves produced tries for John Tilsey (2) and Andy Norman in the 24–6 win over Esher.

Oxford Old Boys secretary Barry Townsend had been trying to improve his club's fixture list due to the expectation that league placings in the future would be decided on the strength of a club's fixture list. For five years the Old Boys had been a little disorganised due to the uncertainty of a ground and clubhouse but, despite these issues being solved, the club was finding it difficult to get their old fixtures back and reported that three major junior clubs in a 35 mile radius were trying to avoid playing them.

The Oxford club's injury list was long again and contributed to home defeats from Clifton, 8–12, a 10–10 draw with Guildford & Godalming before Henley exacted some revenge for previous defeats in beating Oxford 3–23 in the Floodlit Cup Final. A productive trip to Sutton & Epsom at the beginning of April saw John Dunnill score a try on his debut after a crunching tackle from Dai David saved the day in an 18–16 win in which John Butler kicked two penalties and two conversions.

Oxford Old Boys, led by Ray Tapper, reached the finals of the Middlesex Sevens when the team beat Wasps II in the final qualifying round to become the first Oxfordshire side to play at the finals since 1970 when an Oxford RFC side did it. It was also the first time for twenty years that a Wasps side failed to qualify! Sadly the Old Boys lost 10–18 in the first round to London Scottish at Twickenham. And there was little joy when the side lost 10–24 to Oxford University in the final of the Oxford RFC Floodlit Sevens, the third successive year that the students had won the tournament.

The last match of the season, an away match at Lydney, seemed like an 'add on' and the 13–36 defeat was no surprise.

David Fitzpatrick, affectionately known as 'The Colonel', was standing down as Club Chairman as he was due for election at County level as President. His shoes would be difficult to fill – he was also Fixture Secretary and Match Secretary and was formerly Club Secretary for six years. David was proud to recall the club's third successive county cup win which, he said, proved that it is deeds that count and not propaganda.

The club's seasonal record was similar to that immediately previous having won twelve, drawn one and lost sixteen with the major successes coming in cup competitions. This reflected in an attitude that it was only the cup games that mattered and the team let itself down at times with poor performances. Mike Florey had celebrated twenty years with the club while captaining the Nomads and was presented with a tankard at the annual dinner. Under the leadership of John Page the Vikings won over seventy per cent of their games and also showed, with John's 'two thirds jug' as an example, how to play the game off the pitch. Bob Martyn, as Team Secretary, gained the individual distinction of being awarded the Harold Phillips Cup for the second successive season.

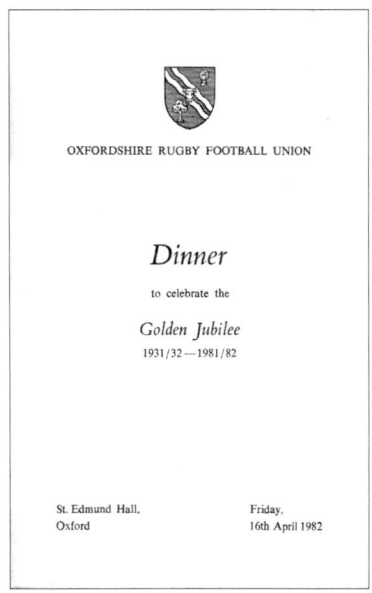

*Oxfordshire Rugby Union Golden Jubilee Dinner Menu.*

# Season 1982–1983

At the beginning of this season it was reported that the Rugby Union's proposals for league rugby had fallen through.

Pre-season training was being taken by Doug Rogers who was also connected to Oxford Marathon, but was not well attended. With new captain Graham Warrington at the helm an unusual side was selected to play Weston-super-Mare due to marriage, moving home, illness, unfit, and plain unavailable. Keith Robinson, a Colt from the previous season, took over the fly half shirt and although the team settled in the second half to show some promise the club team began the season with a 9–16 defeat, the points coming from a Steve Page try converted by Tony Yendole who also kicked a penalty. The next day the club lost prop Peter Mack who had played against Weston, when he stepped back into a pothole while playing in the Abingdon Sevens on Abingdon's notorious riverside pitch. In the week defeat followed again, this time 9–15 against Swindon, and this opening run of losses continued at Worcester, 13–16. In an improved showing the side felt that they were 'robbed' by a try and conversion in the seventh minute of injury time. The Worcester pitch at that time was flanked by a green bank to kill the noise of passing traffic on the M5 motorway and the ball landing beyond the bank was the signal for squadrons of 'daddy long legs' and other associated flies to scramble as they had been disturbed. A 'wag' was heard to say "Just as well that Oxford's touch kicking was not that reliable!"

*Chairman of Selectors, Ron Salter, checks the list with new Captain Graham Warrington with Rhys James and Andy Smith showing an interest.*

In West Oxfordshire the Witney club opened its new clubhouse at a reported cost of £45,000 on a ground owned by the club with a match against a President's XV. This was a big step for the club that had reformed in 1965.

Endless enforced changes made prior to the county trial team's match against the President's XV took its toll on Oxford players and this was partly responsible for a demoralising 7–43 defeat at Stroud and the signs were that there were hard times ahead unless the club could find a settled side, especially in the forwards. The early season record was played four, lost four and was hardly the best preparation for Oxford's John Player Cup match against the Dorset Champions at Wimborne. Allied to this Billy Greenhalgh had recovered from his long term ankle injury but had limped off on his return playing for the Vikings at Didcot, with torn ligaments, and Peter Maton had a gash under his eye. Although former captain Andy Smith was due to leave the area having secured a job at Sussex University, arguably the best and liveliest hooker in the county, Peter Jones, had returned to Littlemore where he was playing at scrum half. But, despite all this, morale amongst the players was high.

The Nomads travelled with the team on 25th September and played against Wimborne II as a curtain raiser at 1pm and were then able to support their club colleagues in the main match.

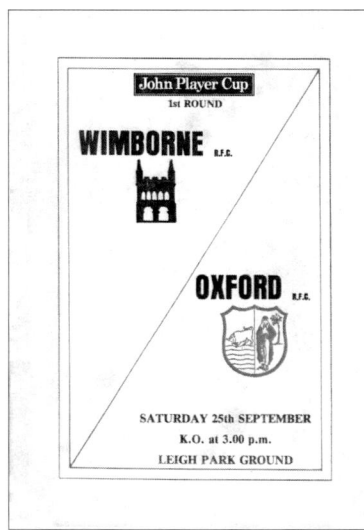

*Wimborne v Oxford in the John Player Cup, match programme.*

The pack was much improved and Warrington and Nick Turner worked tirelessly. After forty three minutes it fell to Gareth Lewis to break the deadlock with what turned out to be a 'Golden Goal' with his penalty kick. Although Wimborne equalised with a late penalty of their own in the second half, it was Oxford who went through under the 'away team' rule. It was not satisfactory after a good team performance but it was progress to the next round. The Oxford team was: D David; G Lewis, S Page, R James, J Tilsey; K Robinson, C Horton; A Staples, A Smith, N Turner, G Warrington (Capt), S Griffiths, K Freeman, R Tucker, N Dobson.

Results wise more gloom followed with home defeats against Oxford University, 9–23, Stafford, 9–17, and then at Rugby, 12–20, where the chance of a surprise win was lost when prop Graham Penny left the field with an arm injury with the score 9–9. Team performances had improved and the club was trying to find the right combinations from a number of players with much the same abilities.

County games were now being played on Saturdays with Oxfordshire in Division 4 along with Berkshire and Buckinghamshire, and several players who had played in recent times had told selectors that they were no longer available. Some first class clubs had told players that if they played county rugby their club replacement would keep the place for at least one more week, and one former Oxfordshire player had told selectors that playing county rugby in Division 4 would not do his first class career any good. With this background Oxfordshire selected James, Page, Horton, Staples, Warrington and Freeman, with the Oxford club's blessing, for the match against Buckinghamshire at Bletchley on Saturday 16th October. In fact the club had a blank Saturday and planned to field two Nomad level teams instead. Oxfordshire's pack did not play well and the team lost 7–13 but the following week there was a complete turnaround with a 31–0 win over Berkshire. How could this be with virtually the same team?

The Oxford side at Sutton Coldfield on the same day had a distinctly Nomadic look about it in a 9–28 defeat but a week later, at the end of October, there was much joy when the team beat Cheltenham 17–5 to record its first win of the season in a club fixture. The result was more pleasing than the performance and the pack was strengthened by the return of props Peter

*Gareth Lewis, scorer of the 'Golden Goal' at Wimborne.*

Maton and Tony Staples after injury which made a big difference. Tries from Andy Walton and Nick Turner, a penalty from Gareth Lewis and two from Tony Yendole secured the win.

Into November a 6–6 draw was the result of a scrappy game with Havant a week before another county weekend was due to clash with Oxford's home fixture with Walsall. It was a match with a dramatic ending as the team beat Walsall, 20–17, with ten points in the last five minutes. Tony Yendole, playing in the centre, created moves for the two late tries scored by Turner and Walton with an earlier try from Tilsey, Lewis kicked two penalties and a conversion while, over at Henley, Oxfordshire beat Buckinghamshire 10–0.

Having won two games from three Oxfordshire were guaranteed promotion but wanted to win the group by beating Berkshire. This created a challenge for Oxford who were due to play Upper Clapton, the last chance to get the team together in preparation for the next John Player Cup match, home again to High Wycombe, the following Saturday.

But before that came an Oxfordshire Cup match at home to Littlemore on 21$^{st}$ November. Oxford picked a strong side and were favourites to beat a side that had been training regularly by arrangement under the Southern Bypass floodlights. It was not a good day for rugby and the horrendous conditions of mud and driving rain proved to be a big leveller in a game largely dictated by the foul weather. Stuart McMinn scored Littlemore's try, converted by Peter Jones, and Malcolm Fitzsimmons added a penalty. A Gareth Lewis penalty was the only response from Oxford who could not match Litllemore's team spirit and will to win. Dick Rudman's players battled away to keep Oxford at bay and only reached Oxford's half of the field twice in the second half but it was enough before John Tilsey scored Oxford's try in injury time. With the conversion missed a draw would not have been enough as the home team in a cup competition and Oxford lost 7–9 anyway. It was a humiliation and the biggest surprise in the history of the Oxfordshire Cup at a bad psychological time on the eve of the High Wycombe match. Oxford lost prestige and status and the loudest cheer at Marston Ferry Road was not because the Old Boys had beaten Oxford Marathon in the cup to preserve their unbeaten record but when the news of Oxford's defeat was received. There were, however, sobering moments when it became known that a Littlemore player, Jim Ackrigg, had been taken to Stoke Mandeville Hospital with a serious back injury after a match during the same weekend with an Oxford Old Boys Fourth XV.

Graham Warrington and Rhys James were selected for Oxfordshire's last championship game against Berkshire but declined as both wanted to play for the club prior to the High Wycombe match, while Karl Freeman accepted. In preparation with a week to go Oxford beat Upper Clapton 9–7 in London while Oxfordshire lost 4–6 to Berkshire but would still be promoted to Division 3.

The High Wycombe team were favourites to win the John Player Cup match through their better record so far, although it couldn't be much worse than Oxford's at that time! And so it proved. With the better pack High Wycombe outclassed and outsmarted Oxford who could have no complaints at the 3–12 defeat. Dai David did his best to stem the flow with some superb crash tackles from full back but Oxford looked little like scoring. High Wycombe's reward was an away tie against Leicester in the next round.

On the same weekend indiscipline led to a first defeat of the season for Oxford Old Boys when the team lost to 4–10 to Henley in the Oxfordshire Cup. It was a difficult result for the now coach Charlie Ede who said "That's two year's work down the drain and we're back to square one." Following the defeat Henley declined the Old Boys request for a First XV fixture, and the Old Boys withdrew from Henley's restricted Oxfordshire Sevens Tournament.

Oxford set the record straight when the pack took control on a muddy pitch in a gale force wind to beat Littlemore, scoring 29 points without reply, in the Floodlit Cup. But it was of little comfort as defeats at US Portsmouth, 7–12, and at home to Solihull, 12–30, saw the losing trend continue. It was Oxford's worst first half season for twenty years. The gloom was lifted by an invitation for the club to join a South East Merit Table due to start during the following season which already contained six clubs on Oxford's fixture list, those being Esher, Havant, Sidcup, Streatham & Croydon, Upper Clapton and US Portsmouth.

Although Old Whitgiftians were beaten by a point, 10–9, things didn't change much in the New Year. A 4–10 defeat at home to Wimborne was hardly inspiration for an away match with London Scottish arranged by Mike Simmie, Oxford's current Chairman and former London Scottish player. This was a morning game played before the England v France International and Oxford gave a good account of themselves leading 9–4 at the break with a Buster Ewart try and John Butler's conversion and penalty. But the Scots' extra fitness told and Oxford crashed to a 9–46 loss.

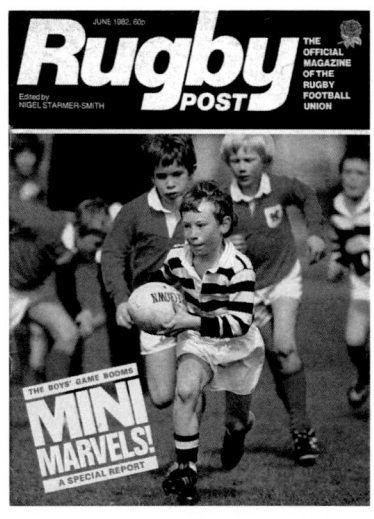

*After the Teacher's Dispute a decade earlier responsibility for producing rugby players now fell to clubs and this was highlighted on the cover of 'Rugby Post' in 1982.*

Ron Grimshaw reported on some 'sniping' at Oxford RFC on his weekly newspaper column. Whilst visiting the Marathons club Ron was approached by a stalwart asking "What's going on at the Bypass? Looks like they've had it" then "Nothing will go right until the players change their attitude" and finally "Well, it's the officials down there who need to change their attitude." All of which Ron put down to the kind of blind pig headed thinking which blights Oxfordshire rugby and which maybe partly explained why local rugby had slumped to such lowly levels. "While there is no focal point or incentive, mediocrity will remain the par" he said.

It could have been argued that these comments, justified or otherwise, were perhaps made in the light of Oxford's poor results and defeats at Sidcup, Clifton and home to Bridgwater & Albion and Fullerians did nothing to change opinions.

The Henley team had to stand and watch a conversion attempt drop just short before they could celebrate a 12–11 win at Banbury while Bicester edged home 6–4 in a dour affair against the Oxford University Greyhounds, both in the county cup semi-finals, before Bicester's spirited performance produced a thrilling final at Iffley Road where Henley won by a point, 8–7.

The 1st team pitch at the club was reported as being a muddy morass, the worst it had been since the club had moved there but the next two matches were away from home. Polytechnic (now Brookes University) student Ian Stevens telephoned to say that he had missed a train from London to Oxford and couldn't get to Nuneaton which left the fly half space open for new recruit Barry Abbott to step in. Barry, a newly appointed Policeman in Oxford who had arrived at the club 48 hours earlier, had previously played for the Army and he scored two tries on his debut in a rejuvenated Oxford side where the pack put in a stirring display. The team fell to a try in the last seconds of the match that was converted from the touchline in the 15–16 defeat. The run of six successive games without a win finally ended the following week, 26th February, when Oxford visited Bournemouth for the first time. This match was a direct result of the John Player Cup match in 1980 and found the pack once more in positive mood. A late car of players meant that there was no time for a warm up but Oxford recovered well from a 0–10 deficit. Warrington, at No 8, picked up to force a break and pass to Reynolds for a try, and Abbott stepped through a gap to pass to James for a second, and Yendole kicked two penalties in the 14–13 win. There was less joy in the week when Banbury beat Oxford 3–10 in the Floodlit Cup on a sodden slippery surface. How could Oxford have won so much ball and lose was a complete mystery.

An innovation was due to be revealed at Twickenham prior to the England v Scotland match where the Rugby Union had installed two forty feet 'Diamond Vision' screens at opposite ends of the ground. These were the first permanent screens in Britain and the largest, at the time, in the world and would show highlights of previous matches and action from the Wales v Ireland game from Cardiff, but not of the game going on in front of the spectators. The Rugby Union was anxious to avoid the possibility of embarrassing the referee if wrong decisions leading to scores were shown. My, how things change!

And it all changed again at the weekend with a 23–3 win at home to Streatham & Croydon. There were rare celebrations as all four Oxford sides won their matches with the Nomads beating Witney 28–10, the Vikings beating Witney II, 12–9 and the Wanderers beating Witney III 14–10 to complete their twentieth win of the season to date.

Charlie Ede resigned his position as Coaching Chairman and selector at Oxford Old Boys 'due to differences in selection policy.' Since he had joined the club from Oxford there had been vastly improved results and status but Charlie remained at the Marston Ferry Road club.

The Oxford team returned to old ways in defeats by Esher, 7–28, Burton, 7–13, and Guildford & Godalming 9–14 while Oxford Old Boys defeated Henley in the Floodlit Cup and then went on to beat Banbury 13–9 in the final.

With the end of a dismal season in sight the club broke new ground when a party of twenty eight went off to Holland for an Easter Tour in early April. After an overnight crossing to Vlissingen, Oxford beat RAF Laarsbruch, 29–9, and the next day a Nomadic looking Oxford side beat Arnhem, whose average age was twenty years, 80–10. The third

*Oxford RFC 1983 in Holland. Back row, l to r: Steve Doyle, Stuart Davies, Peter Maton, Hamish Simpson, Rhys James, Peter Mack, Gareth Lewis, Tony Staples, Nick Turner, Brian Jones, Alan Smith. Front row, l to r: Bill Allen, Shane Tibbetts, Graham Warrington (Capt), Keith Robinson, John Butler, Andy Walton.*

*On Tour! Mike Ryan, Ian McDougal and Bill Allen.*

*Oxford club stalwarts – Phil O'Neill, Phil Kelly, Andy Smith and Stuart Davies.*

and final match against Wageringen was won 39–6 for a total 144 points in the three games with 25 against. Fly half Keith Robinson, who played in all three games, was named as the 'Star of the Tour'.

No 1st team game had been arranged a week later, probably in anticipation of tour recovery, but the Nomads lost 7–22 to Bath United and Oxford retained the Plate in the Henley Closed Sevens. In what was now regarded as the Sevens Season an Oxford team went out early in the Oxfordshire Sevens and the Middlesex Sevens Preliminaries, while Oxford University, winners of the Bagnall Trophy for the previous three years, lost to Borough Road College, renamed West London Institute, who went on to lose to Loughborough College in the Final on sodden ground after heavy storms. The final game of the season followed what was a familiar pattern in an 8–9 defeat at home to Sutton & Epsom where eight kicks at goal were missed.

Chairman Mike Simmie reflected that pre-season training had been poorly attended and lack of personal fitness had stretched long into the campaign when several players were found wanting. Graham Warrington noted the good relationship the club maintained with both RAF Brize Norton and Westminster College in announcing season results of 31 games played with 7 won, 2 drawn and 22 lost with 12 of those games lost by 8 points or less.

At the end of the season Bar Committee Chairman John Cummings left to become Honorary Secretary of Oxfordshire RFU, President John Mawle took a sabbatical after service of 25 years to the club as both a player and administrator, and Ken Morgan stood down as Colts Manager citing disappointment at the Colts not being allowed to play a home game on the John Player Cup match day and there being no mention of the Colts team at the Annual Dinner. Keith Robinson was named as 'The Most Improved Player of the Year' and Ron Salter was recipient of the Harold Phillips Cup.

*Feeling the heat in Holland – Graham Warrington, Tony Staples and Peter Maton take a break.*

# Chapter 9 – 75th Anniversary – with Merit!

Following the demise of the Rugby Union's plans for league rugby, Merit Tables formed by groups of clubs popped up in several parts of the country and Oxford RFC was not left behind in the long and slow lean towards increased competitive rugby when, in July, the news came that the club had been accepted into the newly formed Seven Counties Merit Table due to start this season.

In a threat to the traditional and long established amateur game rumours and reports emerged of an International professional circus being set up by Australian entrepreneur David Lord and sponsorship was reported to be in the region of £20m although there were no details. Hugo McNeil, the Ireland full back returning to Oxford University after the British Lions tour, confirmed that some players had been approached and offered 'big' money while in New Zealand. Lord was alleged to have arranged 31 games in January and February 1984 in England and Ireland with the agreement of 208 players who were promised £90,000 each. The Rugby Football Union hoped that players would "have the allegiance and feeling for the clubs and counties who have helped you achieve the recognition in a world sport which you now enjoy" and demanded a loyalty pledge from the top 120 players to say that they would not be joining the professional circus, and if they didn't sign they wouldn't be considered for England.

## Season 1983–1984

*Oxford's front row, Peter Maton, Peter Jones and Tony Staples get in some pre-season training.*

Amazingly, Oxford opened the season with a plum home match against Harlequins. Andy Norman whose previous season injuries had restricted him to only a few games, was selected on the wing and Barrie Abbott at fly half. Peter Jones had joined from Littlemore to be propped by Tony Staples and Peter Maton while the deposed Kim Bulley joined Oxford Old Boys, and Gareth Lewis sat on the bench. It is said that there is no substitute for class and in the match Oxford were outclassed. In the first twenty minutes the team went well and took the lead with two Abbott penalties before a deluge of points saw a 9–53 defeat in which Staples suffered a broken nose. Key in the result was Harlequins great back row support. In the wake of that opening match, Keith Robinson, selected at full back for the Nomads, left during the week to join Oxford Old Boys.

*Neil Dobson is about to be clattered by Harlequins cover with Barry Abbot unable to get there quick enough.*

Oxford did learn some lessons from the game and the following week beat Worcester 19–9, looking quicker around the field and sharper in the process but a 15–21 home defeat to Stroud followed. Abbott kicked three penalties and converted David Woof's try and there was little doubt that Stroud were the better side although Oxford showed signs of being useful after a 3–40 loss in the corresponding match the previous season. The end of September produced another promising display in 15–28 defeat at Glamorgan Wanderers.

Peter Maton, Simon Stevenson, Graham Warrington and winger Rick Allison were chosen to play for Oxfordshire in an 8–0 warm up win over Buckinghamshire. The Rugby Union had said that the County Championship was its major competition but England selectors were more likely to watch top club sides to pick players at a time of low ebb for the England team. Club places were in jeopardy if the better players declared for county sides and although the RFU had asked clubs to cooperate, the players were left with a difficult decision.

Injuries and non-availabilities led to another loss, this time at Stafford, 0–12. The following weekend the First XV had no fixture but Tony Staples returned from his nose injury to play in the Nomads 17–12 over his old club Bicester on the same day that Oxfordshire lost their Division 3 match 3–15 at Worthing against Sussex.

Chris Clarke made his club debut in monsoon like conditions at Maidenhead and in the lottery that produced Oxford lost again 6–12.

After a futile appeal for help the club was forced into an agonising decision in the middle of October to abandon the Colts fixtures because nobody could be found to run the team. A fixture list with clubs like Moseley, Bath, Northampton, Bedford, Cheltenham, Rosslyn Park and Harlequins on it had taken years of hard work to establish. Steve Lander, a school teacher playing for the Vikings and later to become an International referee of some renown, offered to coach the side but the previous manager, Ken Morgan, had decamped on the well-worn trail to Marston Ferry Road and some of the players had gone with him. These fixtures were now lost to youth players in the county. Ron Grimshaw, again, commented that "The fact that some clubs in the county seem to rejoice in Oxford's misfortune and the present sad situation can only be described as sick."

Oxford's home match with Cross Keys was postponed due to the Oxfordshire v Staffordshire match at the Bypass ground. Simon Stevenson was serving a ban after being sent off playing for RAF Abingdon and Tony Staples took his place in the county team that lost 0–41 in a sorry display of ineptitude. Ron Grimshaw wrote an article in his rugby column "What's happened to the Oxfordshire rugby team? The selectors are doing their best but could reach the point where there are not enough players of the required class to meet the challenge. That is the key. Some players shine in lower grades of rugby but when they move up to county they are just not good enough, this was patently obvious in the match against Staffordshire. This is an echo of the trouble facing England and why there is such a demand for merit tables or leagues which ensures leading players are kept on top line by constantly playing top class rugby. Since what talent there is in Oxfordshire is so fragmented and widely spread the county can only be strong again when there is one club to which all talent is directed. The only club playing anything like the grade required is Oxford. Like it or not that is fact. History proves beyond question that Oxfordshire were at best and most formidable, twice reaching the County Championship semi-final, only when Oxford were strong and provided most members of the county side. The idea of all this co-operating or affiliating was first mooted in 1934 in the George Mallaby plan for the restructure of rugby in England but was largely ignored. Unfortunately the likelihood of it ever coming about has never been less likely than now. There is a great deal of inconsequential rugby being played in Oxfordshire. Clubs may go on piling up points and boasting unbeaten runs but their achievements are in a grade of little consequence."

Billy Greenhalgh returned to full back for his first First XV game of the season after injury and playing through the junior sides for the match at Cheltenham where Oxford vigorously contested the forward exchanges. Abbott missed three penalties and two conversions in the 8–11 defeat but kicked all of Oxford's points in the Town v Gown match at Iffley Road. The University side's greater fitness told in the last quarter to break a 9–9 deadlock and win 12–24. A highly creditable performance, again in defeat, at Walsall again clashed with a county match, Oxfordshire away to Leicestershire. The county's 9–36 defeat condemned the side to the bottom of Division 3 and facing a relegation play-off with Buckinghamshire on 26th November.

By 20th November Oxford had won just one game although team performances had improved. The club again faced Henley in the Oxfordshire Cup and in a typically dour struggle Andy Rogers, son of the club coach Doug Rogers, kicked all the points in a very welcome 12–7 win.

Oxford drew 10–10 with unbeaten Camberley, although the visitor's record should have been shattered through a Peter Jones try, a John Butler drop goal and Andy Rogers's penalty, while Oxfordshire lost 3–11 against Buckinghamshire and were deservedly relegated. It was a spiritless performance played in second gear and lacking cohesion, and future prospects were not bright.

There was further woe at the beginning of December when Henley lost 15–21 at Norwich in the John Player Cup and Oxford were knocked out of the Oxfordshire Cup, losing 9–12 at Bicester in a dour, untidy match. Oxford led 9–0 until Bicester changed tack and ran the ball, the pressure creating a goal and two penalties to come from behind to win. The irony was that the Nomads had twice beaten Bicester so far this season and this was a setback for Oxford as the club was about to start the Seven Counties Merit Table campaign. Neutrals in the local rugby community were left to wonder who could now stop Oxford Old Boys from winning the Oxfordshire Cup. The Oxford team was: D David; C Stone, W Allen, A Yendole, A Norman; J Butler, C Horton; A Staples, P Jones, P Maton, G Warrington,

*Dai David breaks through against Camberley supported by Bill Allen in a photograph that was to appear on the programme cover in the 1987–1988 season.*

C Clarke, A Rogers, N Street, N Dobson.

The Merit Table match at home with US Portsmouth brought no relief in an inconsistent showing but Oxford did improve to beat Solihull 11–9 for the club's first away win of the season with tries from Clarke and Butler while Billy Greenhalgh kicked a penalty in his first senior game this season. The team ended the year by beating Sutton Coldfield 23–0 in a good display of open running rugby to overwhelm the visitors.

Gareth Lewis made known his intention to withdraw from the club as a player because of differences of opinion over selection but, having gained his Preliminary Coaching Award, was prepared to stay on to help with the coaching.

Lt Col David Fitzpatrick, now the County President, grasped the bull by the horns and circulated a letter to all clubs in the county the subject of which was a 'Necessity to

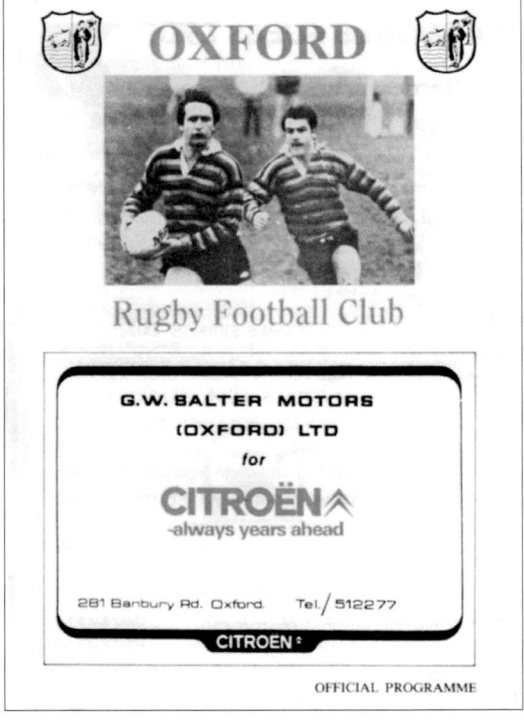

raise the standard of Oxfordshire Rugby.' The letter itemised five points affecting the decline which included individual fitness and the inability to play the full 80 minutes, the effect of low level club fixtures on teams and the inefficient coaching of basic skills. Suggested solutions included fitness tests for players and players playing at a higher level. His remedy was that the Oxford club would be the premier club in a feeder system upon which the County side would be largely based. The letter concluded with two options: accept the present position or take positive action as outlined. A meeting was set for the end of January when all opinions would be discussed. The Club Committee decided that it could make no comment on the letter but would take a role as 'listeners'.

In a 'tongue-in-cheek' distribution of 'Christmas Sporting Goodies' the *Oxford Mail* suggested "For Oxford RFC a package deal of ten players to enable them to field a team capable of maintaining and improving their fixture list. (We'd make it a package of twenty but there weren't that many good players in the County)."

In a bid to improve their lot some of the players had approached former Oxford player Lynn Evans to take a limited number of coaching sessions, offering financial reimbursement which meant a levy of 25p per player. This raised questions over the circumstances regarding Doug Rogers and Gareth Lewis and, of course, any money raised should go to the club but the situation went ahead with Lewis involved and being reimbursed for travelling expenses. Lower down the scale Rodney Staples was still appealing for help on Sunday mornings with Mini Rugby at the club.

Oxford's New Year response was a 16–7 home win against Maidenhead, the third in a row, on a muddy, windswept Southern Bypass Ground. Sleet, Snow and ice came to the county but Oxford played in Croydon against Old Whitgiftians and a much stronger showing from the pack ensured a 27–13 win with Tony Staples backing up well to score two tries. This run of four 'on-the-trot' came to an abrupt end at Stourbridge. PC Barrie Abbott returned to the side after recovering from facial injuries sustained at a discotheque in Kidlington prior to Christmas, only to suffer a knee injury in the second half.

Oxford Old Boys Publicity Officer, Rex Colcutt, wrote to the *Oxford Mail* regarding recent comments to say "Readers may believe that Oxford Old Boys have a weak fixture list. Not so. Fixtures have improved over the last few years and the current list shows a minimum of five sides to have met Oxford RFC in recent seasons with some success. The list could be stronger but it's not bad and getting better".

A conference of all interested in Mini and Junior Rugby in Oxfordshire was held at Abingdon RFC. Due to changes in the education system there had been a sudden and dramatic lack of schoolmasters available to teach the game. The Rugby Football Union realised that they had to take some action to get the game over to boys who were not now getting any rugby tuition at school. Their target was an estimated 10 million boys between the ages of 5 to 9 years to whom they needed to get over the message and basic understanding of the game. Regulations were introduced regarding the number of competitive games (10) and festivals (2) in which mini players were allowed to take part. Reservations were that winning seemed to be becoming too important. Only 20% of the current school population would be taught the game at school which placed a heavy responsibility on clubs.

Both Henley and Oxford had kept 22nd January clear in the hope and prospect of reaching the Oxfordshire Cup semi-finals and it made sense to meet as both had been eliminated. Unfortunately the rivalry spawned in several Cup encounters produced a bad tempered, scrappy game on a very hard pitch at Dry Leas, Henley. Buster Ewart equalised Henley's early try and Andy Rogers and Irvine Gale traded penalties in the 7–7 low standard match.

Cup semi-finals produced a Bicester v Oxford Old Boys final due to be played in February and Oxford beat Sidcup 22–19 in a Merit Table match where the lead changed eight times. A water logged home pitch in Oxford did not affect the side that travelled to Bridgwater and failed to exploit forward advantage, the hard graft in vain in a 4–11 defeat.

Club representatives, at the meeting held to discuss the poor state of rugby in Oxfordshire, were unanimous that something needed to be done to raise the standard but how to do it remained a problem. There was most support, with only one notable vote against and four abstentions, for a feeder system from the clubs to one main club, probably in Oxford. The suggestion that this needed to be a new club found some support until the obvious difficulties of getting and keeping first class fixtures were realised. Working out details of a feeder system seemed to be an almost insoluble challenge. Oxford Old Boys said

*Phil Blake gets the ball away against Nuneaton.*

that they would not contribute to any feeder system and were in isolation on that point. Their suggestion of a senior Merit Table within Oxfordshire met with no support. The meeting dispersed with things very much as they were before with no great hope for the future.

Oxford Old Boys won the County Cup in beating Bicester 20–11 in an excellent and exciting Final and on the same weekend the Oxford team lost the lead, control and the game to a last minute drop goal at home to Salisbury, 7–9. But that just a prelude to an embarrassing 13–61 defeat on the Bypass ground to Nuneaton. The visitors had attracted two players of New Zealand descent who made some difference and although Oxford led three times in the match through kicks, Nuneaton assumed full control to inflict the crushing defeat. Captain Graham Warrington commented after the game that Nuneaton was the best team he had played against including Pontypool and Pontypridd.

The club's enigmatic form continued with wins and losses often by a few points either way and included one inept performance in a 0–36 loss at Esher.

The complete Oxford front row of Staples, Jones and Maton, along with Warrington and Street with Greenhalgh at full back, were selected for Oxfordshire's annual match against Oxford University but the 6–22 defeat prompted David Fitzpatrick to write another paper regarding a feeder system to be presented to the County Committee. The club representatives would be asked to discuss this again in their clubs and then vote at a future meeting. Oxford's club committee felt that, if the system was not adopted, the club should take the initiative and approach the clubs that had already shown an interest.

The beginning of April brought Oxford's Floodlit Cup semi-final against Oxford Old Boys and a real nail biting affair. Hal Cochrane's drop goal gave Oxford an early lead but the score remained at 6–6 until well into the second half. The real difference between the two sides was Warrington's superb lineout dominance and it was then that he made a two handed catch, drove for the line before smuggling the ball for Maton who scored the deciding try. A point which could have hardly gone unnoticed by anyone seriously interested was that any amalgamation of the best of both sides would have provided a sound base for one good club to represent the city.

A week later the club side had to fight to stay in the game in the Floodlit Final running up against a resolute Banbury defence, and never got their game together in losing 9–19.

The restraints of playing ten man rugby and the cares of a disappointing season were thrown away as Oxford beat Rugby 34–10 to record the biggest win in the last home game. The Easter holiday coming in late April provided the club with a southern rugby trip taking in Havant for the final Merit Table match where the side was again in generous mood giving away tries after midfield fumbles, before moving along the coast to renew acquaintances with former club captain Andy Smith, now playing for Brighton. It was the final match and the pack gave a superb display which produced tries for Warrington, Nick Forrester, Rick Allison, Ewart and David Woof in the 25–13 win.

The club had endured a 'Jekyll and Hyde' season, the astonishing inconsistency defying all logic. The front five of the pack had developed into a really strong unit but there was little strength in depth. At least the number of games won had doubled to fourteen, with a mediocre placing in the first Seven Counties Merit Table, despite several players leaving the area through work during the campaign. Amongst those was John Page whose charismatic leadership of the Vikings had become legendary within the club. Who could forget his appearance at the annual dinner replete with Viking helmet? The biggest disappointment of the season was the Oxfordshire County team that had drawn a complete blank in the Championship and couldn't sink any lower. Oxford Old Boys had made it known that they would have no part in any proposed feeder system and had an impressive playing record but were relatively unsuccessful in the second part. They were, though, Oxfordshire Champions and would play in the John Player Cup in the following season. Up in the east of the city Oxford Marathon had probably the clubs worst ever season after the loss of several senior players. Talks of a proposed feeder system continued beyond the end of the season and a question remained – were local players sufficiently dedicated and committed to the requirements of possible regular and, hopefully, top grade rugby? Experience suggested that some likely players were quite happy and satisfied with the easier life and demands of a lower grade game.

*The Squash Court proved to be a popular addition to the club premises. Bob Buckingham won the club's main competition and John Page the Plate.*

TWO winners from Oxford RFC Squash Club's recent tournament. On the left is Bob Buckingham of Cassington who won the main event, with John Page who won the plate competition.

# Season 1984–1985

This was the season that marked the club's 75th Anniversary since formation as Oxfordshire Nomads RUFC in 1909. To mark the occasion an enlargement and refurbishment of the bar area in the clubhouse was due to take place with talks proceeding with the brewery to assist with financing the project through a loan. A special dinner was being arranged and a handbook covering previous years would be prepared.

The matter of the feeder system had rumbled on into the summer months. The County Committee's vote in May had been inconclusive with the club's motives meeting with some distrust. There were misgivings over Oxford's internal setup relating to selection, captains and coaching but the strength and logic of County President David Fitzpatrick's hopes of raising rugby standards in the county inspired the club to go ahead on its' own initiative. An understanding and sporting relationship was being sought with local clubs and a sub committee consisting of Ron Salter, David Bagnall and Peter Richmond was formed. The clubs who had expressed an interest were Abingdon, Bicester, Harwell, Grove and Littlemore with Witney and Thames Valley Police as hopefuls while Banbury had declared an interest with Northampton. It was also known that some individual players had shown an intention of coming to the club irrespective of their particular club's intention. Lynn Evans would coordinate responsibility for coaching and training began on 10th July. Peter Richmond, a Police Officer in Thames Valley and better known in refereeing circles, was a prime mover in the scheme and was not an Oxford club member. He said "We are all completely united to see an improvement in the standard of play in the county."

It was intriguing to see how the club would go with the help of some other county clubs but confidence was high and prospects were bright. Nine 'guest' players were selected to play in the season opener at Weston-super-Mare with six in the Nomads but there was a blow just prior to the start when it was announced that Graham Warrington, earmarked for a third term as captain, had joined Coventry and Peter Maton was named as 'caretaker' captain. Some of the others involved were Sean Murphy (Littlemore), Roy Woodward and Simon Henderson (Cholsey), Richard Howson, Robert Jenkins, David Spencer and Simon Grater (all Bicester), Jonathan Griffiths (Abingdon) and Eugene Gratwohl (Oxford Old Boys), and others in the Nomads included David Wicks and Richard Dolan (Witney).

The season got off to a bad start with a fixture mix up due to a breakdown

*Vic Gordge's role as Club Steward was many and varied. Here he helps to erect the goal posts before the season begins. Whatever happened to Health and Safety?*

in communications. The Oxford team travelled to Weston while the Weston team came to Oxford! The two teams must have passed each other on the M4. In the event Oxford beat Weston 2nds 27–6 while the Nomads lost 0–52. The following week saw no such problems and Oxford scored eight tries in a sparkling 40–3 at Worcester but then lost to an Oxfordshire team 18–20 in a midweek match after leading 18–9 with fifteen minutes to go. This trend continued at the weekend at Stroud with the teams level at 13–13 half way through and Oxford's tackling got weaker and weaker as the stamina ran out for a 19-40 defeat.

Howard Blackett, a former pupil of St Edward's School and latterly of St Edmund Hall, made his club debut for the Nomads and scored all 24 points in the Nomads win over Stroud II with a try, four penalties, a drop goal and two conversions. That performance gained him surprise selection for Oxfordshire's warm up match with Buckinghamshire but, despite an impressive county debut Oxfordshire fell to a decisive 6–19 defeat.

With the John Player Cup match coming up quickly Oxford Old Boys trained with Oxford during the week but an angry Nigel Goodey returned to Oxford after a selection dispute. He had returned home early from holiday in France to replace John Thompson in the match against Ampthill but was then dropped for the Swindon cup game. Feeling he had been given a 'raw deal' he saw himself as a casualty of what he called 'bar room selection' and said "I was thinking of going back to Oxford at the start of the season anyway."

The game with Swindon was the most important match in the thirty eight year old history of Oxford Old Boys. It was the club's first appearance in English rugby's top competition and losing in the first round would be worth £810 plus gate money. It was a close match and the experience of Ray Tapper helped the team to snatch a dramatic win three minutes from time. At 9–12 down the side were awarded a penalty and, realising a draw would not suffice, Tapper kicked high into the corner and, in the scramble, Bernie Calnan touched down for the winning try. The reward was another home draw, this time to Lydney.

On the same day Oxford lost a Merit Table match 12–13 at US Portsmouth when a strong wind blew away any chance of a win and followed this with a similar one point defeat 9–10 at home with Cheltenham. Oxford's team that day was: J Griffiths; E Gratwohl, R Howson, R Woodward, S Murphy; H Blackett, C Horton; P Maton, D Spencer, R Dolan, J Dunnill, C Clarke, G Hopkins, W Jenkins, S Grater.

The club lost a game, to Bournemouth 0–15, and won one, Stafford 16–3 before a break in the fixture list in mid-October. This coincided with Oxfordshire's first Championship match against East Midlands at Leighton Buzzard and proved timely due to the club's growing injury list and the provision of nine players, Gratwohl, Woodward, Murphy, Blackett, Horton, Stevenson, Spencer, Maton and replacement Staples, to the county side. One reason

*Groundsman Alan Davies tells President Brian Deane just how it is.*

for this was that the Old Boys had advised the County Committee that the club would not release any players while the club was still involved in the John Player Cup, the reason being that four county matches would disrupt the club's team planning. It was possible that maybe four of that club's players might have been involved at the higher level. There was an irony in that former Oxford player Paul Ashby, now captain of the Old Boys, was out of the game with a long term injury having broken a bone in his foot while playing for the Blue Boar pub side on a Sunday.

Far from showing signs of improvement on the previous season Oxfordshire were woeful in a 9–23 defeat at East Midlands. Nine Oxford players were again selected for the following Saturday against Berkshire and already the pressure was on with the other two counties having won a match. Although there was no lack of team effort the pack got another lesson in losing 15–23.

Woodford had lost just one match so far but Oxford's Merit Table match was 'demeritised' due to county involvement. Nigel Goodey came into the side for the first time since his return and captained the side that got scant reward for a valiant effort in losing 9–19. After the match Vic and Shirley Gordge were presented with a silver sugar bowl by Club President John Rowell, Vic having been Club Steward for five and a half years. He was due to move the short distance to become Landlord of the Cross Keys pub in South Hinksey village. At the Annual General Meeting in 1985 it was noted that the percentage increase in bar takings was up to 37% but there had been a marked decrease since his leaving.

Having become an integral part of a plan to improve rugby in Oxfordshire the club was now feeling the strain and some senior members were uneasy over supporting the county team. With cup rugby slowly assuming more importance the feeder system was only partially working. The club was fielding understrength teams and the team would have just two games together in six weeks in preparation for the county cup match due at Banbury.

Prior to the Floodlit Cup match at the end of October against Oxford Old Boys the club had just two wins from eight games against the Old Boys seven wins and two draws but, in a thrilling match, the Oxford pack produced a great performance which saw the side win 19–14 to take the Old Boys unbeaten record. But any joy was soon dispersed in a crushing 0–42 defeat at Nuneaton.

With six players injured and six on county duty the feeder system was still strong enough for Oxford to beat visiting Walsall 13–7 with a Sean Murphy try and three Jonathon Griffiths penalties while Oxfordshire lost again at Witney, 10–12 to Eastern Counties who kicked a penalty in injury time for the win. The club used its lights for an extra fixture against Keynsham as a warm up and three tries provided a good tonic in the 19–10 win just prior to the Banbury cup match.

It was a tough cup tie but Howard Blackett and Jonathon Griffiths kept Banbury at bay and frustrated with tactical

*Vic and Shirley Gordge, popular club hosts for more than five years.*

kicking and both added kicks. A third Banbury penalty hit a post and the 6–6 draw saw Oxford go through on the 'away team' rule. The best Banbury player was Gareth Lewis who, probably thinking that he had a point to prove, tackled tenaciously and made several piercing runs but lacked support. In the same round the county champions, Oxford Old Boys, fell at the first hurdle in a 9–9 draw at home to Henley who also progressed under the same rule.

It was announced that the Seven Counties Merit Table would be sponsored by Lombard Shipping to the tune of £25,000 over a five year period, and any of the thirteen clubs taking part who failed to win 25% of their Merit Table games would have to seek re-election. This centred the club's attention leading up to a home Table match with Maidenhead where the team took the lead but were left to rue missed opportunities in a 10–16 defeat after a pre match downpour had left pools of water on the pitch. At Abbey RFC, near Reading, Oxfordshire suffered a humiliating 7–29 defeat to Berkshire to leave the side with a second consecutive disastrous season, again without a single success.

The 43 year old Ray Tapper, dubbed as the 'Peter Pan' of Oxfordshire rugby, was due to lead Oxford Old Boys in the John Player Cup match with Lydney and excitement was high. The President, Aubrey John, announced that the club had already won £1080 in prize money and would dearly like to increase that with another victory. The Old Boys led 12–3 and gave Lydney a fright but cracked under pressure in the second half. After seventy minutes Lydney took the lead to go on to win 12–21 but this was no disgrace to the Old Boys. Sadly the occasion was soured by after match incidents in the clubhouse when a general melee took place after it was alleged that Lydney members were rude to specific Old Boys players and females present were locked behind the bar for safety. As a result the Old Boys Committee decided to cancel an arranged return match under lights at Lydney.

Oxford's lack of cohesion, due in part to the county programme, probably contributed to a 19–41 Merit Table loss at Southend and this was followed by another defeat, 13–18 to Solihull. In between these defeats Thames Valley Police were easily beaten 31–0 under lights in the county cup.

There was seasonal joy when Oxford beat Sutton Coldfield 17–4 on Christmas Eve playing open rugby in the rain. The decisive factor was the pack where the back row of Gethin Williams, Andy Rogers and Russell Tucker revelled on a pitch that churned into a sea of mud but this was not enough to defeat Lydney on

*Action from scrum half Andy Walton against Maidenhead.*

New Year's Eve as the club ended the year losing 0–11.

At the halfway stage of the season the club team had won eight of the twenty games played with one drawn as seasonal cold weather set in. Prop forward Peter Maton was finally confirmed as Club Captain and Old Whitgiftians were due at the Bypass ground on 5th January. The visitors duly arrived and changed for the match but requested that the pitch be rolled, then decided that the pitch was too hard and declined to play. Other games went ahead as planned and the players chose either to watch the Vikings or Colts, who were again operational, on adjoining pitches. The club's game at Stourbridge was cancelled due to the home side's county cup involvement and this was to be replaced by a match with Gordon League. And then it began to snow!

*Stefan Griffiths and Tony Staples concentrate on this lineout with backup from John Dunnill and Russell Tucker.*

The artic conditions put paid to any local rugby for three weeks but despite that the club had good reason to celebrate. 150 people attended the club's 75th Anniversary Dinner held at St Edmund Hall in Oxford on 12th January and speeches from International players Joe McPartlin and Peter Robbins, who had won their last caps playing against each other at Murrayfield in 1962, helped to make the occasion one to remember. An Anniversary brochure, now much sought after, was produced to mark the occasion.

With little to play for locally Oxford Old Boys brought up their idea again of an Oxfordshire Merit Table for four teams and a 2nd Division for the smaller clubs which would be good for the second part of the season for clubs now out of the Oxfordshire Cup. Again the idea found little support partly because it would mean clubs giving up other fixtures to take part.

On 3rd February the Bypass ground was considered fit enough to play and Oxford's cup match against Oxford University Greyhounds went ahead on Pitch 2. The Oxford team had not played for five weeks but neither had the Greyhounds, their break since losing to Cambridge in late November being much longer. Oxford made what looked like a fairly easy task difficult by giving away penalties and not taking advantage of their obvious forward power. The 16–12 win saw the club drawn at home to play Henley – again! It would be the eleventh such meeting and every one at the Bypass ground.

After even more snow a big freeze descended over the country – had it ever thawed out? This time the break lasted for two weeks and Oxford stepped

OXFORD RUGBY FOOTBALL CLUB

75th ANNIVERSARY DINNER

ST. EDMUND HALL

JANUARY 12th 1985

*75th Anniversary Dinner Menu.*

*The Vikings set something of a record when father and son Graham and Andy Barrett joined father and son Phil and Marcus Blake in the same team at Abingdon on 29th December.*

*Oxford Vikings 1984–1985. Back row l to r: Frank Hartley (Referee), Archie Young, Jim Day, Chris Baines, Rodney Staples, Richard Irwin, Charlie Rogers, Mark Maylin, David Rees. Front row l to r: Marcus Blake, David Dillon, Bob Martyn, Graham Barrett, Andy Barrett, Phil Blake, Richard Tyrrell.*

out on 24th February to meet Henley who, of course, had not played either, in the county cup semi-final. The importance of the occasion seemed to affect a tense home side that made mistakes in the first period. Facing a 0–19 half time deficit the side hit back with Griffiths kicking three penalties but he also missed three more and Henley held on in a cliff hanger to win the tie 16–19. Chinnor beat Witney by a point 13–12 to set up the final.

With the perceived stress of the county cup behind them the team found some form to beat Streatham & Croydon 9–7 in the first of four Merit Table matches left to play and, during the week that followed, Ewart, Murphy, Staples, Jones, Maton, Dunnill and

*Oxford RFC 1984–1985. Back row l to r: Nigel Street, Chris Ewart, Steffan Griffiths, Roy Woodward, Richard Howson, Russell Tucker, Andy Rogers, John Dunnill, Howard Blackett. Front row l to r: Gethin Williams, Graham Fairclough, Jonathon Griffiths, David Spencer, Peter Maton (Capt), Sean Murphy, Tony Staples, Chris Horton.*

Henderson played in the Oxfordshire team that lost the annual match to Oxford University 8–19.

In an attempt to centre the players attention the club resurrected the 'no train, no play' rule and some changes were forecast. The Esher club was demolished at the weekend as Oxford romped to a 33–9 Merit Table victory. It was a personal triumph for Howard Blackett who notched twenty one points from five penalties and three conversions of tries from Tony Yendole and Simon Grater, touching down two pushovers. The team followed this with a 22–0 win at Burton and, on the way back, stopped off at the Bicester clubhouse which had become a favourite watering hole in that direction for Oxford, in reciprocation of Bicester's whole hearted support of the feeder system in this season. This was Oxford's first away game this year and defeat followed at the second, at Guildford, Oxford's 'bogey side' where despite Jonathan Griffiths' outstanding game the team lost 13–21.

The club had a quiet Easter but visited Glamorgan Wanderers on Easter Monday where Sean Murphy gave his side the lead with an interception try but were then outclassed as the home side romped home by 7–53. The team found an end to end wind at Rugby the following week where, in the second half, tries from Roy Telling, Murphy again and Andy Walton secured a 14–4 win while five Griffiths penalties and a sound defence gave Oxford a 15–9 Merit Table win over Havant.

Oxford club sides failed to make an impact in local Sevens Tournaments going out in the Pool at the Oxfordshire Sevens, the winners being Bristol, and in the Oxford RFC Floodlit Sevens at the same stage, won by Loughborough College.

The folly of playing rugby the day after the club dinner was highlighted in a 0–23 defeat to Sutton & Epsom refereed by former Oxford member Steve Lander, who was later to make his name as an International Referee. The final act of the season came in the Floodlit Cup Final against Banbury, a repeat of previous season's match and this time there was a different result as Oxford defended grimly. A Griffiths penalty was followed by Tristan White's try involving most of Oxford's backs which Griffiths converted from a difficult angle. All the points came in the first half as Oxford finished the season with a trophy, winning 9–3.

If seasons and the feeder system are judged by results then both would be seen to be successful with the club winning eighteen of its games, losing fifteen with one drawn despite the difficulties encountered with clashing county matches. Ironically the feeder system was set up in an attempt to strengthen county rugby by drawing in talented players to one club so the club could hardly complain that such players were missing on occasions. The Nomads side also enjoyed a good season but there had been rumblings from the Vikings set up, the players of which felt that they were outside of the system and the Wanderers XV had been disbanded after players at that level had drifted away. Peter Maton, appointed as Captain late in the day, stated the need for a permanent coach after sessions led by a variety of coaches failed to provide a settled playing pattern.

## Season 1985–1986

The Oxford Marathon club had been promised the use of four pitches at the Horspath Road ground and, after three lean seasons, were hoping to reap the benefits of seeds sown, especially through the Colts team while Oxford Old Boys had plans to enjoy a Golden Jubilee season. Elsewhere in the county a new club, Carterton RFC, had been formed and were recruiting from RAF Brize Norton. It was also reported that there might be seeding in the county cup competition and that some county games may be played midweek under floodlights.

There was some sad news regarding Simon Grater who suffered a serious back injury when playing for his original club, Bicester, in a pre-season friendly match as part of his fitness programme. No other player was involved as he twisted awkwardly when giving a pass and this caused two discs to pop out crushing nerves. He was destined to remain in hospital for six weeks after an operation, which would then confine him to the side lines.

An early season county tour to Cornwall involved Oxford players Griffiths, Woodward, Maton, Staples, Jones and Grater. The side lost to Penzance, 6–16, and Penryn 12–23 where Griffiths, having kicked four penalties on the tour, dislocated his shoulder.

Oxford had problems getting back into the grove what with holidays, injuries and illness and lost the opening game at Weston-super-Mare 6–17. The forwards did show some promise but the side lost again in mid-week 0–10 to Gordon League. The new scrum laws where heads must be kept above hips were causing some challenges but the now fit again Billy Greenhalgh scored two tries, two

*Tony Staples and Peter Maton seem to be saying "Bring it on then!"*

conversions and a penalty in a 19–9 win over Worcester. Roy Woodward added a further try.

The team paid dearly for giving away two penalties in front of the posts which was the margin of a 7–13 defeat from Stroud. Keith Robinson returned to the club from Oxford Old Boys to contribute to the best display so far this season when Roy Telling scored late in the game to add to Greenhalgh's penalty, and at the end of September it needed Captain Peter Maton's strong words at half time to turn a slender lead into a romp in beating Sutton Coldfield 31–9. On the same weekend, down in Cornwall, Henley came from behind to beat St Ives 22–18 to earn a next round match at Southend in the John Player Cup.

Across the country the Oxford club had been provisionally included in discussions to expand the National Merit Table system into a South and South West Table. This had not been approved by the RFU due to the fear of a promotion and relegation relationship with the Merit Tables A and B cautiously introduced in this season. It could be argued that Oxford already had a foot in the Merit Table door which could be strengthened by good results in the Lombard Shipping Seven Counties Table. It was therefore galling that, in the first meeting between the sides, Oxford lost at home to Maidstone in a Table match by two points, 14–16, after conceding penalties for dissent. With the club attempting to instil a level of discipline in such games the culprit was 'rested' for Oxford's match at Cheltenham where a revival came too late in the game to avoid an 18–27 defeat. Prop Richard Dolan had just won a place in the team when he was injured playing for the Blue Boar Sunday side and joined the growing injury list as an already weakened side was crushed by a big Stafford pack, 4–22.

Southend beat Henley 19–3 to end Oxfordshire's interest in the John Player Cup as a lightweight pack struggled to compete in Oxford's 7–14 defeat at Woodford in the Merit Table.

The club was facing a busy period ahead with county matches on three consecutive November Saturdays and arranged to switch Merit Table matches with Old Askeans and Maidenhead to Sundays in an effort to avoid a clash.

The Oxfordshire Union cautiously agreed to an Oxfordshire Merit Table which was approved by the RFU. Oxford Old Boys were quick to point out their original proposition and wanted to play against the strongest opposition but Oxford, Banbury and Henley were not interested as they already had Merit Table involvement in different directions. The twelve clubs that made up the table were Abingdon, Gosford All Blacks, Oxford Marathon, Bicester, Grove, RMCS Shrivenham, Cholsey, Harwell, Wheatley, Didcot, Littlemore and Witney and each had to play two thirds of the other clubs involved. Some of the clubs had already met on the field and these results were included retrospectively.

A humdrum midweek 6–13 defeat in an unofficial Trial match against a County XV was no preparation for a visit to Cardiff to play the

*Scrum half Andy Walton is held against Maidenhead.*

highly successful Glamorgan Wanderers but Oxford won general approval for their attitude, but not the match, in a fast, open and entertaining 10–42 loss. Peter Maton, Peter Jones, Roy Woodward and David Spencer were selected for Oxfordshire in the opening Division 4 match where lack of tactical awareness cost the team a 24–28 defeat against Dorset & Wiltshire and, on the same afternoon, Oxford lost heavily again, 6–49 at Walsall.

Ten years after conception in 1976, the Littlemore club was due to open a new clubhouse which, in fact, was a former classroom on the Peers School site at a reported cost of £25,000 with a match against a President's XV. Oxfordshire lost again, to Berkshire 3–13 but Oxford had switched Merit Table matches to adjacent Sundays so that the club's county players could take part and this seemed to work with a 10–7 home win against Old Askeans. The same situation occurred the following weekend when Oxfordshire recorded the team's first Championship win in three years in beating Buckinghamshire 22–6, and Oxford's switch paid dividends with a 15–12 Merit Table victory at Maidenhead.

Graham Warrington, having returned to the club from Coventry, had played in the statutory three games to qualify for county cup rugby and Oxford were able to pick the following side from strength for the cup match at Chinnor: Griffiths; Murphy, Woodward, Ashman, Stone; Robinson, Walton; Wilson, Jones, Maton (Capt), Warrington, Dunnill, Turner, Jenkins, Tucker, replacements Telling, Clarke, Staples. The team coped with an end to end wind and restricted Chinnor to a drop goal. In the second half Griffiths kicked four penalties in the 25 to 40 yard range and kept Chinnor pinned back before good handling brought Chinnor a late try as Oxford won 12–7.

The rearranged match at Lydney was played in relentless rain. With three regular backs already missing Oxford collected more injuries with Maton's shoulder and Chris Turner's kick on the head in the 9–28 loss. This reflected against Southend the following weekend with a 3–9 Merit defeat, but all came good as Christmas approached and the constant driving force of the forwards brought a 17–6 win over US Portsmouth, also in the Merit Table. Warrington and Rob Wilson, a student at Westminster College, returned to Wales for the holiday period as Oxford lost Griffiths and Murphy to injury and the match, 7–25, at Solihull.

Seasonal weather conditions brought a cancellation to Oxford's home match with Nuneaton and, as the year drew to a close, the club at this stage showed six wins and eleven defeats which was about average considering the seemingly never ending injury problems but the side was at least in eighth place from thirteen teams in the Merit Table. The club decided that the Nomads would apply to play in the Oxfordshire Merit Table in the next season in an attempt to give this side a competitive edge. Organisers of the Table had agreed a sponsorship for Grape Ideas who were putting up £500 worth of rugby equipment and three trophies from the following season.

Oxford's game at Old Whitgiftians in early January fell foul of the weather and the club, having not played since 21st December, hoped that the match at Stourbridge would go ahead bearing in mind the cup match at Bicester the following week. Poor conditions prevailed and in a scrappy game played in a bitingly cold wind Oxford lost by two penalties to one in the West Midlands.

The programme notes for Bicester's cup match with Oxford spoke of 'A Long Friendship. No account of the club's association would be complete without mention of the Oxford Thursday side which evokes fond memories in older players while newer players are very aware of the contribution Bicester made to the feeder system. Bicester supported Oxford in this positive venture to improve county rugby and most clubs must be disappointed that other stronger clubs in the county did not have the foresight to become involved. In view

*John Dunnill shows an aggressive front on the charge!*

of these links the Bicester club wishes all its past players and contacts at the Oxford club an enjoyable afternoon's rugby, but they will understand more than most that the loyal Bicester supporters will be vociferous in their vocal support for a home win.' The match took place on a wild, wet and windy afternoon which produced a titanic forward struggle. The occasion was not helped when both teams left the pitch for fifteen minutes in the second half due to a neck injury suffered by a Bicester player. Andy Walton touched down for a pushover try before Roy Telling collected a loose ball after a tackle for a try in Oxford's 8–3 win. The 'reward' was a home semi-final tie with Oxford Old Boys!

Ray Tapper, now 45 years on 1st February, made known his intention to retire from the game after twenty five years of club rugby. Another to announce his impending retirement was the *Oxford Mail* reporter Ron Grimshaw who had been following and reporting rugby events since the late 1940s.

Andy Griffiths, brother of Jonathon, had left Northampton and re-joined the club as had the Cholsey hooker Steve Cave. Another to join the fold was a former Wasps junior XV scrum half, Andy Tiplady, who was studying at Westminster College to become a teacher.

Oxford beat Sidcup 7–6 in the Merit Table having spent most of the match in their opponents half but having little to show except an Andy Griffiths penalty who then combined with brother Jonathon to put Roy Telling away for the winning try, but this was followed by a 12–24 defeat at Bridgwater & Albion.

The worst weather of the winter so far was to follow with temperatures barely reaching freezing point. This put paid to local rugby for three weeks until early March when Oxford played a floodlit match with Littlemore which provided the opportunity for both sides to get players qualified for the Oxfordshire Cup matches. It was just one of those familiar afternoons with steady, continuous rain, as both Oxford and the Old Boys ran out onto a soft and muddy pitch for what was a tough semi-final. The visitors had to reshuffle their pack when the Number 8 was forced to leave the field but Ray Tapper booted through a charged down kick for Seretse Williams to score a try against his old club which Tony Edney converted for a half time lead. In the second half the ball ran free after Simon Henderson had tackled Tapper and Keith Robinson picked up to run fifty yards for a try. This lifted the Oxford team which gained momentum and, after laying siege to the Old Boys line, were awarded a penalty try which Andy Griffiths converted for a 10–6 win. It was a sad finale for Ray Tapper who was led from the pitch with concussion and, subsequently advised not to play for a month, called an end to his playing career. Reference was made, yet again, to the old chestnut of the two clubs getting together.

Alas, any such pooling to provide Oxford with one good club was no more viable then than when it was first mooted about half a century earlier which, in turn, would mean that Oxfordshire would probably stay down among the dead men of County Championship rugby.

Henley had won 9–0 at Littlemore with three penalty goals to set up the final at Iffley Road one week later on 16$^{th}$ March. On the same weekend the club's third XV, the Vikings, broke new ground with a 'tour' to Cornwall, staying in Trevone at former club player Ray Mills' hotel, where the team beat a Wadebridge XV 36–12. Most of the players got back to Iffley Road just in time for the 2.30pm Sunday kick off to witness a real cliff hanger of a game. Mike Poulson gave Henley an early penalty kick lead and then scored a great opportunist try from a quickly taken penalty as Oxford struggled to get into the game. But Andy Tiplady kept his side in it with a drop goal and then a penalty to reduce the arrears to one point. There was real drama as Tiplady, only nominated as the kicker on Thursday's training session and having already missed three or four penalties, lined up a 45 yard angled penalty kick in injury time which sailed over the bar to give his side the lead for the first time. Henley surged back in an attempt to regain the lead they had held after only two minutes of the match. Tony Staples dived in to secure a loose ball but Simon Henderson also dived in over the top to concede a penalty right in front of the posts. Mike Poulson stepped up as Oxford heads dropped but he

*Old Boys player Ray Tapper is led dazed from the pitch by Owen Smith in the cup match against Oxford, a sad end if this was to be his last appearance on the Southern Bypass ground.*

drew his kick across the face of the goal and off the left hand post. Oxford players gathered the ball and made safe to become the new Champions of Oxfordshire. The tension was too great that Groundsman Alan Davies and Secretary Ron Martin who couldn't bear to see the end and both went into the changing rooms for the final ten minutes! Oxford's team was: J Griffiths; S Murphy, R Woodward, A Griffiths, R Telling; K Robinson, A Tiplady; A Staples, P Jones, P Maton (Capt), G Warrington, S Griffiths, W Jenkins, S Henderson, R Tucker.

Andy Tiplady's arrival at the club had caused quite a stir and was having an effect on Oxford's play while Andy Walton returned to Oxford Marathon but Phil Randell arrived from Oxford Old Boys and was playing in the Nomads.

It was now known that the RFU were planning to introduce a league system to English rugby after many years of speculating and prevarication while Oxford kept the winning momentum going with a 22–12 win over Guildford & Godalming. The players enjoyed a free Easter and returned for a Merit Table game at Sutton & Epsom. Having already won enough games to avoid seeking re-election Oxford featured in a close game where the

*Peter Maton comes close to dropping the cup after all the excitement!*

home side came from behind to draw level but, in injury time, Andy Griffiths kicked ahead and Roy Telling sprinted in to touch down for the winning 19–15 score.

There had been the odd critical comment from one or two local clubs that the feeder system was 'one way traffic' and 'we never get any players back once they have moved'. This was refuted by the fact that Andy Rogers, Gethin Williams and Andy Walton had all played for Oxford Marathon on the previous Saturday after spells at Oxford RFC, and Nigel Goodey had played his second game for Littlemore against them. Bicester also had players returning to them to prove that the system did work to mutual advantage. A sad point at that time was that Peter Richmond, having done so much to launch the scheme, was standing down just as the system seemed to be working well.

The club recorded its sixth win in succession in beating Rugby 15–12 at the Bypass ground. Full back Tony Yendole linked with the backs, dodged a tackle, cleverly made ground before passing to Telling whose pace took him clear for a try and Tiplady converted to add to his two penalties. Rugby drew level but Tiplady's third penalty gave Oxford the game. It wasn't just his kicking prowess that led to the

*Oxford RFC 1985–1986. Back row, l to r: John Gunter (Coach), Neil Starling, John Dunnill, Steffan Griffiths, Graham Warrington, Chris Clarke, Russell Tucker, Andy Smith, Tony Staples, Andy Lukes (Touch Judge). Middle row, l to r: Ron Martin (Secretary), Roy Woodward, Andy Tiplady, Simon Henderson, Peter Maton (Capt), Andy Griffiths, Jonathon Griffiths, Nigel Wright, Ron Salter (Team Manager). Front row, l to r: Peter Jones, Roy Telling, Sean Murphy, Keith Robinson.*

acknowledgement that Tiplady was probably the best scrum half at the Oxford club for quite a while and, in a short space of time, had helped to transform it.

But tragedy was not far away. Playing against Wasps in the Esher Sevens on Wednesday 16th April, Oxford's long serving utility back, Tony Yendole, badly dislocated his left knee in the opening minute of the match. He was taken to Chertsey Hospital where the knee was re-set before being transferred to the John Radcliffe Hospital in Oxford, and following a further operation on the Friday later died from a thrombosis. Tony, a Maths Teacher at St Bartholomew's School in Eynsham, was 36 years old. He had been the Nomads Captain, had played many First XV matches and was a committed and much valued club man. He left a widow, Joyce, and a 9 year old daughter.

In blustery conditions Oxford conceded a 15–6 lead in a second half collapse at Havant to fall to a 16–22 defeat before the final Saturday of the season which brought warm spring sunshine to the Oxford ground for the Merit Table match with Upper Clapton. The players stood in silence before the kick-off in honour of Tony Yendole. Nigel Wright, who had been playing for Coventry, made his debut for Oxford and featured in a fast and open game which brought a 37–15 win for the club. Murphy scored three tries while Robinson, Woodward and Henderson added one each with Tiplady kicking five conversions and a penalty in the tally.

Loughborough College beat Oxford Old Boys 38–4 to retain the Oxford RFC Floodlit Sevens trophy, the Old Boys having beaten Oxford 16–19 in the semi-final.

Oxford Marathon had to switch their final match against Gosford All Blacks to the Kidlington ground as the field at Horspath Road had been taken over for cricket, and the 36–3 win saw that club become the first winners of the Oxfordshire Merit Table. The Table had been popular and had given some purpose to the twelve clubs that had taken part in it.

Ron Grimshaw, who was set to retire from his life as a Sports Journalist, was presented with a suitably engraved lead crystal hand cut

*Tony Yendole.*

OXFORD MAIL, Monday, April 21, 1986—3

## Injured player dies after knee op

AN Oxfordshire rugby player has died in hospital following a routine operation to an injured knee.

Tony Yendole, 36, one of Oxford RFC's longest serving players, suffered a stroke after the operation at the John Radcliffe Hospital and died on Sunday.

Mr Yendole, of Tower Hill, Witney, leaves a widow, Joyce, and a seven-year-old daughter, Alison.

Mr Yendole was a maths teacher and head of computer studies at Bartholomew School, Eynsham, where the news was broken to staff and pupils during morning assembly today.

He turned out for Oxford RFC in the Esher seven-a-side competition last Wednesday and dislocated his knee in the opening minutes of his first game.

The knee was reset at Chertsey Hospital, but after an operation to restructure the knee at the John Radcliffe Hospital, Mr Yendole suffered a cerebral haemorrage.

He had captained Oxford Nomads team for several years but had also made a large number of first team appearances.

*Roy Woodward was named as the 'Outstanding Player' at the end of the season.*

decanter by President Brian 'Dixie' Deane at the Oxford RFC Annual Dinner to mark his contribution to the game. Simon Henderson was the Most Improved Player, Roy Woodward the Outstanding Player, Graham Barrett was presented with the Harold Phillips Cup for Services on and off the pitch and Groundsman Alan Davies the Bob Cooper Cup for services to the Club.

The First XV returned a record of sixteen games won and seventeen lost in a better than usual playing season, maybe proving that the feeder system could be successful with a respectable sixth place in the Lombard Shipping Merit Table providing a focus. Captain Peter Maton issued a rallying call to the players to be more committed to pre-season training and make the following season, as County Champions, even better.

But it had all been overshadowed by the loss of Tony Yendole. He was to be sadly missed but very fondly remembered.

## Season 1986–1987

A Memorial Fund had been set up for Tony Yendole and the club received many letters of sympathy and offers of help from local clubs, the Oxfordshire Referee's Society, the London Referee's Society, Esher RFC, and many other sources. It was planned to hold a match between teams representing Oxford RFC and Witney RFC, where Tony had worked within the local community particularly in his church, at the start of the season when a bench seat would be placed on the ground.

The local rugby community lost another true stalwart with Ron Grimshaw's untimely passing in June, so soon following his retirement after forty years in local journalism with the *Oxford Mail*. Ron, an Oxford club member, had been reporting on club and county affairs since the late 1940s and was a familiar figure on touch lines and in clubhouses in Oxfordshire which he then replicated in cricket seasons. He proved to be a very hard act to follow.

The club broke with tradition and arranged a pre-season tour on 31st August/1st September against Worthing and Brighton. This attempt to bring the players together was a calculated risk given some players' historic attitude to early training and the results were not good although the weekend was enjoyed by those who went in the late summer sunshine.

Two newcomers to the club, Duncan Nicholl from Grove and Steve Miller who had experience with Bedford, along with the return after some years of Ted Sandbach on the wing, gave the club's three quarter line an unfamiliar look in the traditional opening game against Weston-super-Mare. Nicholl scored on his debut from Keith Robinson's pass after good work by Nigel Wright but Oxford failed to take advantage of the windy conditions and fell to kicks in the second half in a 9–16 defeat.

Nicholl scored again in the week as Oxford lost to a County President's XV 12–28 which doubled as a county trial. There were already selection problems with Billy Greenhalgh's unavailability for the John Player Cup match against Exeter on 27th September and, with Jonathon Griffiths still injured, Ted Sandbach looked favourite to fill that role. That seemed to bring dividends in another wind affected match at Worcester with Oxford, having learnt the lesson from the previous week, coming back from a 0–12 deficit to win 13–12. Winger Duncan Nicholl scored for the third successive match and Peter Maton added a try but it was left to Andy Tiplady to seal the win with a penalty kick. It was a particularly pleasing weekend with the Nomads beating Oxford Marathon 12–0 back at the Bypass ground. The club was 'peeved' at the time by regulations which decreed that club 2nd XVs were unable to play in Merit Tables, in this case the Oxfordshire Merit Table. The Nomads had just beaten the previous season's Merit winners and were due to play most of the other clubs involved. The players felt that the only way would be to beat them all and become 'unofficial' winners.

A bench seat was dedicated prior to the start of a match in memory of Tony Yendole on Tuesday 16th September between Oxford Nomads and a Witney XV. It was a highly enjoyable match with some exciting rugby won fittingly, given Tony's commitment to the club, by the Oxford club team 55–8. For once rugby took second place though as we remembered a loyal and valued friend. The programme circulation realised £70 and donations made this figure up to £130 on the night as people paid their respects.

HGC Scaffolding presented Peter Maton with a set of tracksuits which the team wore at Stroud, watched in the crowd by Derek Manley who won caps in England's back row in 1963, now an Exeter 'spy'. Oxford lost Andy Smith and Duncan Nicholl with facial injuries and also the match 16–18 by a converted try in injury time.

It was felt that Oxford's backs held the key to success against Exeter in the John Player Cup and the strong running Roy Woodward was drafted back into the centre while Brian Kentish had reported back from a mission to Devon that Exeter had a big pack with a mobile back row.

The visitors based their tactics on a sound ten man game and were aided by a very disappointing Oxford performance where the forwards were unable to produce much worthwhile possession. The game turned when prop Tony Staples left the field after twenty minutes with a back injury. Hoping he would recover Oxford did not replace him and by the time he returned to the field Exeter had scored two tries. Tiplady kicked three penalties in Oxford's 9–28 defeat. The Oxford team was: T Sandbach; D Nichol, R Woodward, K Robinson, H Blackett; N Wright, A Tiplady; T Staples, P Jones, P Maton(Capt), G Warrington, S Griffiths, A Smith, S Henderson (C Clarke 7 mins), G Still.

In his weekly column the new *Oxford Mail* rugby correspondent, Alan Birkinshaw, asked "Where do Oxfordshire stand after this?" Writing about the County Champions poor performance against Exeter he referred to Henley's loss at Southend in the previous season. There was praise for club officials who organised events off the field superbly and this reflected well on the club. But the result was, of course, a big disappointment.

Making six changes for the Merit Table match at Maidstone, Oxford lost a winning start after Tiplady's penalty. Number 8 Chris Clarke made an incisive 45 yard run before being bundled into touch, and Tiplady forced a quick tap penalty try but the home side had the last laugh with a penalty and a 7–12 Oxford loss. The unfortunate Howard Blackett broke his shoulder in the Nomads defeat to a young and fit RMCS Shrivenham side. He had expressed a wish to be considered only for First team rugby but was persuaded to play in the Nomads.

Robbie Blain from RAF Brize Norton, understudy to Rory Underwood in the RAF team, made his Oxford debut but could not prevent another defeat, 9–15 against Cheltenham. The Nomads won 28–9 on the adjoining pitch and an Ambulance man, called to the ground, was quoted as saying "Good God, if we have to come back to this place I'll bring a coach" with three Cheltenham players and a referee needing attention. Local referee Peter Richmond took over the First team game and Cheltenham clinched the match with a score in the tenth minute of added time.

Oxford's dismal run continued with another home defeat, this time 10–20 against Stafford and some good news revealed that Andy Griffiths, a former Northampton player was to start playing again after a 'golf sabbatical'. He was seen as replacement for the injured Nigel Wright whose work career had taken him to Bristol. Defeat the following week at Clifton was Oxford's eighth in nine games as the end of October approached with the loss of Jonathon Griffiths, who had a short return at full back but suffered a reoccurrence of his shoulder injury with the prospect of an operation to pin it, to boot. But, locally, Littlemore provided a surprise in beating Banbury 26–23 in the Oxfordshire Cup with Oxford getting a bye as current Champions.

In the week Oxfordshire beat Berkshire 16–11 under Oxford RFC lights in a 'warm up' for the real thing. The team were discussing line out and back row moves in the changing room before the game when one of the players stood up, saying "I think I'm in the wrong changing room" before leaving.

At last, after two months play, the team finally 'clicked' to score six tries in a 35–9 win over Aylesbury on 1st November. There were two tries for John Cahill and Roy Woodward and one each for Chris Stone and Phil Randell while Andy Tiplady added four conversions and a penalty.

Woodward and Tiplady along with Peter Maton and David Spencer were selected to play for Oxfordshire in the first County Championship game against Devon at the County Ground in Exeter. The team caved

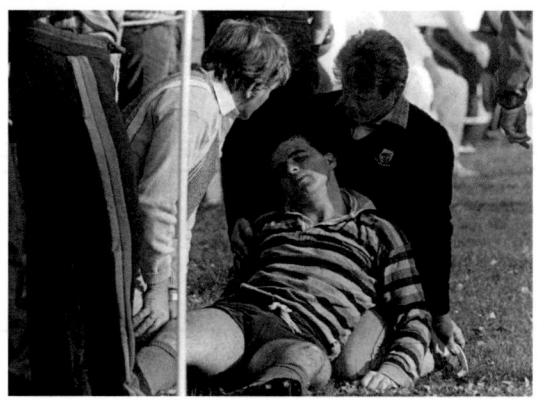

*Simon Henderson in a not too unfamiliar pose, after a knock against Exeter. He took no further part in the game.*

in during the second half to a heavy 15–46 defeat. On the same day, missing those players, Oxford lost 9–17 at home to Walsall.

The club found itself in an un-inspired period and a 3–27 Merit Table defeat followed at Old Askeans who had lost just one game so far in this season. Saturday 22nd November saw one of those infamous fixture mix-ups when the club discovered that the team was expected at Rugby when they thought the day was free due to county calls with the regular match, at home to Maidenhead, moved to Sunday. Wishing to avoid any ill-will a team was sent to a 3–36 defeat at Rugby while a Nomadic looking side lost 10–29 on Sunday in the Merit Table. Andy Tiplady lost his county scrum half place to Bicester's Ian McMillan but that made little difference as Oxfordshire crashed 0–34 at Dorset & Wiltshire. The County's Chairman of Selectors, Jan Maciejewski, thought that the best side was being selected and didn't know where to turn. He said "The better players don't seem to be there. If you look at the playing records of the Oxfordshire clubs you'll see they are all losing more matches than they are winning. Perhaps we'll have to look further afield". Only Blain and Maton kept their places for the final match against Buckinghamshire under lights on a Thursday evening at Oxford's ground and, against the odds, Oxfordshire avoided the wooden spoon with a 6–4 win.

Having been given a bye in the Preliminary Round of the County Cup, Oxford were due to face Oxford Polytechnic, a new team in the competition, on the small pitch at Marston Ferry Road. There was a scare for the club as the team's weight and experience was more than countered by the students fitness and tenacity. In a nail biting finish the Poly team scored a try from a lineout in the fifth minute of injury time to take the lead but Oxford survived through Tiplady's fourth penalty three minutes later, from inside his own half on the shorter pitch in the 12–10 win.

Chris Franks, a former Colt who had been playing in the Vikings, made his First team debut and Henderson returned for the home match with Purley. In Oxford's biggest win of the season thus far, 34–15, Franks scored a try on his first appearance. Another to make his club debut was Steve Lazenby, a full back from RAF Brize Norton, who also scored on his debut and was reported as 'looking promising'. Careless errors accounted for a 12–19 home loss to Bournemouth before Lazenby scored four tries against Solihull to eclipse the Purley win in the 37–18 result as Christmas approached before a 12–32 defeat to the strong Nuneaton club.

It had been a poor first half of the season by Oxford's standards and the side had won just five of the eighteen games played although there were signs that a change of fortune might not be far away. 1987 began with a battling Merit Table performance at Southend where chances were made but not taken in the 3–13 loss. Lionel Crowe made his debut at prop and must have wondered what he'd let himself in for against Southend's enormous 18 stone Captain, John Stokoe.

In the local Oxfordshire Merit Table, Didcot were leading the way with five games won but didn't plan to

*Andy Tiplady, whose four penalties saw Oxford through in the Oxon Cup against Oxford Polytechnic.*

*Newcomer Steve Lazenby who scored four tries in the home win against Solihull.*

play the previous seasons winners, Oxford Marathon, who had offered a challenge to do so. Didcot weren't playing Bicester or Witney either but didn't have to as the club already had sufficient Merit Table games arranged and didn't want to jeopardise their position especially with prizes at stake.

Oxford's home game with Stourbridge was called off due to a frozen ground and the much anticipated cup game at RAF Brize Norton was also called off two weeks in a row for the same reason. This led to a cancellation of Oxford's game with Sidcup on 23rd January and the bizarre situation of three Brize Norton players playing for the Nomads the day before playing for the camp side against Oxford! Graham Still, a Corporal at Brize Norton, elected to play for the club but Steve Lazenby was selected for the home side that played on a wide, flat pitch next to the runway. Oxford had improved since the Polytechnic game but there was a perceived danger in the airmen's backs.

A burst pipe, the result of the cold weather, put Oxford's ground temporarily out of action but the cup team were able to train in a hanger at RAF Benson. On the day Oxford's highly impressive display led to the best display of the season. This was helped by two RAF players being sent off near the end, one for kicking and the other for swearing at the referee over the decision. But it was all over by then and Tiplady added 22 points to the 38-0 total by scoring in every way possible with three penalties, three conversions, one drop goal and a try. The club was now due to play Oxford University Greyhounds who had beaten Henley at Iffley Road with an injury time penalty.

A significant point at this time was that Oxford RFC was not represented in the County Colts Knockout Cup which involved eight teams in the draw. One of the pre-requisites to the proposed league system was that each joining club should have a Colts team and the club intended to contact Simon Grater, the former Oxford back row player who had retired from playing following a back injury while playing for Bicester in the pre-season friendly. Simon was now running a Youth Team at Bicester but nothing came from this approach.

All the Oxfordshire clubs were due to take part in the new league programme due to start in the following season but none had been considered of suitable standard for nomination to the three National leagues or the South Area League and all would come under the South West Division. Oxford was the county's best placed team in South West Division One, comprising of eleven teams. The club might have hoped for a place in the higher ranked South Area League like its regular opponents Cheltenham and Stroud. But Oxford club secretary Ron Martin was realistic and said "I don't feel that there is any case for complaint. We would like to have been higher but our recent results haven't been good enough". Of the other clubs Henley had been placed in South West Division Two, and Banbury, Oxford Old Boys and Oxford Marathon in the Southern Counties League. Oxford Marathon fixtures would be enhanced by this but Oxford Old Boys were slightly disappointed and President Aubrey John said "We felt we might have been a bit higher and certainly not two leagues below Oxford". The league fixtures were causing a big problem as clubs tried to fit games with traditional opponents into fixture lists and Oxford's future membership of the renamed Tandem Computers Seven Counties Merit Table was in the balance.

A 90 metre dash for a try by Roy Telling turned Oxford's game on February 9th with Bridgwater & Albion after a struggle in the pack. The backs were now 'on song' and Telling added another, Griffiths and Lazenby one each and Keith Fowler notched a fifth in the 24–8 win. The backs were again to the fore and Blain, Griffiths, Lazenby and Woodward all scored in another home win, this time 26–4 against Fullerians. Keith Robinson made his debut for Littlemore as Oxford announced an unchanged team for the first time in a long time for a visit to Iffley Road to play Oxford University. Oxford played all the rugby in a

*Peter Jones gets the ball away, despite being tackled against Oxford University Greyhounds, with Maton, Still and Henderson in support.*

determined and decisive 24–10 win, and once again it was the backs who shone, to put the team in good spirits for the cup match the following week.

All of a sudden Oxford looked a different side and had scored 112 points in the last four games with only 22 against. The cup semi-final with Oxford University Greyhounds was won with a score of 34–6 and Andy Tiplady, with 18 points in the match, had now past the 200 point mark for the season. This win set up a final with Oxford Old Boys who beat Oxford Marathon 20–3.

In the week Oxford Nomads lost 6–18 to Banbury in the Floodlit Cup semi-final, it having been decided that the Nomads should represent the club thus giving those players a taste of competitive rugby. Banbury went on to beat Chinnor in the final to win the cup for the fourth time.

Oxford kept the winning run going at Esher on 14th March, coming from behind with Tiplady's five penalties and a late try from Telling after a pass from Ted Sandbach who had come storming into the back line.

There was to be a new trophy up for grabs in the Oxfordshire Cup Final, the Ron Grimshaw Memorial Trophy, to be awarded to the 'Man of the Match' as decided by the *Oxford Mail* reporter covering the game. Oxford were able to pick from strength despite having three players cup-tied and John Cahill was preferred to Roy Telling presumably for his defensive qualities. On the day of the match the weather conditions were appalling with driving rain in a biting wind. Despite that there were four tries, three by Oxford from Chris Stone, Roy Woodward and Andy Griffiths while Tiplady added three penalties in the swirling wind as the club won the match 21–7 to retain the County Cup for the second successive season. Oxford Old Boys put on a brave performance and there was a period in the second half when they clawed back to 7–10 which caused Oxford some concern in the conditions which were a great leveller. Andy Tiplady had a hand in all of Oxford's tries and

*This time Simon Henderson charges away from the back row while Tiplady and Franks watch points.*

was the first recipient of the new Ron Grimshaw Trophy saying "Certainly it's an honour for me and I'm proud to have won such a lovely trophy". Passions ran high off the pitch during the game and the then President of the Oxford Marathon club wrote to the *Oxford Mail* to complain of the 'loutish behaviour' of the Oxford Old Boys supporters who, he said, 'hurled a tirade of vile and filthy language' at the Oxford players throughout the match. Further correspondence suggested that this was due to frustration and indecisive refereeing.

Oxford's seven match winning run ended on 29th March when, due to injuries and un-availabilities, only one of the backs from the cup team played in a 3–14 defeat at Guildford & Godalming but the team got back on track the following week in beating Sutton & Epsom 18-4 with Tiplady and Lazenby to the fore. After that Northampton II provided the opposition on 12th April in a strong end to end wind which saw Oxford 0–22 down at the break and, despite a brave fight back, were short in a 21–26 defeat.

There had been a gradual decline in interest over the years in seven-a-side rugby due, maybe, to an increase in the amount of rugby being played, and in an attempt to regenerate some interest in local clubs the club suggested to the County Committee that the Oxford RFC Annual Floodlit Sevens competition could be restricted to Oxfordshire clubs with the semi-finalists to be included in the Oxfordshire Sevens Tournament, now down to one day with no preliminary rounds. But this idea was declined and the club scrapped its tournament for the season.

Oxford played the RAF team in a midweek fixture as the visitors warmed up for the Inter Services Tournament. It was a hard game that saw a 22–25 defeat for the club side and injuries sustained affected Oxford's last game of the season on 2nd May at Upper Clapton where the depleted side lost 6–17.

There was much sadness when John Rowell passed away at the relatively young age of 57 years in Sobell House after a short illness. John had joined the club as a player in 1955 and had later become the club's Treasurer, Membership Secretary and President for two years and continued to be a strong supporter of the club. Typically he left a legacy of £2000 to the club and an ample amount to be spent on a wake at The Fishes in North Hinksey Village. The club was to perpetrate his memory with a special presidential bar stool and three suitably engraved tankards. Club secretary Ron Martin said "John was always a great person for entertaining the match officials afterwards. It is for this reason that we intend to buy the stool and place it where he used to sit. The tankards will be used by referees who visit the club".

The poor start to the season was recalled by Peter Maton at the club dinner when he said "People's attitudes have got to change if we are to realise our potential. Last season players didn't dedicate themselves to pre-season training and we paid the price. We made a dreadful start to the season and our dismissal from the John Player Cup by Exeter can be attributed to this. With the new leagues starting in September it is imperative all our players get down to training early".

The club team had ended the season strongly after the poor start and some of this success could be attributed to a trickle of new players who had been attracted to the club in the New Year. One by one they began to make a significant difference to the style of play and this brought a turnaround in fortunes. The club definitely benefited from the influence of Maurice 'Geordie' Lowden and his contacts. Geordie had been stationed at RAF Benson but was a 'rugby man' and in his time in the RAF had been kit man for the RAF team and this gave him access to players of some quality stationed locally.

A massive change was about to take place in Rugby Union from this time onwards. The game in England had become stale in a changing world and was certainly in need of revision. The national team had been in the doldrums for a number of seasons and the recently introduced Divisional Championships was not the complete bridge between the County Championship and the clubs on the pathway to international rugby.

The introduction of Merit Tables had not been totally satisfactory because each club did not play every other club in their table. 1200 clubs had applied to join the new league system which had attracted generous sponsorship from Courage Breweries and nobody really knew with any great certainty how the changes from the start of the following season were going to pan out. But, whether you liked it or not, league rugby was going to happen after several years of toing and froing by the Rugby Union, who had introduced strict regulations regarding the registration of players at clubs and this would effectively see the end of the feeder system at Oxford Rugby Club unless players joined as bone fide club members.

On the international front the very first Rugby World Cup was due to take place in June hosted by New Zealand with the assistance of Australia. So, despite everything, there was much to look forward to and many rugby folk in the land were excited and looking forward in great anticipation!

*The influence of former RAF man Geordie Lowden was instrumental in bringing players to the club.*

And finally, to end on a happy note, a 'picture special' from the 1987 Oxfordshire Cup Final!

*We're all off to the Cup Final! Back row, l to r: Brian Cliff, Chris Stone, Roy Woodward, Chris Franks, John Cahill, Graham Warrington, Andy Luke, Ted Sandbach, Richard Howson, Russell Tucker, Roger Whitfield, Graham Still, Peter Rudd, John Gunter, Peter West, Roy Telling, Geordie Lowden, Ron Salter, Richard Tyrrell. Front row l to r: Simon Henderson, Peter Maton, Peter Jones, Andy Griffiths, Andy Tiplady, Geoff Whitfield, Phil Randell.*

OXFORDSHIRE
MORLAND BREWERY
CLUB CHAMPIONSHIP
**FINAL**

OXFORD
v
OXFORD OLD BOYS

on
Sunday 22nd March 1987

O.U.R.F.C.
IFFLEY ROAD, OXFORD

KICK-OFF 2.30 p.m.

£1.00

*The programme from the Final.*  *Coach John Gunter surveys the Iffley Road scene.*

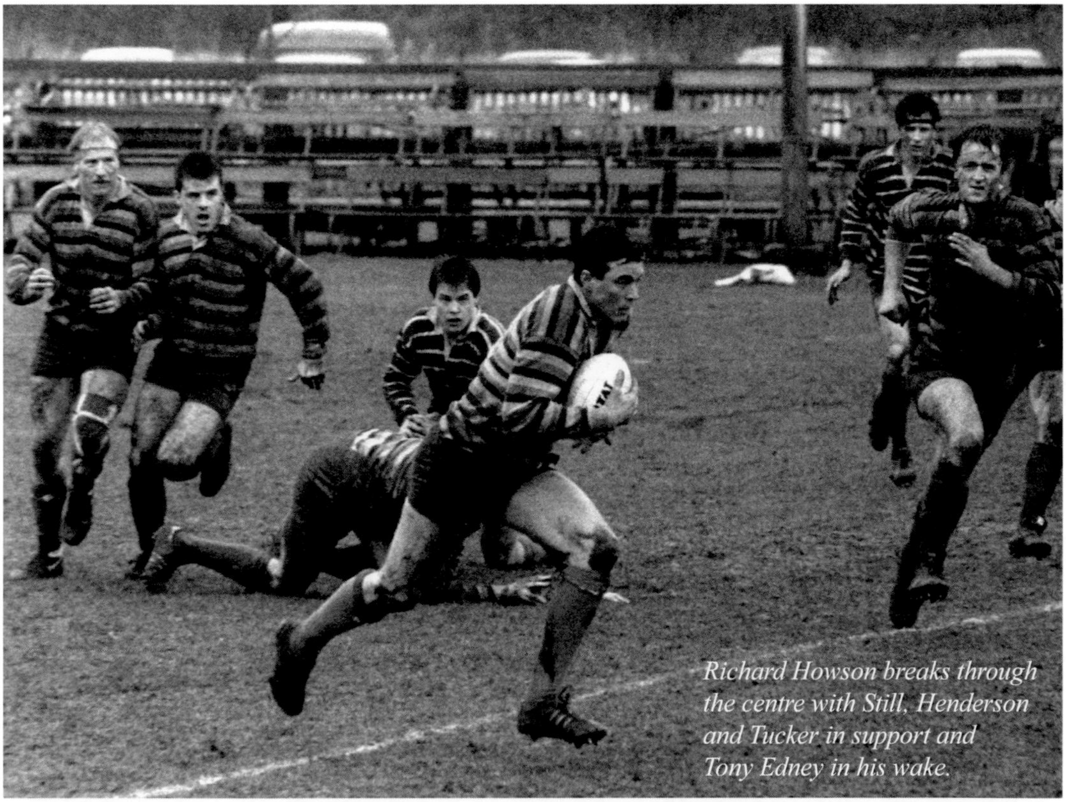

*Richard Howson breaks through the centre with Still, Henderson and Tucker in support and Tony Edney in his wake.*

*Howson gets the ball away as former Oxford player Paul Ashby closes in.*

*Former Oxford Colt Chris Franks wins this lineout.*

*Graham Warrington obviously happy with the result!*

*Andy Tiplady is the first recipient of the Ron Grimshaw Memorial Trophy, presented to the Man of the Match, by Ron's step daughter, Wilfreda Morris. Geordie Lowden and Ron Salter look very happy in the background.*

*Peter Maton collects the cup for the second year running.*

*One for the boys!!*

# The first volume is still available.

**Oxfordshire's oldest Rugby club is brought to life in this look back to 1909, and beyond.**

'The First Fifty Years' covers the trials, tribulations, joys and successes as the club gets going, only to be devastated by World War One. Recovery is made, rugby grows in popularity, the County Union is formed, only for it all to descend into turmoil again by the second conflict. But all this heralds a terrific revival, the change from Oxfordshire Nomads RFC to Oxford RFC and a 'Golden Years' period to 1959.

£14.99 plus £3.00 p+p from:
Stray Cat Publishing, 159, Banbury Road, Kidlington, Oxford, OX5 1AL

Oxford RFC 1981–1982. Back row, l to r: Stefan Griffiths, John Tilsey, Steve Page, Geoff Elliott, Neil Dobson, Graham Warrington, Ian Graham, Rhys James, Billy Greenhalgh. Front row, l to r: Andy Norman, Peter Maton, Andy Smith (Capt), Tony Staples, Phil Blake, Chris Pittaway.

Oxford Captain Nigel Goodey receives the Oxfordshire Cup after beating Henley 10–6 in the 1981 Final.

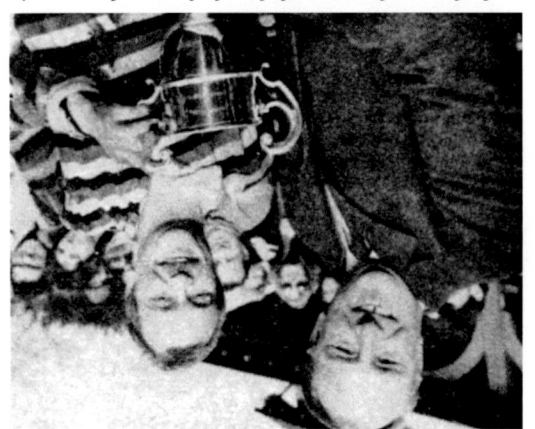

... only to be recovered, with encouragement from Vivienne Goodey...

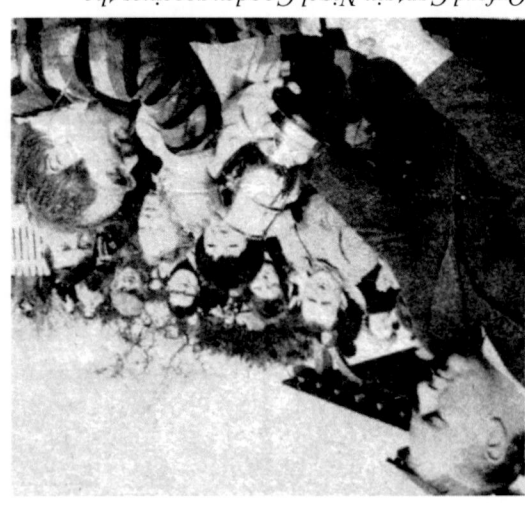

But the cup and plinth part company...

... before ending in safe hands for another year!